ALSO BY ALAN PAUL

Texas Flood

One Way Out

Big in China

BROTHERS
and
SISTERS

THE ALLMAN BROTHERS BAND
AND THE INSIDE STORY OF THE
ALBUM THAT DEFINED THE '70s

ALAN PAUL

ST. MARTIN'S PRESS
NEW YORK

First published in the United States by St. Martin's Press,
an imprint of St. Martin's Publishing Group

BROTHERS AND SISTERS. Copyright © 2023 by Alan Paul. All rights reserved.
Printed in the United States of America. For information, address
St. Martin's Publishing Group, 120 Broadway, New York, NY 10271.

www.stmartins.com

Endpaper credits: profile for Duane Allman © Peter Tarnoff / MediaPunch/Alamy;
Allman Brothers ticket © MediaPunch/Alamy; Gregg Allman and Jimmy Carter ©
Jerome McClendon/Atlanta *Journal-Constitution* via AP; Gregg Allman and Neal
Preston by Neal Preston; smoke © jaideephoto/Shutterstock.com; Grateful Dead with
Allman Brothers on stage © The Estate of David Gahr/Getty Images

The Library of Congress has cataloged the print edition as follows:

Names: Paul, Alan, 1966– author.
Title: Brothers and sisters : the Allman Brothers Band and the inside story of
    the album that defined the '70s / Alan Paul.
Description: First edition. | New York : St. Martin's Press, 2023.
Identifiers: LCCN 2023009384 | ISBN 9781250282699 (hardcover) |
    ISBN 9781250282705 (ebook)
Subjects: LCSH: Allman Brothers Band. Brothers and sisters. | Rock
    music—1971–1980—History and criticism. | Rock music—Southern states—
    History and criticism.
Classification: LCC ML421.A43 P377 2023 | DDC 782.42166092/2—dc23/
    eng/20230228
LC record available at https://lccn.loc.gov/2023009384

Our books may be purchased in bulk for promotional, educational,
or business use. Please contact your local bookseller or the Macmillan Corporate
and Premium Sales Department at 1-800-221-7945, extension 5442, or by email at
MacmillanSpecialMarkets@macmillan.com.

First Edition: 2023

10 9 8 7 6 5 4 3 2 1

For Kirk and Kirsten West, who opened the door,
held my hand, and walked me into wonderland.

For my parents, Suzi and Dixie,
who always let me be me.

And for Rebecca. Always for Rebecca.

CONTENTS

AUTHOR'S NOTE   IX

PREFACE   XI

1. BEGINNINGS   I

2. THE BOYS IN THE BAND   9

3. END OF THE LINE   19

4. WILL THE CIRCLE BE UNBROKEN?   27

5. YOUNGER BROTHER   33

6. TROUBLE IN MIND   47

7. TROUBLE NO MORE   53

8. BROTHERS AND SISTERS   59

9. ALL MY FRIENDS   71

10. BROTHERS IN ARMS   85

11. BIG BOSS MAN   103

12. AMERICAN BEAUTIES   115

13. NEW SPEEDWAY BOOGIE   125

14. EYES OF THE WORLD   139

15. ALL IN THE FAMILY   151

16. DOWN THIS ROAD BEFORE   157

17. HITTIN' THE NOTE   165

18. HE WAS A FRIEND OF MINE   183

19. LET NATURE SING   193

20. DOWN SOUTH JUKIN'   203

21. SOUTHERN BLOOD   215

22. TALES OF ORDINARY MADNESS   223

23. HIGHWAY CALL   233

24. DON'T ASK ME NO QUESTIONS AND I WON'T TELL YOU NO LIES   239

25. SUGAR SWEET   247

26. WIN, LOSE, OR DRAW   253

27. DREAMS   261

28. . . . AND JUSTICE FOR ALL   271

29. THE NIGHT THE LIGHTS WENT OUT IN GEORGIA   281

30. ONE MORE TRY   287

EPILOGUE   293

ACKNOWLEDGMENTS   297

NOTES   301

BIBLIOGRAPHY   317

INDEX   327

AUTHOR'S NOTE

IN SEPTEMBER 2021, I flew back from Macon, Georgia, carrying a dusty suitcase full of hundreds of cassette tapes that an old friend promised would shed new light on the Allman Brothers Band and American culture.

Kirk West, the longtime Allman Brothers insider, had recorded hundreds of hours of interviews with the band in the mid-1980s for a book he never wrote. Some forty years had passed, and no one had ever listened to most of them—not even Kirk. I carried the precious cargo on the plane with tender loving care, as if I were transporting sacred texts. I had already started writing this book, convinced that there was a lot more to be said about the Allman Brothers Band and their impact on America beyond music, even after so much had been written about the group, including my own bestselling oral history *One Way Out*.

The era that was the most crucial yet most underexplored was the time just before and after *Brothers and Sisters,* an album recorded and released in 1973. It became the Allman Brothers Band's first and only true hit, pushing them beyond their devoted circle of hard-core fans to superstardom as they rose above the status of great American rock band to become a national institution. The history of the album reveals a larger story, a story about the nation itself.

I dug into the making of *Brothers and Sisters* and the events of 1971–76, stitching together a broader tale that explains how and why the band was so deeply influential during this period. They helped elect Jimmy

Carter. They hosted the largest rock concert ever. They were at the center of events involving a list of who's who of American celebrities ranging from Cher to the Grateful Dead. I did dozens of fresh interviews and extensive research, but my secret weapon was contained in that suitcase: Kirk's cache of never-before-heard interviews.

The subjects were talking to someone they deeply trusted during a lull in their careers. In the mid-1980s, the band had twice broken up and had no plans to reunite. Everyone was bracingly honest, deeply reflective, and consistently insightful. When the Allman Brothers Band reunited again in 1989, Kirk became a central figure during their final twenty-five years together, serving as "Tour Mystic," photographer, archivist, and historian, as well as conceiving and founding Macon's Allman Brothers Band Museum at the Big House.

Before any of that, he was a major fan researching a book and conducting hundreds of hours of interviews with founding members Dickey Betts, Gregg Allman, Butch Trucks, and Jaimoe, as well as crew members, wives, siblings, and promoters like Bill Graham. When Kirk got hired by the band, he shelved the book and stored his tapes in the two-sided case, which was stashed under a desk in his office and left to gather dust until he entrusted it to me.

I digitized the cassettes and spent endless hours listening to the members and their extended band family tell their stories and share their thoughts. The interviews provided original insights beyond what I could have imagined, leading me to a deeper understanding—not only of this era but of the band's entire history and the members' personalities and motivations as well as their relationships with one another.

There is a symmetry in Kirk's interviews playing such a central role in this book. He is the reason I became an Allman Brothers Band insider in the first place. Our relationship began grounded in mutual professional respect and blossomed over thirty-plus years into one of my most valued and important friendships. Kirk was with me every step of the way in writing *Brothers and Sisters*.

The sources for quotes used in the text are detailed in the book's notes. Anything that is not documented comes from my own interviews.

PREFACE

THE FIVE-YEAR PERIOD between Duane Allman's 1971 death and the Allman Brothers Band's 1976 breakup was a remarkable run for the group, one that helped not only shape rock history but the era's American culture and politics. The band was at the center of several conflicting strands of society, sometimes straddling seemingly disparate divides.

They worked to elect President Carter, a progressive politician who was dedicated to civil rights, even as they used the Confederate flag in their imagery, despite including two Black members. They were intimately linked to both the Grateful Dead and Lynyrd Skynyrd. They were down-home boys basking in communal living even as Gregg Allman married the iconic Los Angeles star Cher and the couple became poster children for a newly emerging celebrity culture.

The Allman Brothers Band was at the center of mid-1970s American culture, rubbing shoulders with the wide range of fascinating, crucial characters who pass through these pages: not only Jimmy Carter and Cher but also Native American activists, Bob Dylan, Jerry Garcia, Geraldo Rivera, promoter Bill Graham, and filmmaker Cameron Crowe. They teamed with the Grateful Dead for a series of massive shows that culminated in the Summer Jam at Watkins Glen, drawing over six hundred thousand people to a small town in New York. The festival, the initial bond between the two bands, and what drove them apart are all explored in depth in the pages that follow.

Remarkably, the Allman Brothers played this central role during a period when most people didn't even think they could still exist, following the death of their inspirational founder and leader, Duane Allman, which occurred just as they were on the verge of stardom.

After a few years of scuffling, the band had broken through with their third release, the live double album *At Fillmore East,* which captured the original six-piece band in full flight, effortlessly mixing rock and blues and an improvisational approach grounded in jazz. Duane described the band's approach as six guys working "for one sound, one direction" and said that *At Fillmore East* was "as close as we've been able to come to a real portrayal of what we are." The sky truly seemed to be the limit, but Duane was killed in a motorcycle accident on October 29, 1971, four months after the album's release and days after it became the band's first gold record. Bassist Berry Oakley's death just a year later again brought the band to its knees.

They were teetering on collapse before, during, and after the recording of 1973's *Brothers and Sisters,* the album that made them superstars. This book explores and explains how all this happened and why it came abruptly crashing down. It is about how the Allman Brothers Band transformed itself and achieved its greatest success in the wake of these tragedies. The book covers the band's evolution from a modern blues group based in Georgia but rooted in the studios and music halls of New York, San Francisco, and Miami to a group forging a new, distinctively Southern sound—a Macon sound. It's about how these children of the '60s became men of the '70s, for better and worse.

But before you can understand *Brothers and Sisters,* and the events that occurred between Duane's death and the band's demise, you have to understand the roots. You have to understand Duane and the band he led, which is where our story begins.

1

BEGINNINGS

DUANE ALLMAN WAITED impatiently for his younger brother, Gregg, to graduate from Seabreeze High in Daytona Beach, Florida. Their band, the Allman Joys, was popular locally, and Duane, one year older, thought his baby brother's insistence on finishing high school showed a lack of faith. He wanted Gregg to drop out like he had, but the boys' mother, Geraldine, refused to allow it.

"I told Duane, 'You didn't want to graduate, but Gregg wants his diploma,'" she said.

Duane had pretty much quit going to school in ninth grade in favor of shooting pool and playing music, working anywhere he could, including as the bassist in a strip-club band. Trying to get him back on track, Geraldine sent both boys back to the Castle Heights Military Academy, which they had attended as young kids. As much as they hated the school the first time, it was far worse as teenagers. They were required to shear their hair and adhere to a strict schedule and disciplinary codes. Being placed in the same sophomore class as his little brother was a final indignity for Duane, who was put back a year due to his school absences.

"To call military school horrible would be kissing it on the cheek," Gregg said. "It is a rich man's reformatory. You're isolated, with a shaved head, and they'll kick your ass in a heartbeat. If the school doesn't do it, your fellow classmates will."

Duane didn't make it through the year, returning home, never to attend school again. When Gregg finally graduated in 1965, the boys got to work. The Allman Joys became popular on the Florida club scene and then slowly expanded their reach across the Southeast. After two years of pounding the circuit with little to show for it other than sharpened skills, they impressed the Nitty Gritty Dirt Band and its manager, Bill McEuen, during a monthlong engagement in Saint Louis in 1967.

Gregg laughed when the manager said that if the band moved to Los Angeles, he could make them "the next Rolling Stones" and was surprised when Duane seemed excited to make the move, but his big brother's overriding point resonated: why not take a chance? They were on a road to nowhere.

In May 1967, the Allman Joys arrived in Hollywood at the beginning of the Summer of Love and signed to Liberty Records, which renamed them Hour Glass. Members included drummer Johnny Sandlin and keyboardist Paul Hornsby, Alabama natives who would remain important collaborators for decades. The band's first California gig was a late-night set following the Doors at the Hullabaloo club on Hollywood's Sunset Boulevard.

"It was the summer of 'Light My Fire,' there were three thousand people in the room, and my knees were shaking," Gregg said. "That's when I was introduced to a magnum first dose of stage fright."

Things seemed to be moving in the right direction for the Hour Glass. They had a record deal and were playing great clubs with popular bands, but they were uneasy with the way Liberty dressed them up like hippie Kewpie dolls and dictated their musical approach. The October 1967 release of their self-titled debut should have been the culmination of years of dreams, but it was a disappointing anticlimax. The band was disgruntled with both the material and the sound pushed upon them.

Stifled in the studio by record company constraints, Hour Glass made their mark onstage, garnering attention from fellow musicians and informed observers. They jammed with Janis Joplin, Eric Burdon, and Paul Butterfield and played shows with Canned Heat, the Animals, and Buffalo Springfield at prime California venues like L.A.'s Whisky a Go Go and San Francisco's Avalon Ballroom and Fillmore Auditorium. Used to making their living playing all night, every night, they chafed at restrictions imposed by the label, which feared overexposure, even as the band's reputation as performers continued to grow.

"They were just a fantastic, hip live band," said Jeff Hanna of the Nitty Gritty Dirt Band. Duane and Gregg both briefly lived in the Dirt Band's "hippie pad" in Beachwood Canyon. "They'd open with Buck Owens' 'Buckaroo' and close with the Yardbirds' 'Over Under Sideways Down' and Duane would throw his Telecaster in the air and walk offstage. It was dramatic and great."

Before he picked up slide, Duane was a "super hot rock guitarist" whose heroes were guys like Jeff Beck and Eric Clapton, Hanna adds, but that didn't come through on the Hour Glass records, where he was saddled with a fuzz-tone sound in the style of Keith Richards on "Satisfaction." "It was nothing like Duane sounded live," Hanna said.

Duane and Gregg were leading a killer progressive blues-rock band, but producer Dallas Smith* had an altogether different vision, envisioning Hour Glass as a "hippie version of the Righteous Brothers," the blue-eyed soul duo who had hits with "You've Lost That Lovin' Feelin'" and "Unchained Melody."

"Duane could sing the low harmony under Gregg, and they could actually do that kind of thing really well," said Hanna. "It was not at all where their hearts were, but in 1967, the artist was at the bottom of the totem pole."

A fed-up Duane came to some sessions for their second album, *Power of Love,* so high he couldn't play, then quit the band and stormed out of the studio, vanishing for a couple of weeks. Following his return and the release of the album, which featured liner notes by Neil Young, Hour Glass went on tour, making it back home for shows in Jacksonville and Daytona Beach and recording strong tracks in Muscle Shoals, Alabama, that included a B.B. King medley and the Gregg original "Been Gone Too Long." Liberty's immediate rejection of this music was the last straw for Duane, who left L.A., headed "back down south," and never looked back.

In September 1968, Gregg briefly joined his brother in Florida, where

---

* Smith's greatest success had been with teen idol Bobby Vee, and his vision of Hour Glass seems to have been limited by his own past experiences.

they recorded a demo with the 31st of February, a folk-rock band that included drummer Butch Trucks, an old friend from the Florida club circuit. That album included the first recorded version of Gregg's "Melissa" and a take on the apocalyptic, antinuke folk song "Morning Dew," which the Grateful Dead had recorded the prior year.* When that album went nowhere, Gregg returned to Los Angeles, feeling obligated to fulfill his contract with Liberty. The brothers did not talk for about six months.

"It was the only time we were ever apart," Gregg said. "Duane wasn't one to write, so half of those months passed before I heard anything from him. He was trying to stay alive."

Back in L.A., Gregg played with a variety of people, including some members of Poco. Duane made his way to Muscle Shoals, where Rick Hall's FAME Studio was cranking out R&B hits. He found work as a session guitarist and immediately made his mark. Working his second session, he proposed that superstar Wilson Pickett record the Beatles' "Hey Jude," a current top 10 hit. It was an audacious suggestion by the new kid, but the song, which Duane arranged, was a hit. His guitar leapt out of the speakers—even though he would be credited on the album as "David Allman, possibly because he was still contractually tied to Liberty." Eric Clapton, arguably the world's most revered electric guitarist at the time, pulled over his car when he heard it on the radio, then rushed home to call Atlantic Records and find out who was playing the wicked licks behind "Wicked Pickett."

Duane became a first-call player in both Muscle Shoals and New York, where he worked with Aretha Franklin, King Curtis, and other Atlantic artists. He was thriving as a session player, and the other musicians at Muscle Shoals were puzzled about why he wanted to move on after such a successful start. They "couldn't understand why I didn't want to lay around and collect five bills a week just playing sessions," Allman told Joel Selvin. He wanted to get a band together and play live. "I've never been the sort of person to just lay around," he said. "Playing on the road broadens your scope."

"He liked that studio thing while he was doing it, but he wanted to pick!" Gregg said. "He wanted to travel. He loved the gigging business."

---

* This album was released in 1973 to capitalize on the success of the Allman Brothers Band. Much to Trucks's dismay, it was deceivingly credited to "Duane and Gregg Allman."

Duane used his time in the studio to hone his tone and sharpen his attack while becoming more disciplined, all necessary skills to excel as a session guitarist. He learned about manipulating tone and getting the sound he wanted out of his guitar. He was getting better, more professional, more seasoned. The producers and managers who saw Allman's obvious talent, charisma, and inner flame wanted him to lead his own band. Rick Hall signed Allman to a management contract, and they began recording solo tracks, but Duane wasn't really a front man and he had bigger ideas than cutting the type of singles-driven album Hall envisioned. Hall recognized Duane's brilliance, but he also quickly realized that the wild-haired, free-spirited rocker was beyond his ability to control—and Hall did not like things he could not control.

He sold the contract and those early tracks to a team of Atlantic's Jerry Wexler and Phil Walden (Otis Redding's former manager) for $15,000, "a steep expenditure," Wexler noted, "because Duane didn't sing, write, nor did he have a band." Wexler was in love with the guitarist and recognized in Duane the talent to be the next Jimi Hendrix or Eric Clapton. Walden, who was bereft after Redding died in a 1967 plane crash, knew he had found his next great talent when Hall played Pickett's "Hey Jude" for him over the phone, screaming to "stop that thing!"

He had one pressing question: *"Who the hell is that guitar player?"*

Hall laughed and replied, "He's a long-haired hippie boy, come in here from California. He's high on something; he's so up there in the clouds that Pickett calls him Skyman."

Pickett's tag combined with "Dog," Duane's nickname due to his mutton-chops, to create the nickname that stuck: Skydog. Nicknames be damned, Walden immediately headed to Muscle Shoals to "try and sign that boy to a management contract."

Walden still managed a great roster of soul stars, including Sam and Dave ("Soul Man," "Hold On I'm Coming") and Clarence Carter ("Slip Away," "Patches"). He had recently founded Capricorn Records at the urging of Wexler, who pushed him to start an Atlantic-distributed boutique label when Walden told him that he was opening a studio during a fishing trip in Miami and would like some production activity.

"I'll do you one better," Wexler replied. "I'll get you a label." He wanted

Walden to start an R&B label with a rhythm section to record singles for Atlantic, and the two of them chose the name Capricorn for their shared zodiac sign. Atlantic needed to replace Stax, the Memphis label and studio where they had recorded hits by Otis Redding, Sam and Dave, and many others. The two labels' relationship was severed when Atlantic was sold to a major conglomerate and Stax learned the awful truth that the New Yorkers that they considered partners now owned all of their master recordings.

Atlantic advanced Walden $75,000 against royalties for exclusive rights to produce and distribute any recordings he made for three years. Walden put up about $250,000 in cash and borrowed $65,000 from Citizen and Southern National Bank. It was a risky move for the stolid Georgia institution since the respectable people of Macon did not initially embrace the rock and roll ambitions of their native son.

"Phil was regarded in town as being pretty far out in those days," the bank vice president who approved the loan said.

Attending the 1967 Monterey Pop Festival with Redding, Walden experienced the power of rock acts like the Jimi Hendrix Experience and the Who and recognized their potential to tap into the massive, lucrative white youth market. Walden's career had largely been spent promoting Black artists to Black audiences. An intense experience at a 1968 Miami Beach conference where Walden and Wexler were among those threatened with violence by rising tensions between Black artists and DJs and mostly white label heads and radio station owners, pushed him towards rock and roll. That suddenly seemed like a smart move.

When he called Bunky Odom, a North Carolina concert promoter he had worked with, and asked him to come work for him in 1969, Walden said, "I'm pivoting from Black to white."

Pickett's "Hey Jude" made it clear to Walden that Duane Allman was his ticket to this new world, and his ambitions for Capricorn grew. First, he had to sign Duane to some sort of a deal.

He traveled to Muscle Shoals, walked into FAME, saw this "real thin redheaded guy with muttonchops" sitting in the corner playing, and walked across the room and politely asked, "Are you Duane Allman?" The guitarist answered yes and stood up to shake hands.

"I'm Phil Walden."

"Yeah, man. I know you. What's up?"

"I thought we might have lunch today. I want to talk a little business with you."

"What about?'"

"About the possibility of me becoming your manager and putting a band together.'"

"You got it." Duane didn't see any need to have a more in-depth conversation, which shocked Walden.

"Wait a minute," he said, "we got to talk about this."

Duane, always ready for action, replied, "No, we don't. You got it! I know all about you, man. Let's go."

The tracks Allman and Hall were already recording for a planned solo album featured Paul Hornsby and Johnny Sandlin, but Phil and Duane both knew these tracks weren't going to cut it. Walden had enough vision to allow Duane to put together the band of his choice, not forcing him into the power-trio format that both Walden and Wexler originally envisioned. Walden also recognized that, while Sandlin and Hornsby weren't the right guys for Duane's new project, they could be great assets to his new label, and he hired them as studio musicians. (They would become Capricorn's in-house producers.) Walden seemed to understand that to get the most out of Duane, he had to support him and stay out of the way.

Duane didn't want to think about business and he didn't want to stop and explain anything. "My brother didn't have a lot of patience with anyone slowing down his trip," Gregg explained.

2

THE BOYS IN THE BAND

DUANE ALLMAN HAD something far grander than a trio in mind and set about assembling his dream band, starting with Jaimoe. Born Johnie Lee Johnson, the drummer from Gulfport, Mississippi, had been living in Macon and touring the "chitlin' circuit" of Black clubs with R&B stars, including Otis Redding, Joe Tex, and Percy Sledge. Fed up with the bad pay and lack of respect these stars showed to their backing musicians, Jaimoe was prepared to move to New York to try to make it as a jazz musician.

Jazz was more than his true love; it was a spiritual quest. He thought that God himself had sent the jazz magazine *Downbeat* to his high school library, where he pored over every issue like a religious text, filling his head with knowledge of the musicians creating the sounds he loved so much. He wanted to find these guys in New York, throw his hat in that ring, and see if he could cut it.

Duane heard a demo featuring guitarist Johnny Jenkins and had just one question: "Who's the drummer?" Jaimoe had backed several of Walden's clients, so Duane asked his new manager about him. Walden replied, "He plays so weird no one here knows if he's good or not."

Duane knew, and Jaimoe was soon on his way to Muscle Shoals. The drummer was leery of Walden after watching interactions he found problematic with Redding, whom Jaimoe knew wasn't thrilled with his manager. But this new guy had serious backing and he remembered the words of wisdom from his mentor Charles "Honeyboy" Otis: "If you want to make some money, play with a white boy."

Johnson walked into FAME's studio B, saw a "skinny little white boy hippie with long straight hair," and knew it was his man. Duane rolled in a Fender Twin Reverb amp and the two commenced jamming. From their first notes together, Jaimoe never again worried about how much money he might make. He didn't need to move to New York to play jazz, because he could make exactly the music he wanted to make with Duane. He moved into Duane's cabin on the Tennessee River, and they began listening to a lot of jazz, starting with Miles Davis and John Coltrane.

The laid-back Black drummer who looked like a hipster bodybuilder, with his well-developed arms and abs, tiny round sunglasses, beret, and bear claw necklace, and the fiery, skinny, redheaded hippie were an Alabama odd couple. They formed a bond that would last forever and change the musical world. Duane sought additional players, telling Walden, "I'm gonna run around. I'm looking for something."

His next stop was Jacksonville, where he had his eye on bassist Berry Oakley, with whom he had felt an immediate bond when Oakley's girlfriend, Linda Coleman, introduced them after Hour Glass played Jacksonville's Comic Book Club in 1968. Oakley, a former guitarist, didn't abandon melody or frontal attack when he switched instruments for a gig with the garage pop band Tommy Roe and the Roemans, with whom the Chicago native had made his way to Florida as a clean-cut teen. His prime influences on his new instrument were the godfathers of progressive, nontraditional bass playing: Jefferson Airplane's Jack Casady, the Grateful Dead's Phil Lesh, and Cream's Jack Bruce.

Oakley's band Second Coming included guitarists Dickey Betts and Larry "Rhino" Reinhardt, who would go on to join Iron Butterfly, and keyboardist Reese Wynans, who would become a member of Stevie Ray Vaughan's Double Trouble. Betts was accustomed to playing with a second lead player, and he and Reinhardt were already playing a lot of harmony parts together. He was influenced in this by western swing music, a subgenre that blended string-band fiddles, country's pedal steel guitars, and jazz's big-band horn sections. It's a hard swinging music that freely mixes genres and it had a deep impact on Betts's musical ideas. When Duane sat in with

Second Coming, he felt a spark, amazed by the harmony lines he and Betts came up with on the fly. His vision was expanding.

Harmonica player Thom Doucette, a close friend who would become a frequent sit-in guest with the Allman Brothers Band, said that South Florida band Blues Image and their lineup of two drummers, two lead guitarists, and a Hammond organ made a big impact on Duane. (They would become one-hit wonders with 1970's "Ride Captain Ride.")

Lead guitarists are like fighter pilots, surgeons, samurai warriors, or heavyweight champions—alpha beings who generally do not seek to share the spotlight. Duane had a different idea; he wanted to see what he and Betts could do together. The two had been well established for years as the hottest guitarists in a Florida club and frat-party scene that included Stephen Stills, Tom Petty, Mike Campbell, Lynyrd Skynyrd's Gary Rossington and Allen Collins, and future Eagles members Bernie Leadon and Don Felder.

Betts's distinctive melodic sense led him to consistently come up with memorable lines, which Duane jumped on, using his perfect pitch and technical facility to add harmony and counterpoint on the fly. This simpatico musical relationship helped create and define one of the greatest guitar partnerships in rock and roll history. Together, they rewrote the book on how two rock guitarists could play together, a dynamic that changed popular music.

While Second Coming excelled at playing modern, progressive rock by the likes of Cream and Jefferson Airplane, Betts had a broad musical range that extended in multiple directions. He had a deep affinity and talent for the acoustic blues of Robert Johnson and Blind Willie McTell and could play urban electric blues with vigor and authenticity. He was also deeply grounded in western swing and jazz, loved country guitarist Roy Clark and jazz pioneers like Charlie Christian and Django Reinhardt, and had a family background in acoustic string music. He played ukulele and fiddle and was even a member of a banjo group long before he ever picked up an electric guitar.

Like Duane, Dickey did not graduate from high school, literally running away to join the circus at age sixteen, playing fifteen thirty-minute shows a day on state fair midways, performing Little Richard and Chuck

Berry songs while doing duck walks and splits and sitting atop bandmates' shoulders. "The barker would introduce us and lure people in by spinning outrageous lies, like we had been on the *Ed Sullivan Show* and were about to be stars," Betts recalled with a laugh.

Betts's time in this band helped him hone his chops and paid him an excellent salary of $125 a week. When that gig ended, Betts made his way to Indiana to play with the Jokers, a hot band on the midwestern circuit whom Rick Derringer memorialized in "Rock and Roll, Hoochie Koo." ("There was a group called the Jokers, they were layin' it down.")

Betts's personality was as complex as his musical background. He was a tightly coiled athlete with a mighty temper as well as a student of Zen Buddhism and karate, which he used to channel and control his compulsiveness, anger, and occasional violent urges. More than once, an audience member made the mistake of making sexual advances at Betts's wife, Dale, Second Coming's singer, only to find themselves in a crumpled heap at set break, when Dickey would leap off the stage, pummel the catcaller, and then calmly retreat backstage to relax with a beer. Despite such behavior, he was also a true believer in the hippie ethos of the era and would go on to write some of the most peaceful, joyful songs in the rock canon, including "Revival," "Blue Sky," and "Jessica."

Betts could be quiet and thoughtful, expounding on Buddhism, jazz, architecture, or country music, and he could disappear into his thoughts, vanishing behind a blank gaze that unnerved people.

"Dickey's a real Charles Bronson type," Gregg Allman said. "It doesn't take long after you meet the guy to realize that there are things he knows about himself that you'll never know, so don't even get close to his space. Which is fine. He's a very intricate guy, Dickey Betts."

Every aspect of Betts's multifaceted musical background and Jekyll and Hyde personality would eventually be evident in his playing, which formed a large part of what came to be the Allman Brothers Band sound. Betts had a genius for inserting bluegrass-type melody into blues and rock songs. His melodic ideas were also shaped by a strong rhythmic drive. As a kid, he dismantled banjos to create a drum set out of the heads, and he never lost his interest in percussion, practicing drum rudiments for years.

"Dickey was a pretty good drummer," said Jaimoe. "When he had an idea for a drum part, I'd just ask him to sit down and play it."

Betts had the ambitious goal of creating a singularly unique voice on the guitar, remaining rooted in the blues without mimicking the masters' ideas and licks. "I tried to use as much of the instrument's scope and range that was outside of the blues form and tie it in with the motions and feeling of the blues," said Betts.

Jaimoe said that from the very start of their relationship, Duane discussed having two drummers and that he had someone in mind. Jacksonville's Butch Trucks had played a few Allman Joys gigs as a sub and Duane and Gregg had recorded with him and the 31st of February just a few months earlier. Trucks was the lone Allman Brothers Band member to have attended college, lasting just one year at Florida State, distracted by the folk-rock music he was playing with his high school friends Scott Boyer and David Brown. (The latter two would go on to play together in the band Cowboy.)

Duane drove Jaimoe to Butch's Jacksonville house, introduced them, and left the two drummers to sort things out. Jaimoe sat silently on the couch and Trucks stared at him, finding him to be impossibly intimidating. For the first time in his white middle-class, southern, born-in-1947 life, Trucks said, he "had to get to know and deal with a black man." It completely changed him, as he wrote in the foreword to my 2014 book *One Way Out: The Inside History of the Allman Brothers Band.*

Their initial communication came through the one thing they both knew how to do without saying much: playing music. "We set the drums up and started playing—and it just worked," Jaimoe said.

"He played what he wanted and I played what I wanted and we never had to discuss it," Trucks said. "It was just like an endless conversation. The syncopations that Jaimoe brought in and his general feel for rhythm were just so fun to play with."

The drummers were forever perplexed that others had such a hard time understanding the simple, simpatico nature of their bond.

"Both of us learned to play in marching bands with a lot more than two drummers," said Jaimoe. "A drum set is like a percussion section in an orchestra; everything in a kit is an instrument."

Trucks soon earned the nickname Freight Train for his power and un-flagging energy, but when they first started playing together nobody but Duane saw these aspects in him—not even Trucks himself. He was planning to return to college and become a music teacher. His background was in far gentler folk-rock, and Trucks said that he initially felt that Duane didn't want him in the band because he was too insecure. But Allman lit the drummer's inner flame at one memorable jam session that Trucks talked about with awe until the day he died in 2017.

A flaccid shuffle was "going nowhere" when Duane turned around, looked Trucks in the eye, and challenged him with a high-toned lick. Trucks pulled back, but Allman kept challenging. The third time, he "got really angry and started pounding the drums like I was hitting him upside his head." The jam took off, and Duane smiled at Trucks, who said that he was never insecure about his drumming again; Allman had "reached inside" him and "flipped a switch."

"I could play whatever was in my head because I knew Butch was there taking care of things I didn't have to worry about," Jaimoe said, comparing his partner to John Coltrane's drummer Elvin Jones. "That motherfucker was driving the car, so I could experiment. And playing with me made him think more musically. We were switching licks around. Always listening. Butch was a great drummer. Almost everything I've ever played that someone said was great was a reaction to something Butch played."

With Butch in the driver's seat and taking command, the whole band quickly began playing at a very high level.

"They were majestic instrumentally," Walden said. "I told Duane, 'You are over everyone's head musically, but you need a vocalist.'"

Betts would emerge a few years later as a strong singer, but he did not initially sing at all. Duane and Oakley were handling the vocals, and their manager knew they needed someone stronger to front the band. Sandlin told Walden how great Gregg was and suggested that he was the simple answer to the band's singer problem, but Duane balked at Walden's suggestion.

"He said that Gregg was not reliable, that he had just got out of a band with him and you could not rely on him," Walden said. "He's my brother and I know him better than anyone," Duane told Walden, to which he replied,

"'Well, you've got to have a singer.'" Walden said that Duane thought about it for a few days, then called his brother in California. Jaimoe rejects this whole idea that Walden or anybody else had to push Duane toward calling Gregg. "He told me from the start, 'My brother is the only guy who can sing in this band,'" says Employee Number One.

Gregg recalled that Duane called him and said, "We got it shaking down here and all we need is you." It wasn't a "hard sell" for Gregg, who said that he was "doing nothing, going nowhere."

Gregg arrived in Jacksonville the week of March 26, 1969* and walked into a rehearsal where the band was cooking. The first song they performed together was a new arrangement of Muddy Waters's "Trouble No More," a song which Gregg had never heard. He felt intimidated to sing with a group that already had such a cohesive feel, but he passed the "audition" with flying colors. Duane's band was now complete.

Everyone in the room knew that Gregg was a fantastic singer, but he had also recently developed into a great songwriter after years of trying and was starting to get on a roll that would define the band's catalog. He came armed with "Dreams" and "It's Not My Cross to Bear," which he had just written and demoed on a Wurlitzer piano in his Los Angeles living room. It's difficult to grasp how someone just twenty-one years old could have written and sung these songs' existential blues, but Gregg had already seen some things. He said that he had reached such a level of despair living alone in Los Angeles that he contemplated ending his life.

"Just before I put the gun to my head, the phone rang," Allman said. It was Duane calling to tell him to come to Jacksonville. All the pain and confusion came pouring out in his music, songwriting, and singing, which were filled with a depth and anguish remarkable for someone so young.

Gregg's bluesy, churchy organ work was also a crucial musical element to the new band's emerging sound, and it was something he had to learn after being assigned the new instrument by his big brother. He had previously played mostly rhythm guitar and some electric piano and Vox organ. Gregg said that while he was thrilled to join Duane's new band because he

---

* For years, Gregg cited various dates before consistently stating that he arrived in Jacksonville on March 26, which was never more than a guesstimate. It has since been celebrated as the official date of the Allman Brothers Band's formation.

"was on a strange, starving trip out in L.A.," he was intimidated that he had to master a new instrument well enough to contribute to the fantastic group he had just joined. Gregg said that Duane assured him he'd be fine on this new instrument and that he replied, "Okay, Doctor. An organ player you want, an organ player you got."

Gregg was not the only member who evinced a maturity well beyond his age. When the Allman Brothers Band formed, Duane was twenty-two, and Gregg and Trucks were both twenty-one. At twenty, Oakley was the youngest member, while Jaimoe and Betts were the oldest at twenty-four and twenty-five, respectively. Despite being young, each member was a seasoned road musician with years of touring and performing experience.

"We were a nightclub band, not a garage band, which gives you a lot more depth," said Betts. "My own nightclub period, from about sixteen to twenty-two years old, was like going to college. That's where I really learned how to play music, how to get along in the world and make things work."

Each member had spent years feeling like the most serious, dedicated member of any band they were in, and now the six musicians immediately recognized they had found kindred spirits, both in musical vision and in dedication to their craft and art.

"It was the first time in my life I was playing in a band where everyone was a totally committed pro," Gregg said. "Everyone had the same sense of self-respect. We didn't know exactly where it was going, but we knew we were going to play our own music and if we starved, so be it."

With everyone in place, the unnamed band played a few informal gigs billed as a "fantastic group" along with Second Coming, absorbing some of that band's fan base and repertoire. That included an instrumental version of the Spencer Davis Group's "Don't Want You No More," which they paired with Gregg's "It's Not My Cross to Bear," with excellent results. Duane called Walden and said, "I got the band together. Get us a place to stay in Macon and let's get started."

The newly christened Allman Brothers Band moved together into an apartment in Twiggs Lyndon's building at 309 College Street. Known as the "hippie crash pad," the apartment became the communal home of all six band members, as well as their original crew of Mike Callahan, Kim Payne, and Joseph "Red Dog" Campbell. Lyndon had worked for Walden as a trusted road manager of soul acts like Arthur Conley and Percy Sledge and he had accompanied Otis Redding's wife and father to identify Otis's body in Madison, Wisconsin, following the plane crash that killed him and most of his band in December 1967. Lyndon became a devoted Duane acolyte as soon as he heard him and was now given the job of shepherding this new band. A tightly wound, meticulous man, Lyndon would prove to be a valuable, extremely loyal ally in the band's early years, right up until he stabbed a Buffalo club owner to death in 1970 when the man refused to pay the group what he owed them for a performance.

Defense attorney John Condon would help Lyndon be found not guilty by reason of temporary insanity, essentially arguing that life on the road with the Allman Brothers Band had made him crazy, but Jaimoe describes the group's early years as "just the greatest thing in the world." It was, he said, like-minded musicians learning from each other, feeding off each other, and constantly spurring one another to new ideas and new heights, rising beyond what any of them could have imagined on their own. All of that began with the spark Duane provided everyone who was fortunate enough to have ever played music with him.

"Duane inspired everyone he ever played with to tap into their deepest selves in their playing," said Bruce Hampton, a friend whose Atlanta-based Hampton Grease Band played regularly with the early Allman Brothers and was signed to Capricorn Records almost solely on Duane's recommendation.

The band had a deep bond; powerful, original music; and Walden's financial backing. They did not, however, have much immediate success. Their self-titled 1969 debut came and went without much notice, though their second album, 1970's *Idlewild South*, cracked the top 40, and they built momentum with maniacal touring and strong word of mouth. Their moment seemed to have arrived with *At Fillmore East*, a release that validated everyone's confidence that the Allman Brothers Band was coming into its own and about to be acknowledged as the greatest band in the land.

3
END OF THE LINE

NO ONE COULD have known that *At Fillmore East* was not a beginning but an end. Three months after its release, in October 1971, the album was climbing the charts. Two and a half years of relentless touring and faith in the face of adversity were paying off. "We'll be farting through velvet underwear," Duane told his bandmates.

"He was riding high," Butch Trucks said.

And then he was gone in an instant. On October 29, 1971, Duane picked up his first significant royalty check—an advance for his work on Derek and the Dominos' *Layla and Other Assorted Love Songs*—from Bunky Odom, and together they went to the bank to cash it. "Big daddy bucks is here!" he proclaimed to the teller. A few hours later, he swerved to avoid a lumber truck and crashed his Harley-Davidson Sportster.

"Duane had incredible drive and liked to live life to the fullest," Walden said. "He wasn't happy unless he was getting the maximum enjoyment out and would push himself to the limit in everything he did."

Ultimately, his impulsive personality probably cost him his life. Duane died at the Macon Medical Center following several hours of surgery. No one knew what would happen next. Continuing without their visionary leader and breaking up were equally unimaginable for the Allman Brothers Band.

"You know what it's like after there is a death in your family: everybody is confused," said Betts. "There wasn't anybody for or against anything: everybody had reservations about the future. There were mixed feelings."

There was plenty of musical talent to go around, and Duane had been the rare band leader who was neither singer nor songwriter. The band could work around the musical hole Duane's death left, but it was going to be far more difficult to replace his leadership, which was natural, not forced. His bandmates followed Duane without his ever having to ask, and his presence provided an emotional equilibrium, no matter how wild his or anyone else's behavior became.

Neither Gregg nor Dickey was well suited to stepping forward as leader. Oakley was the most logical choice do so—Jaimoe called him "just as much the leader of the band as Duane was"—but he was mired in an alarmingly deep depression.

"Nobody had a clue what to do and the entire organization was grief-stricken and lost in tragedy," said Rose Lane (White) Leavell, who worked in the Capricorn Records office at the time and married pianist Chuck Leavell in 1973. "Duane was the only truly strong personality in the band. Butch and Jaimoe didn't know what to do. Gregg was too passive, Dickey too wild, and Berry too drugged out and lost."

"We agreed to take six months off, but we were going crazy almost immediately and started hanging out together," Trucks said. "We needed to play. People like us, that's where you vent it. You have all these emotions, all these feelings, this massive sadness, and the only way to get it out of your system is to go make music. It's what we did."

They would regroup and move forward. Somehow.

IT WOULD BE a mistake to think that everything was fine in the Allman Brothers Band's world before Duane died. Yes, their commercial fortunes were finally looking up. *At Fillmore East* was making clear to the world what people like promoter Bill Graham and critic Lester Bangs had been preaching for years: the Allman Brothers Band were America's greatest, most original rock band.

But they were coming off a period when tensions had been mounting and drug use spiraling out of control, with most members addicted to heroin. Everything got quickly and decidedly worse in the summer and fall of

1971, exacerbated by nearly two consecutive years on the road. In October, following a show at San Francisco's Winterland Ballroom, Duane had barged into Trucks's hotel room and screamed at him, complaining that the rhythm section was "pumping away" for Dickey, but "laying back and not pushing at all" when he played.

Trucks stared down his bandleader and said, "Duane, you're so fucked up on smack that you're not giving us anything to work with." Duane turned heel and left, which Butch believed was evidence that Duane knew that it was true and was what he needed to hear. Producer and father figure Tom Dowd and Atlantic Records executives Jerry Wexler and Ahmet Ertegun were among those observing the increasing heroin use with growing alarm.

"Do you have any fucking idea what you are messing with?" Ertegun and Wexler warned Gregg and Duane after pulling them aside at a New York City party. "It killed Charlie Parker, it killed Billie Holiday and it will kill you, too."

Duane received the message. After a short fall tour concluded on October 17 at the Painters Mill Music Fair in Owings Mills, Maryland, Duane, Oakley, and crew members Red Dog and Kim Payne flew to Buffalo, New York, for a week of drug rehab at the Linwood-Bryant Hospital. Gregg had a plane ticket and a reserved room at the hospital, but he didn't show up at the airport. Betts, Jaimoe, and crew member Joe Dan Petty detoxed on their own in Macon. Trucks was the lone member of the band and crew who didn't have an opiate problem.

This was the dark ages of rehab, and no one in Buffalo approached their problem or the solution to it in a way that would be recognizable to anyone who has attended rehab in more recent decades. Some of their girlfriends and wives visited. They snuck out a window for conjugal visits at a nearby hotel, and after leaving the hospital, no one seemed to think that a dedication to sobriety meant anything other than not using heroin. Cocaine was considered just a good party starter, prescription pills took an edge off, and alcohol . . . well, it was legal, right? During the visit, someone stopped at a liquor store and saved a $3.79 receipt for a bottle of J&B scotch for future reimbursement from the band account.

Duane's leadership had kept the band moving forward, even as they wobbled under the weight of addiction. He had the strength of person-ality, dedication to the music, and long-range vision to keep the train on the rails, no matter how chaotic things got, but those skills were being challenged like never before. He led by example, but never had a chance to do so in terms of sobriety and there's no way to know whether he could or would have. Duane had seen the situation deteriorating and ordered everyone to clean up. Before that, he had banned needles but not the dope itself.

It's not clear just where he drew the line in terms of substance use, but it was far from what we call sobriety today. "You couldn't really say Duane kept people in line because he wasn't too in line himself," said Scott Boyer of Cowboy, another band Capricorn signed on Duane's recommendation. "He certainly didn't keep anybody from getting fucked up, but he kept the band going."

Gregg was devastated and adrift. Duane was not only his big brother but also his father figure, protector, scold, and inspiration. "Gregg defi-nitely needed guidance from Duane—or from somebody," said Joe Dan Petty.

The whole enterprise came perilously close to collapsing on the night of Duane's death. Gregg overdosed and almost died. Oakley flipped his car and could easily have been killed. Walden, too, was shattered by Duane's death, just four years after Redding's passing had shaken him to his core. Decades later, he was still overcome by emotion discussing the two tragic deaths.

"Duane and Otis are the only two people who gave me the feeling that I was in the presence of someone truly special," Walden said. "Either of them could walk into a room of 2,000 people and be noticed by anyone whether they knew who they were or not. They both had little formal edu-cation but were two of the smartest people I ever met. Duane was charm-ing and eloquent. His speaking was like poetry.

"For Otis's life to be over with when he was at the peak was just un-believable, and then to see Duane go just four years later . . ." Walden's voice trailed off, before he began speaking again. "To see those real spe-cial people taken so young when they were so full of life and playing music for all the right reasons was just unfathomable and impossible to understand."

DUANE'S FUNERAL WAS held on November 1 at Snow's Memorial Chapel in Macon. His guitar case sat in front of the casket, with the band's equipment set up behind it, and the surviving Allman Brothers Band members, with Thom Doucette on harmonica, played "The Sky Is Crying," "Key to the Highway," "Stormy Monday," and "In Memory of Elizabeth Reed." They were then joined for a jam by Dr. John on guitar and Bobby Caldwell on drums before Delaney Bramlett led everyone through "Will the Circle Be Unbroken." Bramlett played a solo version of "Come On in My Kitchen," which Duane had recorded with him, then Gregg played "Melissa" on Duane's acoustic guitar, after which the band returned to play "Statesboro Blues."

Afterward, Gregg flew to Jamaica with his friend Deering Howe, an heir to the International Harvester fortune with a sizable trust fund. Howe, who had also hung out with Jimi Hendrix and Mick Jagger, became an indispensable ally to Gregg. "He kept me busy at all times so I couldn't get down," Gregg recalled.

Two and a half weeks later, the band prepared to head to New York to start a run of shows. Everyone in and around the group was extremely apprehensive. "We knew that the fans were pulling for us to come back out on the road and it was the right thing to do," said Betts.

Their first show without Duane was at Long Island's C.W. Post College on November 22, 1971, exactly three weeks after the funeral. Betts described the performance as "not tight, but the music was flowing," and while it was "filled with mistakes," he said, the crowd buoyed them, simply by cheering them on. Their audience reassured the band that they could continue. Three weeks was an absurdly short break, but they all understood that taking more time off was only going to make getting back onstage harder.

"We did exactly what Duane would have done if someone else had been gone: keep on playing," said Jaimoe. The key, he added, was Betts's ability to step forward into the spotlight. "Dickey was possessed, and that pushed us forward."

Betts was suddenly standing alone in the middle of the stage replicating

Allman's slide parts on songs like "Statesboro Blues," a difficult task that he seemed to handle with ease. "I think replacing Duane would have been one of the most uncreative, morbid moves anyone could make," said Betts. "It would have cheapened our whole organization to hire someone and teach him Duane's licks. We just weren't going to get someone else to do it."

Gregg Allman was amazed at the grace with which his musical partner handled this difficult task. It gave him optimism for the band's future. "He showed more strength than anybody," Allman said. "I have never been so high thinking of anyone as I was on that day. He was a superhero."

While he was new to electric slide, Dickey was an accomplished acoustic slide player, excelling at country blues. However, it does not appear that Betts had ever played electric slide onstage before Duane's death—and he definitely had not done so with the Allman Brothers Band. His performance, a remarkable accomplishment, was grueling both emotionally and musically.

"It was difficult to suddenly have to play slide," Betts said. "I've always enjoyed playing acoustic slide, but I never cared much for playing electric slide and I hated having to play Duane's parts. It was uncomfortable, but if we were going to play those songs then I had to play them."

Sadly, in the same interview where Gregg praised Betts so ardently, he also admitted that he had never "to his satisfaction" expressed his admiration for the way Dickey handled Duane's death to the man himself. Gregg knew full well that Betts was essential to the band's ability to forge ahead amidst unthinkable circumstances.

"Dickey was really the champion of that whole thing," he told Kirk West in 1987, adding, "Dickey is one of my best friends in life."

It wasn't long before Allman and Betts would be engaged in a battle for control of the band that would wax and wane for decades before boiling over in 2000, leading to a bitter split, but they rallied together in the aftermath of Duane's passing.

"The time after my brother's death was the hardest time I figure I'll ever have and that's when all the talk of the brotherhood became reality," Allman said. "I was in pretty much of a stupor after my brother was killed. . . . It did a trip on everybody's head, but nobody laid around and whined 'Oh God, we can't make it now.' We all pitched in and built ourselves back up. We stuck together to survive."

Three days after the C.W. Post show, the band performed at Carnegie Hall, then did two more weeks of shows in the mid-Atlantic region and the South. They were back. "Within that one tour we knew it was going to work," said Betts. "People accepted me as the only guitarist—they saw that I could play on my own."

"I really can't remember anything about any of these shows," said Jaimoe. "We just had to play and everyone played and you really didn't know what you missed more about Duane—being onstage with him or just life in general, just being with him and having him as a friend."

4

WILL THE CIRCLE BE UNBROKEN?

BEFORE DUANE'S DEATH, the band had already cut "Stand Back," "Blue Sky," and "Little Martha" for their third studio album, *Eat a Peach*. Following the New York shows, the band returned to Criteria Studios to finish the album, recording "Melissa" and writing and recording Gregg's "Ain't Wastin' Time No More" and Betts's "Les Brers in A Minor." All three were in some way a tribute to Duane, their "way of expressing what they were feeling at that moment," as Trucks said.

Producer Tom Dowd approached these Duaneless sessions with trepidation. He had always gone over songs, concepts, and schedules solely with Duane. "I had no idea as we regrouped if anyone was going to take charge," he said. He found a group being "super delicate" with one another, leery of getting in each other's way. Dowd thought they mostly seemed okay individually, but not collectively.

"The only ones who seemed to have thoughts as to what they needed to do to finish were Berry and Butch," Dowd said.

Johnny Sandlin played a vital role in keeping the sessions on track. Dowd was simultaneously working with Stephen Stills's Manassas on their debut album in the studio next door, and Sandlin's deep roots with the band provided him with a unique ability to navigate such a fraught situation. Dowd was an essential figure to the band, but he was a father figure, not the brother they needed in this tenuous moment. Sandlin "knew them better," Dowd acknowledged.

Betts cut his first studio slide part on "Ain't Wastin' Time No More" and put in considerable practice time crafting a memorable line, which uplifted Gregg's song. His beautiful guitar lines also elevated "Melissa," which Gregg had written in 1967 or 1968 and first recorded on the demo album that Gregg and Duane cut with Trucks's 31st of February in 1968. Gregg had sold the rights to "Melissa" and "God Rest His Soul" (a beautiful tribute to Dr. Martin Luther King Jr.) to producer Steve Alaimo for $250 to buy a ticket back to Los Angeles. Gregg did not want to record a song he did not own, so Walden cut a deal with Alaimo, in which Gregg got half of the "Melissa" publishing rights back.*

Gregg had introduced "Melissa" at his brother's funeral by saying that it was a favorite of Duane's. "I never much cared for it," he said. "But I'm going to sing it to him."

Betts's brilliantly composed fills and solo, which Gregg once called his partner's "finest guitar work," completed the song. "I knew it needed something and told Gregg I would come up with a lead line," recalled Betts. "I took a recording home and started playing around and I came up with that entire lead guitar portion that night, which was Gregg's birthday [December 8]. I walked into the studio the next day and said, 'Happy Birthday, Gregg' and laid that on him."

The group finished the album with Betts's new instrumental "Les Brers in A Minor," which was based on a guitar lick that he had improvised in the breakdown section of his "Whipping Post" solo on *At Fillmore East*, though no one realized that at the moment he wrote and introduced the song. They just thought that it sounded vaguely familiar.

While Gregg rose to the occasion musically, he was withdrawn, almost completely absent emotionally, rarely interacting with his bandmates outside his performances. "He really wasn't among us," Dowd said adding that Gregg recorded his parts and then sat back silently, with little to no interaction with others.

---

* "He was an unprincipled, opportunist son of a bitch," Gregg said of Alaimo, who had a minor hit in 1963 with "Every Day I Have to Cry" for Chess Records and went on to help launch disco music with George McCrae ("Rock Your Baby") and KC and the Sunshine Band. Alaimo accepted the deal to give back half of "Melissa," since owning half a song Gregg was about to record was sure to be more valuable than owning all of a song the actual composer vowed to never perform.

The three new songs pointed the way forward, while the double album was completed with three live Duane-led tracks from the Fillmore East: "One Way Out," from the June 27, 1971, closing of the venue, and "Mountain Jam" and "Trouble No More" from the March shows that yielded the live album. "Mountain Jam" took up two vinyl sides, and they had an excellent single album without it, but the magnificent improvisation spun off the English folk singer Donovan's simple "There Is a Mountain" melody was a landmark of the Duane-era band that they felt compelled to include, even though most members of the group considered this Fillmore version to be a relatively tepid take.

Eat a Peach came out "Dedicated to a Brother, Duane Allman" on February 12, 1972, and became an immediate hit, peaking at number 4 on the *Billboard* album chart. The Allman Brothers toured behind the album as a five-piece band. Gregg came out from behind his organ to play guitar on a few songs every night, but for most of the show, Betts was the sole guitarist and primary soloist. He did heroic work in the ninety shows that the band performed over the ensuing year, and it was noted by his bandmates, even if they didn't always acknowledge it either publicly or privately. In 1987, Gregg said that he and Dickey grew "real close, closer than ever," during this time, and working together they pushed the band ahead.

There is an undercurrent of sadness to these five-man-band shows, an unmistakable hole in the middle that persists despite everyone's best efforts to rise up and fill in the gaps. Trucks described the feeling in those shows simply: "We played some blues, let me tell you."

As impressive as their ability to continue and play at a surprisingly high level was, everyone in the band knew that they were going to have to do something to adapt. This short-handed group could not continue forever. A new member would alter the dynamics and be risky and unpredictable, and any new guitarist would immediately be compared to Duane, not only by fans but by the band themselves—but without an additional voice to focus on, it was hard to look beyond what was absent rather than what was there.

"It was obvious that there was something missing," Trucks said. "There was nothing to latch onto, nowhere new to take the songs."

Quite simply, the Allman Brothers Band needed some help, and they all recognized it. "We all knew that something had to be added," Allman said.

THE BAND MEMBERS also knew that they had a real problem with Oakley. He had been in a deep depression since Duane's death, and they were all wondering if or when he would emerge from the hole.

"That year of Berry's life is better left alone," Gregg said. "Duane's death was hard for all of us. I weighed 136 pounds on my six foot one and three quarters body because I was down in a deep hole, but Oak, he died the same day. I loved Berry, but I didn't see how anyone could base their whole existence around somebody else's existence. I can't really accept that he thought Duane was the whole thing and without him it couldn't be. It never appeared that way to me. Not to Dickey Betts. Not to Butch Trucks. Not to Jai Johnny Johnson.* And Duane Allman would not have thought of it that way. He was gone, but the band was still there."

Berry was unable to finish some shows, and his struggles reached a nadir at the historic Auditorium Theatre in Chicago on February 21, 1972. There, with his extended family present, Oakley toppled over into the orchestra pit. On July 21, at City Park Stadium in New Orleans, Oakley threw up onstage, ending up with puke-stained knees. Crew member Joe Dan Petty finished both of those performances for him.

Tour manager Willie Perkins said that he assigned a crew member to stand in the pit in front of Oakley to catch him in case he fell. "I'm not sure how many times he fell off the stage," said Perkins. "But it was a concern every night."

"It was sad, and it was a piss off," Allman said. "What can you do when a cat walks out onstage too drunk to play so many times that you find yourself saying a few Hail Marys that he comes to the job vertical?" Gregg implied that the group briefly considered replacing Oakley before quickly deciding it would be sacrilegious.

---

* Born Johnie Lee Johnson and nicknamed Jaimoe by Rudolph "Juicy" Carter, a saxophonist in Percy Sledge's band, the drummer went by various names over the years. With Redding, his bass drum read "Jai Johnny Johnson," a name he also used on some Allman Brothers Band albums. At times he also added o's to lend his name a Scandinavian flair: Jai Johanny Johanson. He sometimes signs notes to friends "LJB," for Little Johnie Boy.

As Trucks said, "He was a brother and when a brother is hurting, you try to help him."

"We didn't know what to do, except stand by him, wait and pray," Allman said. "Everyone was wondering what we could do to find a leader in this organization. Everyone went to great lengths to get along, and rehearsals were real good. Communication was at its all-time peak, but Oakley kept dragging us back down. We didn't know if we should book a tour, toss a coin, buy a flower shop, or what the fuck."

Allman said that Oakley drank copious amounts of Michelob and bourbon every day and that he walked into Oakley's room once during that period and found him passed out, his lips turning blue.

"There's a little part of your brain in the back of your head that tells you when to breathe," Allman said. "There's a little man back there and Berry got the little man drunk and he forgot to breathe. I knocked him around and got him through, and Berry came on me angry. I said, 'Berry, you could die that way.' And Berry said, 'What makes you think I don't want to?'"

Trucks, who said that he was never particularly close with Oakley "anywhere but onstage," believed that Oakley's struggles had started before Duane died, then quickly worsened. Oakley's sister Candace said that the problem was larger than Duane's death, that he was tormented by a growing awareness that the band's business was crooked, that they were getting ripped off by Capricorn, and that Walden was exploiting tensions between Gregg and Dickey over who would lead the band.

"It ate at him and tore him apart and he didn't have anyone to talk to about it, because it was always him and Duane who discussed everything and called the band meetings," Candace Oakley said.

Trucks said that while he and the others realized some of Oakley's business concerns were "essentially right," they created a haze of pessimism as the band was trying to push forward into a new era.

"He was paranoid all the time, which was not what we needed as we were trying to put a new band together and keep going through a very difficult time," Trucks said. "After years of pure positivity, we were now listening to that negativity and paranoia night after night, and none of us wanted to hear it."

One way that the rest of the band powered through the loss of their charismatic leader was by trying to ignore what happened to the best of their abilities. Betts spoke to Roy Carr of the *New Musical Express* about "when Duane suddenly split from the band," prompting the writer to note, "that's how the Allman entourage refer to Duane's demise."

"I didn't really accept it for a long time," Betts admitted. "I think a lot of us would have really lost it if we had accepted it. I had a dream for years [in which] the Brothers would go and do a gig with Delaney & Bonnie and there was Duane in their band, and I'd say, 'You son of a bitch! Where've you been?'"

5

YOUNGER BROTHER

FINALLY MAKING SOME real money, the Allman Brothers Band purchased approximately four hundred and fifty acres in Juliette, Georgia, about twenty miles north of Macon, for $160,000 on May 3, 1972. It immediately became a group hangout known as "The Farm." This type of bucolic communal property was one of Oakley's long-held, oft-expressed dreams.

"Berry was the driving force behind the purchase," said Willie Perkins, a former banker who was the group's de facto money manager in addition to overseeing their day-to-day touring. "He wanted a place where everyone would live. We went out to the Macon airport and hired a plane to fly us over the property and the guys just fell in love with the place, which was truly spectacular."

"We were going to call it ABB-ville," Trucks recalled. "Our plan was to start a town out there, where we could all build houses and Red Dog would be the mayor."

Said Oakley's wife, Linda, "We had dreamed of getting this big piece of land where everyone could build a house and then it happened. We drove out there in our new cars and it felt like our dreams were coming true."

There were a lot of practical hurdles to building a communal town, but Perkins said that "when you walked down the main road and entered that place, it felt magical."

Ultimately, only Betts would build a home on the land. Trucks had architectural plans for a house drawn up, but his marriage was on increasingly shaky ground. In the meantime, he moved into a double-wide trailer on the other end of the property from Betts, because he "just wanted to be there."

"It was right on the Ocmulgee River, with a federal wildlife preserve on one side and a huge hunting club on the other," Trucks said. "The nearest neighbors were five miles away and it had everything: high rolling hills, marshes, two pretty lakes, gorgeous woods, and the best hunting in the state of Georgia."

Everyone in the band hung out at the property, riding horses, eating, drinking, target shooting, and occasionally hunting. Gregg said that he enjoyed the farm and he'd "like to live there," but the bumpy dirt road was a problem for him. He didn't want to drive up and back too many times, he explained, because "it tears up my cars."

The band bought horses and enjoyed playing cowboy. They quickly realized, however, that horses required a fair amount of time and money to take care of, as well as someone who knew what they were doing. As much as the members of the Allman Brothers Band and their crew liked to wear wide-brimmed hats and holsters and style themselves as southern gentlemen, they mostly had suburban backgrounds. No one had grown up with horses. Betts solved the problem with a phone call to his ex-wife, Dale, then living in Love Valley, North Carolina, who moved down to the farm and took care of the horses.*

BY THE TIME the Allman Brothers Band bought the farm, they had already performed more than fifty shows in the first four months of 1972. Gregg,

---

* Dale Betts fell in love with and eventually married drummer Joe English. In 1975, Jaimoe received a call asking him to audition for Paul McCartney and Wings, who were in New Orleans recording and needed a drummer. Although the gig was said to be his for the taking, Jaimoe felt obligated to the ABB and recommended English, who balked at giving up a steady gig touring with Bonnie Bramlett for something that wasn't guaranteed and could leave him stranded in New Orleans. Jaimoe called Walden's travel agency and bought English a ticket to New Orleans with a flexible return date, guaranteeing him a way home should the gig not work out. English played on the 1975 *Venus and Mars* album and three more with Paul McCartney and Wings, traveling the world and accumulating wealth and musical success. Then he quit and returned to Macon, eventually replacing an ailing Jaimoe in the post-ABB Sea Level. By 1980, English had undergone a Christian conversion and started playing only religious music. A decade later, he and Dale, still married, became members of the Word of Faith Fellowship, an insular religious group considered by many to be a cult. He credits it with saving his life.

exhausted from what he called "the longest year of my life," was anxious to plunge himself into his greatest shelter from the storm: writing and recording music. He was working on several new songs and was obsessed with "Queen of Hearts," a sweeping, romantic composition rooted in folk but with a grand, jazzy vision that he had been struggling to complete for over a year.

He moved a Hammond B3 organ and a drum kit into his living room and invited Capricorn house drummer Bill Stewart over to work with him as he attempted to marry the song's bluesy opening to its jazzy, swinging interlude, which is played in 11/8 time, unusual for a rock or blues song. "He was working out the changes necessary to make that work," Stewart said.

When the Allman Brothers had a meeting to go over new material, Gregg proudly showed them "Queen of Hearts," and the group promptly rejected it, a dismissal he viewed as "a real mind fuck," one that drove him into "a silent rage."

"It took me a year and a half to write 'Queen of Hearts,' the longest it ever took me to do anything, and the band flat out turned it down," Gregg said. "It was the first time that ever happened, and I believed in that son of a bitch just like I believed in 'Midnight Rider' or 'Whipping Post.' Maybe they didn't mean to spurn me, but it really hurt me."

The rejection spurred Gregg to pursue a solo album he had contemplated for years, a project that would allow him to explore and develop a softer, more lyrical side of himself. He had a name picked out before he started: *Laid Back*.

Allman asked his friend Deering Howe for financial backing so "he'd be free from all the bullshit with Capricorn Records," said Howe, who agreed to help for a producer's credit.

"Gregory was just not in a good place," Howe said. "He was still trying to cope with Duane's loss, and he wanted a change musically as well. He had these songs that didn't fit in with the Brothers and he just wanted to do something different. He *had* to do something different."

Gregg said that he called his bandmates and explained what he was doing before starting work, sensitive to how it could be received both internally and externally. He assured them that he was not abandoning the

Allman Brothers Band and they gave him their blessings. "They all said, 'Do it. We're your cheering section.'"

Allman wanted to get away from Macon to focus on this new project, so he and Howe went to Miami's Criteria Studios on May 12, 1972, in the middle of an off month for the Allman Brothers Band. They were joined by Stewart, Oakley, and Capricorn house bass player Robert Popwell. Why two bass players and no guitarist? "Because Gregg had no idea what he wanted to do other than try to work out some of these songs, which the Brothers didn't want," said Stewart. "He was especially confused about how to pick a guitar player in the absence of Duane."

The band stayed at the musician-friendly Thunderbird Motel and hung out with former Jimi Hendrix drummer Mitch Mitchell, who was recording the band Ramatam's debut album, with Tom Dowd producing. One night, Allman, Mitchell, and Ramatam guitarist Mike Pinera, formerly of Iron Butterfly and Blues Image, jammed in the studio.

Gregg cut a handful of band demos, but most of what emerged featured him alone on acoustic guitar. He cut raw, unguarded recordings of a few of his own gentle songs, along with tunes by Muddy Waters and Jackson Browne, some of which eventually came out on the out-of-print *One More Try* collection and/or the *Laid Back* deluxe edition, released in 2019. While none of the tracks from the Criteria sessions were used on the final album, they started to form the template of what Gregg wanted to explore on his solo debut.

On July 5, Howe and Allman spent a day together at New York's Advantage Street Studios without making much progress. "Quite frankly, Gregory was pretty drunk the whole time, and it was hard to get anything done," Howe said.

A busy Allman Brothers Band summer tour wrapped up on August 31 at Atlanta's Municipal Auditorium, and they returned home to Macon. Worn out from the grind, the band took a break, uncertain just when they'd get back to work. Still pursuing his solo project, Gregg went into Capricorn Studios alone with Stewart for two long sessions, which left him exhausted and frustrated. Then Stewart made a simple suggestion: ask Sandlin for help. It turned out to be sage advice that forever altered Gregg's solo career.

Sandlin assembled a band that included Stewart, bassist Charlie Hayward (who would go on to be a member of the Charlie Daniels Band for over forty years), and Cowboy's Tommy Talton and Scott Boyer on guitars. For keyboards, Sandlin called Chuck Leavell, the twenty-year-old phenom who had already made his mark in Macon but was then back home in Tuscaloosa, Alabama, visiting his mother and contemplating his next move.

Leavell had moved to middle Georgia two years prior at the invitation of his mentor and former bandmate Paul Hornsby, who said that Macon was the place to be for a young southern musician. Leavell and Hayward packed up Chuck's 1965 Oldsmobile Cutlass station wagon and drove 285 miles into another world. They met Walden, who welcomed them to town and said he thought there would be plenty of work for them both.

Hornsby helped Leavell and Hayward land gigs with the band Sundown, which put out a record and toured for almost a year without notable success. When that fell apart, Leavell quickly landed a gig with Capricorn artist Alex Taylor, James's older brother and first musical inspiration. Chuck was nineteen and had a good thing going with Taylor, a wonderful singer and songwriter who paired his little brother's sense of empathy and folk storytelling with a bluesy edge and R&B swagger.

"Alex was really deeply into it," said James Taylor. "He was immersed in Southern soul music."

The elder Taylor cut two records for Capricorn, 1971's *With Friends and Neighbors* and 1972's *Dinnertime*, which featured Leavell and Stewart.

"Alex was a really wonderful man with a great laugh and spirit who really made us all feel valued as musicians," Leavell said. "He was harder-edged musically than James, but very kind and welcoming."

The time on the road with Taylor helped Leavell learn the ropes of being a professional touring musician. It was a time of tremendous musical growth for him, a key moment in his becoming one of the greatest rock and roll keyboardists of all time. "Chuck just kind of left us behind when we were on the road with Alex," said Hayward. "He went to another level right in front of our eyes."

When Taylor left Macon following a rift with Walden, his group became Dr. John's backing band, with Leavell sliding over to play Hammond organ behind the master New Orleans musician and piano player, another big step in his growth. "He sat and watched and added some second-line flair," says Hayward.

Despite his successes, Leavell suddenly found himself without a job when Dr. John took a touring break. He was home with his mom when Sandlin called and said that Gregg was doing a solo record and wondered if he'd like to return and play on it.

"The answer was, 'Hell, yes!'" Leavell said.

Word that Gregg was working on a solo album intensified already-swirling rumors around Macon that the Allman Brothers Band was breaking up. Guitarist Les Dudek came to town from Florida looking to join the new group he had heard Dickey Betts would be forming.

"There was a cloud of uncertainty over the future of the band and people were talking about that around town," said Leavell.

Working with a core band under Sandlin's direction, Allman's solo tracks started to take shape. Betts was also writing new material, and the Allman Brothers Band started getting together for studio jams after the *Laid Back* sessions, which Jaimoe was also participating in. Leavell and Dudek regularly joined in.

"We were recording *Laid Back* and as we'd finish a session, Dickey, Berry, and Butch would show up," said Leavell. "They'd hop on their instruments, we'd pick a key and a groove, and jam. It was very exciting for me."

PRIOR TO THE release of *Eat a Peach* in February 1972, Capricorn signed a new distribution deal with Warner Bros, ending the label's connection to Atlantic Records. Jerry Wexler had delivered a moving, heartfelt eulogy at Duane's funeral that made clear his love and respect for the guitarist and his incandescent talent. "This young beautiful man who we love so much is not lost to us because we have his music and the music is imperishable," Wexler said.

Wexler seemed to think that Duane's death marked the end of his band, however. "His eulogy was all about Duane's session work and Derek and the Dominos' *Layla* and barely even mentioned the Allman Brothers," Trucks said. "After the funeral he went up to Phil and said, 'Well, I guess that's the end of the Allman Brothers' and Phil [Walden] said, 'You can count on that being the end of the Allman Brothers and Atlantic Records' and he went out and made the deal with Warner Bros."

Walden may well have been insulted and spurred to push back at Wexler, and he certainly may have used the Atlantic executive's comments to make himself look good to Trucks and his bandmates, but the story is more complex than that. Capricorn's distribution deal with Atlantic was up for renewal, and he had reason to expect a better deal the second time around. The label was certainly in a stronger position than in 1969 when the band was an Atlantic concept and it would be in an even stronger position if the Allman Brothers Band remained active. Rose Lane Leavell said that Walden explored his options widely, speaking with almost every major label there was, before agreeing to the deal with Warner Bros, which included a much better royalty rate.

"Anyone will leave if he's not getting an ample share of the profits," said Walden, who added that he thought that Wexler had a "paternalistic view of Southerners." Walden believed that Wexler thought he should be happy to be part of the Atlantic family, that their friendship bonded them, and possibly even that he was lucky to still have a nationally distributed label with Duane gone. Under its Atlantic deal, Capricorn earned a 12 to 13 percent royalty rate on each album sold, and Walden wanted more. When Wexler refused, Walden cut a deal with Warner Bros that made them profit-sharing partners.

"They gave Phil a joint venture partnership as opposed to a straight distribution deal," said Perkins. "As close as Phil was to Ahmet Ertegun and Jerry Wexler, he just couldn't refuse the deal."

Warners also advanced Capricorn money for operating expenses, which allowed the label to expand its roster to about twenty-five wide-ranging artists, including Derek and the Dominos' keyboardist Bobby Whitlock, country singer Kitty Wells, and comedian Martin Mull. None of them had notable success.

Eat a Peach was the first Allman Brothers album distributed by Warner Bros and released with a new logo and cream-colored label. Its follow-up would be the first one they cut in Macon, at Capricorn Studios. This allowed Gregg to continue recording *Laid Back* as the band was working on new material. The Allman Brothers Band needed this level of informality and benefited from the comfort and ease of working with Sandlin.

A renegotiated deal with Capricorn also provided the band with free time at the label's studio, which was a significant perk. "The way they were working at that point, with a lot of jamming and different people coming and going at all hours meant the sessions for any album went on for months," said Perkins. "That free studio time was worth $100,000 or more per album."*

Leavell's work with Gregg on *Laid Back* and his participation in the informal Allman Brothers Band jam sessions were making him indispensable to what was going on in the studio. Unbeknownst to him, Gregg had suggested adding him to the Allman Brothers lineup. Betts was the slowest to warm up to the idea of adding a pianist. During the jams, Betts largely remained aloof and would sometimes mockingly call Leavell "Chopin," but he recognized the vitality that Leavell's energy, enthusiasm, and graceful playing were bringing to the band. "Dickey was a little resistant about adding Chuck, but we all knew it was time for a change," Allman said. "After we tried it, Dickey really dug it. He came to love having Chuck in there."

One night during the Allman solo sessions, two or three hours into working on "Queen of Hearts," Gregg turned to Leavell and said, "Chuck, I forgot to tell you, but the band is in town and we want to hire you."

"He looks at me with a priceless look on his face," Gregg recalled. "A look of shock, I guess, but he didn't say much. I stopped after a while and said, 'Well, shit what do you want me to tell them?' He came over and hugged me. That was a good night for him!"

---

* The building that housed the studio at 530 Broadway, around the corner from the label's offices, also housed Braswell's Barber Shop. During their earliest sessions at the studio, Jaimoe was amused when he saw Chank Middleton working as the joint's shoeshine man. "I knew him since he was a tall, skinny fifteen-year-old with a basketball afro," said Jaimoe, who had been in and out of Macon for several years. "His girlfriend's daddy owned the shop and there he was. Everyone loved Chank."

Middleton quickly became close with Duane, since the band would come into the barbershop, which had air-conditioning, to cool off from the still-under-construction studio, which did not. "We had never seen a hippie before, so I was fascinated by them," Middleton said. He and Gregg would soon bond and become lifetime friends.

Still, Leavell had not received a formal invitation and kept his expectations in check until he received a call from Walden's secretary, Carolyn Brown, saying, "Phil wants to see you in his office." It felt ominous—like a kid being called to the principal's office. Despite the conversation with Gregg, his first thought was, "Oh, crap, what have I done?"

Leavell walked into Walden's office and saw the entire Allman Brothers Band sitting around the room. Walden quickly got to the point: "The guys have been enjoying these jam sessions and they feel like you're adding an interesting element. We know no one could replace Duane, but this is a different direction and they like what's happening. Would you be interested in finishing this record and going on tour?"

Despite all the jam sessions, and Gregg's earlier invitation, Leavell was stunned into virtual silence. He felt as if he were being invited into the knighthood. "I went from unemployed to playing with one of the greatest bands of the day," he said. "I was on top of the world. I knew we had something cool going on, but I thought it was just good-time jamming."

With Leavell on board, sessions for the follow-up to *Eat a Peach* began in earnest. Gregg paused work on his solo album, although Talton, Boyer, Sandlin, Leavell, and others continued to work on arrangements, songs, and ideas both with and without Gregg. Everyone's focus shifted to the Allman Brothers Band recording taking place in the same studio.

Leavell was the first-ever new member of the Allman Brothers Band. By the time the group retired in 2014, there had been twenty members, but in 1972 there had only been the original six. "I felt both the immensity of the moment and the opportunity," Leavell said. "I had followed Gregg and Duane since I saw them in the Allman Joys when I was thirteen. It was quite heady to be asked to be a member of the Allman Brothers Band, but I was determined not to let that immensity interfere with the musical possibilities. I had to let that big picture go, focus on the music and take it one song at a time. I was too young and dumb to understand that I should feel pressure. I just wanted to play."

Leavell's impact was immediately clear. "Everything was completely different as soon as we added Chuck," Trucks said. "There was a whole new texture and rhythm to latch on to and he played so damn well. His presence sparked us. I don't think too much else would have happened if we hadn't added Chuck, which was Gregg's idea. We would have kept latching on to the hole—the negativity of what was missing. Chuck added something positive to latch on to."

The pianist's musical imprint is unmistakable on the first two tracks the band recorded, Gregg's "Wasted Words" and Betts's "Ramblin' Man." He added a bounce that elevated "Wasted Words," undergirding Betts's slide guitar, which was less fluid and expansive than Duane's and more attuned to playing a defined melodic part. Gregg had recorded a demo of "Wasted Words" in Los Angeles on August 9, with Johnny Winter on guitar and Buddy Miles on drums. Betts's slide line sounds like it was inspired by what Winter had played on the demo.

The lyrics of the song are a brutal kiss-off to Gregg's first wife, Shelly Winters (not the actress), including his own admission of failure:

Well, I ain't no saint and you sure as hell ain't no savior.... Don't ask me to be mister clean, baby, I don't know how.

This was followed by a brutal line:

Your wasted words, so absurd / Are you really Satan, yes or no?

The song kicked off the sessions with swagger, which continued in a totally different vein with "Ramblin' Man." The two songs, one an Allman rock blues, the other a Betts country rocker, are entirely different but sonically linked by Leavell's honky-tonk bravado. His sound is singular, even as you hear elements of the musicians the pianist cites as his prime inspirations: Ray Charles, Nicky Hopkins, Dr. John, Leon Russell, and Elton John. He wasn't particularly influenced by country music, but his instincts naturally took him to some traditional playing on "Ramblin' Man," bringing to the song a genuine country swing.

"I just followed my ear and played what seemed appropriate," Leavell said.

"Ramblin' Man" was different from anything the band had ever recorded before. The only thing close was "Blue Sky," another major-key song with a country bounce. But "Blue Sky" wasn't all *that* country, as Betts would note. "It was more of that country/rock thing that was popular at that time. It could have been done by Poco or the Dead."

"Ramblin' Man" was much closer to being an actual country tune. Betts said the Hank Williams song of the same name inspired his initial idea, with Dickey's lyrics adapting Williams's "when the Lord made me, He made a ramblin' man." Betts originally thought he'd offer it to a country artist but was surprised to learn that he was the only guy in the band who thought it was too country for the Allman Brothers Band to record. "I was going to show it to Hank Williams Jr. and ask if he wanted to cut it," he said.

Gregg had no issues adding the song and broadening the band's range. "Hell, that song cooked," he said. He was glad the band recorded it and that Dickey didn't save it for a solo album, as he had suggested he might do.

Decades later, after years of conflict with Betts, Trucks would scoff at the song, alluding to Dickey's initial inclination to give it to a country artist, by saying the band thought they were "recording it as a demo for Merle Haggard or someone." But all indications are that the song was always intended to be an Allman Brothers release and that the group almost immediately knew that they had hit on something beautifully different.

"I can't remember any discussion whatsoever about 'Ramblin' Man' being too country to include," said Leavell. "I certainly didn't feel that way. I thought it was a marker of how great of a band it was that you could do a song like 'Melissa' followed by 'Liz Reed' followed by 'One Way Out'—and now Dickey was pushing that out to country rock."

As much of a departure as it was, "Ramblin' Man" was not a new song. Betts had been working on it for a few years and had played an embryonic version for Duane. He can be heard working through the song on *The Gatlinburg Tapes*, a bootleg of the band jamming in April 1971 in Gatlinburg, Tennessee, during *Eat a Peach* songwriting sessions. At that stage, the lyrics refer to a "ramblin' country man," but the chords, structure, and concept are all in place. He finished writing the song about a year later in the kitchen of the Big House, the Allman Brothers' communal home at 2321 Vineville Avenue (which now houses the Allman Brothers Band Museum at the Big House). He had written "Blue Sky" in the living room.

Betts said that he carried the germ of the idea around in his head for several years. Before the Allman Brothers Band's formation, whenever he didn't have a place to sleep, he'd crash at the Sarasota apartment of his friend Kenny Hartwick, whom he described as "a friendly, hayseed-cowboy kind of guy who built fences and liked to answer his own questions before you had a chance."

"One day," Betts recalled, "he asked me how I was doing with my music and said, 'I bet you're just tryin' to make a livin' and doin' the best you can.' I liked how that sounded and carried the line around in my head for about three years. Except for Kenny's line, the rest of the lyrics were auto-biographical. When I was a kid, my dad was in construction and used to move the family back and forth between central Florida's east and west coasts. I'd go to one school for a year and another the next. I had two sets of friends and spent a lot of time in the back of a Greyhound bus. Ramblin' was in my blood."

On the final version, Les Dudek, who still thought he might be hired for the band, plays sterling guitar harmonies with Betts, making a huge contribution to the song's success. The two guitarists had worked out all the parts together, but then Betts decided to play them all himself, cutting multiple tracks.

Dudek was in the control room watching as Betts repeatedly came in and asked his opinion about various takes, before finally just saying, "Why don't you just come out and play?" Dudek said that he walked out to the recording floor and they played their harmonies live, with Oakley "staring a hole" through him. The sight of another guitarist playing with Betts seemed to hit Oakley hard. "That was very intense and heavy," Dudek said.

Sandlin agreed that the entire band knew they had something special the moment Dudek and Betts finished their guitar parts. "We all knew it was really good," he said. "The guitar playing on the song is just amazing."

As Trucks said, "Les added a lot to 'Ramblin' Man.' He was a good, slick player and he and Dickey worked well together."

In addition to its obvious country influences, "Ramblin' Man" also shows Betts's love of jazz big bands. For the coda, he wanted an orchestral approach with a huge sound. The song's instrumental section had four guitars playing two different harmonies an octave apart and Betts's final overdub, which was a slide guitar line. "I added that long instrumental ending in the studio to try and make it sound more like an Allman Brothers song," said Betts.

Knowing that the song needed a strong intro to "grab the listener," Betts turned toward the string-band music he played with his family as a boy in Florida. He wrote a fiddle-style major pentatonic guitar line, which he then worked out as a call and response with Leavell. The pianist's "Ramblin' Man" contributions and his bouncy, swinging work that elevated the blues structure of "Wasted Words" illustrate the brilliant decision to add Leavell instead of replacing Duane with another guitarist. His role at the heart of the music would only grow over the rest of the album sessions.

"It was just a happy accident—certainly nothing that was by design," said Leavell. "Nobody said, 'Let's get a piano guy!' It happened by osmosis, more or less out of the blue from an unexpected direction, which is maybe why it wound up working as it did."

EARLY IN THE sessions, engineer Buddy Thornton brought a new date to the studio, a stunning woman named Janice Blair. It was an early, casual date, which was a good thing because she left with Gregg and was soon his girlfriend.

"We went out to dinner and I stopped by the studio to make cassette tape copies of some *Laid Back* rough mixes and brought Jan to show her around," says Thornton. Allman met him there pulling his newly built chopper with "fancy paint and ape hangar handlebars" onto the sidewalk. "He told me he would wait for me to make the copies and I introduced him to Jan and went into the back room. When I came out with the copies, there was no one around, but Gregg's bike was still there. I was so mad that I poured my Mountain Dew into the fuel tank of his ugly chopper and left."

Allman said that it was literally love at first sight. "I just walked right up to her and said, 'Look, it's you and me,'" he said. "I'm sure I scared the piss out of her, but I kept after her. I loved that woman before I could call her name."

In February 1973, Janice Blair would become the second Mrs. Gregory Allman. Gregg and Shelly Winters, whose son, Devon, was born on December 10, 1972, had gotten divorced after less than a year of marriage.

6
TROUBLE IN MIND

EVEN AS THE recording sessions were going well, the band remained concerned about Oakley and his drinking. Sandlin said that many of the initial sessions had to wrap up early because Berry became too inebriated to continue. The producer said that he played bass as the band learned "Ramblin' Man" because Oakley hadn't shown up and that the band even questioned whether Oakley "would be able to be on the album at all."

They were all aware without openly discussing it that the first anniversary of Duane's death was approaching. Heaviness hung in the air, particularly around Oakley. Still, his playing on "Wasted Words" and "Ramblin' Man" was excellent, and there was hope that he was coming out of the year-long depression. Oakley was particularly buoyed by Leavell's arrival. "He started playing his ass off again after Chuck joined," said Jaimoe. "It was like he saw the light and the old Berry was back."

An enthused Oakley went out of his way to make the new member feel at home. "Berry and Jaimoe were the first ones to really welcome me into the band," said Leavell. "Berry would put his arm around me, check on me, make sure I felt comfortable. He was very keyed into the dynamics of being the new guy and smoothing over that transition. He was also just the coolest guy."

Thom Doucette was at the first rehearsal the band had after Duane's death. There to support his friends and maybe to be a part of the new band, he sensed heavy tension between Gregg and Dickey over who was in charge the moment he walked into the room. It was a feeling that Oakley shared, Doucette said.

"Berry and I looked at each other and understood what the other was thinking," said Doucette. "What was, is now over. It's gone. It was just too weird. With Duane around, the Dickey/Gregg rivalry was never an issue, but without him, it was inevitable."

WITH TWO SONGS in the can, the group played live for the first time after a nearly two-month hiatus on November 2, flying to New York for a short set at Hofstra University, as part of Don Kirshner's *In Concert* TV show, which also featured Blood, Sweat & Tears; Chuck Berry; and Poco. They debuted not only "Ramblin' Man" but also their new lineup, back to six pieces and featuring Leavell. The pianist was thrilled to finally be onstage as a member of the Allman Brothers Band and was particularly keyed into Oakley's distinctive playing.

"Berry was the most unique bass player I had ever played with," said Leavell. "Rather than holding down the bottom end, he was very adventurous, constantly listening to the other instruments and popping out with great melodies. He was there to support anyone's improvisation. I could feel Berry following me when I started a melody and it was just fantastic. He also had the most powerful rig and the coolest bass sound; you could *feel* it inside."

While the characteristics of Oakley's playing were apparent in the studio, Leavell said that they were especially evident onstage, where he drove the band. Leavell would only perform in concert with Oakley that one time. Just nine days later, on November 11, 1972—one year and thirteen days after Duane's crash—Oakley, too, was killed in a motorcycle accident when he sideswiped a city bus, less than a quarter mile away from Duane's crash site. Like Duane, Oakley was just twenty-four years old when he died.

Despite everyone's acute knowledge of and concerns over Berry's struggles, his death jolted the band. As they pondered their next moves, they immediately canceled two shows with the Grateful Dead, which would have represented their first official billing together since February 1970.

"We had finally gotten some good positive energy going again," said Trucks. "The dynamic had turned with Chuck. Dickey was writing and singing his ass off. Everything felt like it was moving in the right direction for the first time since Duane's death and then, bam, we were right back in it again."

The band once again stood at a seemingly unthinkable crossroads. Not only had they lost two of the original six band members in one year, but they were essentially missing their corporate board. Duane and Berry were the group's undisputed leaders, a general and his colonel, the two everyone else looked to for direction. "Duane had the vision and Berry got it done," said Doucette. "They were so close."

"Duane was very outspoken and Berry was a lot easier to deal with," Jaimoe said. "You couldn't talk Duane out of anything once he made his mind up. He was just so intense. Berry was more the voice of reason, a bit more diplomatic. In fact, Berry Oakley was the brains behind the Allman Brothers Band. He knew enough about how to do business, and he knew how to deal with people. Duane didn't have Berry's patience."

Oakley's loss left everyone in and around the band reeling. Gregg was in New York, on his way to Jamaica with his new girlfriend, Janice Blair, when he got word of Oakley's death from Carolyn Brown, Walden's secretary. "She called me and said, 'Honey, if I was you, I'd go right on to Jamaica. You don't need this, not again,'" Gregg recalled. He did not attend Oakley's funeral, held at Macon's St. Joseph Catholic Church on November 15. The remaining band played a desultory set of music, with Joe Dan Petty on bass.

"Berry's death fucked me up the way Duane's death did to him," said Jaimoe. "Berry was my man. I got high on smack just to go to his funeral. Later that night, I nodded out in my car."

Sleeping at a red light in downtown Macon, Jaimoe was rescued by a friend who happened to see him, ran to the car, and drove Jaimoe home to the Big House. It was a reflection of how deeply impacted the entire group was by this second tragic death.

"It was just like when Duane died," said Sandlin. "Suddenly you're just going through the motions of daily life. I really didn't know how much more any of us could deal with. At that time, at our age, we didn't know how to grieve properly. Most of us had not lost many people yet."

"It was so hard to get into anything after that second loss," Gregg said. "I even caught myself thinking that it's narrowing down, that maybe I'm next."

Walden said that while they never doubted the band's will to continue, in a very real sense, things were never quite the same again after Oakley's passing. "The brotherhood part of it sort of died with Berry," he said. "That was a real thing to him."

Just as Duane had upon his death, Oakley left behind two women who had good reason to consider themselves his wife. Linda Oakley, to whom he was still married, was the Allman Brothers Band's den mother, the de facto head of the Big House and the mother of his three-year-old daughter, Brittany. Julia Densmore had spent much of the previous year traveling with the band and was pregnant with Oakley's child. Their son, Berry Duane Oakley, would be born on March 30, 1973, almost five months after his father's death.

Oakley was buried at Rose Hill Cemetery next to Duane Allman, whose body had remained in the morgue for a year as his estate was contested. Dixie Meadows, with whom Duane had lived for most of his last year, staked a claim as his common law wife. Eventually, that claim was tossed aside when it was learned that Meadows had been married and never legally divorced, negating her claim. Donna, the mother of Duane's two-year-old daughter, Galadrielle, his only heir, was back in Macon to try and break this impasse and move his burial along when Oakley died. She and her close friend Linda Oakley took control of arrangements. They had Duane and Berry buried side by side in Rose Hill Cemetery, on a beautiful bluff overlooking the Ocmulgee River. It is just around the corner from the grave of Elizabeth Jones Reed, the nineteenth-century Maconite whose name graced Betts's monumental instrumental "In Memory of Elizabeth Reed."*

THE GRIEVING BAND took a couple of weeks off before reconvening to audition bassists. Joe Dan Petty, Betts's childhood friend who had filled in for Oakley on the nights he was too inebriated to finish shows and played at his funeral, did not try out for the gig. Petty, an excellent musician, would soon be a founding member of Grinderswitch, which released three albums on Capricorn between 1974 and 1976 and continued until at least 1982.† "No

---

* The enlarged Rose Hill burial plot now also includes Gregg Allman, as well as Butch Trucks's ashes.

† Interestingly, the core of Grinderswitch consisted of Les Dudek's former Florida band. Dudek eventually moved to San Francisco to join Boz Scaggs's band.

one knew those songs better than Joe Dan," said Jaimoe. "But he had too much respect for the whole thing to even think about trying out."

That's Jaimoe speak for "Joe Dan was too close to the band and had too much respect for Berry and the music to want to put his own touch on it." Petty needed to keep a distance and did not want to take on a different role with people he was so close with.

The band initially tried out four bassists at Capricorn Studios, most suggested by different members: Gregg brought in Mark Andes of Spirit and Jo Jo Gunne, who would go on to play with Firefall and Heart; Trucks suggested Buzzy Meekins, who had replaced Oakley in Second Coming; Betts called in Stray Straton, a friend who would play on his 1974 solo album, *Highway Call*; and everyone agreed on Kenny Gradney, who had just left Delaney & Bonnie and was soon to join Little Feat. They all played well enough, but there was no agreement on who was the best fit.

"We were all a little confused about who was even in the lead," said Leavell. Before they reached a decision, Jaimoe asked the band to consider Lamar Williams, his childhood friend from Gulfport, Mississippi.

Jaimoe was the first member Duane hired, and everyone in the Allman Brothers Band revered his musical acumen and purity of intent. "The feeling was simply if Jai said we need to check this guy out, then we need to check this guy out," said Leavell.

The band agreed to audition Williams, then playing in club bands around Gulfport and Charlotte, North Carolina. Jaimoe reached him in New York, where Lamar was in search of a record deal for his Fungus Blues Band. He was also auditioning for singer Eddie Vernon, who was trying to put together a new version of his influential but unsuccessful protofusion band Dreams, which had featured Billy Cobham and the Brecker Brothers. Williams immediately headed for Macon.

Williams and Jaimoe met up at Bunky Odom's house and rehearsed together for a couple of days. "I knew Lamar had the job when I heard him and Jaimoe practicing," Odom said. There was one additional hurdle to overcome. Like Oakley, Williams also played with a pick. Unlike Oakley's thumb pick, Williams made his own picks from the neck of Clorox bottles. He decided to make some new picks at Odom's house when his hand slipped and he sliced his finger. "He almost cut his damn finger off,"

Jaimoe recalled. "I went, 'Aw, shit. This is all we need.' It was terrible. It felt like he cut his damn arm off."

Williams walked into his audition with an air of confidence, bandaged finger and all. Said Leavell, "Lamar didn't seem nervous or concerned about who the Allman Brothers were. He just played music. He was presented with an opportunity, and he made the most of it."

It quickly became clear that he was the right man for the job. After playing two or three songs, Trucks asked Williams if he had ever played the material before. He said he had heard the songs but never played them. Butch then asked Lamar to leave so they could have a band meeting. He said, "This guy doesn't even know these songs and he's playing them like he wrote them. Let's end this audition and make it a rehearsal."

"That was the greatest thing I ever saw Butch do!" said Jaimoe. "I was so worried about Lamar's cut finger, but he could have been in there drunk and standing on his head. He was that good. Two of the other guys knew the material so well they could have started an Allman Brothers tribute band and Lamar, who had never played any of these songs, blew them away."

No one disagreed, which did not surprise Trucks. "It was obvious," he explained. "No one could miss it."

"Berry's death was almost unbearable but Lamar was the perfect replacement," Allman said. "It's amazing we found him."

With their new lineup set, the band returned to Capricorn, and studio tapes show them working on both new and old songs by December 3. Williams was beginning one of the most remarkable transitions in rock history, replacing a founding cornerstone of a great band without missing a beat. While extraordinary to those who didn't know Williams, who seemed to have come out of nowhere, it was exactly what Jaimoe and anyone else from the Gulf Coast music community would have expected. There, Lamar Williams had been a first-call bassist since he was fifteen.

7
TROUBLE NO MORE

J **AIMOE AND LAMAR** Williams were more than just old friends. They were musical soulmates. Though Johnson was five years older and an experienced drummer by the time they met, Williams taught him how to play with a bassist—most crucially, how the kick drum should align with a bassist's picking hand to create a groove. This alignment is how a rhythm section in rock, blues, and R&B creates a "pocket," the very essence of these genres' sound and the key reason why a drummer and bassist work together to form the backbone of any band.

"I had studied jazz drumming, where there was nothing definitive about where to put the beat, unlike in rock or R&B," said Jaimoe. "Lamar explained that to me. He made me wake up and pay more attention. It was like, 'Shit, man, something's happening here.'"

While Williams had an instinctive musical knowledge, Jaimoe had far more experience playing live shows, and they each benefited from playing together. "I taught him a lot about being a musician, but I learned so much from him in return," Jaimoe said. "I had a lot more experience than him and had been playing gigs for several years, but he was just a hell of a bass player."

Lamar was the eldest of nine siblings; three of his younger brothers were also bass players. Their father, Lemon, was a renowned local gospel singer, fronting a group called the Deep South Spiritual Singers, who played with national stars like the Mighty Clouds of Joy. "Dad's group sang on the radio every Sunday morning and we'd all sit around and listen," said Lamar's brother James.

After meeting through a mutual family friend, Lamar started coming over to hang out with Jaimoe, and the two would listen to records together and play along, with Lamar plucking an upright bass sitting in the corner of the Johnsons' house. By age fourteen, Lamar was playing with his father's gospel band, and he quickly became the de facto musical director.

Lamar was soon also playing with top-shelf local musicians in the thriving Gulf Coast club scene, mostly with Jaimoe in an R&B group called the Sounds of Soul. "Lamar was just a kid but nobody noticed that because he had a full beard and wild hair, a giant afro," said Jaimoe. "We had a real hot little band and it was a tremendous experience for both of us."

Williams quit school after ninth grade to focus on music, just as Duane Allman had done. "No matter his lack of education, Lamar was a smart motherfucker," said Jaimoe. "He was making more money playing with us and some others than his dad was making and just decided if he could do that doing what he loved, he was quitting school."

When Duane met Jaimoe in Muscle Shoals in January 1969, he asked the drummer if he knew any musicians they should check out. Jaimoe immediately thought of Lamar. "He was the only cat I knew who was good enough to even consider," said Jaimoe. "It's interesting to think what would have happened if Lamar had joined up with us in 1969. Musically, he would have been great but different, but he wasn't an outspoken leader like Berry was."

This was all just an intellectual exercise because Williams was serving in Vietnam then, having been drafted into the army the year before. "It was very sad to watch him have to shave off his beard and cut his hair," James Williams said of his brother. "He was so upset about being drafted."

Williams's enlistment was part of a surge that saw the United States build up to almost half a million troops on the ground in Southeast Asia in 1969. Throughout the war, African Americans were disproportionately drafted and sent to fight: they "represented approximately 11 percent of the civilian population. Yet in 1967, they represented 16.3 percent of all draftees and 23 percent of all combat troops in Vietnam."

While Williams had been drafted and unhappily joined the army,

Jaimoe had tried and failed to enlist in the armed services multiple times after graduating high school in 1962. He wanted to improve his drum fundamentals and thought a military band would be a great place to do so. He had taken and passed the air force musical test but was rejected because of poor vision in his left eye, the result of a childhood accident with a rubber ball. The navy rejected him for the same reason. The fact that Jaimoe tried so hard to enlist in two branches of the military in the early 1960s reflects how the later expansion of the war in Vietnam and the rapid increase in U.S. involvement changed many young Americans' views on serving. Jaimoe was five years older than Lamar and three years older than Gregg Allman, who famously had a foot-shooting party to avoid the draft.

"A few years later my friends would be shooting themselves in the foot and eating soap to spike their blood pressure to avoid getting drafted and there I was scuffling to get in," Jaimoe said. "It was peacetime and I didn't want to shoot nobody. I wanted to play in the band, but they classified me as 1-Y, which means the only way we will put a gun in your hand is if motherfuckers land here."*

Williams was initially assigned to a Special Services band, which helped him expand his musical vocabulary. "The interesting thing about all this was we did everything from ragtime to country and western music," he said. "I think it's important to have perspectives on different types of music and not let yourself get into a rut by playing only one style. I keep track of all of it."

Eventually, however, Williams joined a combat unit and was sent to Vietnam. Opposed to the war and repulsed by the idea of killing anyone, he went AWOL once he arrived in Southeast Asia, a classification for soldiers who are absent for thirty days or less and which applied to as many as 10 percent of soldiers in this period. He walked away from his base and into the jungle, his real base for his entire tour of duty. "He told me that he immediately integrated himself into Vietnam," said Jaimoe. "He wasn't in any particular unit and the way that he lived was like a lot of cats lived over there. They just survived."

---

* The official designation of 1-Y was "available for military service but qualified only in the event of war or national emergency," so Jaimoe's colorful description is not far off.

Lamar told friends he would wander to different American bases, say that he had been separated from his unit, stay there for a few weeks, and wander back into the jungle. The army punished Williams by extending his tour by six months.

After receiving an honorable discharge, Lamar returned from Vietnam in 1970 with a taste for heroin. The heroin in Vietnam was extremely pure and mainly came from Cambodia, from which it flowed more readily after the country fell into civil war in 1970 in the wake of American bombardment. Use by U.S. soldiers ticked up accordingly, fueled both by the drug's easy availability and the increasingly bad situation on the ground. By 1973, 34 percent of U.S. soldiers used heroin and up to 20 percent were "dependent" on the drug while serving in Vietnam.

"There was an incredible culture of heroin use among soldiers over there," said Jaimoe's brother Leroy Johnson, who also served in Vietnam. "That shit over in Vietnam was so pure that it would build your tolerance up so high that snorting heroin was just like smoking a joint. When your tolerance becomes that high, you just function on it, and most people don't even notice that you're using."

When Williams returned to Mississippi in 1970, the Allman Brothers Band was in its second year of relentless touring. Williams started playing with the Kings of Soul, a group that included Rudolph "Juicy" Carter, a saxophonist who had been in Percy Sledge's band with Jaimoe and who had sat in with the Allman Brothers regularly, including the shows in New York that made up *At Fillmore East*. Williams's family became concerned about his rootlessness, his heroin problem, and his continuing search for a steady musical home.

"He said he was going to give it until his twenty-fifth birthday and if it didn't work he'd try to do something else," recalled his brother James. Two months before his twenty-fifth birthday, Jaimoe called Lamar to Macon to audition. Within days, he was rehearsing with the Allman Brothers, and it wasn't long before the band was back on the road.

The Allman Brothers Band played their first gig with Lamar on December 9, 1972, at sold-out Crisler Arena in Ann Arbor, Michigan. It was less than a month after losing Oakley. Around the same time, they started recording again. With the additions of Leavell and Williams, the new Allman Brothers Band was complete.

Once the band started touring and playing their back catalog, Oakley's and Williams's different approaches would become clear. Oakley played with an expansive, free-range mentality, like the Phil Lesh devotee he was, while Williams stayed more on the root and in the pocket, creating grooves with the drummers. But Oakley had stayed closer to home on "Wasted Words" and "Ramblin' Man," the two *Brothers and Sisters* tracks he recorded, adapting his style to the material. This made for a remarkably smooth transition; there is no difference in the feel of the bass or the band's overall sound from Oakley's tracks to Williams's work on *Brothers and Sisters*.

Lamar himself described his playing as essentially doing whatever it took to serve the song. "I like to fill all the holes—keep it padded and just hold the bottom," he said. "If there's a specific song that requires some flair, then I'll go for it, but I always like to keep the sound rounded."

Williams's easygoing personality helped ensure his transition into the group. His stellar ear and well-rounded musicality were key assets as well. Leavell said that Williams could listen to any song once and develop a perfect bass line. He could play back the most complex melodic lines after a single listen, and he heard everything that everyone else was playing.

"If somebody played a note wrong, it was always Lamar who picked up where the mistake had been made," Leavell said. "He just had an innate gift for music and was a more melodic player than most people realize. In that way, he was very similar to Berry. He played much more with the drums than Berry did, but he was also willing to explore and experiment."

As the bass player for the Allman Brothers from 1996 to 2014, Oteil Burbridge studied Oakley's and Williams's work as much as anyone ever has, and he sees the brilliance of what Williams brought to the band: he straddled Allman's and Betts's differing demands from a bassist and further developed his "natural rhythmic hookup with Jaimoe."

"Lamar had all the facility, the great chops, and creativity to take the music out far, which Dickey liked to do, as well as the natural inclination to stay home in the pocket, which Gregg really favored," said Burbridge. "Lamar was a perfect player to help the band launch a new chapter by giving both Dickey and Gregg what they wanted, which is a tricky balance to maintain."

Everyone understood that this music could only work as intended if each musician was free to express themselves, to adopt the band's ethos without copying his predecessor. Sandlin described the thought process perfectly: "The guy who was driving the bus is gone. Let's go down a different road."

Jaimoe, with jazz ever on his mind, compares the shift to Miles Davis and his different groups. The music was different with John Coltrane and Cannonball Adderley on *Kind of Blue* than it was later with Herbie Hancock and Wayne Shorter on *Miles Smiles*. "Directions change when personnel changes," he said. "Duane died and Chuck came in. Berry died and Lamar came in. Dickey started writing more songs. There was a natural flow. Moving with the flow of the current reality makes more sense than trying to re-create the old reality."

The Allman Brothers Band was entering a new stage. While it felt good to everyone, no one could have anticipated just how smooth the transition would be or how successful the new iteration would become. That success was being worked out in real time onstage and in Capricorn Studios, as Lamar and Chuck settled into their roles.

8

BROTHERS AND SISTERS

I**T TOOK ALMOST** a year to record *Brothers and Sisters,* far longer than anything the band had done previously. That doesn't sound like a particularly long time, but they had released their first four albums—*Allman Brothers Band, Idlewild South, At Fillmore East,* and *Eat a Peach*—in a span of two and a half years. This was not an unusual production schedule for the time. Creedence Clearwater Revival put out three hit-laden albums—*Bayou Country, Green River,* and *Willy and the Poor Boys*—in 1969 alone. The Beatles released their three final albums—*Yellow Submarine, Abbey Road,* and *Let It Be*—in fifteen months despite their well-documented conflicts and problems.

Taking over a year to record a single album seemed extravagant. The length of time was even more pronounced because Warner Bros had mistakenly launched an advertising campaign that sent buyers into stores looking for a nonexistent album. It had been reported a year earlier that the album, tentatively titled *Lightnin' Rod,* would be out by September 1972, which came and went without much progress.

Under the circumstances, the delay was understandable. The recording was interrupted by the death of one of the band's leaders and the addition and integration of two new members. In addition, they were consistently touring throughout the process, and one of their two key songwriters and lead singers was simultaneously writing and recording a solo album. The band was also taking advantage of the free studio time promised in their contract, which took the heat off in ways both good and bad. Booking a week in a studio, traveling to it, and staying in a hotel tends to focus the mind.

They worked at night, often until sunrise. Sandlin was thrilled to finally be producing the band. His work on *Eat a Peach* had been uncredited, reduced to a thank-you, and it wasn't his first disappointment with the band. Sandlin had been told by Walden, Duane, and Gregg that he would coproduce *Idlewild South* at Capricorn with Tom Dowd. Unfortunately, no one ever discussed this with Dowd, leading to an embarrassing day of studio miscommunication before Dowd moved the project to his better-equipped home base at Miami's Criteria.

"Deciding to record *Idlewild South* with just Tommy was fine and understandable," Sandlin said. "Not telling me about it and allowing me to make an ass out of myself with someone I really admired was not. I was hurt and angry."

Now they were recording on Sandlin's home turf with him behind the board. Years later, he would reflect that the open-ended nature of working at home with free studio time had its downside. There didn't seem to be any urgency or deadlines to complete songs, and things often bogged down to a glacial pace. It was easy for band members—generally, Gregg or Dickey—to rationalize showing up hours late or not showing up at all for any given session.

"It was almost like a prestige thing for them: *we're so big, we can just take over a studio and wait for a magic moment to happen*," Sandlin said. "It is not an efficient, productive way to work."

Betts, however, expressed relief at not having to "get in there with a deadline. For the first time in a long while, we [were] just taking it easy."

As the new Chuck and Lamar lineup found its legs, they recorded "Southbound," their first keeper track together, which was written by Betts and sung by Allman. The band had cut a crisp instrumental version with Oakley on November 8, in what may have been his last recording. The song leans toward what was soon to be known as southern rock. The fine playing, Betts's stop-time arrangement, and Gregg's vocals saved it from being generic.

Betts said that he wrote the song for his then wife, Sandy. He was inspired by a short run of shows when the band rented buses to do four or five gigs "that were just too close to fly to." Thinking about heading back south to his home and wife led him to put pen to paper. The song is not one of Betts's or the band's more original tunes, but it has held up well, and it remained in the Allman Brothers stage repertoire until the end, often as a vehicle for guest jamming.

The Kirshner show performance, Oakley's last, aired on national TV in December, while the band was still in the studio. It was the first time the world heard "Ramblin' Man," over six months before the single's release. Betts said that he and the band were amused watching themselves on TV. "We looked so nervous," he said. "We looked scared—because we were."

As they contemplated finishing the album they had started with Oakley, the band got the idea of assembling "Wasted Words" and "Ramblin' Man" with a studio jam, dubbed "Berry's Tune" after his passing, on one side of the album. The concept was to honor Oakley by collecting his final recordings together. They decided to hold off on "Berry's Tune," Sandlin explained, because it was a ten-minute jam and not a true composition.

"After the long wait, we just didn't want people to feel they were getting ripped off," Sandlin said. "There'll be a time to put it out. It's certainly worthy." The song has still not seen the light of day fifty years later, despite plenty of other studio outtakes being released, so maybe wiser heads prevailed. "Berry's Tune" didn't make the cut for 2019's expanded *Brothers and Sisters* release, which included an entire disc of studio outtakes and jams.

At some point in the recording process, Walden mentioned to Betts that the album did not yet have a signature instrumental along the lines of "In Memory of Elizabeth Reed," "Hot 'Lanta," or "Les Brers in A Minor." Betts told Walden that not every album needed an instrumental and that he couldn't just create one without having a vision. "I really need to have an image in my head before I can start writing an instrumental because otherwise it's too vague," Betts said. "I get an emotion or an idea I want to express and see what I can come up with."

"Jessica" was no different. The song began as an experiment Betts was conducting: to write a piece of music that he could play with just two fingers on his fretting hand in honor of Django Reinhardt. It gained form, however, from the sight of his baby daughter, Jessica.

Reinhardt, the Romani jazz guitar master, played with just two usable fingers on his left hand, after the others were rendered useless from severe burns suffered in a wagon fire. He could use his fourth (ring) and fifth (pinkie) fingers to chord but not to play single note leads. This led to his creating a new style using just his index and middle fingers for single note playing, a technique that he used to produce some of the greatest music of all time. In doing so, he became a major inspiration to countless guitarists, including B.B. King and Betts.

Trying to write a song using this technique, Betts came up with a simple but distinctive melody but no further structure. It did not take flight until Jessica came crawling across the floor and he started playing along to her natural rhythm. "I was trying to capture musically the way she looked bouncing around the room, and the song came together," Betts said. Before that, he said, it was "just a bunch of notes going nowhere." One of the greatest rock instrumentals ever written and recorded, "Jessica" is a contender for the world's happiest song, reflecting its origins.

Les Dudek, who had already helped light up "Ramblin' Man" and would contribute acoustic guitar to "Jessica," said that he helped finish the song, turning a good sketch into a completed composition. "I co-wrote 'Jessica' with Dickey," Dudek insists.

The guitarist said that the two of them had been doing a lot of jamming when Betts invited him and his girlfriend over for dinner, telling him to bring his acoustic guitar. Before the group sat down to eat, Betts demonstrated the opening rhythm and main verse riff of "Jessica," telling him he was stuck there. Dudek said that he continued to work on the song after a frustrated Betts walked away, coming up with a bridge, which switched the two-chord change from A-D to D-G for the guitar solo. Dudek said that as soon as they worked it out, an ecstatic Betts ran to his pickup truck, and the two guitarists went off in search of bandmates to play the song. They were ready to record a demo while the composition was fresh but couldn't rustle up the group. Dudek and Betts went to the studio together the next day to play the song for the band, a fact no one disputes. No other band member fully supported Dudek's claim that he helped write the song, but he notes that they were not there when this session happened.

They may also have had different standards as to what constituted songwriting. There's no way to know what went down between Dudek and Betts, but it's quite possible that they were both right. Dudek could have contributed a significant idea that led to finishing the song, which Betts may have considered just buddies jamming or "arrangement" work. It would not be out of line with how the band did things. Berry Oakley did not even receive a writing credit for "Whipping Post," which Gregg brought in as a slow blues song and which Oakley transformed with a signature bass line in a unique 11/8 time signature. "Whipping Post" is not "Whipping Post" without that thundering bass intro, but Gregg is the sole credited composer.

"Dickey would often come in with an idea or a really nice melody and we'd all play our parts and make it into a song," said Jaimoe. "I don't know how much you have to put in a song to have a credit, but that's not how we did things. I believe Les may have helped him write the song."

This is a common practice in bands, and it has created major tension and disputes in many groups, notably the Band. Although Robbie Robertson received the songwriting credits for most of their songs and thus the associated revenue, many of the band members contended that he initiated songs but that they were often finalized by the group working through them together. Levon Helm felt strongly that "all the hot ideas, from the basic song concepts to the mixing and sequencing were not always exclusively" Robertson's. The Allman Brothers Band often worked in a similar fashion, considering that final process to be arranging rather than songwriting. In the 1960s and 1970s, most people did not yet realize just how much money the songwriting credits of a hit song could generate or how long they would continue to do so. The Doors, R.E.M., and U2 are among the small minority of iconic rock bands to credit most songs to all members so that everyone shares in the songwriters' income. Robertson sold the rights to his song catalog in February 2022 for a reported $25 million.

Royalties are paid to band members who perform on recorded songs, while studio musicians almost always receive day rates, with no further income. Songwriters earn separate, additional income, and the money generated by a hit can be significant, especially one with a long life. "Publishing" income derives from collecting this income for the songwriter. Traditional deals like Walden's gave the publisher an equal 50 percent share of songwriting royalties collected.

"Songwriting always has some gray areas," said Leavell. "If someone plays a particular riff, is it part of the song or part of the arrangement? We all contributed to the arrangement of 'Jessica,' but it was Dickey's song and I'm forever indebted to him for writing it. It's probably what I'm best known for."

Dudek showed up at the studio expecting to play the guitar harmonies he and Betts had painstakingly worked out, but said that Dickey told him he'd be handling them himself, with Leavell adding harmony parts as well. He said that Betts acknowledged his writing contributions but said, "You already played all those harmonies on 'Ramblin' Man,' so if you play the harmonies on 'Jessica' the critics might think you're gonna be in the band. I want you to play the acoustic rhythm guitar part instead."

"I was very disappointed, but there was nothing I could say about it, so I played the acoustic guitar," said Dudek. He added a simple but excellent and effective acoustic part throughout the song. In the studio, "Jessica" became something entirely different from anything the Allman Brothers Band had ever recorded: a major-key romp. The song is fueled by its beautiful and joyous structure and Betts's precise playing. It is elevated by Leavell's now iconic piano solo (a moment that, Sandlin noted, "gave Chuck a chance to stretch out and shine right away"), which leads to Betts's solo, blasting the song into the stratosphere.

Leavell said the song provided both a challenge and a unique opportunity, because it was "more light-hearted and less serious in nature" than the band's previous instrumentals. "The question," he said, "was how do we make this a little more intense and make it work as an Allman Brothers song?"

The group made another innovation to the song, largely replacing their famed two-part guitar harmonies with three-part harmonies, featuring two keyboards and a guitar.

"They were very difficult to work out and Gregg had to figure his parts out on a Hammond B3, which is not easy," said Leavell. Gregg demonstrated here that he was not just a singer playing the organ but also an important musical contributor.

"Gregg was a great B3 player," said Leavell. "He had a magnificent sense of how to properly use the instrument and a great ability to find the right colors—when to darken and when to lighten the tone and intensity."

Allman also had masterful control over the Hammond's draw bars, which alter the instrument's tones. While many rock organists mostly ignore them, Leavell said, Gregg "changed the sound a lot to go with the words or different parts of the music. He used the organ to its full effect."

Despite his strengths on the organ and as a musician, Allman still had some lingering insecurity from his earlier experience of having joined a hot band and being told by Duane that he had to learn a new instrument. Jaimoe notes that while "Gregory was insecure about his musicianship, he was a very great organ player, always in the groove."

"He was a master of the Leslie cabinet," said keyboardist Peter Levin, who played in Allman's last solo band and closely studied his playing. "He knew exactly when to kick it into fast, and exactly when to slow it down, which added a huge soulful element, in addition to his playing. It was so subtle, but so perfect."

While Allman took a back seat to Betts in terms of songwriting on *Brothers and Sisters*, he did contribute one of his finest songs to the album, "Come and Go Blues." The song is a beautifully constructed piece of music complemented by lyrics that convey the insecurity of being enmeshed in a failing relationship while still trying to follow your heart.

As he sings plaintively in some of the opening lines:

> *If only you would make up your mind.*
> *Take me where you go or leave me behind.*

Gregg would go on to record various versions of the song, including a gorgeous solo finger-picked acoustic take that he sadly never formally released. That version represents the song's true origin. The version on *Brothers and Sisters* is cast a bit differently, with a Betts-added bridge. Williams's soulful, loping bass line pulls the song back behind the beat as the drummers push it forward. That rhythmic drive and Leavell's elegant piano playing make "Come and Go Blues" one of the signature songs of this era of the band. It would have sounded radically different performed by the Duane-led group, and it's the one track that would have been equally at home on *Laid Back,* the solo album Gregg was simultaneously crafting. He would, in fact, record a slightly different version on his second solo album, 1977's *Playin' Up a Storm.*

Betts's playing and the bridge he added to "Come and Go Blues" and Allman's excellent organ work on "Jessica" are great examples of each musician lifting the others' compositions. It's something that became increasingly difficult to achieve in the years ahead as the musicians became more siloed from one another, according to Sandlin.

By late May 1973, the Allman Brothers Band needed one more song to complete the album. Gregg kept saying that he was finishing up two tunes: "Double Cross" and "Early Morning Blues." Demos of both songs were cut, but they remained works in progress.

"Double Cross" vanished into the Allman Brothers ether, despite a strong demo cut during the sessions, but Gregg performed it on his 1974 solo tour. "Early Morning Blues," however, was very much in the band's plans. Gregg said the lyrics were almost done, and the band laid down the musical tracks—a deep, slow blues in B that sounded suspiciously like Gregg and Duane's old arrangement of "Outskirts of Town." That blues standard was first recorded by Casey Bill Weldon in 1936, popularized by Louis Jordan in 1941, and subsequently recorded by many, including Ray Charles, whose version Duane and Gregg learned.

They recorded a great take of "Outskirts of Town" with Hour Glass in 1968, and the Allman Brothers Band even rehearsed the song during early sessions for *Brothers and Sisters.* That version is excellent, extended and loose, with everyone taking lengthy solos. The box containing the tape is labeled "Breaking in Chuck Leavell to Old Songs and Working Up New Songs." Sandlin said that he kept asking Gregg about the "Early Morning Blues" lyrics and that Gregg continued to say they were nearly completed, with three set verses and parts of a few others. But when it came time to lay down a finished vocal, "he didn't have much at all."

The struggle to get "Double Cross" and "Early Morning Blues" done was reflective of Allman's struggles during this time. "It got real hard to get Gregg in the studio," Trucks said. "We'd start at eleven PM and he'd show up at three or four in the morning. He said he had more songs for us, then basically just disappeared."

Gregg was simultaneously incredibly productive—concurrently recording two great albums—and a subject of concern for his friends, bandmates, and management. On May 27, 1973, he sang a three-verse version of "Early Morning Blues" that sounded nearly complete, far more so than Sandlin or anyone involved seemed to recall, as heard on the *Brothers and Sisters* deluxe edition. The song follows the "Outskirts of Town" slow blues pattern through the verses and solos, including a swinging, surging organ chorus by Gregg and a biting blues flight by Betts. But then, instead of ending, it flows into an extended double-time outro that veers into a "Whipping Post" feel, just the type of riff-driven crescendo that the Allman Brothers regularly used to turn blues covers into original songs. Steered by Betts, the coda jam fades out with him and Leavell playing stirring call and response with each other.

Although it doesn't sound too far from being complete, said Leavell, "My sense was that Gregg didn't really have a finished song and was basically mumbling some lyrics over the tracks we cut."

Maybe Gregg lacked the confidence to deliver the vocal with gusto, because the next day, with time running out to complete the album, he came in and sang the words to "Jelly Jelly" over the original "Early Morning Blues" track. "Jelly Jelly" was a 1940 hit written and first cut by jazz giants Earl "Fatha" Hines and Billy Eckstine.* Bobby "Blue" Bland later cut a version for Duke Records that made subtle changes in the first verse, and Gregg sang a slightly modified version of Bland's song. It had already been cut by everyone from acoustic bluesman Dave Van Ronk to saxophone giant Dexter Gordon to blues rock band Pacific Gas and Electric to singer Track Martin, who somehow ended up with the songwriting credit.

"Everyone was pushing me to complete the recording," Sandlin said. "Capricorn and Warner Bros wanted that album, so I was bugging Gregg. Finally, out of desperation, Gregg just sang the words to 'Jelly Jelly.' When

---

* Eckstine was a Pittsburgh native whose big band was the font of bebop, the place where Dizzy Gillespie and Charlie Parker connected in the horn section and started playing unison lines that changed the musical world.

we finished that vocal, I breathed a huge sigh of relief, as did Phil and Frank [Fenter, Capricorn president]."

Sandlin said that Bunky Odom was waiting in the studio to take Gregg to a drug and alcohol rehab facility in Buffalo as soon as he finished the "Jelly Jelly" vocal track. He spent most of a month there. "It was just a sad situation," Sandlin said.

Early pressings of *Brothers and Sisters* listing "Early Morning Blues" quickly became collector's items. "Jelly Jelly" would eventually close the first side. The album closer would be another left turn for the band: Betts's foot-stomping acoustic blues "Pony Boy." Engineer Buddy Thornton said that he was in the studio one day when Betts ran in with his wood-body resonator guitar, the same one that Duane had played on "Little Martha," and announced, "I've got this new song I've got to record real fast before I forget it."

Thornton got a stool and set up a direct microphone over Betts's dobro, and Betts played and sang "Pony Boy" by himself. "We were just going to cut this new tune of Dickey's so that he didn't forget it," Thornton said. "But that's the track we ended up using."

The song displays Betts's deft touch and mastery of acoustic slide playing. He describes the song as being heavily influenced by Robert Johnson's guitar playing. "I've always enjoyed playing in that style," said Betts. "Back in the early days of the Brothers we used to hang out with [acoustic blues man] John Hammond Jr. quite a bit, and he taught us a lot about traditional country blues playing."

Lyrically, Betts adds, the song was influenced by Blind Willie McTell's sense of humor. It tells the story of a pony trained to carry his drunken owner home safely after a night of carousing. As fanciful as the tale sounds, Betts said it's based on a true story regarding his uncle. "When I was a kid, the family lore was he would take his horse out when he went drinking to avoid DUI charges and the horse knew just how to take him home," he said.

Sandlin had Leavell, Williams, and Trucks come in and add piano, acoustic bass, and "drums" in the form of playing a piece of plywood on the floor; there is no actual drum kit on the song. Cowboy's Tommy Talton played acoustic guitar. "I ended up playing on 'Pony Boy' simply because I was in the studio all the time and Dickey and I played acoustics together," said Talton.

The song was finished off by Trucks and Betts, who sat down in chairs facing each other and played a hambone coda, slapping their legs percussively. "They did it live together, laughing and just having fun," Thornton recalled. Their laughter remains a part of the song and Trucks's only regret is that they didn't let the sound of their joy echo for longer.

"We were so serious about it, and at some point we just looked at each other and burst out laughing," Trucks said.

"Pony Boy" gave the album a gentler acoustic coda, reminiscent of *Eat a Peach*'s "Little Martha," and again opened up new territory for the band. It was a uniquely Betts song, as were "Jessica" and "Ramblin' Man," all of which helped redefine what the Allman Brothers Band's music was and what it could be. They also contributed to the feeling that Betts was taking more control of the group.

Dickey's growing role as front man, singer, and songwriter would create tensions with Gregg, but his original emergence was out of necessity. Allman's struggles with substance abuse and grief combined with the significant creativity he was pouring into *Laid Back* meant that there weren't a lot of other options to get the album done. Betts's new songs were also superb, as was his singing and guitar playing, which were increasingly spotlighted.

"We needed a song to finish the album and Dickey wrote 'Pony Boy,'" Trucks said. "Gregg eventually got mad that he only had two songs on there, but we couldn't wait around forever for him to finish more and present them to us."

As they passed the one-year anniversary of *Eat a Peach*'s February 12, 1972, release, everyone at Capricorn and Warner Bros was growing antsy to get *Brothers and Sisters* out. Capricorn's head of publicity, Mike Hyland, said that the label had the record jackets printed and waiting to be filled "for a long time." (That explains why "Early Morning Blues" was erroneously listed on those initial albums.)

The label would have to wait a few more months to press the records that could be slipped into those jackets and shipped around the country. After the recording was largely finished, there was still plenty of work to be done to complete *Brothers and Sisters*. This included mixing, the crucial art of layering and balancing each instrumental and vocal track, and mastering, the final act of post-production, which involves equalization and compression, with the goal of creating a unified sound and volume across all tracks. Sandlin, who was never fully happy with the sound of *Brothers and Sisters*, went to work, with various members of the band coming to sit at the board with him as he toiled late into the night. They were also cutting new parts to augment or replace previous sessions until at least June 29.

9

ALL MY FRIENDS

AS THE BAND was finishing up *Brothers and Sisters,* Allman and Sandlin were also completing his solo album, which had a very different sound and feel, though recorded in the same studio with the same producer. With nary an extended solo, *Laid Back* intitially confused some listeners expecting the harder-edged sound of the Allman Brothers Band. It was an album more suited to late nights and early mornings than Saturday-night partying or rolling down the highway—more "under the covers" than "tailgate party" material.

You wouldn't think that people would be surprised that an album named *Laid Back* sounded laid back, but in 1973 few outside the band's inner circle knew this side of Gregg Allman. "A certain side of me has always viewed myself as a folk singer with a rock and roll band," he said. Though it would become more obvious as he toured with various solo projects and released additional solo albums, *Laid Back*'s diversion from the Allman Brothers' sound stunned critics and listeners alike.

Gregg developed his approach of singing like Bobby Bland or Little Milton and writing songs like Tim Buckley, Stephen Stills, and Jackson Browne when he lived in Los Angeles in 1967–69. The L.A. scene was brimming with creativity, and Gregg learned much from these folk and folk-rock artists, several of whom became his friends.

"Gregg so easily slipped into that singer/songwriter, denim shirt / turquoise jewelry, Laurel Canyon vibe," said Jeff Hanna of the Nitty Gritty

Dirt Band. "That was very comfortable for him. When he was out there, Neil Young and Stephen Stills were already fully formed, Joni Mitchell was writing fabulous songs, and Jackson Browne was coming into his own. That Laurel Canyon sound was in the air and water of Southern California, and it had a real impact on Gregg."

His love for the acoustic guitar as both a player and a listener developed during that era. Gregg once told me that, though best known as a keyboardist, he considered guitar his "main instrument." That love affair had a rocky beginning, however. Gregg grew up in Nashville until he was about twelve and associated the acoustic guitar with country music, which he "had shoved down [his] throat and couldn't stand," associating it with "rednecks" in uncomfortable wooden Ryman Auditorium seats. The Ryman, home of the Grand Ole Opry, is now a revered American institution, but it represented everything a youthful Gregg wanted to escape, an old-fashioned temple to a bygone rural era. He wanted nothing to do with country music.

"I hate to speak ill of such a place, but as a kid, it was all String Bean and the Foggy Mountain Boys and crying in your beer stuff, so the last thing I wanted to see was a Tennessee flat top box, which is what they called the Martin-style guitar," Allman said. "Before I went out to L.A. and came across these guys, I didn't think of the acoustic guitar as something you could make art with. I thought it was something you lightly strummed or picked the blues on, which I often heard my brother do."

The transformation of his relationship with the acoustic guitar really began with Browne, who was Allman's roommate in Los Angeles for a brief but important time. The brothers Allman were in Los Angeles recording with Hour Glass. Their manager was Bill McEuen, who also managed the Nitty Gritty Dirt Band, which included his brother John. Both acts were signed to Liberty Records, and Hour Glass recorded Browne's "Cast Off All My Fears" on their debut album.

A year younger than Gregg, Jackson Browne had already written "These Days." The German singer Nico, formerly of the Velvet Underground, had a small hit with the song in 1967. Browne, who was briefly a member of the Nitty Gritty Dirt Band and was still friends with the band members, met Gregg through the McEuen connection. Liberty had set up Hour Glass with apartments, though Browne did not have one. "That's why Jackson was crashing with me," Allman said. "He was too proud to go home, and I really admired him for that."

Watching Browne's approach to songwriting had a huge impact on Allman. "He really influenced me to try my hand at writing more seriously," Gregg said. "He was already so good at it."

Just after Browne moved out of Gregg's apartment and Duane left Los Angeles, Gregg wrote "Melissa." Gregg often said that he had written it several years earlier in a Pensacola, Florida, hotel room, but no recording of it exists before the 31st of February's 1968 demo. And when he performed it publicly for the first time at Duane's funeral, Gregg said it was a song he "wrote three years ago." He also told me in 1996 that Browne was a huge influence on the song. After writing and tossing away over four hundred songs, Gregg said, he had penned the first song that could possibly stand up to the work of his peers. "Before that it was just, 'I wanna swoon with you / under the moon / in June,'" he said. Watching Browne work had completely altered his perspective.

"I really admired the way he played and picked and wrote songs about shit that I think about and have gone through and stuff that hurts you, just different ways of saying it," Allman said. "That's what I learned from him. It's knockin' thirty-five words down to four and having them really mean something. That is part of being a poet. Real poets might read this and laugh, but I think poetry is the art of saying something in a different way. People consider Shakespeare profound for saying, 'A rose by any other name is still a rose,' but Jackson wrote things I consider just as profound. He really touched a soft side of me, and I enjoyed every minute I ever spent with him."

In Los Angeles, Gregg also became a huge fan of Buffalo Springfield, featuring Stills and Young. Hour Glass opened a three-show run for them at the Fillmore in December 1967. Young's guitar playing did not much impress Duane, who thought he should "stick to rhythm work," but his singing and songwriting made a huge impression on Gregg, particularly "Expecting to Fly" and "Broken Arrow."

"'Expecting to Fly' is a piece of art . . . certainly just as potent to me as *Sgt.*

Pepper's Lonely Hearts Club Band," Allman said. He was just as enthusiastic about Tim Buckley, a unique singer and guitarist who could play accompanied just by a gentle percussionist and "sound like a choir."*

Allman was also greatly influenced by Buckley's songwriting. For years, he used Buckley's "Once I Was" as a warm-up song to prep his voice and guitar playing, recording it on his final album, 2017's *Southern Blood*. Allman was also fascinated by Buckley's use of finger picks on a twelve-string Martin guitar, inspiring him to learn how to Travis pick, the most popular style of fingerpicking.

"I developed my style from combining these things—folky songs with soulful-style vocals," Allman said. "I wrote 'Midnight Rider' and 'Come and Go Blues' by Travis picking in natural [open] G, and I don't think I ever would have written songs like them or 'Multi-Colored Lady' had I not gotten involved in a more serious way with the acoustic guitar. I learned so much and met so many wonderful people out there, and it really broadened my musical horizons. All I had known was R&B and blues, and these guys turned me on to a more folk-oriented approach and it's always stuck with me."

While most Allman Brothers Band fans never associated Gregg with California singer-songwriters, you can hear it clearly in songs like "Midnight Rider" and "Melissa." It was also visible in some of his lyrics, where Gregg, for all his macho swagger, was not afraid to show his vulnerability in a manner more familiar to singer-songwriters than to the blues tradition. He explored this softer, more lyrical side on "Come and Go Blues" and throughout *Laid Back*.

The integration of these different sides of Gregg's musical personality is perhaps the main reason *Laid Back* sounds so timeless and has endured as a significant artistic statement. It's hard to fathom just exactly how he recorded it in the middle of incorporating two new members into the Allman Brothers Band, grieving Oakley, recording *Brothers and Sisters*, and touring—all while continuing to wrestle with his own demons in the aftermath of Duane's death. To even begin understand-

---

* The same description could apply to Tim Buckley's son, Jeff. Both died tragically young— Tim at twenty-eight in 1975 and Jeff at thirty in 1997.

ing how this all happened, one has to grasp just how loose things were around Capricorn Studios and the deep bonds that existed between the core musicians.

Bill Stewart, the lone musician on *Laid Back* who had also been with Gregg in Miami for his initial solo sessions, said "the ball started rolling" when they got back to Macon. He credits much of the shift to Sandlin, whose help with arrangements, assisted in important ways by Scott Boyer and Tommy Talton, enabled Gregg to fulfill his vision. After working off and on for months, they recorded most of the final tracks in March 1973.

Laid Back and *Brothers and Sisters* overlapped often. All of this activity was happening inside a one-room studio in a nondescript building in downtown Macon, which unsuspecting people passed by every day without even noticing. When Buddy Thornton first arrived in Macon from Alabama to start working with Sandlin, he drove up and down Broadway looking for the studio, seeing nothing but dilapidated buildings. He felt increasingly certain he had the address wrong until he spied someone emerging from an unmarked door carrying a guitar.

From the street, the studio looked "like a nesting place for indiscriminate winos," Ben Edmonds wrote in *Creem*. "The only clue to the studio's existence is a small hand-lettered sign scotch taped on a bare window. Expectations call for a couple of tape machines propped on wobbly chairs to protect them from the spilled beer and cigarette butts. . . . Inside, however . . . the board room [had] a circular feel, almost like a diving bell. The orange carpeting is so thick you can feel your feet sink in with every step." The studio had multicolored lights, helping contribute to a space "as comfortable as the overstuffed couch in your grandmother's sitting room."

That comfortable room became the center of Macon's musical activity, with Paul Hornsby holding court as in-house producer during the day and Sandlin, a night owl, taking over after dark. The studio was originally built to cut R&B singles and adapted into a rehearsal space and a convenient low-tech facility for bands to record demos. By 1972, Capricorn completely renovated and updated the studio. It was a place, Sandlin said, that "always felt right."

"Capricorn Studios was our playhouse, our man cave, our tree fort," said Talton. "Everything was informal. When Gregg decided he had these songs that the Brothers quite frankly didn't care about, he knew that he wanted to get them recorded and Johnny's attitude was simply, 'Let's do it!'"

Everyone else's involvement was similarily organic, Talton explained. He and Boyer were constantly hanging out in the studio anyhow, and they were both friends with Gregg. "It wasn't like, 'Mr. Talton, Mr. Allman would like you to play acoustic, electric and slide on his next project. Be there on Tuesday at 4:30 with your instruments tuned, ready to record,'" Talton said. "It was, 'Hey man, are you around? Let's go in with Johnny and see what we can get down.'"

Boyer was in the studio constantly, sometimes recording and often-times just hanging out or waiting to see what would happen next. "It was nicer than my house," he said. "One night Tommy and I were in there and Johnny came in and said Gregg was going to record a solo album and we could probably play on it. He suggested we work something up, so we did a version of 'These Days,' because we knew Gregg was working on it and how much he loved Jackson, who had visited him in Macon."

The version he and Talton worked up featured Boyer on pedal steel guitar and was similar to the final take. Boyer had a "thrown-together" pedal steel that a young Ronnie Van Zant had given him in Jacksonville in 1969, which he played on several *Laid Back* tracks. Gregg liked his work on it so much that he bought him a high-end Sho-Bud instrument.

During the nights when the Allman Brothers Band was not recording, efforts on *Laid Back* continued, often with the musicians working out arrangements and laying down basic tracks without Gregg in the studio. They kept recording when the Brothers toured, with Boyer on scratch vocals. "We called him the stunt singer," said Stewart.

It all worked, in part because of Sandlin, whom Talton describes as the "glue or duct tape" that held the album together. He produced with a firm hand yet a relaxed approach, creating an atmosphere that inspired excellence and remained focused. He was keyed into the vibe Gregg sought and seemed to always know when to call for a break, intuitively sensing when someone needed a cup of coffee, a cigarette, a drink, or a bite to eat.

"He was great with the music, but he also had a knack for the other intangibles that make someone a great producer," said Talton.

"It was really relaxing to work with Johnny," said bassist Charlie Hayward. "He made it so comfortable, not at all intimidating as studio work can be. It was like being in his living room. If it had been a lesser producer, just rolling in there and doing his job, I don't think the album would have ever worked."

"Johnny had a very clear vision of what Gregg wanted," Boyer said. "They were in lockstep, and it was usually Johnny who conveyed it to us." Gregg described it as Sandlin's simply asking him what he wanted to hear and then providing solutions. Sandlin was much happier with the sonics of *Laid Back* and Betts's 1974 album *Highway Call* than he ever was with *Brothers and Sisters*. The difference, he said, was that the solo recordings were much more relaxed efforts on which it was easier for him to mic and record things exactly how he wanted, compared to the more raucous, late-night, catch-it-when-you-could Allman Brothers Band sessions.

Sandlin's hands-on approach to *Laid Back* was necessary because Gregg came and went from the studio for a variety of reasons, including his own lack of adherence to any schedule, and because the Allman Brothers Band continued to tour, an activity that remained the financial backbone not only of the band but also of the entire Phil Walden industry. "Even while recording two albums, the Brothers still had to go on the road because they made the money that kept the whole operation afloat," said Stewart.

Another factor that necessitated a firm producer's hand with *Laid Back* was that the musicians were working out the material on the fly in the studio. This was in contrast to the Allman Brothers, who often road tested and tweaked songs onstage before recording them.

"Everything on *Laid Back* developed in the room," said Leavell. "It was so exciting just sitting there going over the material with Gregg and Johnny, then discussing the arrangements, and who might be best to do a solo. We'd try different things and if it didn't work, go on to something else."

Much of the *Laid Back* band's core—Leavell, Hayward, and Stewart—had an easy familiarity and cohesiveness with one another, having spent much of the last two years on the road with Alex Taylor and Dr. John. Talton and Boyer were longtime bandmates whose Cowboy was part of the Capricorn family. The pair had been roommates with Leavell in an apartment around the corner from the Big House. Boyer later lived at

Idlewild South, the lakeside cabin that had been the Allman Brothers' rented getaway and which their second album was named after. "We all knew each other and had spent a lot of time jamming together," said Talton.

All of the musicians were close with one another and to varying degrees with Gregg. Everyone had worked often with Sandlin. The relationships made working together easy.

"We were just playing music," said Talton. "The suits were in the office two blocks up the street. They didn't come down and bother us and they could care less about what we were doing."

It was a relaxed approach that reflected the album's title: a two-word mission statement from Gregg to Sandlin and the band. *Laid Back* established Gregg Allman's own musical vision and identity, separate from his partners in the band that made him famous. "The big-amp thing is one thing, and then there's my thing, which you could call a small-amp thing," Allman said. "To get total musical fulfillment, I need both."

Despite its cohesive sound, *Laid Back* only features two new compositions from the man who had provided the bulk of the Allman Brothers Band's original material on its first four albums: "Queen of Hearts" and "Multi-Colored Lady." The rest of the material includes the Carter Family's "Will the Circle Be Unbroken"; new arrangements of "Midnight Rider" and "Please Call Home," songs Allman recorded just three years earlier on *Idlewild South*; a cover of a 1965 R&B hit, "Don't Mess Up a Good Thing"; and interpretations of two ballads, Boyer's "All My Friends" and Browne's "These Days."

It wasn't a big leap for Gregg to record "All My Friends." Its title was an apt description of what was unfolding at Capricorn Studios. The track originally appeared on Cowboy's 1971 album, *5'll Getcha Ten,* which had been in regular rotation at the Big House and included one of Duane's final recorded performances, "Please Be with Me." Gregg makes the song his own without radically altering it, taking it to church. Talton double tracked a guitar solo at Sandlin's suggestion.

Unlike "All My Friends," Allman completely remade his friend Jackson Browne's "These Days." Browne cut his own version of the tune on *For Everyman,* released in October 1973, the same month as *Laid Back.*

Browne preferred Allman's version to his own. He noted how Gregg slowed it down, "felt it deeply," and made the "song twice as good as it was before he sang it." Allman "unlocked a power" in the song, so much so that he paid his old friend the highest compliment a songwriter can give: Browne "strove to emulate" Gregg's version in his own performances of the song.

Gregg's interpretation of "These Days" is yet another example of the way a gifted artist can create fantastic, highly personal art by recording the work of others. Interpreting is an art in and of itself. Frank Sinatra and Billie Holiday made indelible art largely recording the work of other songwriters. Bonnie Raitt made John Prine's "Angel from Montgomery" her signature song.* Gregg's "These Days" belongs in that pantheon of interpretations that are impossible not to hear as coming from the singer's very essence, his or her deepest soul. Like most great interpreters, Gregg made small changes to make anything he sang his own—slightly altered vocal melodies, tweaked words, subtly shifted lyrical emphasis.

As he'd do with all his subsequent solo efforts, Allman also reinterpreted his own work on *Laid Back*. The Allman Brothers Band's "Please Call Home" went from a straight guitar blues to a gospel-infused, grandly orchestrated lament, featuring strings, horns, and a choir of female backup singers anchored by gospel legend Cissy Houston (mother of Whitney). Leavell played a big part in that reinterpretation.

Allman described the *Laid Back* version of "Midnight Rider," which featured him playing an open-tuned acoustic, as "the original version." "That was how I always heard the song," he said. Talton said that Allman came into the studio one day with an idea to play the song's signature riff a bit differently than in the Allman Brothers Band version, picked up his acoustic guitar, and showed the band. On *Laid Back*, "Midnight Rider" is simultaneously spare and lushly orchestrated, a testament to Sandlin's masterful mixing. There's a lot going on throughout the album, but the songs never sound cluttered.

"Midnight Rider" centers on Gregg's voice, Boyer's ringing acoustic guitar playing Gregg's new lick, Leavell's electric piano, and Talton's slide guitar.

---

* Allman's own philosophy was, "If you can make it yours, you can do it. I don't care if it's 'Mary Had a Little Lamb.' Hello, Stevie Ray." (Stevie Ray Vaughan performed a brilliant version of the nursery rhyme, which was actually a cover of Buddy Guy's arrangement.)

Sandlin augmented it with string and horn sections and backup singers. Jaimoe's congas come more to the fore on the ride out, subtly propelling the song. Unlike the swagger of the Allman Brothers Band's "Midnight Rider," Gregg's eerie, haunted vocal delivery hints that the hellhounds that had long been on his trail were nipping at his heels. The performance provides some insight into Gregg's mental state during these sessions, which took place in the lingering emotional aftermath of Duane's death.

Hayward believed "the darkness of 'Midnight Rider' had a lot to do with Gregg's state of mind. I thought he was singing his heart out for Duane." That sense of loss permeated everything around Capricorn and Macon music at the time, and it certainly impacted *Laid Back.*

"We knew that Gregory was hurting because of Duane and we wanted to make this record special for him," said Talton. "Everyone in Macon was hurting because of Duane, so I couldn't imagine what Gregory was going through. We knew this was going to be an important record."

If his performance of "Midnight Rider" indicated that Gregg's demons were closing in, then his response came with the album-closing "Will the Circle Be Unbroken," the Carter Family song that had been so central to the brotherhood and that mourners sang at Duane's funeral. Gregg's version is a moving prayer for solace in the religion of music and universal brotherhood. The song was a coda not only to *Laid Back* but also to Duane's time in the Allman Brothers Band. It was no coincidence that forty-one years later, during their final run at New York's Beacon Theatre in October 2014, the Allman Brothers Band slipped the melody of "Will the Circle Be Unbroken" into a song every night, climaxing in a full-on vocal version of the song near the end of the final set at the last show the band would play.

"It just seemed appropriate given that it was such an important song in the history of the band, seemingly played at every important occasion and by Gregg on *Laid Back*," said Warren Haynes, who helped resurrect the Allman Brothers Band in 1989 and was a crucial member in its final incarnation. "It's a song that always had a way of appearing."

The *Laid Back* version starts with Leavell's gospel piano accompanied only by Gregg's Hammond organ, which lets a single note drone through his Leslie cabinet. It's the sound of a Sunday service, the keyboards carrying the song from beginning to end. Gregg's vocals gather power as the song progresses, moving from a mournful lament to a hopeful, almost optimistic plea. Stewart's drums and Leavell's piano pick up a joyful feeling as the tempo slowly increases throughout the song. Cowboy bassist David Brown plays subtly. Lifting it all up is a Macon gospel choir that sings and claps, supplemented with the voices of various Capricorn musicians and employees.

Laid Back contained just two new Gregg Allman originals, but what songs they are—compositions and performances that defined the album and set the contours for Allman's solo career. "Multi-Colored Lady" is a gorgeous ballad that fades in with Talton's delicately finger-picked acoustic guitar and then Leavell's graceful piano, after which Gregg enters with a gentle vocal.

"The intro I put on that was spur of the moment," Talton said. "Johnny just said, 'Tommy, why don't you give us an intro?' and I started picking." Sandlin's handling of the introduction gives the listener a feeling of drifting into a gentle sleep or awakening from a dream. It's an enigmatic song, absent any blues form, with lyrics about the narrator boarding a bus in Memphis and sitting down next to a "broken-hearted bride" sobbing over a recent heartbreak. Touched by her sorrow and beauty, he comforts and maybe seduces her. Gregg's lyrics are heartfelt and romantic. They feel deeply personal even while not being particularly clear and quite possibly metaphorical: *("Multicolored lady, you ain't like no rainbow I've ever seen. Multicolored lady, angry red, passion blue, but mostly shades of green.")* Sandlin polished the track off with a string section that emphasizes its lush romanticism.

"Queen of Hearts," the song whose rejection by the Allman Brothers Band kick-started Gregg's desire to make a solo album, is another strikingly unguarded romantic ballad. The song became a masterpiece when it was completed with guitar parts by Buzzy Feiten and a saxophone solo by jazz giant David "Fathead" Newman. Sandlin and Allman also traveled to New York to record strings and horns.

Leavell said that the addition of a string section arranged and conducted by a prominent outsider—Ed Freeman, who had produced Don

McLean's 1971 hit "American Pie"—was exciting. It made clear just how different this project really was: a ballad-based album with a less fierce, more mellow approach.

Gregg started *Laid Back* with the idea of not having any lead guitar, but it became clear that some songs would benefit from a true soloist. Sandlin called Feiten, and the Los Angeles–based guitarist flew to New York and added his licks to both "Please Call Home" and "Queen of Hearts." Feiten was a top-flight studio guitarist revered for his spectacular solos on Stevie Wonder's 1972 "Superwoman" and his tandem playing with Jeff Beck on Wonder's "Looking for Another Pure Love." He had already talked to Gregg about playing in his solo band, a collaboration that never took place but led to Feiten's being on this album.

Per Gregg's wishes, Feiten played no extended solos. But his lyrical intro transformed "Queen of Hearts," and Sandlin mixed more of his blazing licks throughout the song.

Newman, who cut his solo on the same New York sessions, was one of the masters of the "big tenor" sound and a key member of Ray Charles's early bands. His pithy solos enlivened hits like "Lonely Avenue," "Night Time Is the Right Time," and "Unchain My Heart." Atlantic's Jerry Wexler called Newman "Ray Charles' alter ego."

Gregg was excited to have him on "Queen of Hearts" and was deeply moved sitting in the control room listening to him play over the song that Gregg had spent so much time crafting. When he learned that the saxophonist was being paid the union day rate, Gregg said, he reached into his pocket and pulled several hundred dollars off a money roll and handed it to him in gratitude. Fathead's solo, Feiten's intro and lead fills, and Jaimoe's conga playing finished the moody, complex "Queen of Hearts."

Hearing the completed song had a powerful impact on Allman. He once went so far as to say that it saved his life by helping him realize he still had something to say in Duane's absence. "For the first time I realized I wasn't the no-talent, procrastinating, don't-take-care-of-business flunky sheep I thought I was after my brother died," he said.

Allman was clear in later years that he welcomed the opportunity to develop aspects of his music that he couldn't really explore with the Allman Brothers Band. The solo albums, he said, were "like an open field" where he could try anything.

"With the Brothers, what you hear on stage and record have always been pretty much the same thing, but with my own records, I feel free about sweetening it with strings and voices, or to go the other way, and just have just my acoustic guitar and voice," Allman said. "A lot of it was just an adventure to see how I would like it. There's always something else to try."

10
BROTHERS IN ARMS

THE **ALLMAN BROTHERS** Band and the Grateful Dead had a close bond long before their relationship blossomed with a series of very large high-profile shows in 1973 just before the release of *Brothers and Sisters*. The Dead, which formed in 1965, were a primary influence on the Allman Brothers Band, particularly Duane Allman, Dickey Betts, and Berry Oakley.

Paul Hornsby, the Capricorn producer who played keyboards in Hour Glass, said that the band saw the Grateful Dead shortly after arriving in Los Angeles in June 1967 and were less than impressed. This experience seems to have been forgotten by Duane two years later, when the Grateful Dead and the Allman Brothers Band first appeared on the same bill on July 7, 1969. The Allman Brothers had only existed for a few months when both groups played in Atlanta's Piedmont Park, the day after the first Atlanta International Pop Festival closed. Flyers handed out to departing festival attendees read simply, "Come to Piedmont Park, Monday 1 PM."

Promoter Alex Cooley had organized the free show as a thank-you after his three-day festival, a landmark Southern musical and cultural gathering, featuring Janis Joplin, Johnny Winter, Creedence Clearwater Revival, the Staples Singers, and Led Zeppelin, among others. The Allman Brothers and Dead were the only bands to play at Piedmont who had *not* been at the festival. Already well-established hippie heroes, the Dead were the day's final performers, capping an incredible run of free music that included the Hampton Grease Band, Chicago Transit Authority, the Allman Brothers Band, Spirit, and Delaney & Bonnie and Friends. The Dead closed their set by inviting members of all the other bands onto the stage; Duane and Dickey joined Spirit's Ed Cassidy, Chicago's Terry Kath, Delaney Bramlett, and many others for a jam.

Although there were significant differences in their approaches, the Grateful Dead and the Allman Brothers Band were both rock bands grounded in improvisation more common to jazz and known for free-flowing live shows that could last for hours. Both bands have continued to exert strong influence on music and culture for more than fifty years, with catalogs that have become as foundational as the old-time blues and standards that were both bands' cornerstones.

Though there were significant differences in the playing and leadership styles of Jerry Garcia and Duane Allman, both were bandleaders who liked to emphasize that they were really just another band member. Both guitarists had an aura that led people to follow them without ever having to be asked. Duane, however, was not shy about telling people what to do, which, as Dead drummer Bill Kreutzmann notes, "Jerry did not like to do."

"Duane laid it down and it was done, but he never once had to say it was his band," said Thom Doucette. "He was so fucking magnetic. This was a guy connected to the higher order of the world, with absolute self-confidence but no ego."

Sam Cutler, who comanaged the Dead from 1969 to 1974, draws a distinct line between Garcia's leadership on and off the stage. When it came to anything not related to music, especially business decisions, he said, "Jerry was hopeless. He would sit there with a gnome-like grin watching the mud being stirred by Machiavellian power plays." Onstage or in the studio, however, Garcia was "a psychedelic fascist."

"He led the band, just like Miles Davis led his band," Cutler said. "Jerry determined where it was headed. Other people had some influence, especially Phil [Lesh], but when it came to musical decisions, Jerry's word was law and no one questioned it."

Adds Kreutzmann, "I don't know how to describe it, but there's a spark in some people that you can't deny, and Jerry had that, big-time."

Garcia's Allman Brothers counterpart was similarly wired. Everyone who knew and interacted with Duane described the same kind of magnetism, although, unlike Garcia, his was accompanied by a whirling dervish energy.

"Duane was very different from Jerry Garcia, who was very easygoing. Duane didn't have time to be easygoing; there was much more urgency to his personality," said Betts. "You gained a lot of respect from him if you proved you could keep up with him. He led by example, not by giving orders."

Whatever their differences, Garcia and Allman saw each other as musical brothers, "friends with a deep respect for one another," as Butch Trucks said.

The entire Grateful Dead recognized the Allman Brothers as "kindred spirits," said Bob Weir. "We always loved playing with them. Our connection was clear from the first time we played together."

Cutler, who was a key part of the Dead/Allman collaborations, notes that both bands were actively redefining Americana during "that magic period around the end of the '60s." An Englishman who came to the Dead via the Rolling Stones, Cutler was fascinated by the way serious American artists constantly questioned what it means to be an American. "It's not an English thing," he said. "No one sets out to discover England, whereas it is very American to search for the heart of a nation which constantly reinvents itself."

At their founding, Garcia and the Dead found inspiration from the Beat Generation, writers like Allen Ginsberg, William S. Burroughs, and Jack Kerouac, who were casting about for a new vision of postwar America. Kerouac's 1957 novel *On the Road* was based in large part on the author's relationship with Neal Cassady, who also became a Grateful Dead mentor and inspiration. The book was a statement of postwar disillusion, a new-generation template of peripatetic purpose. Hearing a recording of Kerouac reading the book was a major turning point in Garcia's conception of the world and its possibilities.

"I'd read this stuff, but I hadn't heard it, the cadences, the flow, the endlessness of the prose, the way it just poured off," Garcia said. "It was really stunning to me. His way of perceiving music . . . and the romance of the American highway, it struck me. It struck a primal chord. It felt familiar, something I wanted to join in. It wasn't like a club. It was a way of seeing."

The impact was so immense, Garcia said, that it couldn't really be measured. Kerouac had so deeply penetrated his essence that it was impossible to parse exactly what the influence was and who Garcia had been before he heard him read his work. "I don't know if I would ever have had the courage or the vision to do something outside with my life—or even [have] suspected the possibilities existed—if it weren't for Kerouac opening those doors," he said.

The possibility of taking to the road to find or reinvent yourself was a powerful, uniquely American concept, one that the Allman Brothers Band and the Grateful Dead embraced both consciously and unconsciously. "The Allman Brothers were sort of the Southern version of what the Grateful Dead were in California," said Cutler. "There was an intense sympathy between the two sets of musicians."

The bands shared a love for improvisational music that was based in roots and blues but limited only by the imagination. And although there were significant differences in sound and approach, there were also similarities among them. Oakley drew inspiration from Lesh's inventive style, which freed the bass from playing root notes locked in with the kick drum—the two bassists greatly admired each other. Both bands also had two drummers, although they approached their craft in very different ways. While Trucks and Jaimoe took pride in working out their parts on the fly by "just playing," Kreutzmann and Mickey Hart took the opposite tack, carefully crafting the drum tracks.

"Jaimoe and I studied what Bill and Mickey were doing, but it was much more contrived than what we did," said Trucks. "That worked very well for them, but not for us. Our styles mesh in a way where we don't talk about it or work it out. We've always each played what we wanted, and it just works."

Trucks emphasized that he "wasn't criticizing" the Dead's approach, and Kreutzmann readily agreed with his assessment. "We worked stuff out!" he said. "We improvised with each other—like if Mickey was on the low tones, big drums, I'd go to the high tone, small drums, and we'd have conversations, but whether it looked easy or not, we worked hard. There's really no comparison, no similarity to what we did and what the Allman Brothers did, other than having two drummers."

Oteil Burbridge is in a unique position to analyze the similarities and differences between the two sets of drummers. The bassist played with Jaimoe and Trucks for seventeen years in the Allman Brothers and has played with Kreutzmann and Hart in Dead and Company from 2015 to 2023. "They are very different, almost to the point of being yin and yang," said Burbridge. "In both cases the two-drummer thing is a big part of the music and the pairs having played together for so long gives them a level of communication that is truly beautiful to witness. The tiniest shared glances can take on such depth."

And while both bands had two guitarists who approached their partnerships very differently than one another, neither band favored the standard rhythm guitarist / lead relationship. The Dead hewed closer to this model, with Garcia as the soloist and Weir the accompanist, but Weir favored counterpoints, chord inversions, and distinctive parts to traditional rhythm playing, a method inspired largely by pianist McCoy Tyner of the John Coltrane Quartet. Betts and Allman altogether ignored the rock and roll convention of having one dominant soloist and one supportive rhythm player, swapping and sharing lead lines while pushing each other with aggressive, creative rhythm playing.

"I wish everyone could hear what I heard standing behind their amps listening to what Dickey and Duane played behind one another's solos," said Doucette. "Their rhythm playing was endlessly inventive and inspiring."

They also excelled at playing harmony lines that echoed both jazz horns and western swing instrumentation, a seemingly natural and intuitive approach, but one that set them apart and helped create new possibilities for rock and roll guitar playing.

BY THE TIME the Allman Brothers Band formed in 1969, the Dead was coming out of its heavy psychedelic phase and headed toward the emerging Americana of *Workingman's Dead* and *American Beauty*. The two song-oriented, country-tinged albums were released within five months of each other in 1970 and are the pinnacle of the band's studio career. The tunes reveal the heavy influence of the Allman Brothers Band's first two releases, which made a huge impact on Garcia and lyricist Robert Hunter, the Dead's primary songwriters.

The quieter songs were also a reaction to the band's tumultuous 1969, when they released two primo psychedelic recordings: the studio *Aoxomoxoa* and the free-flowing *Live Dead*. That August, the Dead played a weak set at Woodstock that they refused to appear on the album and movie. In December, the band played a central role in planning a free concert at California's Altamont Raceway that was to feature them; Santana; Crosby, Stills, Nash, and Young; Jefferson Airplane; and the Rolling Stones. Some 300,000 fans arrived to find insufficient facilities and chaos. During the Stones' headlining set, Meredith Curly Hunter was stabbed to death by a member of the Hell's Angels. The motorcycle gang oversaw security at the suggestion of the Dead. The fiasco scarred the band. Although scheduled to play before the Stones, they left the premises after hearing that a member of the Hell's Angels assaulted Jefferson Airplane singer Marty Balin and never took the Altamont stage. Altamont also brought them Cutler, who stuck around when the Stones fled back to London and was hired by the Dead, who admired his integrity.

In the wake of such a turbulent year, the Dead looked to scale back, turn inward, and make more personal music as a new decade dawned. "All music played at any given time is a reflection of what is going on in that person's life, and we are the kind of musicians who play how we feel," said Kreutzmann.

With the band ready for a change of direction, owing Warner Bros almost $200,000 after *Aoxomoxoa*, and not wanting to get deeper into debt, Garcia suggested the Dead approach their next album "like a country record . . . a few instruments, relatively simple and easy to perform songs." It was, he said, a conscious effort to work fast and cheap and also to "expose a side of us that we hadn't exposed very much."

Garcia's suggestion was consistent with the rootsier direction in which the Dead was already heading. He had learned pedal steel guitar and formed the New Riders of the Purple Sage, whose acoustic-based roots music both reflected his outlook and impacted his songwriting. In the summer and fall of 1969, the Dead added country songs like Merle Haggard's "Mama Tried" and debuted rootsy new originals like "Dire Wolf," "Casey Jones," "Cumberland Blues," and "Uncle John's Band."

Another influential change was the band's growing friendship with David Crosby, Stephen Stills, and Graham Nash, who were frequent guests at Mickey Hart's Marin County ranch. Garcia played the beautiful pedal steel on Crosby, Stills, Nash, and Young's 1970 hit "Teach Your Children," and the group's guidance on how to perform stacked vocal harmonies "changed the ballgame entirely," said Kreutzmann.

Crosby said that the assistance wasn't in the form of "formal lessons," but instead something far more casual and intuitive. "They were brilliant musicians who saw something they could adopt," he said. "We all just liked each other and were hanging out a lot and they paid attention to what we were doing."

The Grateful Dead entered San Francisco's Pacific High Studios in February 1970 and, true to Garcia's expressed vision, finished *Workingman's Dead* in just ten days. The music was far more approachable than their prior work, pulling listeners into an intimate communion from the opening acoustic guitar and three-part vocal harmonies of "Uncle John's Band" to the final notes of "Casey Jones." The songs harkened back to the Dead's roots in traditional music, an approach that was in sync with the ongoing evolution taking place in popular music. Rock inflected with country and acoustic blues emanated from coast to coast. The Band basically invented Americana in 1968 in Woodstock, New York, decades before the term came into vogue. Los Angeles also had a thriving country rock scene, with Poco, the Byrds, and the Flying Burrito Brothers, featuring ex-Byrds Gram Parsons and Chris Hillman.* In 1969, Bob Dylan recorded *Nashville Skyline*, featuring Johnny Cash and A-list Nashville studio musicians. Delaney and Bonnie Bramlett and their gospel-infused good-time blues attracted Beatles member George Harrison and guitar god Eric Clapton as part-time members.

The band took the *Workingman's Dead* concepts even further with the mostly acoustic *American Beauty*, on which Garcia takes no guitar solos.

---

* The Burritos were the first to record the Rolling Stones' "Wild Horses," Gram Parsons having learned it from a brief but significant collaboration with Keith Richards.

(The lone electric guitar solo, on "Box of Rain," is by David Nelson, of the New Riders.) Bob Weir describes "Sugar Magnolia," his most famous composition, as his "take on southern rock, an attempt to do a rock and roll version of a Cajun fiddle tune à la Doug Kershaw."

"We were influenced by anything that came our way," said Weir. "Anything that came within pissing distance of us would be sucked up and incorporated into our music. We sort of forgot our roots during our psychedelic era, but as soon as we stopped taking psychedelics with absurd regularity and put our feet back on the ground, our love of American music took back over. We osmosed it right up through our systems and it came out of our pores and into those songs."

As the *American Beauty* recording sessions began in September 1970, Weir had recently lost both his parents, Lesh's father and Garcia's mother were dying, and Ron "Pigpen" McKernan's health was faltering. The sense of mortality is felt on songs like "Ripple," "Box of Rain," and "Attics of My Life." The album also contained a trio of the band's most resonant, upbeat commercial tunes: "Truckin'," "Sugar Magnolia," and "Friend of the Devil,"* but the overall feeling was one of depth and reflection, so much so that shortly after the album's release, Garcia said that he could barely listen to *American Beauty*.

"There's a lot of emotional trips happening in that record," Garcia said. "There was this rash of parent deaths where everybody's parents croaked in the space of about two or three months. It was just Tragedy City—bad news every day, really."

DICKEY BETTS SHARED more sounds, influences, and ideas with Garcia than did Duane. Both Dickey and Jerry had deep roots in traditional acoustic guitar playing and mixed minor-key blues playing with the strongly melodic major keys more common in bluegrass and folk music. Betts grew up playing traditional acoustic music with his family, while Garcia was a

---

* Hunter had presented the "Friend of the Devil" lyrics to New Riders of the Purple Sage's David Nelson and John "Marmaduke" Dawson, who quickly wrote the music. The final version of this now classic song came about through serendipity and insight; the descending G scale that opens it was just Nelson warming up, but Hunter insisted it become part of the song. Garcia's old friend David Grisman added a beautiful mandolin part after bumping into the band at a Dead / Jefferson Airplane softball game.

"local hero" for his bluegrass playing, said Weir, before the two formed a jug band together with Pigpen. Though Garcia and Betts were about the same age, the Dead were recording years before Betts entered a real studio.

"I was studying those guys before I ever made a record," he said. "Garcia influenced me a lot and I was kind of tipping my hat to Jerry all the time, which he got a kick out of. I was trying to play electric rock guitar that incorporated some of the old-time acoustic melodies, and when I heard Garcia I felt like he had beat me to it!"

Betts said that the music he always had running through his mind was "string music," which we now call bluegrass.* The music derives from Scottish and Irish reels and is "all melody," he notes. Even when playing a straight urban blues, Betts leaned into melodic leads, more in the style of acoustic finger pickers like Blind Willie McTell than electric masters like B.B. King and T-Bone Walker, who also strongly influenced Betts. "I played mandolin, ukulele and fiddle before I ever touched a guitar, which is where a lot of the major keys I play come from," he said. "Garcia seemed to be doing a very similar thing."

As their relationship grew in 1972 and 1973, Garcia told Betts that the Allman Brothers had caught up. The Dead may have been an influence, but they were also peers, and the two guitarists welcomed every opportunity to jam, onstage or off. Jerry always had a guitar in his hands, Betts said, and every memory he had of a conversation together involved playing as well as talking.

Even as they developed into electric guitar heroes, Betts and Garcia maintained their love for traditional acoustic music. Each took a break from their main gigs by undertaking quieter, more contemplative solo projects. These efforts reveal the two guitarists' similar musical visions, which focused on traditional American music—bluegrass for Garcia, country and western swing for Betts. The connections extended to musicians as well. Bluegrass fiddler Vassar Clements played with Garcia's Old and in the Way

---

* In 1938, mandolinist Bill Monroe, a Kentucky native, named his band the Bluegrass Boys and the name stuck to the traditional string music he played. After banjo player Earl Scruggs joined in 1945, the sound of what we now know as bluegrass was clearly defined. This is often considered the start of that musical idiom.

bluegrass band in 1973–74, before joining Betts for 1974's *Highway Call* album and subsequent American Music Show tour.*

THE ALLMAN BROTHERS Band made their Fillmore East debut opening for Blood, Sweat & Tears in December 1969. The Fillmore staff were taken aback by the life-size nude photos of the band standing in a creek displayed in the lobby as promo and were further aggravated that these "hillbillies they had never heard of" had the gall to show up late for sound check, said Allan Arkush, of the Fillmore East stage crew. That was a major no-no at a venue that was rightfully viewed as a sort of temple devoted to rock and roll. As soon as they started their sound check, however, employees stopped working, left their offices, and watched in awe. "We thought they were fabulous," said Arkush.[†]

Graham himself was wowed by the Allman Brothers Band, especially Duane. "You put that glass thing on his finger and it was just magic," he said. "Duane was the one. Anyone can boil a potato, but not everyone can make gravy. There's only a few bands you can say that on any given night they are the best fucking band you can hear. The Allman Brothers Band always did that for me."[‡]

The Grateful Dead was another Graham favorite, and the two bands' first official shows together were a run of three at the Fillmore East, on February 11, 13, and 14, 1970. The Allman Brothers opened. Love played the middle set. "The Allman Brothers were still unheard and unknown," Arkush said. "But these were legendary shows."

Dead soundman (and legendary LSD chemist) Owsley "Bear" Stanley was already a fan of the Allman Brothers Band, so he taped their sets. On

---

* One difference between the two guitarists noted by Weir was their relationship with rock and roll volume. "The one notable difference is that though they both played loud, Jerry did so because he had to, because the band was loud, while Dickey was loud because he wanted to be, and there's a big difference," said Weir. "Playing loud is very gratifying for you as the player, but I'm not sure how much that transfers to the listeners' ears."

† The staff recognized that Blood, Sweat & Tears were not a good fit for the Allman Brothers Band and, after the show, apologized to Twiggs Lyndon and asked who they liked. He said Albert King, B.B. King, and the Grateful Dead. They soon played with all three of them in both New York and San Francisco.

‡ The interview with Graham was conducted in San Francisco on the day he died, October 25, 1991, by John Ogden for *Hittin' the Note* magazine.

the way to the first show, Garcia hipped bassist Phil Lesh to the opening act. "Hey, Phil, make sure you check these guys out," he said. "They're kinda like us: two drummers, two guitars, bass and organ, and I hear they jam hard."

No one was more excited or understood the pairing's simpatico nature better than Graham, who booked virtually every contemporary band of note at his venues and favored these two. "When the Dead and the Allman Brothers played the Fillmore East, it was rock at its very best," he said. "They both had something undeniable that you can't buy: the ability to excel and just completely captivate a crowd with no production of any sort. It was all in the greatness and intensity of the music and the focus and intent. They exemplified communal pleasure, where everyone had the same idea. And it didn't matter what they played. It was like going to your sister's house; whatever she serves is going to be good because you're so comfortable. I loved to take someone who thought they didn't like either of those bands and set them up on the side of the stage. A half hour later they were transported."

The Allman Brothers' original and infamous road crew member Red Dog described the two bands' alchemic formula in his own inimitable style: "For sure, anytime the Dead and the Brothers played together . . . it would gather the spirits, past and present."

In between the first and second shows on February 11, the Dead met Gregg, Duane, Butch, and Jaimoe backstage. Fleetwood Mac also were in town, to play Madison Square Garden on February 13 in support of Sly and the Family Stone on a bill that included Grand Funk Railroad and Richard Pryor. The Dead and Fleetwood Mac had played the Warehouse in New Orleans together less than two weeks earlier, and after the first night, January 30, the Dead were famously "busted down on Bourbon Street." The February 1 performance became a drug-bust fundraiser, with Peter Green sitting in that night on "Turn on Your Love Light."

Lesh was pleasantly surprised when he heard the Allman Brothers play "Mountain Jam" during a blistering set that kicked off the midnight show. The extended instrumental, which took different flight paths every time the group performed it, is based on the melody of the English folk singer Donovan's "There Is a Mountain." The Dead had been playing around with the simple, catchy lick for years, with Garcia regularly quoting it in "Alligator." Lesh thought it was hip that the Allmans had crafted an entire monumental jam song from the same few notes. "It was quite an eye-opener," Lesh said. "It was really cool. The Allman Brothers were doing it their own way, but there was obviously a common denominator. It was a shock of recognition that the Allman Brothers Band was out there performing that same line of inquiry into the art of music."

The first and arguably greatest jam between the two bands occurred at the end of the Dead's late show, in the wee hours of the morning of February 12. During the quiet section of "Dark Star," Lesh was startled by the clarion sound of Duane's slide guitar. Garcia had not told him about any planned sit-ins. As Allman was finding his footing, Peter Green also plugged in, and he and Duane took off as the song turned the corner toward its minor-key segment. The rhythm section, now including Garcia and Weir, locked into a groove, and the song took flight before shifting into the four-bar pattern the band dubbed "Spanish Jam" because they took the riff from the Miles Davis / Gil Evans album *Sketches of Spain*.

Garcia and Allman were trading licks when Gregg appeared on the organ bench, adding some sustained notes followed by quick licks. By the time Gregg and Duane were playing call and response, Trucks had also joined on drums and Mickey Hart was literally banging his gong. As Green brought the song to a climax, Lesh and Weir launched into the familiar riff of Bobby Bland's "Turn on Your Love Light," which had been not only a highlight of Dead shows for years but also a frequent cover in Gregg and Duane's previous bands like the Escorts, the Allman Joys, and Hour Glass. The Dead had steered the music right into Gregg's sweet spot, and he sounded suitably juiced.

By that time, Fleetwood Mac drummer Mick Fleetwood and guitarist Danny Kirwan were also onstage, though Fleetwood was heavily tripping and did not play, roaming the stage with a grin plastered across his face. "I had a tom-tom and a snare drum and I was gooning around on the stage," Fleetwood recalled. Bill Graham also emerged, tripping hard, smiling and hitting a cowbell.

Pigpen, who walked off for "Dark Star," returned to sing atop a band that now included five guitarists and four drummers. He sang two verses, then Gregg took the third, finishing with a guttural howl that cut deep, before he and Pigpen traded vocals. Halfway through the song, Oakley took over on bass, because Lesh "just want(ed) to listen for a while," he wrote. As the band segued in and out of Howlin' Wolf and Hubert Sumlin's "Smokestack Lightning" riff, Lesh distinctly remembered the sound of "everyone flat out wailing."

The bassist felt his mind stretching out of shape as the megaband drove the song to a frenzied climax, Jerry Garcia, Duane Allman, and Peter Green egging one another on. When the song finally came to its wild conclusion, Weir took the mic and energetically proclaimed, "From all of us to you, thanks and good night."

But the crowd had not had enough and kept cheering, as a dazed Fleetwood, who would later describe this as a "crazed night," sat on the lip of the stage, microphone in hand, repeating: "The Grateful Dead are fucking great!" Garcia, Lesh, and Weir came out to wrap things up with a single acoustic guitar. The bassist said, "If you folks would all be kind enough to be quiet for a while, we're gonna sing a purty little old song with only an acoustic guitar." They played "Uncle John's Band," and the night was finally over.

After the dazed crowd filed out, someone opened the door behind the stage, and the musicians looked out at the New York City streets bathed in golden early-morning light, snow gently falling. Lesh, Weir, and Garcia embraced in a group hug, and one thought ran through the bassist's head: "This is what it's all about."

Joe Rosenberg was a twenty-year-old college student at the midnight show, seeing all three bands for the first time. He was mesmerized by the Allman Brothers' performance from the first note of the show-opening "In Memory of Elizabeth Reed," but he dozed off during the Dead's wee-hour performance, waking up in the middle of the amazing "Dark Star" jam with Duane and Jerry wailing and Fleetwood dancing around the stage. It was a mystical, magical experience, like a euphoric dream. Stumbling out in the morning, he found himself walking behind two members of Love and eavesdropped on their conversation. "They were talking about how incredible the jam was and how remarkable the Allman Brothers had been," Rosenberg recalled.

Also there was Bruce Kaufer, a sixteen-year-old high school senior in town on a school trip to see a Broadway play. He had been at Woodstock, where he saw the Dead, but it was this night at the Fillmore East that made a huge impression; it changed his life, he said. "Those shows lit the fire inside to pursue live music in all its shapes and genres," said Kaufer. "Ending up at the Fillmore that night was a simple twist of fate."

The next day, Duane sat down for an interview at *Crawdaddy* magazine's New York office, still glowing from the jam. "Peter Green, Garcia, Bob Weir—so beautiful, what it's all about," he said. "Just getting down to that good note, man. Just grooving and looking along on that one good note."

The members of the Dead were similarly enthusiastic. Owsley described the Allman Brothers performances as "fantastic" and "a real inspiration for the boys." After a night off, the Dead played two more shows on this run, February 13 and 14, turning in some of their most memorable performances of the Pigpen era. They were good enough to be released twice, in 1973 as *History of the Grateful Dead, Volume One (Bear's Choice)* and in 1996 as *Dick's Picks, Volume Four.** A couple of months later, on May 10, 1970, the Dead played the Sports Arena in Atlanta, with Bruce Hampton's Hampton Grease Band opening.† When the Dead's gear didn't make it, the Allman Brothers sprang into action and drove their stuff up from Macon.

"The Dead arrived in Atlanta without their equipment, and I called Duane at home in Macon early on Sunday morning to ask him if I could rent his sound system," recalled the show's promoter, Murray Silver. "He asked me who it was for, and when I told him, he [said] that I could have it for free. The Brothers brought their equipment to Atlanta."

"I had to borrow a bass; I didn't even have my instrument," Lesh said. "Talk about thumb up your ass!"

---

* Grateful Dead Records released a compilation disc of Owsley's recordings of the Allman Brothers in 1997, and a more extensive three-disc version was released by the Owsley Stanley Foundation in 2021.

† Duane loved the Hampton Grease Band and helped them get a deal with Capricorn. Decades later, Hampton, now calling himself Col. Bruce Hampton, became first an Atlanta fixture and then a major inspiration to a new generation of jam band musicians. Future Allman Brothers Band members Oteil Burbridge and Jimmy Herring started in Hampton's Aquarium Rescue Unit.

Oakley, Trucks, Gregg, and Duane watched the show from the stage and sat in for a show-closing jam on "Mountain Jam" > "Will the Circle Be Unbroken." Silver described that jam as "unlike anything that has been heard before or since." *The Great Speckled Bird,* the main chronicler of Atlanta's underground scene, agreed, calling the show "one of the great musical/sensual experiences the Atlanta hip community has ever had." Unfortunately, there is no known recording of this show.

Making their sound system available for free was emblematic of Duane and the Allman Brothers' esteem for their San Francisco friends. "I love the Dead!" Duane said in a 1970 on-air interview with a New York DJ. He added that "Jerry Garcia could walk on water. He could do anything any man could ever do. He's a prince."

At least once, on July 10, 1970, at SUNY Stony Brook, Duane clearly quoted "Dark Star" during "Mountain Jam." Lesh said that Garcia returned Duane's appreciation and respect and that the two had an obvious bond and similarities. "Duane and Jerry just knew what to do, as musicians on that level do—when to play, when not to play," Lesh said. "Jerry had an immense amount of respect for Duane, who was truly a master. His spirit, his fluency . . . listening to Duane play was like watching a flower grow. We all felt that way about his playing. Beauty is truth, truth is beauty."

Duane and Jerry's relationship was grounded in mutual respect but was growing into something more, above and beyond the music. They had a budding friendship, which was clear on November 21, 1970, when Duane popped into the studios of WBCN in Boston as Weir and Garcia performed. Recalled disc jockey Charles Laquidara, "I was working the 10–2 shift and the person answering our listener line said that there are a bunch of musicians at the door saying they played two different clubs and want to come up and hang. It was Bob Weir, Jerry Garcia, Gregg and Duane Allman, and Pigpen. It was a great, laid-back evening!" With Duane guitarless, Jerry passed him his acoustic so he could participate musically, but the two could not play together.

Duane turned up onstage in New York on April 26, 1971, during the Dead's final week of shows at the Fillmore East, a month after the Allman Brothers had recorded their landmark live album there. He joined the band for three tunes: "Sugar Magnolia," "It Hurts Me Too," and "Beat

It on Down the Line." Duane's slide naturally dominated Elmore James's "It Hurts Me Too," while he and Garcia took flight together on the other two songs, playing with graceful ferocity. It would have been impossible for anyone to believe it would be their last time onstage together. The burgeoning friendship was just one more victim of Duane's death on October 29. "We developed a close relationship with Duane that unfortunately never had the time to blossom," said Weir.

Still, the relationship between the two bands was just getting started. When the Dead played Hartford's Dillon Stadium on July 16, 1972, Betts, Oakley, and Jaimoe drove up from New York on an off day, with Jaimoe's kit in the back of the limousine. They watched the show from the side stage, then joined in to play "Not Fade Away," "Goin' Down the Road Feeling Bad," "Hey Bo Diddley," and an encore of Chuck Berry's "Johnny B. Goode." Oakley replaced Lesh on bass, and Garcia and Betts gleefully riffed off each other, while Jaimoe and Kreutzmann locked into each other with ease.

"There's only ever been three drummers I enjoyed playing with: Butch Trucks, Bill Kreutzmann, and Buddy Miles," said Jaimoe. "Because they listen and if you do that, it really doesn't matter if there are 13 guitars, 15 basses, 20 sets of drums. I always loved playing with Bill."

The next night, Weir, Garcia, and Kreutzmann returned the favor, showing up at the Allman Brothers Band's show at Gaelic Park in the Bronx and playing an aggressive "Mountain Jam" to close the show. The bands were growing closer. When *Melody Maker* interviewer Chris Charlesworth mentioned that the Brothers and the Dead had some similarities, Gregg readily agreed. "He loved the Dead, and respected Garcia a lot," Charlesworth wrote.

The bands planned shows together in the wake of Duane's death, which Dead crew member Steve Parish describes as "trying to support our friends" during a difficult transition. When Oakley died a week before, the Allman Brothers pulled out of a two-night joint show in Houston on November 18–19, 1972, which was to include two hours of "open jam" at the end of each night. The Dead played that show alone, but a joint appearance in Athens, Georgia, was canceled outright. The Allman Brothers also pulled out of their scheduled slot opening three shows for the Dead at Winterland on December 10–12, 1972.

Even with Allman and Oakley shockingly gone, the groups' mutual admiration was unconstrained, and lines of communication remained open. "We wanted to work together even more after the shows were called off," said Bunky Odom. "We kept talking and talking."

When the Allman Brothers resumed touring with their regular vigor in 1973, they scheduled some very large shows with their California brothers. "Playing shows together was just an obvious and natural desire," said Cutler. "We realized that if we added our energies together, it was like one plus one makes three. It would be mutually beneficial to both bands."

The first scheduled show was Bill Graham's inaugural Day on the Green, May 27, 1973, at California's Ontario Motor Speedway. Advance tickets sold for $7.50. A crowd of 150,000 was expected. The *Pomona Progress-Bulletin* reported on May 8, "The Grateful Dead, the Allman Brothers, and Waylon Jennings will take part in the first rock concert at the Ontario Motor Speedway."

Two weeks later, the concert was canceled. Local police and civic officials demanded the show end three hours before sundown, which would have meant wrapping up at about 5:00 PM, making the timing simply too tight. The groups found more accommodating municipalities on the East Coast, with three giant shows—two at RFK Stadium in Washington, D.C., followed six weeks later by the Summer Jam at Watkins Glen, featuring both groups and the Band.

"The Dead were as big as the Beatles in the Northeast, from D.C. on up," said Odom. "The Allman Brothers Band were just beginning to get big up there—they were huge in New York City, and it was starting to spread, but the Dead was already huge in the entire region. They helped the Allman Brothers develop in a very hip section of the country that we didn't completely understand in the South."

Cutler similarly saw the Dead's collaboration with the Allman Brothers as an opportunity to expand their reach, as well as proof that it was possible to be a national band, not just a coastal phenomenon. "I was trying to take the band to a much larger space, to the national fan base we knew was out there," said Cutler. "We knew that the alternative society was everywhere, and the Allman Brothers were proof of that. They represented the Southern tribe of freaks."

As the managers looked at tapping both bands' fan bases to expand their popularity into different regions of the country, the musicians simply enjoyed one another's company and any opportunity to interact.

"The Dead's philosophy was always very similar to ours," Betts said. "We sound very different, because we're from different roots. They're from a folk music, jug band, and country thing. We're from an urban blues / jazz bag. We don't wait for it to happen; we make it happen. But we've always had a similar fan base and philosophy—keeping music honest and fun and trying to make it a transcendental experience for the audience."

11

BIG BOSS MAN

STEVE MASSARSKY WAS an unlikely person to become a central figure in the history of the Allman Brothers Band. In March 1973 he was a twenty-five-year-old law school dropout who answered the phone in the office of Peter Yarrow (of Peter, Paul and Mary fame) to find Phil Walden looking for him. They had been in contact over the previous year as Massarsky unsuccessfully sought the Allman Brothers Band's involvement in various benefit concerts he organized on behalf of Yarrow. Massarsky was surprised that Walden, having turned down every previous request he had made, was now seeking him out.

"You know, Steve," Walden said, "you always call me about having the Allman Brothers do benefits for these organizations you're involved in. What if we were going to put together an organization that did benefits for American Indians? Would you be willing to help?"

When Massarsky said it sounded interesting, Walden replied that a ticket was already waiting for him at the airport for a flight to Macon. A meeting was scheduled to organize the North American Indian Foundation on March 13, just a few days away, and Walden wanted him there for it.

Massarsky got involved in the music business the same way that many of his generation did: by booking bands in college. At Brown University, he promoted shows with Janis Joplin, Diana Ross, James Taylor, Ray Charles, and others. With no clear path to a music biz job, he decided to attend Rutgers Law School in Newark, New Jersey. But before starting, he stumbled upon a one-week gig filling in as a Peter, Paul and Mary roadie. The experience only stoked his desire to work in music.

Midway through his second semester of law school, Yarrow asked Massarsky to assist in putting together nationwide rallies to register eighteen-year-olds, who had just been granted the right to vote. After doing this for almost a year while also attending law school, he dropped out and became Yarrow's road manager on his first solo tour. Yarrow's manager was Albert Grossman, one of the most powerful figures in rock music, and visits to his Woodstock, New York, office were always educational and interesting for Massarsky, who found Grossman clients like Bob Dylan, and members of the Band lounging around.

Yarrow's tour floundered, but it helped introduce Massarsky to actor Warren Beatty, who hired him as entertainment director for Democratic nominee George McGovern's 1972 presidential campaign. That led to a job putting together benefits, which eventually connected him to Walden.

Intrigued by the idea of the North American Indian Foundation, Massarsky flew to Macon with little knowledge of the city, the region, or even the Allman Brothers Band. Betts, who picked him up at the airport, spearheaded the North American Indian Foundation after his longtime interest in Native American culture deepened when he started dating Sandy Wabegijig, a First Nation Wiikwemkoong from Manitoulin Island in Northern Ontario, Canada. (Native Canadian Indigenous people are referred to as First Nations.) They had met in March 1971 at a party in New York the weekend the band was recording *At Fillmore East*. The next year she gave birth to their daughter, Jessica. Wabegijig then went by the name Sandy "Blue Sky," which she described as the shortest way to translate her last name. Betts wrote "Blue Sky" for her.

"When I met Richard, I was regularly attending gatherings of North American Indigenous elders and medicine people with my sister and brother-in-law, Rolland and Carol Nadjiwon, who were part of the foundation that set up the gatherings," said Wabegijig. "He became very intrigued and started attending the events, where he met several of the people there that became part of the Foundation's Board of Directors."*

---

* Betts went by Richard during this era, and that was how Wabegijig usually referred to him.

Inspired by his discussions with Rolland and after listening to the Native elders discussing their concerns, Betts told Walden to schedule some benefit concerts to direct funds to Native causes. Willie Perkins said that to do this properly, they would have to set up a tax-exempt nonprofit corporation. Walden knew just the man for the job: that guy from Peter Yarrow's office who kept calling asking the Allman Brothers to perform at benefits. That's what led to Walden's phone call to Massarsky.

"The Foundation was Dickey's idea, but everyone in the band was on the board of directors," Massarsky said. "The idea was to do benefit concerts with the Allmans and other bands to raise money for things that American Indians needed, specifically preserving Indian culture by teaching the dances, having retreats, and doing sweat lodges."

On April 14, 1973, approximately a month after Walden first contacted Massarsky, Betts and Wabegijig were due to be married on the Allman Brothers Band's farm in Juliette. In preparation, over 300 handwritten invitations were sent out. On the advice of Stanley Smith, a Creek medicine man and Baptist minister who would conduct the traditional Native ceremony, Betts flew to Oklahoma to purchase a traditional wedding gown for Sandy, which the medicine man helped make almost fifty years earlier and which had been on display in the store's front window since the 1930s.

Despite the careful planning, on the day of the event guests had to wait for the nuptials to begin. Smith was late because no ticket was waiting for him at the airport in Green Bay, Michigan.* When he finally arrived at the farm, well after the wedding's scheduled starting time, Smith said that Betts had to personally sacrifice a duck before the ceremony could begin.

"Finding a duck in the growing dusk wasn't such an easy task," the *Macon News* reported. The guests, anxious for the ceremony to begin, cheered the sound of every gunshot, until Betts finally emerged holding up a duck, "resplendent in traditional Indian wedding shirt and feathers in his hair." Thus commenced the wedding.

Smith positioned the couple's relatives to the west and east in a large

---

* The *Macon News* reported that when Smith realized there was no ticket, he called Frank Fenter at Capricorn, who dispatched a cab. It is unclear if the car made the thousand-mile drive to Macon or took him to another, larger airport, probably in Milwaukee, Chicago, or Detroit.

circle around an open fire lit by the guests. He made an offering of earth and corn before he gifted Betts and Blue Sky with medicine pouches and pronounced them man and wife. A traditional Creek dance followed, with the bride and groom and their families and friends—including Betts's Allman Brothers bandmates—circling the flames four times. All the band members joined in the celebration that followed.

Jaimoe and Lamar also got married that summer: Jaimoe in May to Candy Oakley, Berry's sister, and Lamar on July 6 to his girlfriend, Marian Belina. The officiant for both was crew member Gerald "Buffalo" Evans. In June 1974, the band played its first benefit for the foundation at the Omni in Atlanta, raising about $50,000. "Anytime anybody makes a lot of money, it's awfully nice if they share some of it," Betts said. He pointed out that he had an "Indian wife and baby," but insisted that what really spurred him to action was not his marriage but the uprising at Wounded Knee, South Dakota, in February 1973. Indian activists had taken over the Oglala Pine Ridge Reservation, only to be surrounded by a massive military and law enforcement cordon. Two Native leaders were killed, and the siege lasted about three months, garnering widespread national attention. "It was the last straw," he said.

Betts shrugged off suggestions that the foundation was a public relations stunt. "I have four gold records and three platinum records on the wall and I've been named the second best guitar player in the world, after Eric Clapton," he said. "We don't need the publicity."

Betts believed that he had Native American ancestry, which had been his family's handed-down oral tradition. He asked Massarsky to do some genealogical research on the Betts family. Although he did not discover any Native roots, he did find that the first Betts in America was a "redheaded Jew" who somehow survived an Indian scalping, a surprisingly common occurrence.

"For the next year or so, every time a business issue came up, Dickey would look at me and say, 'Us Jewish guys are better at this stuff. We'll handle it,'" Massarsky said with a laugh.

GIVEN BETTS'S GROWING interest in Native culture and his increasing centrality to the band, Massarsky immediately became an important Allman Brothers Band insider. A native New Jerseyan and Ivy League graduate who had rarely been to the South and who had never seen the band play before joining forces with them, his introduction to the group came quickly.

A few days after he arrived in Macon, someone with the band asked if he'd like to come to a show in Tuscaloosa, Alabama, about three hundred miles away. By Massarsky's recollection, they all piled onto "a little yellow school bus that looked like it belonged to a new band just getting together." They arrived and checked into their hotel at 2 AM without much fanfare. In the morning, Massarsky was shocked to find himself in the middle of a Southern Beatlemania.

"There were people running up and down the hallway yelling things like 'I just saw Butch Trucks in his underwear!' and 'Dickey put his room service tray in the hallway! I saw his head!'" Massarsky said. "This was a giant order of magnitude bigger than I had understood."

The crew asked Massarsky if he wanted to tag along with them when they left for the venue. He was shocked, almost speechless, to walk into a twenty-thousand-seat arena and learn that it was sold out. He had assumed they would be playing a theater. "That was my first exposure to the Allman Brothers Band," he said. "I had no idea how big they were, but I learned quickly."

From that simple, naive beginning, Massarsky would become an important yet somewhat overlooked character in Allman Brothers Band history. He moved to Macon and immediately took stock of the power and glory of association with the Allman Brothers and with Capricorn Records. The city was at the height of its attractiveness to musicians, artists, freethinkers, and freaks, who were flocking there from all over the country, particularly the South. "It was just a wild time to be living in Macon," Massarsky said.

Walden was at the center of all band and label activity, and Massarsky looked at him with awe. He was running an empire out of a single office with a handful of employees and had managed to put Macon on the map as a musician's destination. "I thought he was a magical person," said drummer Bill Stewart. "Phil seemed to have an incredible sense of what needed to be done."

Simply put, the Allman Brothers Band would not have existed without

Walden and certainly would not have survived until 1973 without his support, financial and otherwise. "Phil had a very interesting relationship with everybody in the band," Massarsky said. "He started the band, and he was a father figure. He did a lot of things for them that were very good, and you can't take that away from him."

Walden funded their existence for their first two years. He kept the band together, on the road, and with good gear long enough to grow their audience show by show, city by city, until *At Fillmore East* broke through in fall 1971. "*Fillmore East* just kind of caught everyone up," said Rose Lane Leavell. "Phil had put a lot of money into the band."

Willie Perkins said that after a few months on the job, he did an internal audit and discovered that the band owed Walden about $150,000 (equivalent to approximately $1 million in 2023), which included commissions earned but not taken on relatively low performance fees. They all went on the books, and Walden was genuinely shocked to realize he was in so deep. By 1973, the band had repaid him several times over, with the debts being subtracted from their incoming earnings, but not before some bumpy years.

How did the band end up so deep in the hole to their manager? By late 1970, they paid everyone—six band members and five crew—a weekly salary of $90 while on the road, plus a $5-to-$10 per diem each day they traveled. As spartan as that might seem, Walden probably fronted more than $60,000 a year to keep the Allman Brothers Band on the road. The amount doesn't include travel expenses, constant requests for advances on royalties, and even alimony and/or child support payments for Betts ($20 a month to Dale Betts) and Duane ($100 a month to Donna).

"Anything we needed, Phil would just shell out the money," Trucks said. "He just about bottomed out before we made a penny. He had a lot of faith in us. I think he had a better idea than we did of the band's commercial potential."

Jaimoe had known Walden for years, having worked in the touring bands of several of the soul singers on his roster, including Otis Redding and Percy Sledge. He was also the only one to really question the largesse and resist the temptation to keep taking Walden's money. "They were buying instruments for everyone and putting it on the tab," said Jaimoe. "Berry got a new amp and told me to come to the music store and I just said, 'No thanks. I've got my own damn drums.'"

Jaimoe put his money where his mouth was. He was the only member of the original band who declined to sign a management contract with Walden in 1969, concerned about being legally bound to someone he didn't trust.

"I read in magazines about the things that managers did to take advantage of their artists," Jaimoe said. "And I saw things myself."

One thing he saw was a heated argument between Walden and Otis Redding that was almost certainly money related. He accidentally opened the door to Walden's office to the sight of "Otis leaning over him with his finger in his face and they were having a serious disagreement."

Redding was saying, "If you ever do that again . . ." and Phil's face, Jaimoe said, was "red as a boiling lobster."

"After that, I saw what went on with Sledge and Phil, so when we all moved to Macon and Phil gave us the contracts, I told Duane, 'We only gonna get fucked by these guys,'" Jaimoe recalled. "Duane heard me and just nodded. He wanted to get to making music together."

Whatever Walden's flaws, he rarely meddled with the music, putting his faith in his artists. This was no small thing, especially to Duane after his Liberty Records experience with Hour Glass. Walden also continued to advance them money long after they started really earning. The amounts just got higher to keep up with changing lifestyles. It all went on the tab, though the band members seemed to view it as free money or forgot they had received it when Capricorn deducted it from their paychecks.

"There was no accounting for what we were really making or should have had because we all had enough pocket money and just asked for money and took it," Trucks said. "I could go out and raise hell every night, so I was happy—and yeah, that was a dumb way to be!"

In the early days, Duane and the band never had an outside business manager or lawyer advising them beyond unrelated civil and criminal affairs—divorce, custody, criminal charges. As they started to make real money in 1971, Perkins, who had worked as a bank auditor in Atlanta before quitting to jump on their pirate ship, oversaw the group's finances. "There probably should have been three or four people doing what I did," said Perkins. "Most of us working for Phil or the band wore a lot of hats."

Walden held the band and the company together in part by sheer force of personality. Paul Hornsby described Walden as a charismatic character on the level of Duane Allman. "He could make you like something," Hornsby said. "He could talk you into anything."

Odom saw another similarity between Walden and Duane: their self-confidence and leadership. "Nothing was democratic with Phil Walden and Associates, and nothing was democratic with Duane," said Odom. "Duane was a natural born leader, with a philosophy that everyone should climb on his back, and so was Phil."

When Walden founded Capricorn Records, he enticed Frank Fenter to leave his job as Atlantic's managing director for Europe with a 20 percent equity stake in his new label. Fenter took the leap of faith after hearing demos of the Allman Brothers Band's debut album, calling the band "a knockout" that he "knew would make it."

South Africa–born and a former actor, Fenter had played a major role at Atlantic in signing Led Zeppelin, King Crimson, and Yes and helping to bring soul music to the United Kingdom and Europe. He had met Walden when Fenter promoted Otis Redding's 1966 tour of Britain and France, a breakthrough for Redding abroad *and* at home.

Fenter's involvement in Capricorn was essential, as Walden's experience was solely in artist management. Fenter's ties with Atlantic, the label that initially distributed Capricorn, were also crucial. "Phil was a great manager and talent-side person . . . [and] really needed someone who understood the record business," said Atlantic cofounder and president Ahmet Ertegun. "Together Frank and Phil formed a great partnership."

Dick Wooley, who worked with Fenter at Atlantic and joined him at Capricorn in 1972 as vice president of promotion in charge of getting songs played on the radio, said that Ertegun and his brother Nesuhi thought very highly of both Fenter and Walden. "They were grooming Frank for a presidential seat, and they were shocked when he left the company and moved to Macon," said Wooley.

The Erteguns weren't the only ones surprised to learn that Fenter was moving to a sleepy midsize Georgia city eighty miles south of Atlanta. His wife, Baroness Ulla von Blixen-Finecke, was thrilled when he said they would be moving from the chic London neighborhood of West Kensington to a small town called Macon. "She said, 'Lovely! I love France! Macôn, France. We'll be on the Rhône, we'll drink wine, it'll be fantastic!'" said their son Robin Duner-Fenter. "It was a little bit of a shock for her to realize he meant Macon, Georgia."

Fenter opened Macon's first two French-style restaurants, Le Bistro and Le Brasserie, in part to help keep the baroness, known as Kiki, happy in her strange new environment. They were both frustrated by the lack of fine dining options in Macon and wanted somewhere to comfortably entertain visiting business associates and friends. Together, the couple made a strong impression.

"Frank and Kiki were the center of the social hub of the Macon music phenomena," said Sandy Blue Sky. "They were the primary hosts of parties and dinners for the Allman Brothers and other musicians."

However important Fenter became to Macon nightlife, it paled in comparison to what he was doing at Capricorn, where he was the key person running day-to-day operations. "Frank was Executive Vice President, and the head of the record company," said Rose Lane Leavell. "Phil owned the label, but he had limited experience in the deep details of running a record company. He was the manager and that's what he did."

Fenter took to running an American label and working for an independent maverick like Walden. Sipping a late-afternoon scotch and water at his desk, he told a reporter in 1974 that the British record industry "treated music like the banking business." Coming to America, he said, was "like stepping out of kindergarten and into university. . . . The sheer awesomeness [and] volume of it is staggering. It's like being in front of a bulldozer all the time. But I dig it, man."

"Basically, the label was Frank and Phil in their tiny little offices," said Wooley. "It was a primitive setup—an old chicken slaughterhouse that had a floor that slanted in the middle where the drain was. It was a sad-looking place, but Frank and Phil knew what they were doing."

Walden also approached Jon Landau, a Boston rock journalist and aspiring producer, about moving to Macon and becoming the head of

Capricorn A&R (artists and repertoire), in charge of procuring and working with talent. He had produced one of Capricorn's earliest releases, Livingston Taylor's self-titled debut. "I was very taken with Phil," said Landau. "He was a very charismatic, very smart man. We just hit it off and I enjoyed Macon, which had a great feel. It was fun to hang out in his office with all these great musicians wandering in and out."

In 1969 and 1970, as Walden worked to get the Allman Brothers Band off the ground, he remained a major player in soul music but was still learning about rock and roll. "Phil knew his R&B world better than anybody and correctly saw the Allman Brothers as a major national rock band that could be enormous, the biggest thing that he had ever done," said Landau. "He didn't know exactly how to go about it and realized that I knew a whole lot about that world."

The way great musicians of various stripes were constantly walking in and out of the Capricorn offices made a huge impression on Landau when he visited Macon. "There were people everywhere, Tony Joe White and Clarence Carter popping in, everyone headed out for a barbecue," Landau recalled. "It was very intoxicating."

He wasn't sure if Walden had staged the guest appearances to recruit him, but the opportunity to make the leap from journalist and occasional producer to label executive tempted Landau. He hesitated after meeting Fenter, however. "The idea of going to work for Phil was one thing, but working for Frank was another," said Landau. "Frank was a classic promotion man, who woke up in the morning selling records. He was pushing records when he was asleep, in his dreams. He was a talented guy, but I had misgivings about him and his presence just was not a positive in the equation of deciding whether or not to go work at Capricorn."

"Frank had a lot of experience at labels—he had been the first Managing Director for Atlantic Records in Europe—but he was a bullshitter," said Rose Lane Leavell. "He was a guy who could talk all the young guys into signing the deal."

Landau may have sensed that there wasn't really room for another smart, ambitious executive at Capricorn, and he declined Walden's offer. By 1975, he was working with Bruce Springsteen on *Born to Run*, the start of a close relationship as producer, confidant, and manager.

In a 1974 *Melody Maker* feature, Chris Charlesworth described the Capricorn dynamic: "Walden is the boss of everything—manager of the Allmans, boss of the record company and also owner of sundry other Macon enterprises—while Fenter is his right hand, running the day-to-day business of the label while Walden is sorting out the numerous problems surrounding the Brothers."

Jaimoe said, "I used to call Frank 'Mr. Kissinger' because he had to constantly do shuttle diplomacy. Phil would go crazy on someone, and Frank had to smooth it out. He had a role similar to Berry, who had to take care of a lot of the tensions Duane created with his intensity."

Fenter was more accessible to the artists than Walden. He was the guy they turned to for guidance or financial help. "He would cut you a check for a hundred dollars for groceries," said Chuck Leavell.

In meetings, Walden and Fenter could also switch roles in an instant, with an easy rapport that transcended the need to ask one another questions or work out a plan. "Good cop / bad cop was their MO," said Wooley. "They switched it around depending on the circumstance. They were very talented at that. It was awesome to watch them work someone over."

Wooley was also an important partner in the label's success. "The three of us could work a room with a wink and a nod; we could all communicate silently to one another. No one had to tell us what to do: Phil knew how to manage, Frank knew how to run a record company, and I knew how to get records on the radio."

Walden ran each of his businesses as separate entities. Capricorn was the record label, Capricorn Studios the recording studio, Walden and Associates the management company, No Exit the publishing company, and Paragon the booking agency. He held a minority interest in Great Southern, the merch company originally started by band wives at the dawn of that ancillary business. Through 1970, Walden had six people running three companies. That represented significant growth since 1960, when Walden opened "Phil Walden & Associates" to book Redding with no associates, sometimes feigning a woman's voice when answering the phone before "transferring the call to Mr. Walden."

"I handled the bookkeeping and accounting, which is a joke," said Rose Lane Leavell. "I can't even balance my checkbook. There was no one else to do it after Phil had a falling-out with his brother Blue [real name Clark], who had been doing them. He started paying Blue, who drank a lot, to not come to work and asked me to do the books."

Though it was several years after the 1964 Civil Rights and 1965 Voting Rights Acts were enacted into law, the mixing of Black and white artists was highly unusual in Macon and throughout the Deep South. Like the Allman Brothers, their flagship band, the Capricorn offices on Cotton Street were integrated. Rose Lane Leavell, a white woman, and Carolyn Brown, a Black woman, were desk mates in Capricorn's reception area. Brown had started as Redding's secretary and worked closely with Walden, eventually handling much of the publishing office.

"Absolutely nothing else was integrated in Macon at the time," said Rose Lane, who was twenty-two when she had a chance meeting with Frank and Kiki Fenter. "He asked if I was a good secretary. I said 'The best,' and he offered me a job," she recalled with a laugh. "All he knew was I had long legs and I looked good. I fit the image they wanted and that's all he cared about, adding a pretty white girl to work with the pretty black girl."

She added, "I went from a job where they wouldn't let you wear pants to wearing hot pants and go-go boots to work. For Macon, that office was another world."

ABOVE: Duane Allman was the undisputed leader of the Allman Brothers Band. No one knew how the band could continue after his death on October 29, 1971, but they were determined to do so. Chapel Hill, North Carolina, May 1, 1971.

PHOTO BY JOHN GELLMAN

AT RIGHT: Duane Allman's funeral, November 1, 1971. Snow's Memorial Chapel, Macon, Georgia.

JEFF ALBERTSON PHOTOGRAPH COLLECTION, ROBERT S. COX SPECIAL COLLECTIONS AND UNIVERSITY ARCHIVES RESEARCH CENTER, UMASS AMHERST LIBRARIES

The five-man Allman Brothers Band, which performed from November 1971 through November 1972. From left: Jaimoe, Gregg Allman, Berry Oakley, Dickey Betts, and Butch Trucks.

TWIGGS LYNDON, COURTESY OF THE BIG HOUSE MUSEUM ARCHIVES

RIGHT: Producer Tom Dowd, Berry Oakley, and Dickey Betts during the *Eat A Peach* sessions, Criteria Studios, Miami, December 1971.

TWIGGS LYNDON, COURTESY OF THE BIG HOUSE MUSEUM ARCHIVES

LEFT: After Duane Allman's death, Dickey Betts stepped to the fore. His new responsibilities included playing slide on stage for the first time. Hollywood, Florida, December 27, 1972.

SIDNEY SMITH/ALLMANBROTHERSBOOKBYSIDNEYSMITH.COM

THE ALLMAN BROTHERS BAND

An early publicity photo of the Allman Brothers Band Mach 2, featuring new members Chuck Leavell and Lamar Williams. COURTESY OF THE BIG HOUSE MUSEUM ARCHIVES

Lamar Williams, 1973.
KIRK WEST

Chuck Leavell, 1973.
SIDNEY SMITH/ALLMANBROTHERSBOOKBYSIDNEYSMITH.COM

The Grateful Dead's Jerry Garcia, Bob Weir, and Bill Kreutzmann sat in with the Allman Brothers Band in Gaelic Park, Bronx, New York, on July 17, 1972.

PHOTOS BY DINA REGINE

The Allman Brothers Band and the Grateful Dead drew over 80,000 people over two days to R.F.K. Memorial Stadium in Washington, D.C., on June 9 and 10, 1973.

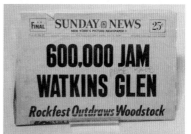

TOP: The Summer Jam at Watkins Glen, New York, drew over 600,000 people to a racetrack in New York's Fingers Lake region to see the Grateful Dead, The Band, and the Allman Brothers Band. RANDALL S. HOUSER

ABOVE: Front-page news.
PHOTO COURTESY OF THE BIG HOUSE MUSEUM ARCHIVES

AT LEFT: It was estimated that 30 percent of people between the ages of seventeen and twenty-four living between Boston and New York were at Watkins Glen. A good time was had by most. RANDALL S. HOUSER

RIGHT: Grateful Dead sound guru Owsley "Bear" Stanley used this motorbike to traverse the massive Watkins Glen grounds.
RANDALL S. HOUSER

BELOW: Bill Graham, who was very close with all three bands, did not promote Watkins Glen, but he was in charge of staging and backstage facilities. RANDALL S. HOUSER

LEFT: The Grateful Dead's "coven of hi-fi wizards" designed the massive Watkins Glen sound system, a precursor of the Wall of Sound.
RANDALL S. HOUSER

By the time the Allman Brothers Band took the Watkins Glen stage at 9:30 p.m., a cold, biting wind had moved in behind the blown-away thunderstorms.

The New York Times reported that, "half-naked bodies coated with brown slime moving rhythmically to the music amid huddled figures curled up sleeping in the mud at their feet in barbiturate or alcohol-induced stupors."

The Times described the post-jam festival site as a "giant garbage dump," where the debris was so thick that the ground was not visible.

RANDALL S. HOUSER

ABOVE: "The syncopations that Jaimoe brought in and his general feel for rhythm were just so fun to play with." –Butch Trucks

RIGHT: "Butch was a great drummer. Almost everything I've ever played that someone said was great was a reaction to something Butch played." –Jaimoe

SIDNEY SMITH/
ALLMANBROTHERSBOOKBYSIDNEYSMITH.COM

LEFT: Though Jaimoe's childhood friend from Gulfport, Mississippi, Lamar Williams, seemed to come out of nowhere when he joined the Allman Brothers Band in November 1972, he had been a first-call bassist around his hometown since he was 14.

SIDNEY SMITH/
ALLMANBROTHERSBOOKBYSIDNEYSMITH.COM

BELOW: Lamar and Marian Williams, London, 1974.

COURTESY OF THE MARIAN WILLIAMS
COLLECTION

Lamar and Marian Williams' wedding, July 6, 1974.

COURTESY OF THE MARIAN WILLIAMS
COLLECTION

ABOVE: Dickey's father, Harold Betts, on the farm.

RIGHT: Dickey, Butch, and friends hanging out at the farm, April 1973.

BELOW LEFT: Vaylor and Melody Trucks play on the farm.

BELOW RIGHT: Dickey and Jessica Betts.

SIDNEY SMITH/
ALLMANBROTHERSBOOKBYSIDNEYSMITH.COM

ABOVE LEFT: Gregg with his second wife, Jan Blair
Allman, 1973.

ABOVE RIGHT: Gregg Allman and ABB manager Phil Walden,
at the Capricorn Music Weekend, September 1973.

BELOW: Dickey Betts hanging out at the farm with
crew members (from left) Kim Payne, Buffalo Evans
and Tuffy Phillips, Spring 1973.

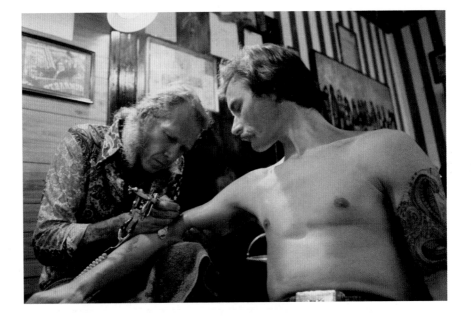

Dickey Betts visiting the studio of tattoo legend Lyle Tuttle, San Francisco, September 1973. Tuttle had given the band their mushroom tattoos two years earlier. NEAL PRESTON

ABOVE: Cameron Crowe and Gregg Allman, Phoenix, Arizona, September 1973.

BELOW: Gregg in his Phoenix, Arizona, hotel room while being interviewed by Cameron Crowe, who called him "a generational rock star—a towering, suspicious, incredibly vivid guy." September 23, 1973.
NEAL PRESTON

Gregg Allman in his Phoenix, Arizona, hotel room while
being interviewed by Cameron Crowe, September 23, 1973.
NEAL PRESTON

12

AMERICAN BEAUTIES

ON JUNE 9 and 10, 1973, the Allman Brothers Band and the Grateful Dead co-headlined RFK Stadium in Washington, D.C., alternating opening and closing slots. Tickets for each day were $7 (about $45 in 2023). The headliners (Allman Brothers Band on day 1 and the Dead on day 2) played long sets, stretching the shows, which began in the sweltering afternoon heat, until midnight. More than 80,000 people attended, with 53,000 people there on Saturday and 30,000 on Sunday, even though the bands were only six weeks away from playing the largest music festival ever held just three hundred miles away.

"Every rock & roller on the East Coast worth his or her faded jeans showed up," *Rolling Stone* reviewer Gordon Fletcher wrote. "The emphasis was so much on scene-making that the music frequently seemed incidental to the conspicuous consumption of reefers, reds and Ripple." With the masses rolling in from up and down the East Coast, D.C. police let concertgoers spend the night in the areas surrounding the stadium.

"If 2,000 kids show up and sit on the grass all night, there's not a hell of a lot you can do about it," Lieutenant Albert Yowell told *The Washington Post*. The next day's newspaper showed a photo of campers spread out around a tent and noted that "by midnight, an encampment of more than 3,000 rock fans had encircled RFK Stadium." Crowds partied all night, sleeping in and around their cars so they could be in the front of the line when doors opened at noon for the general admission seating. They left mounds of garbage in their wake.

The *Post* reported that a crowd of two thousand tore down a gate and forced their way into the stadium almost an hour before the scheduled noon opening on day 1. Edward Steven Weissman, seventeen at the time, said that he helped rip the gate open—not to get in early but to prevent getting trampled by the surging crowd.

"We were being pushed up against the gates," Weissman recalled. "With the pressure behind us mounting, we put our hands underneath and started rocking. I was young and strong and just kept pulling up with all my strength with my friends pushing me and all at once the gate started moving. It went up and everyone ran into the stadium. My friend lost his boot and lifted himself up and out of the way to avoid being trampled. We all got separated as we fought forward just to get out of the way and be safe. We regathered inside—my friend with one boot on!"

Police blocked that entrance, but the stadium authorities realized that trying to hold back the masses was hopeless and fans rushed in carrying coolers of beer and wine. Dealers did brisk business during the show, openly selling joints and Quaaludes as if they were hot dogs and beer at a ball game.

Texas legend Doug Sahm, of the Sir Douglas Quintet, got things started on Saturday in front of a crowd that included Caroline Kennedy, the fifteen-year-old daughter of late president John F. Kennedy. "Marijuana was plainly in evidence in the Stadium, smoked in rolled joints, in pipes, in hookahs and in bongs (large water pipes usually made from bamboo)," the *Post* reported. An undercover policeman, well ahead of his time, told the reporters that if he tried to arrest everyone smoking weed, he'd "have to arrest 35,000 kids," adding with a shrug that "it's a crime without victims."

The paper also noted the prevalence of wine (especially fruit-flavored) and "sopors," which it described as downers that "[parallel] the effects of liquor: users become incoherent, sleepy and often obnoxious." It was referring to Quaaludes and described their users as "staggering around the stadium in a daze, eyes barely focused on the ground one step ahead." Backstage, the bands were served catered dinner by waiters in black tie.

The Dead played two excellent sets, starting around 3 PM with "The Promised Land" and ending three hours later with "Sugar Magnolia." Dead tape archivist Dick Latvala termed the show a "certified killer." After a stage turnover, Sam Cutler introduced the Allman Brothers at 7 PM, saying, "A lot of energy's been put out over the years to bring these bands together, and prior to this day it hasn't happened for a while. Everybody from our end of the music is real happy that at long last we've been able to welcome on the same bill as the Grateful Dead—the Allman Brothers Band."

The Allman Brothers opened with "Wasted Words," one of four songs from the still-unreleased *Brothers and Sisters* that they would play, along with "Ramblin' Man," "Jessica," and "Southbound." Cutler again introduced the band for their encore, saying, "This is where the scene gets a little loose and various people from various well-known and unknown outfits will be joining the folks onstage to play a little." No guests joined for "Whipping Post," but Weir and guitarist Ronnie Montrose came out for an extended "Mountain Jam" to close the show.

The *Post*'s review of the first day's performance noted that while "the Grateful Dead carried the crowd through Saturday's afternoon heat with the relatively relaxed style of San Francisco soaring rock, the Allman Brothers clearly stole the show with high-power boogie music that had the audience undulating throughout the night."

After the music ended at about 11:15 PM on Saturday, June 9, an announcement came that anyone who filled a trash bag would receive a free ticket for the next day. The tactic cleaned up the infield in an hour. Thousands of kids continued their partying around the stadium, playing frisbee and blasting music into the late hours. The *Post* described it as "a jamboree of freaks" and "a carnival atmosphere." People again slept all around the stadium and its parking lots.

The smaller crowd on Sunday packed the infield, making it "as uncomfortable as a New York subway car during rush hour," said the *Post*. "Many of the passageways to the grandstands contained youths who were sprawled out on the concrete with their eyes closed." The throng was "half naked and happy. . . . Mostly white, middle class and under 25, and saffron-robed members of the International Society for Krishna Consciousness joined the crowd in their dancing as they handed out incense sticks."

Wet Willie opened and impressed *Rolling Stone*'s Fletcher, who wrote that the band "surprised everyone with the most lively, vibrant music of the weekend—an energetic brand of Southern R&B." The Allman Brothers' set was almost a mirror of the previous day's show in a slightly abbreviated form. In these settings, the differences between the two bands' approaches to set-list construction were vividly illustrated. Since their formation, the Allman Brothers Band played virtually the same show night after night on any given tour, while the Dead consistently dipped into their catalog, playing different songs each night and taking greater risks.

On Sunday, the Dead dared to open with the powerful, laconic ballad "Morning Dew." They gave a marathon six-hour performance. Betts and Trucks joined for the third set, a tour of American roots music that started with Dylan ("It Takes a Lot to Laugh, It Takes a Train to Cry"); steered through some Arthur Crudup/Elvis Presley ("That's Alright Mama"), Chuck Berry ("Promised Land"), the traditional American songbook ("Goin' Down the Road Feeling Bad"), and Buddy Holly ("Not Fade Away"); and then landed right back on Berry for a show-ending "Johnny B. Goode." It was a rousing closer to the weekend.

Garcia sure thought so. A few months later, writer Cameron Crowe described Garcia as "ecstatic about the experience" of the RFK Stadium shows. "It's kind of like playing with us the way we were five years ago," Garcia said. "We really inspired them and they've patterned a lot of their trip after us. They're like a younger, Southern version of us in some ways musically. I really enjoy playing with those guys. . . . They're good." *

THE RFK STADIUM shows were not only a momentous elevation of the long-standing Allman Brothers/Dead friendship but also a turning point for the Allman Brothers Band and their internal power dynamics. By then, the road crew had established itself as a power structure within the band.

From the beginning and at Duane's insistence, the Allman Brothers'

---

* Crowe also reported that as the Dead had launched their own label, which hired its first employees in April 1973, there were "definite plans afoot to release an album of a monumental Dead-Allmans jam session." (We're still waiting.) Grateful Dead archivist Dick Latvala and Allman Brothers Band archivist Kirk West were working on this planned multiple-CD project when Latvala died in 1999.

road crew personnel had always been viewed as veritable equals to the band members. It was a unique relationship they shared with the Dead. The road crew had begun to cause problems for the Allman Brothers organization, and things came to a head at RFK Stadium when Kim Payne assaulted Dick Wooley during the band's set.

Payne said that he was on painkillers for a foot injury sustained in a recent motorcycle crash and was hobbling around, grumpy and in pain. His primary concern, he said, was the potential for the stage collapsing under the weight of too many people, including up to 150 in the Dead entourage. He took matters into his own hands when Wooley tried to come up onto a stage that the band had ordered closed. He said that he had told driver Tuffy Phillips that nobody else could come on the stage, before being told that "there was a guy who said he's with the label and wants to come up."

Said Payne, "I hobbled over and saw this guy I had never seen before, with short hair wearing a suit and holding a briefcase." [Wooley was almost certainly neither wearing a suit nor carrying a briefcase.] "He said he was with the label and he was coming up and I just said, 'No you're not' and punched him in the nose."

A fight ensued. Wooley, who studied martial arts, said he was getting the best of a stoned Payne until others jumped on him and started kicking him. He was thoroughly pummeled and thrown off the stage, where he was further kicked and punched.

"The Allman Brothers were always great and very easy to deal with, but the roadies had started thinking they were rock stars instead of baggage handlers," said Wooley. "They got big heads and I wasn't going to take it, so we got into it and they just beat the fuck out of me."

Wooley said that he was saved, perhaps literally, by "a large Grateful Dead crew member" who pulled him from the pile and carried him to safety.

"I probably shouldn't have pressed the matter, but I was kind of drunk myself and I thought it was important to make a statement," said Wooley. "I wasn't permanently damaged, but it just brought to a head the tensions between the roadies and everyone else. It had just gotten out of hand. If success don't change you, nothing will."

The beatdown of an important executive who was crucial to getting the band, and all Capricorn acts, radio play was the culmination of a steady disintegration in behavior and control. This breakdown was fueled by prodigious substance abuse and likely compounded by exhaustion and pent-up anger, pain, and sadness from the losses of Allman and Oakley. The problems extended well beyond the band and their crew. "Everyone in our organization was out of control," said Wooley.

Seeing the need to rein in the road crew, Walden ordered Willie Perkins to fire Payne, Phillips, and sound man Mike Callahan. No one was under any illusion that this would solve all the problems, but as Perkins said, "You can't fire the band." They were less than a month away from two shows at Madison Square Garden and headlining the Summer Jam at Watkins Glen. *Brothers and Sisters* would be released in two months, with a major national tour to follow. With all that on tap, the Allman Brothers Band and their entire operation, right up to Walden, were in turmoil, as even a casual reader of the *Macon Telegraph* would have ascertained.

"Everyone dealt with drugs in their own way, but it took its toll on everyone," said Wooley.

Insiders were growing increasingly worried that the whole house of cards might topple over, but the public only saw a band on the rise in the summer of 1973. The relationship between the Grateful Dead and the Allman Brothers Band was also on the way up, with Summer Jam at Watkins Glen, the nation's largest rock festival, just around the corner.

But first the Allman Brothers Band had some serious housekeeping to do. With three crew members gone and major shows on the horizon, the band needed some help, pronto. Studio producer and engineers Johnny Sandlin and Buddy Thornton joined the band on the road to run sound and Twiggs Lyndon and Willie Perkins started rustling up some new stage help.

Lyndon called his twenty-two-year-old brother A.J. and offered him a job.* He headed to New York, where he would begin his job by working two shows at Madison Square Garden, July 20–21. After the first night's

---

* The younger Lyndon was excited, but his wife burst into tears at news of the job offer. "She didn't want me gone and she knew what life was going to be like out there," A.J. said. He initially declined the offer, but when his mother said that he was being a fool, he accepted the job.

performance, Betts assigned A.J. Lyndon to keep an eye on Wabegijig while he caroused with Waylon Jennings. It was a harrowing night: Betts trashed his hotel room, threatened his wife, and attacked A.J. when he tried to intervene.*

"That whole mess of an evening was spurred by too much cocaine and too many Golden Cadillacs, which was the cocktail Dickey was drinking," A.J. recalled.

It was all too much for the young man, who told his brother, Twiggs, that he quit. "I said I was not cut out for this work and that I wanted out of this nuthouse," A.J. said.

Twiggs called Perkins, who asked A.J. to stay on through Watkins Glen. "He said they needed all hands on deck and would take it as a personal favor if I could stick around," A.J. recalled. "They needed someone to drive the truck back to Macon afterwards. I promised to stay on for that."

IT WAS NOT a coincidence that Betts's sound had inched closer to Garcia's crystalline guitar tone on *Brothers and Sisters*. He had asked his sound people to learn some of Garcia's sonic secrets, recalled Thornton, a Capricorn Studios engineer. Before their joint shows, Dead sound man Dan Healy showed Thornton Garcia's custom-made cabinets, and the Allman Brothers Band's crew built replicas back in Macon.

"Betts' playing style emulated Jerry's a lot," said Healy, who also worked on Garcia's custom amps. "We could all hear that, and we were happy to help Dickey in any way we could with his sound. We weren't a hoarding kind of people, and we considered those guys, both band and crew, our friends."

The Dead and their sound crew were inveterate tinkerers. "They fucked with everything," Cutler said. "The simple position that they came from was: How can we make this better? Fender made that amp? Big deal. Let's crack it open and see how we can improve on it. That's how they approached every aspect of sound." This piqued Betts's curiosity.

The crew members readily shared information, technical and other-

---

* In 1990, Kirk West had a similar experience with Betts on his first night as the Allman Brothers Band's assistant tour manager. It's an interesting pattern, possibly a form of hazing.

wise, with one another. Both organizations could be hard to penetrate but treated friends like brothers. If you were in, you were in, and the Allmans were definitely in with the Dead, who were constantly fiddling with their sound and gear in search of the elusive perfect tone. Thornton and the other members of the Allman Brothers crew were always excited to discuss gear development and sound concepts with what *Rolling Stone* termed "the Grateful Dead family's coven of hi-fi wizards."

Fueled by sound guru Owsley, the Dead had long been on a nonstop quest for sonic nirvana. They pursued audio improvement with a single-minded devotion that was unlike anything else in rock and roll and led to countless sonic advancements. The experimentation reached a zenith in 1974 with the "wall of sound," which combined six independent sound systems using eleven separate channels in an attempt at a distortion-free system that would also eliminate the need to use front-of-stage monitors. It was only used from March to October 1974, because it weighed seventy-five tons and was so time-consuming to set up and take down that two systems and two crews were required, so they could leapfrog each other on tour.

"Those guys were brilliant," said Thornton. "The opportunity to learn what they were up to as we worked on both Dickey's tone and building a new sound system, which incorporated some of their ideas, was priceless."*

Ron Wickersham designed the first multitrack mixing console for San Francisco's Pacific Recorders Studio while working for Ampex. By 1969, he had formed Alembic and begun working extensively with the Grateful Dead. Betts's quest for Garcia's tone also led him to commission Alembic to build him a guitar in 1973. He received it the next year, an ornately

---

* Healy describes Garcia's custom-made amps as "essentially Fender Twin Reverbs," which he used as a preamp in conjunction with a variety of different power amps over the years. Garcia previously played Twin Reverbs modified by Healy, Ron Wickersham, and others, and he loved the sound, but they were all troubled by the amps' inconsistencies and lack of road worthiness.

"Early on we discovered that there's a horrible variance between the Twin Reverbs Jerry loved and that they weren't particularly reliable on the road," said Healy. He and other crew members began disassembling Twins and rebuilding them to make them sturdier, "so you could play them really hard," retaining the amps' essence while making them both tougher and clearer-toned.

carved and decorated instrument with an Allman Brothers Band mushroom on the back of the headstock and a sterling silver RICHARD BETTS inlay across the fretboard.

The instrument was built by Rick Turner, who said that Betts never really took a liking to the guitar because it "just didn't sound like a Les Paul." Betts rarely played the guitar and within a few years gave it to a golf pro who offered him some pointers and slipped him in for tee times. Lamar Williams also had an Alembic built for him at Betts's urging.*

Betts's love of Garcia's tone and playing was obvious on *Brothers and Sisters*, where his sound, always brighter and cleaner than Duane's, took on a more bell-like, Garcia-style tone. Betts's guitar is alone on most of the album, with Les Dudek's harmony parts on "Ramblin' Man" standing out as the only other electric guitar on the album. In that setting, with his Les Paul paired with Leavell's piano and Gregg's organ rather than a second guitar, Betts occupies a more central point and the new tone takes center stage. It is loud, crisp, and clean, a sound clearly influenced by Garcia.

---

* Williams's stage rig also incorporated the Alembic tube preamps into fifteen-inch cabinets built by Thornton and other members of the sound crew after consulting with Healy and other Dead gurus.

13

NEW SPEEDWAY BOOGIE

ON JULY 28, 1973, just six weeks after the RFK Stadium shows, the Allman Brothers and the Grateful Dead hosted the Summer Jam at Watkins Glen, at a grand prix racetrack in New York's beautiful but remote Finger Lakes region. The genesis of the event was Betts, Oakley, and Jaimoe's July 1972 Hartford sit-in with the Dead, which caught the attention of that show's young promoters, Jim Koplik, just twenty-three, and Shelly Finkel, twenty-nine.

"I loved both bands and had great relationships with both the musicians and the management," said Koplik.

Cutler said that the idea of playing their own festival together was an organic outgrowth of their relationship and mutual respect, "a natural constituency for both bands—and it worked," he said. "Every time the Allman Brothers and Grateful Dead played together, it was special. Doing something grand like Watkins Glen was not a hard decision! Making it happen was another story."

Koplik and Finkel originally planned to hold the concert in Springfield, Massachusetts, but city fathers quickly rejected that idea, aghast at the idea of the area being flooded with hippies. Ticketron, an early version of today's Ticketmaster, recommended the Watkins Glen racetrack, which hosted more than 100,000 people annually on its ninety-five-acre grounds. Moreover, there were plenty of nearby campgrounds and a state park next door. In February, Finkel met with local government and racetrack officials and got the go-ahead to proceed. Promoters had higher organizational barriers to climb because municipalities from coast to coast were cautious after the giant but peaceful crowds of Woodstock and the utter chaos and tragedy of Altamont, and few of them wanted to deal with the potential headaches surrounding such an event. The extra work would pay off when the crowds swelled far beyond expectations at Watkins Glen, according to Finkel.

It was clear from the start that the two bands would have to be co-billed as headliners and paid equally, an arrangement known as "most favored nation." They eventually settled on a fee of $117,500 each. The matter of which band would close the show remained unresolved. Koplik said that he knew that he'd need a third act to make the event an all-day festival and lessen the potential controversy of who opened and closed. Added Finkel: "The assumption from the start [was] that the third band would be the opener, so that we didn't have to ask the Dead or the Allman Brothers to do so." Once both headliners agreed to the event, working out the details fell to the Dead's Cutler and the Allman Brothers Band's Bunky Odom.

"Me and Bunky kind of plotted that together because we felt instinctively that there was this huge demand for it out there—and there was!" Cutler said. "The audience recognized the kind of magic that comes about from combining different audiences and when the Allman Brothers and the Grateful Dead got together the flame burned a lot brighter."

Odom said that he made multiple trips to San Francisco and that Cutler came to Macon twice to work out the details. "It was not an easy process, because the Dead were really paranoid about everything," said Odom. "It was like pulling teeth. On my first trip to San Francisco, I was afraid to drink the water or eat the food because we had heard so much about them dosing everything. But never ever have I enjoyed such a great bunch of people. Once they got to know you, the Dead were just super."

Just as Odom was preparing to go to San Francisco for one last sit-down to complete all the details and sign the contracts, Walden told him that he would not accept the deal unless the Allman Brothers Band closed. "I told Phil that insisting on closing could be a deal breaker and that it wasn't necessarily the best slot anyway, that you want to play from 5:30 to sundown, after which people would be too fucked up to listen," Odom said. "Phil blew up and just wouldn't listen to me, so I had to go there and tell them that we insisted on closing."

Odom sat down in the Dead office at a table with Cutler, comanager Rock Scully, Bill Graham, Lesh, Garcia, Finkel, and Koplik. He was badly outnumbered, but they all quickly agreed to list the bands in alphabetical order, which advantaged the Allman Brothers. Odom then grew uneasy as the subject of playing times and slots came up.

"Fuck this," he thought. "What am I going to do?"

As he squirmed in his seat, mind racing, preparing to speak, he was shocked to hear Jerry Garcia suddenly jump into the conversation, saying, "We'll take the first six hours to test the P.A. out."

Odom couldn't believe his luck. "Problem solved!" he thought, suppressing a smile. "The Dead would open and the Allman Brothers would close—just as Phil wanted."

Cutler chuckled at this memory decades later, noting that it is a perfect example of Garcia's high emotional intelligence and ability to foresee problems and navigate around them. "Jerry was intuitively brilliant," Cutler said. "He would have known instinctively that who's going to close the show is going to come up as a big fucking issue, because it always does. It's one of the biggest causes of things breaking apart in rock and roll. Jerry came up with the perfect way to defuse the typical straight Hollywood questions that the Phil Waldens of the world who haven't taken enough LSD would ask. Jerry could see that coming a mile away and he came up with a suggestion that had two advantages: it was a good idea and it defused all those ego issues before they could take hold."

The Allman Brothers Band's contract stipulated they would play one 150-minute set beginning at 10 PM. At the meeting, everyone also agreed that the Band should be the third act rather than Leon Russell, whom Finkel and Koplik had already hired, and to extend an invitation to Bob Dylan, who had not toured since 1966. The promoters went along with this although Russell had already signed a contract, because they were sure that the Band, who had not performed live in eighteen months, would decline, just as Dylan did. When the Band surprisingly agreed to play for a fee of $75,000, Koplik had to cancel Russell, whose contract was for the same amount. "He was not pleased," said the promoter. "We had to pay him half to not play."

"We didn't want to play Watkins Glen," said the Band's Robbie Robertson. "We were in a mood and felt that the only reason to do things like that was the money. But we were talked into it: 'Oh come on. It's just up the road.'"

The Dead insisted that the promoters hire Bill Graham, a figure trusted by all three bands, to handle the staging and backstage hospitality. The creation of the sound system fell to the Dead's able crew. Dan Healy and his team spent two weeks on-site working everything out. "That site was basically just a patch of ground, not a venue," said Healy. "We created every aspect of it."

Red Dog described the stage as "one you dream about as a roadie, about 20 feet high, 80 feet wide and 60 feet deep, with 25 foot P.A. wings on each side." As the stage was under construction, Healy "dug trenches to lay all the snakes and cables underground, connecting the stage to the booth, which was one hundred and fifty feet out, and then to a series of three delay towers" that he built. These buried cables would prove to be crucial as the field filled with hundreds of thousands of spectators and inches of mud.

The rest of the Allman Brothers and Dead crews arrived three days before the event and treated it as a gathering of the brotherhood. "It was two big families getting together to party and musically knock the world off its feet," Red Dog said.

The camaraderie was vital. "Taking a fucking band like the Allman Brothers or Grateful Dead to the dizzying heights of Watkins Glen is not for lightweights or the weak of heart," he said. "This is a serious business. You're humping four tons of gear in and out of venues. It's a huge, physically demanding job."

Red Dog was especially impressed by the massive PA system Healy was constructing, with the aid of what Alembic's Rick Turner termed the Dead's "PA Consulting Committee," which included him, Wickersham, Owsley, Mark "Sparky" Raizene, and John Curl. "There was one hell of a lot of P.A.s," Red Dog said. The system needed to not only be powerful but to have a built-in delay going back from the stage so that the crowd would hear the music together, without echoes.

"The sound from the stage speakers [was] doubled 200 feet from the stage by four delay towers," Turner said. "The [tower] speakers were wired to the stage amps but with a 0.175 second delay built in, so that by the time the sound from the stage speakers reaches the tower area through the air, the signal broadcast from the towers [was] synchronized with it. There were six more delay towers arranged radially 200 feet farther from those towers—400 feet from the stage—and six more towers 200 feet farther out. Sixteen delay towers in all, plus the main PA."

All of that power was fueled by massive McIntosh 2,300-power amps, the Dead's preferred high-end audio component. As they continued to build what Cutler proudly calls "the best sound system there has ever been for an event," they realized that they were still underpowered and were going to need reinforcements. Janet Furman of Alembic was dispatched to the McIntosh factory, which luckily was located only seventy-eight miles away in Binghamton, New York. Still, with every road in and out of Watkins Glen clogged, Furman was going to have to travel there by helicopter. "My assignment was to get five more of those giant amps, any way I could," Furman said, adding that Cutler handed over $6,000 in cash and the use of a helicopter. The McIntosh factory was closed for the weekend, but Furman tracked down the owner at home and took off in the copter.

"The pilot flew me from the venue to downtown Binghamton," Furman said. "I met up with the owner, who drove me to the factory and sold me the amps off the production floor. We drove back to town in his station wagon, his wife and kids aboard on their way to a summer vacation, and transferred the amps into the copter. At over 100 pounds each . . . it was a heavy load for a small helicopter. We had a very scary moment as we took off, coming within inches of crashing into a high-rise building. But back at Watkins Glen, the sight of that enormous crowd from the air was unforgettable. In the moment I landed, delivering the goods, I became an instant hero."

The effort put into constructing the massive sound system paid off. As Healy proudly notes, "the sound never went off despite the enormity of the event, the weather, and the crowd. It worked perfectly, even though the mud became half-knee deep." Koplik calls Healy's sound design nothing less than genius. He built giant scaffolding structures with sound towers atop them, each wrapped with security fencing to discourage the crowd from climbing up to get a better view. People would have to be talked down off the towers anyhow.

"We had to tell everyone to get off the scaffolding because we knew it was going to get wet and people were gonna fall," said Koplik. "That became one of our biggest concerns."

Even as the crews bonded and worked together, things weren't all kumbaya between them. Conflict erupted over Healy's and the Dead guys' proprietary attitude toward their sound gear. The Record Plant mobile truck was there to record the Allman Brothers Band, and the Dead did not want to provide them with a feed, which would ever so slightly degrade the live sound. Sandlin, who was there to oversee the live recording, described what ensued as "a fight about microphones as to who got the best split." One signal went to the sound system and one went to the recording, which Healy objected to providing. He and Record Plant engineer Frank Hubach, there to work with Sandlin on the live recording, almost came to blows before the Allman Brothers and their remote truck got their feed. Sandlin viewed it all as an unnecessary hassle, but, he readily acknowledged, "The Grateful Dead were the best at recording live and their shows always sounded good."

Interestingly, there were problems with Gregg's vocals on the first several songs, which hampered efforts to release the full set in later years. Some in the Allman Brothers Band's camp believed that the Dead sound crew had intentionally sabotaged their feed.

THE PROMOTERS SOLD 200,000 tickets at ten dollars, but the crowd exploded to three times that number. With people piling into the area and lining up behind the closed gates for days, Koplik and Finkel huddled with Graham and decided to open the gates a day early to relieve the pressure and help keep things calm. By Friday, July 27, the day before the festival was supposed to start, the expected two hundred thousand people were already on the grounds, with thousands more flooding in by the hour. It was becoming increasingly clear that the attendance was going to be far beyond anyone's estimate or imagination.

Matt Burt was a high school senior in nearby Ithaca, New York, who traveled to the festival with friends. Late in the afternoon of July 27, they pulled off the road leading to the grounds and threw down their bedrolls, establishing a rudimentary campsite. Then they watched the area fill up.

"By that night cars had parked along our road and cut us off from anyone else camping near us, and about ten groups had the field to ourselves," said Burt. "As I walked around that night, I was stunned to see that lots and lots of folks had arrived. There were bonfires raging, flags fluttering. I felt like I was in the battle camp the night before Agincourt."

Even as the fields around the festival site filled up, there were tens of thousands more people streaming toward the grounds, and an unknown number stuck in heavy traffic extending in all directions. Watkins Glen is less than three hours from the Rainbow Bridge crossing at the Canadian border, where traffic backups turned away an unknown number of northern neighbors. Bill Irvine was an eighteen-year-old driving with friends from Hamilton, Ontario, and listening to a Buffalo radio station, which was reporting eight-to-ten-hour waits.

"We couldn't get closer than 10 miles from the border when traffic just stopped," recalled Irvine. "I got out and walked and the word was it was like this all the way to Watkins Glen, so the driver turned around."

The band members were well aware of what was developing. "It was hard to get in and out of that place," said Bob Weir. "It got way bigger than we intended. We thought maybe if we're lucky we'd get 100,000 people; 60–70,000 would be nice and handle-able. Six hundred thousand was beyond anyone's imagination or thoughts."

Andy Aledort, a guitarist who would go on to play with Dickey Betts for ten years (and who is my coauthor of *Texas Flood: The Inside Story of Stevie Ray Vaughan*) was at the jam as a seventeen-year-old college freshman. He took a bus from Manhattan to Schenectady to meet up with a friend, and the two of them then hitchhiked the almost two hundred miles to the festival, joining the masses walking the last stretch.

"Cars were moving very slowly and we were all jumping on the hoods and riding along for a while," he recalled. "At one point we even got into a car and they gave us a few beers and then we hopped out and kept walking when they got stopped by traffic. That's what the scene was like, a very friendly atmosphere. It was an event, a happening."

Aledort said that it wasn't lost on anyone that the jam was becoming something much larger than anticipated and that the explosion was a result of people his age, teenagers who were too young to attend Woodstock but old enough to be fully aware while it was happening four years earlier and just over 150 miles to the east.

"We wanted in!" he said. "We wanted our own event. The whole notion that a counterculture existed was intoxicating. It may well have been over, but we didn't know that. The storm surge was over, but the water hadn't receded. The Jam was a vestige of the sixties that we were desperate to experience, and that's why it became so big."

Writing in *Crawdaddy,* Patrick Snyder-Scumpy took note of the crowd's youth and the fact that they were in it for a party more than for a spiritual awakening, with booze and downers being more popular than the psychedelics that helped fuel its predecessor.

"The crowd seemed less diverse than at Woodstock," he wrote. "This was the youth of the nation . . . not a gathering of disaffected weirdos. . . . Watkins Glen was a ritual re-creation of a past event with the sole purpose of providing a good time for its participants."

Odom said that 30 percent of people between the ages of seventeen and twenty-four living between Boston and New York were there, as well as one of every 350 Americans. The giant crowds made an impression on local businesses, of course. Jack "the Baron" Mullaney owned the Beverage Baron, a liquor store on Main Street. Sensing that the Summer Jam was going to be a huge event, he bought every can of beer his distributor would deliver, filling his store with cases from floor to ceiling. It was a risky move for a small business, but the Baron's hunch proved prescient, and business was brisk.

Fearful of making his way through the crowd with a bagful of money, Mullaney asked for and received a police escort to the bank to make a deposit, then returned to the store, where he and some friends slept on stacks of emptied cardboard beer cases armed with baseball bats to protect the stock. The caution was unnecessary.

"Family legend said my dad made more money that one weekend than in an entire year of business at the store," said Mullaney's daughter, Becky Chalk.

Of course, beer and other legal beverages were not the only intoxicants being consumed. "It was the biggest drug market on the planet," recalled Brad Perkins, who was a nineteen-year-old army radio operator at the time. He and three friends drove to the festival armed with homemade wooden pipes they intended to share.

"We had to park a long way away and by the time we got there, the night before, the sun was setting," said Perkins. "From the opening gate to the actual stage area was about four miles. The entire walk was shoulder to shoulder with people. Everyone was imbibing some kind of intoxicant. We traded our pipes for good pot, opium, speed, and LSD."

As the crowds continued to stream in, Healy and his crew were above the masses in their sound booth, which they did not leave for two days. "There was no way to come and go, so we stayed there, looking down at people standing knee deep in mud and feces," Healy said. "We had food passed to us, and we pissed and shit in a can at the bottom of the booth. It was crude, but it was the only way to operate. I climbed to the top of my booth, and I could not see the edge of the audience, which extended to the horizon on three sides. There were solid, wall-to-wall people as far as I could see."

The small country lanes leading to the concert site became parking lots—first figuratively, then literally, as many people abandoned their vehicles and walked miles to the concert, effectively closing the roads. The bands were staying at various places off-site, with the Allman Brothers Band eighteen miles away in a small motel in Horseheads, New York.

A week before the show, *The New York Times* reported that eighty thousand ten-dollar tickets had already been purchased and they were selling an average of five thousand a day, leading Koplik to predict a crowd of one hundred and fifty thousand, which was *supposed* to be the sales cap. Finkel admits now that they sold about two hundred thousand tickets. The promoters started turning fans away from the site two weeks before the event.

"This is the son of Woodstock . . . a happening, which will be the place to be," Koplik told the *Times*. He added that "in agreement with the New York state officials, advanced ticket sales would be cut off at 125,000 but an additional 25,000 tickets would be sold on the day of the concert . . . with police roadblocks designed to screen out those without tickets 20 miles from Watkins Glen."

Whatever the advance planning had been, it seemed to break down as the show day grew closer, with the highways jammed with kids desperate to join the generational event. "When we first got there, we were able to drive in and out of the site, but the road became like Armageddon overnight," said Willie Perkins. "It was like there had been a nuclear attack and people had just abandoned their cars."

It was obvious that the band and crew would not be driving to the concert ground. Helicopters were summoned, with Odom placed in charge of flight scheduling. "Bunky was the unsung hero of Watkins Glen," said Koplik. "Watkins Glen would not have happened without him. Bunky is the most organized man I've ever met in my life and the best road manager I ever dealt with. He had everything down to a T and everyone's trust, including all bands and us, the promoters. That's why he was in charge of the copters."

Most important, Koplik adds, Odom was a consistently calm port in a turbulent sea. "He was the guy who was of sane mind in the middle of a bunch of insane people—and that included Bill Graham, who was insane, and Sam Cutler, who was insane. Bunky had this magic of getting everyone into a room and talking sense to them."

As the helicopters ferrying the bands drew close to the site, the passengers asked the pilot to circle the area, their minds blown by the sea of humanity stretched out beneath them.

"We wanted to soak it in and it was absolutely stunning, exhilarating, and exciting to see this incredible mass of human beings," recalled Chuck Leavell. "It was an ocean of bodies. We were all just really buzzed by the whole scene and situation."

While Leavell, Trucks, and most of the other members of the Allman Brothers Band and their entourage were amazed by the crowd and wanted to stay up in the air to take it all in, Gregg Allman felt otherwise. He was "petrified," he said, noting that he'd "rather ride a camel than a helicopter."

The helicopters ferrying musicians and production people in were also being used to fly injured, sick, or otherwise incapacitated people out to receive medical care. Karen Dibble Whitman was a nine-year-old living in Elmira, twenty-five miles from Watkins Glen. She rode her bike down to Amot Ogden Hospital to watch them unload people. "I've always remembered a girl with long blond hair wearing a black top and jean shorts, her arm hanging over the stretcher," said Whitman.

Rain Thursday night had delayed the completion of the construction of the stage and the planned sound checks had never taken place. With crowds still pouring in, and close to two hundred thousand people already on-site twenty-four hours before the concert was scheduled to begin, Graham suggested that the sound checks take place on Friday, July 27, as public performances.

"Everybody agreed," he said. "My theory was that rather than have a stampede, open up at dawn, and those that were up could come in and those that were sleeping could sleep, then get up and not be in the middle of a crowd. I knew if they got out there and saw all those people, they weren't just going to sound check by saying 'Gimme an A.'"

Graham's instincts were correct. The Dead played for about two hours, followed by the Band, who played for close to an hour, and then, feeling some pressure to match the Dead, the Allman Brothers, who also performed a two-hour set. The one-day festival had organically doubled in length. "By Friday night 150,000 people had gotten a five-hour show," Graham said. "They'd gotten a taste, an appetizer, and they knew their heroes were there."

They got more than just proof that the bands were around; the Dead delivered a signature epic performance that has resonated for half a century.

"The sound check just blew all of us away," said Jeff Schein, who was there as a seventeen-year-old from Queens. "It was totally unexpected and lasted for hours."

The sound checks also made an intense impression on all the performers.

Forty years later, Butch Trucks was still in awe: "That afternoon rehearsal ended up being my most powerful memory because in daylight you could see the mass of people stretched out in front of you and my God! What a sight!" he exclaimed. "Everyone should get up in front of 600,000 people sometime in their life. It's sort of intimidating, but also very, very inspiring."

Betts described the crowd in similarly awestruck terms: "It was like looking at the Grand Canyon," he said. "There were people as far as you could see—over one hill and down and back up and over the next hill."

"It looked like a little town out there," the Band's drummer, Levon Helm, said, noting that people were spread out across a huge area, estimated as close to one hundred acres.

Jaimoe, too, marveled at the sprawl of the crowd as seen from the sky, calling it simultaneously "scary and inspiring."

"There were people until the horizon, people everywhere as far as you could see," he said. "I'm sure I'll never see that many people in one place again."

Despite the sprawl, the bulk of the crowd could hear the music, even if they couldn't see the stage, thanks to Healy's ingenious design. One of the keys to this was that Healy set up the delay towers to cover width as well as depth.

"The sound went sideways so everyone didn't try to squeeze into the middle, which would have created a horrible situation," said Koplik. "The stage was only 60 feet wide but the audience was at least 300 feet wide. Dan and the Dead crew truly cared about the kid in the last row being able to hear."*

Throughout the day of the sound checks and well into the night, people continued to stream toward the grounds, pushing toward the gates and creating the very real threat that fences could come down, resulting in a

---

* Healy said that the attention to detail of the sound construction relates directly to the Grateful Dead's entire ethos of holistically serving the audience. "There's a responsibility that goes above and beyond making the music as good as possible, which we always worked on," he said. "With that many people there, the sound system is your only means of controlling the crowd, conveying information and making sure people are informed and under control. If you fail to take that seriously, people can die. We took that responsibility very seriously."

stampede or other unsafe situation, and possibly even breaching the stage and backstage fences.

"I was frantic because we had really lost control of the gates and I was worried about the stage," said Koplik. "Bill Graham told me that we had to open the gates and abandon ticketing or else the fences would come down and many people would be hurt. It was momentarily a difficult decision but clearly the right one."

Graham's biographer Robert Greenfield notes that "Bill had learned the lessons of Woodstock. He hated free, so his insistence that it was the right approach just shows how convinced he was."

Even as ground transportation became impossible and amenities like food and water became scarce and as the fences around the festival grounds came down, the bands themselves never felt threatened or endangered. "It became a serious security situation for the crowd, but the stage was secure," said Dead crew member Steve Parish.

Giving Graham the responsibility to construct the backstage proved to be another stroke of genius. He was well-known for treating acts well and he had taken his usual care in creating a welcoming hospitality area, which Perkins recalled as "idyllic," and which also maintained a secure perimeter as the crowd swelled outside its fences. Koplik and Finkel ran the festival from a backstage command post in an air-conditioned trailer named "Born Free," which had small golden lions embedded on its sides. Graham brought in palm trees and provided most band members with their own trailers. This resulted in their traipsing in and out of one another's spaces, with endlessly mutating jams and hangout sessions. Leavell, Kreutzmann, Garcia, and Jaimoe particularly enjoyed playing together.

Said Kreutzmann, "My best memories of Watkins Glen were playing with Jaimoe backstage. I love that guy!"

"Everybody was in a great mood," said Koplik. "We had volleyball backstage. We had a swimming pool. We had an array of drugs—instead of being drug-free, it was free drugs, with a trailer with free coke and pot for anyone in the band. It was 1973 and it was quite festive, with naked women running around. The bands got along great. They all hung together, and everybody loved everybody."

While the bands were enjoying each other's company, the crowd kept growing. People entered the site from all directions, filling Watkins Glen and other towns, camping in people's yards, bathing in rivers, dropping acid and sitting on rocks staring into space, searching for friends, meeting future spouses, getting separated from their crew, and doing everything else you can imagine vast hordes of people aged seventeen to twenty-five doing. The weather alternated between high heat and humidity that left people panting—water was hard to find—and downpours that soaked the crowd to their bones and had them shivering. "Sweltering one minute and freezing the next," recalled Aledort.

AFTER THE ALLMAN Brothers Band's sound check, A. J. Lyndon was in the crew room, which was a Winnebago, enjoying a beer with fellow new road-crew recruits Mike Artz and Larry Brantley when Betts appeared in the doorway and asked to have a private word with him.

"Mike and Larry cleared out and Dickey said, 'I want to apologize for my behavior in New York,'" Lyndon recalled. "'There's no excuse for it and I would take it as a personal favor if you would stick with the band.' I wasn't stupid enough to not understand that this was because of Twiggs; I'm sure that was 90 percent of the reason he came and apologized. But I did stay and Dickey and I never had any more issues, though I did come to realize that the night was not an isolated incident, unfortunately."

14
EYES OF THE WORLD

AS THE DEAD were preparing to take the stage, Cutler approached Koplik and demanded an additional $25,000 in cash, making it clear that the band would not take the stage without it. His logic was that the agreed-upon fee had been struck based on an expected crowd of 150,000–200,000 and there were many times more than that in attendance.

"I tried to explain that the additional people were there for free and we hadn't made a dime off of them, but he was not persuaded," recalled Koplik.

Koplik and Finkel retreated to their trailer and pulled $25,000 out of a safe, which they handed to Cutler in a bag. With that, the Grateful Dead took the stage and the promoters thought they had dodged a bullet, but another financial confrontation was looming. As the Dead played, a helicopter bearing Walden landed backstage. He did not calm things down. Without even knowing that the most favored nation clause had been violated with the additional payment to the Dead, Walden took one look at the massive audience laid out beneath his eyes and determined that his band would either be getting more money or packing up their gear and heading south.

"When Phil arrived and found out it was now a free concert and we didn't know how many tickets had been sold, he exploded," recalled Odom. "He said, 'We ain't fucking playing; we're going home.'"

Odom assured Walden that they could work out the situation, while also quietly telling Red Dog and Twiggs Lyndon that there was a huge problem being worked on and they should be prepared to take everything off the stage and load it onto their equipment truck—or at least make sure the promoters knew they were ready to do so. "I told them that we're not going to leave but we might have to threaten to leave, so be ready to start packing gear," Odom said. He then found Finkel and Koplik, and the three of them sat down in the back of a limousine to discuss the problem and the fact that Walden was ready to pull the band if they didn't receive more money considering the giant crowd.

"I just said, 'This is not a free concert!' and pushed them on how many tickets they had actually sold," said Odom. "That's when I found out that because Ticketron didn't stay open all the time, they also sold tickets out the back door of mom-and-pop places in cash deals that were never counted. They admitted they had enough money. They sold 150,000–200,000 tickets, but we never knew the exact number, in part because of those side deals. Once I could assure Phil that we were going to be paid more, he agreed to let the band play."

Perkins said that Walden and the promoters agreed to an additional $75,000 payment, which the band received in August, plus an additional $11,136 in ticket-outlet revenue when everything was settled in November.* That put the Allman Brothers' total payment over $200,000, shattering the agreement that each band would be paid the same. Cutler's reaction upon learning this decades later was simple: "Good on 'em!"

"My whole point—and Bunky's—was they sold hundreds of thousands of tickets for $10," said Cutler. "They made fortunes, and our musicians are standing onstage going, 'There's 600,000 people out there. Don't we get more?' We'd all have been fools not to make that demand."

Decades later, Odom said he's relieved that Cutler bears no ill will—and that he always felt bad about cutting a deal behind his partner's back, not knowing that the Dead had already done the same to him.

"Honestly, I didn't know the Dead had that cash payment and I always felt bad about us brokering a separate deal because of the favored nations contract, which was agreed in principle from the very first conversation," he said. "We were all doing what we felt we had to do."

---

* Perkins still has the books and receipts to back all the payment information up.

The impossibly large crowd remained mostly calm and friendly, impressing all the bands, as well as the police. Though the gathering was more than five times greater than the hundred thousand who attended races at the track, they had markedly fewer problems.

"I'd rather deal with these kids than the race crowd any day," a mounted officer said. "I've never been called 'Sir' so many times in my life."

Locals made the same observation as they watched the masses of young people pouring into the festival grounds. "All through Watkins Glen, townspeople perched on lawn chairs and bridge chairs, sitting in their yards, watching the hippies," *Rolling Stone*'s Joel Siegel wrote. "No one saw a fight."

Mary Moulthrop Heidemann was a twenty-five-year-old ICU nurse who worked in the medical tent. She also recalled a largely peaceful event. "We had a few crises, including a couple of overdoses, but it was mostly lacerations, puncture wounds, bad trips, GI upsets and dehydrations, as a result of lack of food and water and some emotional crises," said Heidemann. "People were able to enjoy themselves, partly because law enforcement learned a great deal from Woodstock. They were there but not trying to bust everyone every minute."

One reason for the peaceful, relatively calm crowd was the Mass Gathering Act, which the New York State Legislature passed in the wake of Woodstock to howls of protest from the underground press, which considered the measure reactionary and anti-youth. The law forced Finkel and Koplik to spend $100,000 on portable toilets and fifty thousand dollars on bottled water, the type of action that allowed systems to remain more or less functional. Facilities and resources were "strained to the breaking point but never did collapse completely," *Crawdaddy*'s Patrick Snyder-Scumpy reported.

Finkel said that the law came close to canceling the event before it began. As the site was being readied, inspectors came to check on preparation, including counting the portable toilets on hand. "We had to have 1,000 johns, which is what we ordered, but the state counted only 960 and said the permit would be revoked if we couldn't find the other 40," Finkel said. "The company said there were no more johns in the state of New York and I said they had to expand their search."

The additional toilets were located in Pennsylvania and arrived on flat-bed trucks a few days before the jam. Before they could be removed from the trucks, Finkel said that he was surprised to see movement in the units. They opened the doors to find "kids who had managed to sneak onto the grounds inside the johns."

Though there were no reports of significant violence at Watkins Glen, there was one death, but it occurred in the air, not on the grounds. Veteran skydiver Willard Smith, thirty-five, jumped out of an airplane with others. Looking to make a big impression, he was armed with an "artillery simulator," which is similar to a hand grenade and designed to create a large boom. It seems to have detonated on him, causing massive chest injuries, and his lifeless body floated into a tree about a half mile from the stage. A group of fifteen-year-olds from Oswego, New York, found him after one friendly if naive father loaded them into a packed station wagon, dropped them off, and wished them a good time. Tom Tobin, one of those kids, said that he and his friends were the first people to find the body hanging from a tree following the fiery descent.

"We got him down and waited for help to arrive," Tobin said. "We were a little freaked out, but we knew he had to come out of the tree."

The other abiding tragedy of the event involved Mitchel Weiser and Bonnie Bickwit, teen lovers from Brooklyn who disappeared hitchhiking to the Summer Jam, a case that has never been solved. But, as Koplik said, the festival itself remained peaceful, something he remains proud of, calling it "the epitome of the hippie movement."

SANDLIN LOOKED OUT at the crowd and felt frightened. Beyond the first fifty rows, the people blended into one sealike mass. He wondered what would happen if such a giant gathering decided to rush the stage and was relieved that everyone was peaceful. Trucks had the same fear, contemplating the impact of everyone pushing forward at the same time. "I took note of where the helicopter was in case I had to make a mad dash for it," he said.

"The news reported there were 600,000 there and maybe 2 million people in the area and it was declared a disaster area," recalled Weir. "As disaster areas go, it was nice, but people who were interested in going home, for instance, well, they couldn't. If they wanted to leave, it just wasn't possible. People had to be peeled away layer by layer."

Weir is not exactly right about departure being impossible. Though many people certainly had vehicles that were blocked in, rendering them stuck, many others did make their way out before the performances were over. Some had to return to work or other forms of reality on Monday morning. Some could no longer tolerate the desperate conditions.

"We left while the Allman Brothers were still playing because we had spent two days tripping on acid, not eating or sleeping," said Aledort. "Who we were going to see became very secondary to the event itself. The music was like a blip compared to the whole experience, which was indelible and unbelievable."

"Watkins Glen was not a place to come hear music," Snyder-Scumpy wrote. "It was more of a place to be with the music in an environment that epitomized its message."

Healy echoes the view that the scope of the event overwhelmed the actual music that was played, comparing Watkins Glen to the Dead's 1978 trip to perform in front of the pyramids in Giza, Egypt. "There are some shows where the event outweighs the actual music—a show becomes a fracas or an event—and Watkins Glen was certainly one of those," said Healy. "The magnitude of the event outweighed the actual show, and I doubt if anybody even remembers what the music was like." Most attendees who recall the music at the jam refer to the sound checks—both because they were better performances, especially in the case of the Dead, and because they were such a surprise. (It also didn't hurt that they were perhaps still coherent enough to listen to the music.)

During the jam itself, each of the bands performed long sets. The Dead opened. As legend and the band's own self-deprecatory comments indicate, it was not their best performance, as with Monterey Pop in 1967 and Woodstock in 1969. There is no video recording of the day, because the Dead refused to allow cameras. Koplik and Finkel's original plan had included releasing both a movie and an audio soundtrack, which is how the Woodstock promoters profited from an otherwise money-losing event, but the Dead emphatically rejected that idea.

Afterward, amid persistent questions whether a concert movie would be released, Cutler released the following statement: "The Grateful Dead are sick and tired of being given cornball ideas for rock movies. The Grateful Dead are delighted that Watkins Glen is only a fond memory and that there will be no further commercial exploitation of what was a tasteful musical trip."

While the show was never officially released, widely circulated recordings indicate that it was stronger than the band recalled—not fantastic, but by no means a disaster. They took the stage almost on time, at 12:20 PM, opened with "Bertha," and played for four hours. The sound check performance was indeed more powerful. "We usually do pretty bad at the big ones," Garcia said. "We played terribly at Woodstock, at Monterey Pop—all the milestones."

John Swenson, reviewing the Jam for the *Village Voice*, noted that the crowd of Deadheads, "a tangled mass of bodies, trapped against the cyclone fences in front of the stage," waited "hopefully to have the magic worked on them." But, he added, "expectations often exceed possibilities and the Dead, perhaps a little awed by the massive crowd they had to project themselves onto, played a soporific, lackluster set through the hottest part of the afternoon. Toward the end they started to come on strong, playing a particularly inspired version of 'Sugar Magnolia,' but it was too little, too late."

The Band, who had not played together publicly in eighteen months, started their performance at 5:00 PM under low clouds, threatening skies, and increasing humidity. As they were finishing their eighth song, "Endless Highway," a new tune inspired by Robbie Robertson's dislike of touring, the skies finally opened and the band ran off the stage, instruments in hand, as the crowd was drenched by rain. The break helped them solve one problem: singer/pianist Richard Manuel had enjoyed himself a bit too much during the Dead's long set and was so drunk he could barely walk to the stage. The pause allowed Jonathan Taplin, their former tour manager who had returned to assist at Watkins Glen, time to try and sober Manuel up, plying him with coffee.

Meanwhile, some of the other members of the Band were standing on the side of the stage when a friend appeared with a bottle of Glenfiddich single malt scotch. They passed the bottle, having a few slugs each, "then it began to rain like a cow pissing on a flat rock," as Levon Helm memorably wrote. As they stood there looking out at the crowd and contemplating the likelihood of Watkins Glen devolving into "another Woodstock-style mud bath," keyboardist Garth Hudson took a few long pulls from the bottle and suddenly sent roadies scrambling to move plastic sheeting as he took to his instruments and improvised some cosmic classical blues, playing what Helm described as "shape-note singing gospel, J.S. Bach, Art Tatum, Slim Gaillard. Cool stuff."

"The immense throng of kids loved this," Helm wrote. "And then the rain petered out. Just like that. It seemed clear to me that master dowser Garth had stopped the rain."

Hudson's swirling improvisations morphed into "The Genetic Method," an instrumental that is wild and eerie under any circumstances and that Hudson on this day took to the edge of outer space. He entertained the crowd, paving the way for a dramatic return to the stage by the entire band, who synced up with Hudson and segued into "Chest Fever." It's a performance that resonates with many concertgoers half a century later.

"The entire venue hunkered down," recalled Jay Corcoran, who was nineteen and drove to the festival with a crew of friends from the Jersey Shore, where they all worked as garbage collectors for Stone Harbor Island Trash (SHIT). "As the rain eased Garth came out and played Beethoven on the organ. We were still covered up with heads down when this little instrumental morphed into 'Chest Fever.' It was grand."

The Band played seven more songs before Robertson shouted to the crowd, "You're the most fantastic thing we've ever seen!" They played a one-song encore, "Rag Mama Rag," before walking offstage energized and amazed. The performance made a huge impression on Gregg Allman, who called it "the high point of that scene," noting that "they got the right name: THE Band, 'cause that's what they are."

"There was an alertness to the audience that I could not believe," Robertson said afterward. The success of their performance, followed by two shows in Jersey City, New Jersey, at Roosevelt Stadium with the Dead, influenced the group's decision to return to the road the following year, backing Bob Dylan. Dylan was curious about the Watkins Glen experience, questioning

Robertson about "every aspect of the festival as he weighed the prospect of going back on the road for the first time in eight years."

Walden's demands that the Allman Brothers Band close the festival were misguided. As Odom noted, "the Band had the best time slot." At 9:30, Cutler came out and introduced the final band, yelling: "And now a band with balls! The Allman Brothers! A band with balls!" The sun was down, and a cold, biting wind had moved in behind the blown-away thunderstorms. The crowd, which had "thinned considerably," shivered their "wet, exhausted bodies," noted John Swenson.

"At times the scene in the moist darkness resembled a Bosch painting," *The New York Times* reported, "half-naked bodies coated with brown slime moving rhythmically to the music amid huddled figures curled up sleeping in the mud at their feet in barbiturate or alcohol-induced stupors."

The Allman Brothers Band played a strong set that included five songs from the still-unreleased *Brothers and Sisters*. They opened with "Wasted Words" and also performed "Southbound," "Come and Go Blues," "Jessica," and "Ramblin' Man," which was still almost a month away from being released as the album's lead single. The large puddle in front of the stage filled with mud-slicked dancers as the band delivered an excellent, lengthy set, even if, as Swenson wrote, "only the most insensibly stoned participants were able to give attention" by then.

"It was an awesome experience," Trucks said. "That was the second largest city in New York for that day. Once you're on your instrument in the dark, though, it just became a performance, and we gave a pretty good one! We didn't have any problem keeping the audience's attention and pulling in the same direction, which really helps trouble from starting."

After the Allman Brothers Band wrapped up their three-hour set with "Whipping Post," they returned to the stage with most members from the other two bands in tow. The libertine backstage environment and tricky transportation had kept everyone around until the end, which they were not contractually obligated to do.

"We ultimately didn't care if we delivered the jam at the end or not," said Koplik. "It had been the plan and we did mention it to them all several times, but by then we were fixated on people's safety—getting everyone out of there in one piece."

The combined groups played an extended encore of "Not Fade Away," "Mountain Jam," and "Johnny B. Goode."

"The jam at the end was spectacularly wiggy," recalled Weir. One can debate whether he meant to say the jam was great or terrible. Trucks was far more direct: "It was just garbage."

"By the time we all got together everyone was fucked up—and fucked up on different drugs," Trucks explained. "The Band was all drunk as skunks and sloppy loose, the Dead were full of acid and wired in that far-out way, and we were all full of coke and cranked up. While we were playing, we thought it was the greatest thing the world had ever heard, but then we listened to the playbacks."

Trucks was being harsh. The jam is sloppy and at times teeters toward incoherence, but it's mostly a good time, and there are moments of transcendence, especially as they lock into an intense groove on the simple vamp of "Not Fade Away" and the guitarists take flight together. While the jam may not have delivered on the promise of America's three greatest rock bands collaborating, it had its moments, and the remaining crowd greeted it with ecstatic applause. As it ended, the musicians waved to the masses and made their way backstage to party some more and to begin lining up for helicopter rides back to whatever constituted normal life. The crowd began to melt away, going back to their own daily realities, turning a steady trickle of departees into a flood, with everyone navigating trash-strewn fields and abandoned vehicles blocking the way.

The show was recorded on multitracks but has never been released in full, which is surprising given the quality of the performance. The Allman Brothers did use the Watkins Glen performance of "Come and Go Blues" on their 1976 live album *Wipe the Windows, Check the Oil, Dollar Gas,* and the terrific "Mountain Jam," featuring Garcia, Weir, and Robertson, was included in the fiftieth anniversary *Trouble No More* box set. The rest was never officially released. The Band's *Live at Watkins Glen,* released in 1995, is a fraud, composed mostly of studio outtakes with fake crowd noise added and performances from other shows, including one song from

Woodstock. An eighteen-minute jam from the Dead's July 27 sound check was included on the *So Many Roads* box set, representing the only music from the Summer Jam ever released by the band.

THE POLICE WORKED with the departing masses to help them get out safely, even trying to arrange rides for some of the many kids heading out on foot. "As we walked out there were state troopers stopping everyone and we were all high and/or carrying drugs and thought we were about to be busted, but they were being helpful," said Aledort. "They'd ask where you were headed, direct you to stand in the right group, then stop cars and ask them if they had any room. I imagine that they didn't want masses of people walking on the highways and getting run over."

Aledort and his friend got two short rides en route to Syracuse, eighty miles away, while walking much of the journey. Many of the six hundred thousand fans had similarly harrowing journeys home. The day after the festival, the streets of Watkins Glen were filled with bedraggled, muddy youth walking around after emerging from spending the night in twenty-four-hour laundromats and anywhere else they could find shelter. More kids lined every nearby highway and byway holding signs for their intended destinations, including Florida, Ann Arbor, Montreal, and Cape Cod. In their wake, they left behind a sea of trash.

"The aftermath was horrible," said Heidemann, the nurse. "There were cars just left all over and piles of garbage. The mess was huge."

The New York Times described the site as a "giant garbage dump," where the debris was so thick that the ground was not visible. *Rolling Stone* said that the scene looked like a "war had been fought there. A war fought with beer cans and plastic water jugs, whiskey bottles and Cracker Jack boxes and 10,000 jars of Skippy Peanut Butter."

Said Koplik, "We took to the stage and looked out and the field in front of us was an absolute dump. One thing Shelly and I massively fucked up is we forgot to put garbage cans out there. Every single thing consumed was just dropped on the ground. The cleanup was a real concern. We had an agreement with Schmata Cleaners out of New York for $5,000 and they took one look and demanded $50,000! We fought them on the principle of a deal's a deal, but then the health department came up because it really started to stink and was on the verge of becoming a major situation, so we paid the money and they went to work."

Rolling Stone reported that other expenses for the event included "$30,000 for helicopters; $50,000 for police; $100,000 for rental of 1000 portable toilets; $40,000 for water . . . Bill Graham's FM Productions earned $200,000 for the stage, lighting and 50,000-watt sound system." The promoters made out quite well, despite letting a majority of the crowd in for free; Finkel said that their profit was about $1,000,000.

There was one last drama in store for a few members of the Allman Brothers Band entourage, including Johnny Sandlin. Shortly after takeoff, the helicopter pilot said that he was almost out of gas. He assured his passengers he could run on regular gas until he got back for a proper refueling. A low pass over one gas station revealed it was closed, and he pulled back up. A few minutes later, the motor sputtered and quit, and the pilot calmly said he "was just going to set the helicopter down." After a jarring landing in a Holiday Inn parking lot, he told the frightened but unharmed passengers that he'd return shortly with some gas. They instead found alternate transportation.

Garcia took a helicopter directly to Mount Holly, New Jersey, where he faced charges stemming from a March stop on the New Jersey Turnpike, when he and Robert Hunter were pulled over for speeding. While opening his briefcase to procure his driver's license, small amounts of marijuana, LSD, and cocaine were revealed, resulting in a search of his briefcase. Garcia was wisely not overly concerned at court, signing autographs and chatting with reporters. He received a suspended one-year sentence, the charges to be dropped after that time if he avoided further criminal charges. Two days later, he and the Dead were onstage for two sold-out shows at New Jersey's Roosevelt Stadium, with the Band opening.

On December 31, 1973, five months after the landmark concert, the Allman Brothers Band played the Cow Palace in San Francisco. Garcia and Kreutzmann sat in for much of the second set and encore. The friendships between the two legendary institutions of the jam-rock world seemed to be growing, but they would never again share a bill. To this day, no one can quite explain why that was the case.

Cutler believed that a slightly competitive vibe developed at Watkins

Glen, with both bands essentially assuming they were responsible for the massive success. Also, he said, "the size of it all went to everyone's heads. The management of both bands took it upon themselves to think it was a golden opportunity to establish their credentials, to consolidate the major step up they had taken in public perception."

Cutler also thought that there was something else to it, something more fundamental. The Dead, he said, were "always looking for the next thing," and they had taken the collaboration with the Allman Brothers as far as it could go. "Magic moments occur and the attempt to re-create them could kind of destroy them," Cutler said. "It's like having your first fuck or your first acid trip. The second time is never quite as good as the first. We did RFK Stadium, we did Watkins Glen. What do you do after that? We played for six hundred fucking thousand people! The Grateful Dead were always looking for the next thing. Jerry and Phil especially loved the experimental stuff and new things to explore."

On a practical level, the Dead took a touring hiatus in 1974, coinciding with Cutler's leaving the group. By the time they returned to the road in 1976, the Allman Brothers Band was teetering. The two bands' careers were never quite in sync again, and they didn't have Sam Cutler and Bunky Odom around to call each other up and rekindle such a beautiful affair.

The New York Times covered the Summer Jam at Watkins Glen on the front page, with a headline reading, "Festival at Watkins Glen Ends in Mud and Elation." But the headline that Walden no doubt cared most about ran a week later in the *Macon Telegraph*: "Allmans Get Record Pay at Mammoth Rock Festival."

The article included a photo of Walden, the type of coverage almost as important to him as the actual money that was made. Walden refused to say how much the band received, only stating, "I know it's more than anybody else has ever been paid." For Walden, that was a mission accomplished.

The Allman Brothers returned home to Macon after the Summer Jam, almost a month before their next show and before the release of *Brothers and Sisters* and its lead single, "Ramblin' Man." The British magazine *Melody Maker* summed up the impact of Watkins Glen on the band's status within the rock world simply: "They've made the aristocracy."

15

ALL IN THE FAMILY

THROUGHOUT MUCH OF the recording of *Brothers and Sisters,* the album's working title was *Lightnin' Rod.* As they were finishing up, Twiggs Lyndon was on fire with cover image ideas. Twiggs had an active mind and seemed to come up with new concepts every hour. He shared all of them with his girlfriend, Judi Reeve. But Reeve had an idea of her own. Take a picture of the bands' entire extended family at the farm—members, crew, friends, spouses, girlfriends, and kids—and put them all on the gatefold. The front cover would feature Trucks's almost-three-year-old son, Vaylor, while Oakley's three-year-old daughter, Brittany, would grace the back.

Reeve presented the idea to Betts, telling him it was Lyndon's because she thought he would be more likely to take it seriously that way. The guitarist immediately loved the concept. When Betts complimented Lyndon on it, he directed credit to Reeve. Betts was so tickled by the whole thing that he made sure Reeve was credited on the album for the "graphic concept." The artwork also led to a new title for the album, *Brothers and Sisters.* The cover created a soft yet powerful image of a family living and working together in harmony.

"The family is very tight," Betts said just after the album's release. "We've left our blood families and formed our own with this band. We're trying to hang on to that old thing. It comes out in the music too. When you get right down to it, music is just a reflection of a musician's lifestyle."

Said bassist Lamar Williams, "Most folks probably can't comprehend how close the band is. We really live this brothers and sisters concept."

For all the turmoil that existed in the Allman Brothers Band and all that was soon to come, the album title and photos captured the reality of the moment. The band had rallied together in the face of tremendous loss; they had pulled together in a family bond and created more art in the spirit Duane intended. But, like most things in the Allman Brothers Band world, nothing was ever as easy or straightforward as it looked in the *Brothers and Sisters* gatefold.

Betts's wife and daughter, Sandy Wabegijig and Jessica, are not in the photo because Wabegijig and Betts were fighting and, when she arrived to join the photo, Betts turned her away. She left the farm and drove into Macon. As they were getting ready to take the pictures, Betts had second thoughts and sent crew member Buffalo Evans in search of his wife. "Buffalo probably had a few words with Dickey after I left," Wabegijig said. "He was very ethical and would stand up to anyone, including Dickey, which not many people would do."

By the time Evans returned from town alone, the harsh late-afternoon light cast shadows and led to an unbalanced look. The poor lighting adds to a down-home vibe. The band members are spread throughout the photo, mixed within the extended family rather than featured together in the center. Everyone had equal billing. Gregg's friend Deering Howe sits front and center, often mistaken by fans for a lost Allman sibling. Some longtime family members were offended by the absence of Sandy and Jessica, Dale Betts and Joe English, and Lamar's wife, Marian, but the familial image portrayed in the photograph was not false.

Millions bought this album and studied this simple image of Southern family togetherness with the same intensity with which they pored over *Eat a Peach*'s psychedelic fantasia. The differing images told the story of a new era and a new reality. Once again, the album carried the epigraph "Dedicated to a Brother," this time Berry Oakley.

The title *Brothers and Sisters*, Allman explained, reflected the fact "that even though we have had two great losses, we were still a family. . . . We didn't band together because we thought if we musicians stuck it out, we'd all be driving Rolls Royces. This is no advertisement for communes . . .

but there's a lot of love between us. We knew that we had something and that no matter how far the bullshit went, we would survive if we hung together."

The down-home vibe continued with some of Betts's new, more rural-sounding music. "Pony Boy" and "Ramblin' Man" were different forms of country songs recalibrated in the band's own image. Under Duane, they were Macon-based but rooted in the cosmopolitan centers of New York, San Francisco, and Miami and playing modern, sophisticated blues rock. *Brothers and Sisters* established a distinctly Macon sound and vibe, one that would affect both rock and country music for decades to come. The album was an immediate hit. *Record World* magazine reported that nothing matched the intensity of *Brothers and Sisters* sales since the last Beatles release. By the end of its second week, Capricorn had shipped 1.3 million copies.

The vibe on *Brothers and Sisters* was unknowingly tapping into a national mood. The country sought tranquility, togetherness, and a simpler, more peaceful time after being torn apart in the '60s by social upheaval, including Vietnam, political assassinations, and the struggle for civil rights and its attendant white backlash. The country was also grappling with the Watergate scandal that was soon to force President Richard Nixon's resignation. *The Waltons,* which portrayed a fictional 1930s rural Virginia family, became the nation's second-highest-rated television program in its second season, a month after the release of *Brothers and Sisters. Little House on the Prairie,* a show about the nineteenth-century frontier that debuted as a hit in 1974, also reflected this zeitgeist. These programs focused on the American ideals of family and simpler times, the same thing the gatefold image in *Brothers and Sisters* conveyed to audiences.

The band's music was undergoing a similar transition. "Ramblin' Man" was a departure not only in its country composition but also in its polished commercial sheen, which would make the song especially palatable to radio programmers. Betts was pleased that the song represented one of the first times that he and the group fully utilized the advantages of being in a studio, rather than just trying to play as they did onstage.

Part of that process involved the multitracking of guitars on the track, as well as speeding the track up using a Vari-Speed, a then new tool that controlled tempo and pitch. The mixing of the song was arduous, Sandlin remembered. And it was Dickey Betts who asked him to speed "Ramblin' Man" up. The tempo seemed too slow, he insisted. He and Sandlin worked with the Vari-Speed and made the song faster.

Sandlin finished mixing the album and asked everyone to come listen before he sent it to New York to be mastered, the final step in the recording process. Betts never showed up, but about a week later, he finally came over to listen to a test pressing of the album. As soon as he heard "Ramblin' Man," he started screaming, "That's too fast!" Never mind that he himself had set the tempo.

Sandlin had to remix the song at its original speed, but when the single and album were both released just a few weeks later, "Ramblin' Man" was the original version with the faster tempo, which also raised the pitch and stretched Betts's voice to be a little thin, which was his real source of discomfort with it.

"They ultimately used the wrong mix—the sped-up one," Sandlin said. "Dickey never said another word to me about it. It was hard to complain after the song became a hit. As different of a sound as 'Ramblin' Man' was for the band, it worked."

Dick Wooley, the radio promo man, had tried out "Ramblin' Man" and "Wasted Words" with stations in Boston and Atlanta, and the choice was resoundingly clear: "Ramblin' Man" had to be the lead single. The phones rang nonstop every time the stations played it. The Allman Brothers Band had their first true hit single. As the song began to take hold, Betts was away from all forms of communication on a Sioux reservation outside Alberta, Canada, for a gathering of the American Indian Ecumenical Council. The Allman Brothers Band's North American Indian Foundation funded travel for more than two hundred Native Americans from various nations.

"We went into town one day and I called the Capricorn office to see what was going on," Betts said. "I spoke with Frank Fenter and he was just elated. He told me, 'We've got a hit single!' I said, 'That's nice,' and Frank said, 'That's all you can say?' I was happy about it, but it hadn't really dawned on me what it meant. I didn't realize what a huge difference having a top-five song would make because we had never had a hit single."

"Ramblin' Man" made its first appearance in the Top 40 the first week of September and peaked at number 2 in mid-October; only Cher's "Half Breed" prevented it from reaching number 1. The Allman Brothers Band had at long last crossed over to the then ubiquitous AM stations. All previous attempts at hit singles had fizzled. "Black Hearted Woman" failed to chart in 1969; 1970's "Revival" peaked at number 92, while that year's release of "Midnight Rider" never even hit the bottom of the charts.* The three singles released off *Eat a Peach*—"Ain't Wastin' Time No More," "Melissa," and "One Way Out"—all peaked at number 77. Asked why the band finally broke through, Gregg gave a very honest answer in 1974: maybe it was because Betts finally started writing and singing some songs.

AM radio predominated in the early 1970s. FM remained an underground phenomenon. Most cars lacked FM radios. A hit song blasting on AM radio could become pervasive in a way that's impossible for someone only familiar with contemporary atomized listening habits to understand. Attention on AM radio rocketed the band, already stars, to superstardom.

"When 'Ramblin' Man' became a hit everything changed," said Betts. "The band reached a whole other level. The places we played got bigger, the crowds were huge and the money was just pouring in."

Betts's accomplishment impressed Phil Walden, who said, "A number one single was something totally alien to the Allman Brothers, and he did it with a country rock song! Dickey Betts put the Allman Brothers on pop radio. He walked into a very traumatic situation post-Duane and said, 'I'll show you what I can do.'"

Kirk West, one of the most significant members of the Allman Brothers Band organization throughout its final twenty-five years, was just another hard-core fan in the summer of 1973. West drove a VW bug from Chicago to San Francisco, where he photographed the Allman Brothers Band for the first time at the Winterland Ballroom on September 26. Flipping the radio dial to keep himself occupied as he drove across the country, he was struck by his favorite band's rapid penetration of mainstream radio via "Ramblin' Man." "It was on the radio about every 45 minutes," he said. "You couldn't escape it."

---

* Joe Cocker had the first hit with "Midnight Rider" in 1973, and Gregg's solo version from *Laid Back* rose to number 19 in 1974.

The band essentially quit playing "Ramblin' Man" after they split with Betts in 2000. Well before that, some fans cringed at the song, and the other band members at times resented being so closely associated with such an anomalous tune. But it's just a great song. Bob Dylan, the greatest songwriter in rock history, loved "Ramblin' Man" and called it "one of the best songs ever written." Betts was shocked and rightfully pleased when Dylan not only suggested they sing it together in 1995 in Tampa but also knew all the words. "I should have written that song," Dylan told Betts.

"That was one hell of a compliment," Betts said.

16

DOWN THIS ROAD BEFORE

THE ALLMAN BROTHERS Band was not the only Capricorn act for which Phil Walden wore many hats. He had similar relationships with Wet Willie and the Marshall Tucker Band (MTB), the label's two other most successful artists.

Wet Willie, a high-energy group from Mobile, Alabama, who patterned themselves after the Rolling Stones and featured brothers Jack and Jimmy Hall, was one of Walden's first signings in 1970. A few years later came Spartanburg, South Carolina's, Marshall Tucker Band, led by another pair of brothers, Toy and Tommy Caldwell. They were brought to the label after the Hall brothers met bassist Tommy Caldwell and rhythm guitarist George McCorkle the afternoon of their performance at a Spartanburg club called the Ruins. The Tucker boys said they had a demo tape ready to send to Capricorn and the Halls invited them to open the show later that night. Impressed by what they heard, they promised to give Walden a good report.

The Caldwell brothers, who both worked at the Spartanburg Water Department, drove four hours down to Macon and then waited, insisting that Walden and Fenter listen to the tape while they were there. Pleased with what he heard Walden booked the Marshall Tucker Band a showcase gig at Grant's Lounge, the unofficial Capricorn clubhouse on Poplar Street, around the corner from the label's Cotton Street office. That performance sealed the deal. "As soon as I heard them live, I knew they were the next band I was going to sign," Walden said.

He sent them into the studio to record a demo with Sandlin, but the producer had a hard time relating to the band's music and was unnerved by them calling him "sir," despite being about the same age. This was probably because both Toy Caldwell and singer Doug Gray were veterans who had served in Vietnam, but the formality was just a distraction. The real problem was a lack of chemistry and the band's minimal studio experience. "They were used to playing onstage and played everything 120 miles an hour," Walden said. "We had to try and cut it again."

The band returned to work with Capricorn's other in-house producer, Paul Hornsby. The combination immediately clicked. "They loved Paul," Walden said. "He did well by them and they did well by him." Hornsby's background was more in tune with the band's country-influenced sound, and his piano helped to lighten the mood and brighten the tunes. Everyone felt good about these recordings, but Walden and Fenter couldn't quite figure out what to make of a band that mixed country and jazz with rock and featured a flute and a saxophone. Lead guitarist and chief songwriter Toy Caldwell penned country-tinged songs but played with his thumb like jazz great Wes Montgomery and sophisticated country legends Merle Travis and Chet Atkins, influences that could be heard in his picking, along with those of jazz greats Grant Green and Tal Farlow. Closer to home, Caldwell's playing echoed Betts's major-key country swing, albeit less bright in tone. Caldwell said that he avoided listening to Dickey, lest he start copying his licks, which was exactly Betts's view regarding Jerry Garcia.

"Toy only wanted to sound like himself," said Marshall Tucker Band drummer Paul T. Riddle. "He didn't play slide, because he knew that if he did, he would just copy Duane, and Toy did not want to copy anyone." Caldwell picked up pedal steel instead. The same aspects that made the Marshall Tucker Band's sound intriguing and original made them hard to market. Capricorn struggled to find the right path. Walden played the demo for some people in Nashville, including producer Buddy Killen, who told him, "Well, it's not country and I really don't know what it is."

"They didn't like it," Walden recalled. "You had rules up in Nashville." Those rules did not cover country-influenced rock in 1973, so the MTB was viewed as a tweener act: too rock for country and too country for rock. Walden and Fenter were on the verge of selling the Marshall Tucker Band's contract to Polygram to generate some much-needed cash flow when Capricorn promotions man Dick Wooley stepped in. Wooley said that he heard "Can't You See" and told Walden it could be a hit and the label should put it out: "I played it for the Warner Bros executives in L.A. who would be in charge of distributing the record and they liked it," Wooley said. "It was reminiscent of the country rock stuff happening out there and they could grasp what it was. I guarantee you no one would have ever heard of the Marshall Tucker Band if the contract had been sold to Polygram, who would have been clueless about what to do with them."

Riddle said that he didn't know Capricorn almost sold the band's contract, and he doesn't think any of his bandmates did either, but he's sure of one thing: "Many thought 'Can't You See' was a hit. Everyone was in agreement it was a good song."

Like the Allman Brothers Band, the Marshall Tucker Band developed an audience by playing as many shows as they could. It was only after Tucker had grown their following that Capricorn released their self-titled debut in April 1973, months after they'd completed it.

"We would open for anyone anywhere," said Riddle. "Sometimes the headlining band would worry about us being too hot and cut our set down—that happened with Three Dog Night at the L.A. Forum, where we got fifteen minutes. We still believed that it was always worth it to get in front of people."

Though Tucker didn't do extended runs with the Allman Brothers Band, they were boosted by opening some very high-profile shows, including at Madison Square Garden, which Toy Caldwell called "the greatest exposure you could possibly have." As he told *Rolling Stone* in 1974, "The audience is really gonna like what we do if they like the Allman Brothers."

"Everyone tells me that this rock and roll business is 'gonna fuck you over' and that it's a nasty way to earn a living," Caldwell said. "I don't know, but everywhere we go we're treated like good old people. Everybody's been so kind to us, we feel at home just about anywhere we play. I can see how this business could make you crazy if you let it, but then I guess that's one of the advantages to living in Spartanburg."

Spartanburg at the time was a mill town of about fifty thousand people in the Blue Ridge foothills of nothern South Carolina, and the Marshall Tucker Band members continued to live there throughout their career, eschewing the more glamorous lifestyle that their newly found fame and fortune could have brought them.

By early 1974, the Marshall Tucker Band's self-titled debut was nearing gold status with five hundred thousand copies sold, and its followup *A New Life* was starting to take off. In *Rolling Stone*, Cameron Crowe called them "the South's second most popular band." Caldwell sounded dazed by his band's success. "We were six musicians that nobody ever heard of," he said. "We had hardly played live at all before the album came out, so we had no following. We sold this band through our own constant touring. We went out there night after night and played our asses off."

ONCE STEVE MASSARSKY had the North American Indian Foundation up and running, he planned on returning to New Jersey and reenrolling at Rutgers Law. Worried that the foundation, which was crucial to keeping Betts involved and happy, would not survive the loss of Massarsky, Walden promised to pay his tuition if he would attend Macon's Mercer University School of Law rather than Rutgers.

That was almost an offer he couldn't refuse, but Massarsky was worried that the Mercer law degree, which carried weight in Georgia, would be far less meaningful in New York, where he planned to eventually return. "This is going to work out; I'll make you my house counsel when you get out," Walden promised. "You'll be the first major entertainment lawyer in the Southeast and I'll steer everything I can to you."

Massarsky said that when he agreed to this plan, he told Walden, "You have to understand that I'm taking a big chance. If this doesn't work out between you and me, I'll have to go to a firm in New York and tell them I went to a law school in Macon, Georgia, that none of them had ever heard of."

This wouldn't be a problem, Walden assured Massarsky, because he was "a man of [his] word." With these assurances, Massarsky enrolled at Mercer, where he became friends with Dick Wooley's wife, Joan, who was a classmate. She immediately sized him up as "a genius." "They got the books and Steve read them all in the first week, then never cracked them open the rest of the term," Wooley said. "He had a photographic memory and that's how he could go to law school and do so many other things at the same time."

Massarsky was not the type of person to underestimate. Unfortunately for Walden, he did so, treating him the way he treated his bands and most of his business associates. "Phil had a genius for picking up talent—and for pissing people off," Wooley said. "He was an equal opportunity pisser-offer."

Walden wasn't afraid to use his temper strategically. Jon Landau described him as "pre anger management era," noting that "Phil had an aggressive side, and he could turn up the heat quickly." His outbursts were not helped by the fact that he shared his artists' penchant for J&B scotch and cocaine.

Bunky Odom describes Walden as "a screamer" who'd get so worked up during phone conversations that he couldn't remain seated, and merely standing up wasn't powerful enough. "He'd get so mad he'd stand on his desk screaming into the phone," he said.

Alex Cooley, the dean of Atlanta music promoters, responsible for the two Atlanta Pop Festivals and much more, recalled that the first time he ever met Walden in person, he sat in his office and listened to Walden scream at someone who owed the Redding estate money. "I have never ever in my life seen someone get so much hell from someone else," Cooley said. "I was scared to death at the end of that conversation. Phil was a force of nature when he wanted to be, and I admired him for that. Phil was the best arm twister over the phone that there ever was."

Walden also was an all-or-nothing guy. You were either on his team or you were the enemy. "Once somebody turned against him, it was holy shit!" said Odom. "You turn against him and it's over with. He had the mentality that it's my way or no way."

"I loved Phil, but he was mercurial," said Peter Conlon, an Atlanta concert promoter who worked closely with Walden for many years. "He was a genius, but this was a bipolar guy doing cocaine. We went through extended periods where he wouldn't speak to me. He'd get mad, call you every name in the book, hang up on you, then not talk for a long time."

One of those times, Conlon recalled, after several months of not speaking to each other he received a letter in which Walden said that he didn't remember what the fight was about and that they should make up. "We should be friends," he wrote, "because we dislike so many of the same people."

Jonny Podell learned about Walden's temperament in their very first conversation, when the Allman Brothers Band account fell to the young booking agent after another Associated Booking agent left the firm. Podell said that Walden told him, "Look, motherfucker—the last thing that I need in my life is a skinny little Jew representing my ass. I have all my money tied up in this band and it's blood money. I can't lose it. I've got a one-year contract and there are six months left until you're fired."

"No conversation has ever scared me half as much in my life," Podell said. Properly motivated, Podell busted his ass for the band, and when the contract came to an end, Walden kept him on and they became close friends. Eventually, Podell split the booking with Walden's own Paragon Booking Agency, which he started in 1970 out of the ashes of his original R&B agency. Alex Hodges had left the music business after Redding's death and was working for the Republican Party in Atlanta when Walden asked him to return. When he declined, Walden played him the Allman Brothers Band's debut album, as he had for Fenter. Hodges, too, soon quit his job and headed for Macon.

The controlled fury and occasional bursts of rage were a part of Walden's management style that he rarely turned on the band. For years, they only saw Walden's personality traits working *for* them. However, he was not only the group's manager. He was also their record label, booking agent, merchandise company, and publishing company. This presented serious conflicts of interest, but handling everything in-house limited the number of people to deal with and guaranteed that everyone involved understood every aspect of the band's business. Walden believed this allowed him, and the Allman Brothers Band, to capitalize on the right markets at the right time.

He told *Melody Maker* magazine that, from the start, Capricorn "had a different approach and different attitudes to other record companies." He said that they wanted to be "a company rather than a label" and bragged about their in-house producers, press office, and promotion department. Though it all sounded good, the business model was fraught with conflicts of interest, all benefiting Walden.

Capricorn essentially provided its artists with what are now known as "360 deals," where a single entity supports, but also profits from, all aspects of an artist's career: recording, touring, publishing, and merch sales. Hodges said that there were "various iterations" of relationships, with some Capricorn acts not booked by Paragon and many Paragon acts not signed to the label or managed by Walden, including Bobby Womack, Lynyrd Skynyrd, and the Charlie Daniels Band.

"I viewed it as an advantage to book a Capricorn artist, because I knew I had the ear of Frank and Phil," said Hodges. "It benefited the artists because of the honest communication and truth about where an artist was strong and weak, information that managers and labels are not always truthful about, even with their booking agents."

Walden controlled virtually every source of income for the Allman Brothers Band. A manager's role is to negotiate deals in the best interest of his or her client, and they receive a percentage of money generated, generally 15 percent at the time. With Walden controlling the booking agency and record and publishing companies, it is impossible to know whose interests he was looking after, his or the band's. It was easy for Walden to negotiate favorable deals for his entities at the expense of the band. The Allman Brothers Band never had any outside legal counsel advising them or vetting the contracts with the various Walden-controlled entities. Walden clearly enriched himself by negotiating on both sides of the table.

Decades later, Butch Trucks said that if he could change one thing about the Allman Brothers Band's career, it would be to have had a "lawyer look at those contracts in the very beginning because our manager owned our record company. One of the main functions of your manager is to make sure your record company isn't screwing you over. When your manager owns your record company, you can be pretty sure you're getting screwed over, and we were."

"Phil was the only one they had to look to," Massarsky said. "If you and I are making a deal, and I ask what you think it means, you'll tell me what it means based on what's good for you. If you ask me, I'll tell you what's good for me. The interpretation that Capricorn put on every contract benefited Capricorn. That's natural, but there was no one in there saying what could be the Allman Brothers' interpretation."

The arrangement was also not atypical, as the music industry was still in its infancy and not yet a mature corporate business. Capricorn's business practices weren't too far removed from Chess Records buying Muddy Waters a Cadillac in lieu of royalty payments, and they weren't all that different from what a lot of other artists were contending with.

"I don't think that Phil was staying up nights worrying if he was doing the right thing," said Landau. "I think this is how he learned to do business and artists were soon to become more powerful and better educated by learning from other people's experience. Even the Beatles and Stones had terrible deals at that point, and the whole industry of music lawyers barely existed."

The complicated web of commercial relationships also kept Walden extremely invested in the success of the Allman Brothers Band, which was the cornerstone of his growing empire. And even as the band's success grew, they never got particularly interested or involved in the business side of things.

"The importance of money never took over the band—unfortunately," Betts said. "Maybe in the early days, it was really healthy not to be that concerned about the business end of things, but at the point we had success, we were making so much money that I wish that for the sake of everybody in the band that we had started paying closer attention to it."

17
HITTIN' THE NOTE

THE ALLMAN BROTHERS Band was riding high in 1973 even before the great success of *Brothers and Sisters*. By the time of its August release, they had already played twenty-three shows, including the monster Summer Jam at Watkins Glen, the two RFK Stadium appearances with the Dead, four in New York (including two at Madison Square Garden), and two more at Denver's massive Mile High Stadium.

The band would play sixty-seven concerts that year, never having more than three weeks off. After Watkins Glen, held on July 28, the tour resumed on August 17 in Little Rock. A week later, they played Pittsburgh's cavernous Three Rivers Stadium. Les Dudek, who was playing with opening act Boz Scaggs, sat in on the tracks he'd recorded with the Allman Brothers: "Ramblin' Man" and "Jessica."

The band settled into their new lineup, developing a powerful, slightly altered identity. Betts was usually alone at center stage, and even his appearance spoke to the fact that this was a new era. As Cameron Crowe wrote in *Rolling Stone*, Betts had "taken to dressing a bit like a young Nashville sideman." His long hair, jeans, and T-shirts were gone in favor of short hair, neatly groomed mustache, and natty western wear. Gregg, too, had a newly emerged sense of style, favoring white suits.

Having taken control of the band's creative direction on *Brothers and Sisters,* Betts now became the band's visual focus and musical director onstage.

He and Leavell engaged in endless musical conversations, spurring each other on, buoyed by the ever more limber rhythm section, now rooted in Williams's in-the-pocket bass playing as well as Trucks's rock-solid time-keeping.

Williams's style was vastly different from Oakley's. "Berry was the most unique bass there ever was and he didn't play it like a bass," Trucks explained. Tom Dowd described Oakley's playing as being so free-form during some improvisational sections that it was like "there was no bass part anymore. He was all over the damn place!" Dowd said. "He was playing trombone parts or string parts, and he was completely spontaneous, making it flow better, making it feel better or just getting in the pocket and driving." Williams stayed closer to home, holding down the groove, which gave the drummers the freedom to roam off the backbeat.

"The differences between them really shifted how we played," Trucks said. "They were both unique and fantastic players, but quite different. Playing with Berry, I had to be straight ahead, because if I started getting out there, things would fall apart. He'd take off at any time and somebody had to hold down the fort. With Lamar, I could really stretch out. He was so rock solid that I could get lost, look at his left foot and land right back where I needed to be."

Leavell likewise influenced the music. Not only did he provide another lead soloist, but he played innovatively behind Betts's solos, spurring creativity in the band. "My role was really being a catalyst," said Leavell. "I never felt suppressed at all. I'm a good listener and tried to help the song-writer or soloist achieve what they wanted."

The level of autonomy that Leavell and Williams were granted started the trend of the group allowing new members full artistic freedom, a practice that would continue throughout the band's forty-five-year career and that is extremely unusual for legacy groups, where replacement players are generally expected to play as their predecessors did.

Leavell's presence also freed Allman, who immediately abandoned his Wurlitzer electric piano to focus on the organ. He also would come up front and play electric guitar for a few songs each night, something he enjoyed tremendously and could not have done without the presence of another keyboardist.

"My job got a little less complicated," said Allman, who enjoyed the presence of his new keyboard accomplice, who he said taught him a lot, an education that provided "a key to a bigger room."

"Having two keyboardists was just so interesting," said Leavell. "It's just like the two drummer or two lead guitar thing—not many bands had it and it opened up a lot of possibilities. Gregg and I inspired each other."

Listening to Stevie Wonder also influenced Gregg to add a Clavinet to his stage rig.* He used this instrument to double Williams's bass lines. "It puts a little bit of bite into the sound and enables you to have the bass line coming from both sides of the stage," Allman explained.

The band also gave Leavell tremendous leeway as they honed arrangements of tunes both new and old. "I was good at coming up with interesting ways to get from point A to point B instead of just changing chords," he said. "And that was respected."

As he settled into the band and thrived musically, Leavell was also having a blast on the road and pinching himself about the change in his status, going from unemployed to member of rock and roll nobility.

"Joining the Brothers was like being admitted into an elite club," he said. "They had a very different lifestyle than that of the struggling musicians they had been and I still was until the moment I went out on the road with them. It was all foreign to me and the glamorous aspects could be really distracting, so I just tried to focus on the music. Jaimoe was very clued into that."

Jaimoe told Leavell that there was a difference between musicians and rock stars, and some, but not all, are both. It was food for thought, and Leavell quickly decided the Allman Brothers Band were both musicians *and* rock stars.

In this new lineup, any combination of players could lock into grooves with one another at various times, and Leavell's driving chordal work was as stellar as his solos. Williams's playing was as clever as it was fluid, hopping around, locking into patterns and playing harmony with different bandmates at different times. Leavell, Jaimoe, and Williams were consistently

---

* If you don't know what a Clavinet sounds like, think Stevie Wonder's "Superstition" or Bill Withers's "Use Me."

in sync and at the center of many of the musical adventures. Freed from some of his other responsibilities, Allman played terrific organ. Betts, an absolutely monster guitarist playing with confidence and creativity, stood atop this musical juggernaut.

People who had previously credited a lot of Betts's ideas and playing to Duane Allman were now beginning to understand that they were always coequals in the original band. The guy whose last name was not part of the band's moniker had created many of its distinctive riffs.

"Dickey Betts contributed the most of anyone to the sound of the Allman Brothers Band," said Joe Dan Petty. "Duane Allman was not a humble person and Dickey scared the hell out of him. When [Duane] returned from playing some shows with Derek and the Dominos [in 1970], I asked him what kind of guitar player Eric Clapton is, and Duane said, 'Dickey Betts would wear him out in five minutes.'"

Phil Walden said that Duane used to joke with him that he had it made because he got credit not only for everything he played but also "for what Dickey played as well." If people credited Allman for Betts's work, it wasn't because Duane was seeking it, as the Nitty Gritty Dirt Band's Jeff Hanna learned in May 1971 when he saw the Allman Brothers Band in Mississippi. He had a great backstage visit with his old friend Duane before the show. They talked shop, Duane showed him his guitars, and Duane told Hanna about overdosing and coming close to death the previous year in Nashville. He said he was now "mostly living clean except for a little vitamin C [cocaine]."

The old friends were happy to see one another, and Hanna was excited to finally see the Allman Brothers Band perform. Duane had some viewing advice for him. "Keep your eye on Dickey tonight," he said. "I'm the guy up there doing the skate but Dickey's over there playing amazing shit. He's a monster."

When the show started, Hanna quickly realized that Allman's respect for his guitar partner was well earned. "Duane was magnetic, and your eye was drawn to him, but Dickey's playing was just remarkable," said Hanna. "He had such a great tone and that great compositional skill that came through in the phrasing of his solos, along with that groovy, subtly country thing.

His playing was blues and jazz all at once, with a little Garcia in there as well."

That is the Betts who emerged from the ashes of Duane's and Berry's deaths and stepped to the fore, bringing the band along with him and altering its sound to more explicitly feature his own brand of Americana. It was a powerful brew, which an increasing number of people noticed. After witnessing a four-hour performance headlining the September 19, 1973, North American Indian Foundation benefit at the Forum in Inglewood, California, Chris Charlesworth wrote in *Melody Maker,* "The Allman Brothers today are *the* American Band."

GREGG ALLMAN'S SOLO debut, *Laid Back,* was released in October 1973 during a relatively quiet month for the Allman Brothers Band, who only played one show, at the New Jersey State Fairgrounds. It was less than three months after the release of *Brothers and Sisters,* which was well on its way to platinum status, marking one million units sold. The reimagined "Midnight Rider" off *Laid Back* started getting airplay and reached the top 20. The album hit number 13 and was certified gold, with five hundred thousand copies sold. Despite his struggles, Gregg had simultaneous hits, a remarkable situation given the tragedies he and the band had experienced in the previous two years.

Fenter reflected on this late in 1973. The band's motivation, Fenter said, came from "a lot of things deep down inside them," and their success "said something" about both their resiliency and their singular sound. "Four years, two tragedies and . . . they're still together and bigger than ever," Fenter said. "There's no good bullshitting. This has been no easy trip, especially for the Brothers themselves. It ain't no fashion show when they get up on stage. The trip is making great music."

THE ALLMAN BROTHERS Band was the hottest, most popular rock act in the country. This presented a problem for *Rolling Stone,* the country's most important rock magazine, because the group would not talk to them. They were nursing an understandable grudge over a story by writer Grover Lewis, which not only portrayed the band as bored, drugged-out rednecks but did so in the November 25, 1971, issue that also included Duane's obit-uary. Billed on the cover as "Duane Allman's Final Days on the Road," the article captured the band at a low point just before Duane and Oakley went to rehab in Buffalo, when they were snorting coke like it was lifeblood.

There's no reason to doubt the heavy drug use Lewis described or his portrayal of Oakley seeming worn out at age twenty-three, but the writer clearly exaggerated the dialogue. The portrayal of ex-banker Willie Perkins as a kindly hick, some sort of cracker rube, was a red flag to anyone who had ever spoken to the tour manager. Running the piece in the same issue that mourned Duane's death seemed like a nasty turn of the knife.

"We had some bad experiences with *Rolling Stone*," Betts said. "We had invited [Lewis] to travel on the road with us and he really took advantage of it. He just wrote a really bad article."

Trucks summed up the band's feelings about the piece in a 2005 letter to *The New York Times,* in response to a review of a collection of Lewis's writ-ing: "I am sure that [Lewis] was used to bands falling all over themselves at having one of the great writers from *Rolling Stone* magazine around. He was somewhat taken aback by our lack of interest in his presence. What he wound up writing under the guise of journalism could have been hu-morous satire, at best, if it weren't for one very tragic fact: it was published within weeks of Duane Allman's death, and the people at *Rolling Stone* had time to pull the article but did nothing. . . . In Lewis's article, all the dialogue among members of our group seemed to be taken directly from Faulkner. We are from the South. We did and still do have Southern ac-cents. We are not stupid. The people in the article were creations of Grover Lewis. They did not exist in reality."

If the band felt that strongly in 2005, imagine their attitude in 1973, riding their commercial peak and just two years after the publication of Lewis's article. They didn't need any help selling records or tickets and they simply were not going to talk to anyone from *Rolling Stone*. A long-haired sixteen-year-old kid in San Diego softened their stance.

CAMERON CROWE'S MOTHER, Alice, did not allow rock and roll records in her house. The college sociology and literature instructor felt so strongly about the music's lack of redeeming value that she wrote a letter to NBC complaining when she saw Simon and Garfunkel perform "The 59th Street Bridge Song (Feelin' Groovy)" on *The Smothers Brothers Comedy Hour*. But Crowe's big sister Cindy hid records under her bed and bequeathed them to him when she left home. Crowe thought he would be a lawyer until he discovered *Creem* magazine. Then Cindy introduced him to a staff member of the underground newspaper the *San Diego Door*, which led to his not only writing record reviews but also becoming a protégé of *Creem* editor Lester Bangs, a fellow San Diego native who had been an editor of the *Door*. Crowe kept writing for a wide range of magazines, including *Creem*, *Crawdaddy*, *Circus*, and *Hit Parader*.

When he started conducting interviews, Crowe was too young to even have a learner's driving permit, so he would take the Greyhound bus from San Diego to Los Angeles, where photographer Neal Preston would pick him up at the Greyhound station and drive him to wherever they had an assignment. Their destination was often the Hyatt House on Sunset Boulevard in West Hollywood, lovingly referred to as the Riot House, the scene of much rock and roll mayhem. Crowe was used to being the youngest person in the room, having skipped kindergarten and two grades in elementary school and graduated high school in 1972 at age fifteen.

The young writer developed a good relationship with Capricorn Records vice president of publicity Mike Hyland, who arranged phone interviews for him with the Marshall Tucker Band, Wet Willie, and Cowboy. "He knew I was a big fan of the Allman Brothers Band, and I'd kind of dreamt aloud that I'd one day like to write about them," Crowe said. Hyland arranged a phone interview with Betts for *Rock* magazine, which went well. The next step was a short backstage interview, on the condition that he only speak about the North American Indian Foundation and the guitarist's involvement with Native causes. When they spoke, the writer made sure to refer to Betts only as Richard, then his preferred name. As the guitarist got comfortable, he began discussing how hard it had been to carry on the band after Duane's death.

"Holy shit!" Crowe thought, well aware that neither Betts nor Gregg had discussed this topic in detail. He immediately called *Rolling Stone* senior editor Ben Fong-Torres, who told Crowe that if he could get more material, the magazine would be interested in a major feature, maybe even a cover story. The only problem now was to convince the Allman Brothers Band to allow any journalist—much less one representing *Rolling Stone*—to go on the road with them again. Crowe's earnestness and youth worked to his advantage, as did good words from Hyland and, most importantly, from Betts himself.

"I took to Cameron Crowe," said Betts. "I liked him. He was a young kid trying to make a big break for himself. The band was really gun shy about having anyone come on the road with us . . . [but] I said, 'This is a good guy. I had real good luck with him. He did a nice article.' I was vouching for him and finally talked the guys into letting him come out with us."

Betts's instincts were spot-on. Crowe was in the process of becoming one of the best rock journalists of his era. His stories focused on the music and how it was created; he cared more about the rock and roll than he did about the sex and drugs.

"I always felt like as a journalist, I got a seat in the front row, and I wanted to serve all the people like me that wanted to be there," Crowe said. "I wanted to be a fly on the wall and bring that experience to the fans of the bands I was writing about."

The editors of *Rolling Stone* also saw the advantage of using the earnest youngster to mend fences with bands they had insulted and enraged in various ways. The Allman Brothers Band weren't the only group who fell into this category. The magazine had also disparaged and angered Led Zeppelin, the Eagles, Jethro Tull, and Deep Purple. Crowe profiled all of them, as the older editors handed the decade's most important bands and their stories to the kid.

"They were like, 'Who wants to write about Jethro Tull?' Give it to the kid. They wanted the record company ads, but were happy to outsource the coverage. I was aware of that situation, and I wore it like a badge of honor," Crowe said. "I loved those bands and would have bought the magazine looking for the type of article I wanted to write. I felt like I was performing a service for fans like me. I thought those bands were as deserving and passionate as the acts that had gotten such great play in *Rolling Stone*. I wanted to put my guys on the team. And the Allman Brothers took the biggest risk in trusting me."

Crowe joined the Allman Brothers Band for their September 1973 West

Coast run. "After 20 minutes with those guys, it was obvious that Grover Lewis had taken such a snobby approach to writing about Duane and Gregg, in what would be Duane's final run," said Crowe. "He'd thrown that golden opportunity away for a novelty story."

Crowe fictionalized his experiences on the road in his 2000 film *Almost Famous*. While the movie's details were a composite of multiple bands and reporting trips, the story followed that first, epic road trip with the Allman Brothers Band. "So much of that became the movie," he said. "It was the first time I left home for an extended time, and I kept calling my mom from the road saying I just needed one more day."

The movie's tension surrounding the fictional journalist's inability to secure an interview with a key band member and the group's subsequent accusation that their quotes were made up were straight from Crowe's experiences with the Allman Brothers Band. Gregg Allman had taken a simpler route to denying his quotes: he confiscated Crowe's interview tapes.

Crowe had spent a lot of time on the road with Betts, who continued to look out for him, and with Red Dog, who also took a liking to the young writer. In the process, the roadie taught the writer some valuable lessons. "Red Dog showed me how to pick my moments," Crowe said. "He treated me as an insider and that allowed the band to trust me."

Still, Gregg remained elusive, with Crowe constantly seeking an interview, knowing that he didn't have much of a story without one. "Gregg was unlike anyone I'd ever met," Neal Preston said. "He exuded an ethereal magnetism so strong it cut through the druggy haze that always seemed to surround him. His eyes, whether glazed or not, were piercing and tinged with suspicions." The pain Gregg carried from Duane's and Oakley's deaths was always apparent, Preston adds, and seemed to be "the quiet resignation of someone who had no choice but to soldier on."

Others who spent time around Gregg also realized that much of his elusiveness was really a form of melancholy. "There's an air of loneliness about Gregg that many mistake for cruelty," wrote Madeline Hirsiger, who covered the band for years for the *Macon Telegraph* and *Macon News* newspapers and knew them well.

"Gregg was a generational rock star—this towering, suspicious, incredibly vivid guy," Crowe recalled. "He cut a figure; when he walked through the back door of a venue, it was almost like he was a hologram. There was something about this guy."

Janice Blair Allman, constantly by her husband's side, also cut a striking, mysterious figure to Crowe, "very tall and very beautiful" but equally remote. "She was always around but sort of removed," Crowe said.

Crowe finally cracked Allman's code by telling him how much he liked Gregg's version of "These Days." They did a short interview in Gregg's Phoenix, Arizona, hotel room that included a wonderful acoustic performance, but Gregg's answers remained vague, only scratching the surface of his true thoughts and emotions. Preston, on assignment as Crowe's photographer, was with them snapping pictures. As they spoke, Gregg would pick up a vial of white powder every few minutes, take a healthy hit, and offer it to his guests, Preston said. The writer declined, and the photographer accepted. "It was not my style to look a gift horse in the mouth," Preston said.

The photographer later followed Betts, Leavell, and Red Dog to the shop of famed tattoo artist Lyle Tuttle, who had tattooed mushrooms on the calves of the band and crew in 1970. Tuttle branded Leavell with the Allman Brothers Band mushroom, and Red Dog offered to pay for any tattoo the photographer wanted, an offer Preston still regrets turning down.

Despite all the great access, Crowe still did not have the truly substantive Gregg interview he needed, and time was running out. Crowe's last scheduled show with the band was on September 26 at San Francisco's Winterland Ballroom, a performance that was recorded for a live album but not released until years later as part of the expanded *Brothers and Sisters*. Afterward, late at night at the Miyako Hotel, the phone rang in the room Crowe and Preston were sharing. Gregg was ready to talk. Crowe ran up to Gregg's room with his tape recorder, and Preston followed shortly after, snapping some quick photos—one of which ended up on the cover of Allman's 2012 memoir, *My Cross to Bear*.* Crowe interviewed Allman for a couple of hours, and the singer opened up about many topics, including the death of Duane just two years prior.

---

* Several of Preston's photos from this assignment are featured in this book's photo section. He also took the book's cover photo in 1975.

"We did a long, soulful, haunting interview in which he talked about missing his brother and the loneliness that he felt," Crowe said. "Things that I don't think he had ever told a journalist before."

The writer returned to his room thrilled and buzzing with excitement. "What an interview!" he exclaimed. "Gregg was really out there, but he was talking about Duane, and it was the real shit."

Then the phone rang again. Preston answered, and it was Red Dog, who asked, "Is your little buddy there?" Preston handed Crowe the phone, then watched the color drain out of his partner's face as he spoke to the roadie. Hanging up, he explained that Gregg had requested he come back upstairs—with his tapes. He reluctantly returned, and when Gregg answered the door, "he looked like he was just in another place," said Crowe. "'Fucked up' doesn't do it justice. He looked like he had seen a vision."

Allman told the writer to sit down and asked to see his ID, then seemed shocked by what he saw. "Gregg said, 'Who are you? You're 16! How do we know you're not a cop? We could be arrested for having you out here with us,'" Crowe recounted. Gregg continued: "How dare you not tell us your age! You see that empty chair? My brother is sitting there right now, laughing at you!" As Crowe admitted, "I had never been more scared in my entire life."

Crowe doesn't think that Gregg was really worried he was a cop. "It was his pain being manifested. His pain was palpable," said Crowe. "He had opened up so much and I was such a willing listener, a passionate collector of all the stories. That made him stop and think, 'Wait a minute. Who is this guy?' I had their secrets in my orange bag and that freaked him out."

The idea that Crowe was a sixteen-year-old cop seems preposterous, even comical, and Crowe laughs at it now. But in the heat of the moment, it was anything but funny. "Why did Gregg think Cameron could be a cop?" Preston asks rhetorically. "Very simply because during that first interview, the only one of us who got loaded with him was me."

Gregg assured Crowe that he wasn't going to destroy the tapes; he was going to send them to his mother for safekeeping. "He had his bodyguard [likely Scooter Herring] write out a statement that he had the tapes and he signed it," said Crowe, who turned over the cassettes and returned to his room empty-handed and shell-shocked.

"We were both distraught," said Preston, who had hidden his film under his mattress while Crowe was gone in case they asked for that as well. "This is a disaster. First cover story. You've now given Gregg all the tapes back. You've got killer shit on the tapes, but you'll never be able to use it."

The writer wrote a straight, rather dry history of the band, lacking almost any quotes, and turned it in to Fong-Torres, who found the story flat and boring. "Ben kept saying, 'Didn't more happen?'" Crowe said. "I couldn't tell him; it would have ruined me. It would have been curtains if it got to Jann [Wenner, Rolling Stone's editor]. It would have become the I-couldn't-get-the-interview story, which is a subgenre of journalism. I didn't want to see my favorite band or me get thrown under the bus for a novelty story. I wanted to make good on the Grover Lewis promise."

Relinquishing his tapes at a subject's request had violated a core rule in journalism: never lose possession of your reporting notes and recordings. Gregg and Red Dog had taken advantage of the kid. But, the writer knew, "the whole reason the band was giving me the story is that I was the kid."

Back in San Diego, while visiting a friend, Crowe received a call from Phil Walden; his mother had given Walden the number. Speaking to Walden on his friend's family's kitchen phone made it all the more surreal. "I can remember Phil's voice so clearly," Crowe said. "He said, 'Hey, you know what, buddy? Ol' Gregg found this bag of tapes and he doesn't know how he got 'em, man, but they're yours. We gotta get 'em back to you.'"

The band, however, was already on their way to their next gig—which was in Honolulu. With Crowe back home with his family and forbidden by his mother to leave again, Preston flew to Hawaii to reclaim the cassettes and continue his efforts to get an all-group shot, which had eluded him.

"I'm happy to say that I saw the greatest show of the entire tour," said Preston. "They were smoking hot. And I got the tapes back."

He also got the group photo that had eluded him—although, as with most such photos taken in this era, the band was disinterested in the process and couldn't bother to really line up or pose.

Recalled Crowe, "Neal called to say the tapes were on their way, and that Gregg didn't even remember why he had them. When I got them back, they were in an envelope addressed to Mama A. Gregg was going to send them to his mother, just like he said."

Crowe's story—his and the band's first *Rolling Stone* cover feature—ran in the December 6, 1973, issue. The cover was a drawing of Gregg, which did not much please Betts or the other members; maybe they should have been more cooperative photo subjects. The piece itself was an in-depth, sympathetic portrayal of the Allman Brothers Band that presented much of their now familiar history for the first time. None of the drama about securing the interview or losing and then recovering the tapes saw the light of day.

"We had our story—nobody else had that story," Crowe said. "But there was another story to be told, and that became *Almost Famous*. Without the story of the tapes and everything that Gregg did, there is no *Almost Famous*."

Allman's fear of speaking honestly and showing his vulnerability, and his working to retract his interview before changing his mind and handing back the tapes, became the movie's central point of conflict. In both real life and the film version, the conflict illustrates an inherent tension in the journalist/subject relationship. Even the best-intentioned interviewers are trying to seduce the person across from them into opening up and revealing insights they have never shared before. Interviewees juggle their desire to trust the interviewer and their instincts to be open and honest about their true, inner selves with a fear that they could be screwed over at any moment. This is true of most such encounters and was particularly stark in the case of an intense, sincere young writer and a once-bitten, twice-shy rock star.

The heart of Crowe's article was Gregg's honest, emotional thoughts on the band's ability to continue and even reach new heights of success in the wake of Duane's and Oakley's deaths. "The real question is not why we're so popular," he said, adding:

I try not to think about that too much. The question is what made the Allman Brothers keep on going. I've had guys come up to me and say, "Man, it just doesn't seem like losing those two fine cats affected you people at all."

Why? Because I still have my wits about me? Because I can still play? Well, that's the key right there. We'd all have turned into fucking vegetables if we hadn't been able to get out there and play. *That's* when the success was, Jack. Success was being able to keep your brain inside your head.

The whole experience was eye-opening for Crowe, a true turning point in his life and career. "It was my first glimpse of the darkness in this world," he said. "Before that it was all a realized dream: 'I can do this!' Then I had to face the fact that my family could not protect me from everything, I did not have shoes that fly—and you can end up in a room with a person you admire ending your career."

Crowe's love of Gregg and the Allman Brothers Band's music made the experience more agonizing. This wasn't just another assignment for him. "I felt Gregg's music in my soul and he was in a position to end it all for me," Crowe said. "It was a moment of reckoning, a searing experience. I think that if a man from the future had caught me in the elevator that night and said I'd be talking about this for 50 years I would have believed him. There was so much going on in that little room at the Miyako: it's going to the cover of Gregg's autobiography and it's also the *Rolling Stone* story and it's the beginning of *Almost Famous*. I knew it was monumental."

THE WEEK THE story came out, the Allman Brothers Band was back on the road, becoming the first group to play the new Capital Centre in Landover, Maryland, on December 4. Tampa Stadium on December 9 marked the band's tenth stadium show of 1973.

The band was maintaining a breakneck pace, despite constant hiccups. The dangers of substance abuse were ever present, sometimes in the most frightening ways. Gregg overdosed in New York and was revived by new crew member Scooter Herring, who saved the day, resuscitating Allman as they waited for an ambulance. "It was crazy," recalled Perkins. "Bunky was getting calls in Macon from people in New York asking if Gregg 'had died up here.'"

Life was no less hectic back home in Macon. Sidney Smith was a young photographer who had gotten to know the band while shooting them in his hometown of New Orleans. Trucks and Betts encouraged him to move to Macon, where he became something of a house photographer for the group. He took family portraits for Butch, captured life on the farm, and shot the pictures at Betts and Sandy Blue Sky's 1974 wedding.

Gregg also had some special assignments for him. Once, he gave Smith a hundred dollars and his grandmother's address in Nashville and asked him to send her photographs. He did, and Gregg was pleased, and soon had another job in mind. "Gregg called me over to his house one day," Smith recalled. "It was just the two of us sitting in his little living room shooting the shit, and he said, 'Listen, man, I'm gonna be on the road and I need you to hide out in the bushes or a tree and take pictures of everyone who walks in the front door of my house. My wife's fucking somebody and I need to know who it is.'"

Smith immediately knew he was not going to do this job, but was unclear how to get out of it, so he humored Allman, saying neither yes nor no. He was bailed out a few days later by Gregg's mercurial decision-making. "I was in the Capricorn office when the band came in," Smith said. "Gregg summoned me over and said, 'Remember what we talked about the other day? Don't do it.'"

WHEN THE GRATEFUL Dead played Atlanta on Betts's thirtieth birthday, December 12, 1973, Garcia told the crowd, "I'd like to wish Dickey Betts a happy birthday." The band then launched into "Happy Birthday," greeted by cheers from the crowd in the Allmans' home base. A few weeks later, the Allman Brothers Band closed out the year with two Bill Graham–promoted shows at San Francisco's Cow Palace, on December 31 and January 1.

The band's travel had gotten considerably easier since they started flying on the *Starship,* a former United Airlines Boeing 720 jet bought by pop singer Bobby Sherman and his manager and leased to touring musicians. After playing two sold-out shows at Philadelphia's Spectrum Arena just before New Year's, Perkins recalled that the band members invited "about 100 people to fly to San Francisco on a plane that held 43 passengers." It was up to him to turn people away.

The Grateful Dead, who had played legendary New Year's Eve shows every year since 1967, took the holiday off despite having been offered the venue first. Jerry Garcia and Bill Kreutzmann were in attendance, along with several members of the Dead's extended family. Garcia did an interview on the radio broadcast before the Allman Brothers Band started, saying that he was happy to have the night off and laughing at the idea of making a New Year's resolution. "I could never get into that whole 'I'm going to do this or that better' thing," Garcia said. He did have one standing resolution, however: "I'm going to try and play better."

The Marshall Tucker Band and the Charlie Daniels Band opened the show, making for a long night of music, which the Allman Brothers Band happily extended far beyond their obligation, playing from about 10 PM– to almost 4 AM (1–7 AM on the East Coast). San Francisco's KSAN broadcast the show nationally (and worldwide via Armed Forces Radio). *Radio and Records* magazine estimated that the broadcast reached 40 million people around the world.

"I believe it is still the largest radio audience for a live rock and roll event," said Capricorn's Dick Wooley, who organized the broadcast. "The fact that 40 million people heard the Allman Brothers Band was not lost on music retailers and show promoters. Foreign and domestic album sales skyrocketed after the show, which also helped launch the career of the Marshall Tucker Band."

The Allman Brothers Band played an excellent, somewhat conventional seventy-minute first set, starting with "Wasted Words" and ending with "In Memory of Elizabeth Reed." Listeners included the Crowe family of San Diego, for whom it represented a significant breakthrough of parental acceptance of the music Cameron loved so much.

"I was taping it and when I went to a friend's house, my dad* said he would flip the tape and when I came home he was still listening to the broadcast," said Crowe. "That show changed the dynamics in my house. My mom also came around—we all ended up listening to 'Mountain Jam' together the next day!"

The Allman Brothers Band came back on just before midnight, celebrated the new year, then played a stellar set that started to get increasingly far out during an extended "Les Brers in A Minor," which also featured Garcia, who would stay onstage the rest of the night. As he was getting

---

* Many people think that Crowe was raised without a father, like his alter ego William Miller in *Almost Famous*, but it is not so. That was a writerly decision, not a reflection of reality. Crowe's father, James, was a real estate agent.

ready for an extended drum duet with Jaimoe, Trucks realized that he had been dosed with acid. He said that he only drank from his own bottle of wine, which he carried to his drum riser and kept at his feet after previous experiences. An enterprising acid evangelist had used a squirt gun filled with liquid LSD to dose his wine.

"My drums started just drifting off into space," Trucks said. "When I could hit one it felt like hitting a marshmallow. I turned around and there stood Bill Kreutzmann looking just like Jesus, complete with the halo, and I held out my sticks and asked him if he would play my drums, because I couldn't catch them. He went on to play what was to be my big time in the sun before a [radio] audience of millions. I moved to the side of the stage and thoroughly enjoyed the rest of the show."

Allman was also dosed and freaked out at the midnight sight of Graham emerging as Father Time, which he did at most New Year's Eve shows. "I caught a good one," Allman said. He held on through a spacey yet powerful "Les Brers," which segued into an unusually jazzy "Whipping Post." The song remained instrumental, likely the only time in band history, as Gregg walked off the stage and never returned. "I was running the spotlight and it went to Gregg and he wasn't there," recalled A. J. Lyndon.

Boz Scaggs, who had been watching from the wings, replaced Allman at the organ and handled the rest of the singing for the hour-long blues jam that followed. They played bedrock blues classics, including B.B. King's "You Upset Me," Freddie King's "Hideaway," and Bo Diddley's "Hey! Bo Diddley."

Betts was the third member of the band dosed with acid. His "guitar neck suddenly started growing longer and longer," he told Sidney Smith, who was there shooting the show. But unlike his mates, Betts was able to perform at a peak level, enjoying playing with his friend Garcia. Deep into the morning, Graham came back out and announced that a couple backstage had decided to get married. KSAN stayed on the air, even as some stations dropped the feed, and the band came back for a final instrumental set with a lineup featuring Garcia, Betts, Leavell, Lamar Williams, Jaimoe, and Kreutzmann, with Scaggs joining on some songs as well. The show seemed to finally be over when they played "And We Bid You Goodnight," but Garcia and Betts steered the band into a gorgeous instrumental take on "Will the Circle Be Unbroken," which segued into "Mountain Jam" as the clock hit 4 AM.

The two guitarists' evident pleasure in playing together fueled the extensive all-night jamming.

It was anything but a perfunctory sit-in for Garcia, and it was the last time he would ever share a stage with anyone from the Allman Brothers Band. On January 1, 1974, the Allman Brothers Band took the stage again for a second sellout of the 16,500-seat venue. Only the hardiest, most popular band would dare to play again on January 1, a veritable national holiday of do-nothing. Their guests included John Lee Hooker, Steve Miller, Elvin Bishop, Charlie Daniels, and Buddy Miles, a calvacade of stars that reminded Jaimoe of "one of the great old rhythm and blues reviews." "It was a hell of a show," he said, but no one from the Dead appeared. They left it all onstage the night before.

18

HE WAS A FRIEND OF MINE

ON JANUARY 21, 1974, Bob Dylan and the Band played the first of two shows at the Omni in Atlanta as part of Dylan's triumphant return to the stage after an eight-year hiatus. Georgia governor Jimmy Carter attended the show, having purchased sixteen sixth-row seats, which he insisted on paying for. Afterward, he hosted a reception at the governor's mansion, having invited Dylan the previous month via a handwritten note. Surprised by Carter's invitation, Bill Graham, who was producing the tour, called Phil Walden seeking some information and guidance.

"He asked me what the hell was up with this Georgia governor," Walden said. Graham said that he was surprised by Carter's invitation and wanted to know if "it was for real" because he had to recommend what to do.

"I told him that Jimmy Carter was my buddy [and] Bill asked me to check this invitation out," Walden said. "I called Jimmy, who said he was a big fan of Dylan's and he'd love for him to come. When I told him they were late night guys and they're going to be boozing and whatever else they're going to do, Jimmy said, 'That's ok. I want them to feel comfortable.'"

Walden was happy to broker this meeting and looked forward to being there himself. He had met Dylan at the Monterey Pop Festival, when the songwriter presented "Just Like a Woman" to Redding to record. The two artists had an amiable exchange, and Dylan left thinking that Redding would likely cut the tune; however, while Otis told Walden that he liked the song, there were too many words for him to remember. He'd pass.

(Many years later, Gregg Allman performed "Just Like a Woman," hinting at what a Redding version might have sounded like.)

Walden and Carter's relationship had started in 1971, when the newly elected governor stopped in Macon for a meeting, partly to discuss how best to support the state's growing entertainment industry. That meeting was brokered by Cloyd Hall, who worked for Carter and had also been Walden's elementary school football coach. Walden told Carter that while the state was wooing filmmakers to work in Georgia, which would eventually become an industry leader, it was ignoring the already thriving local music industry. Walden was sick of being treated like a stepchild and saw Carter as someone he could do business with.

Carter's young executive secretary, Hamilton Jordan, also knew Walden from back in the day. As a high school sophomore in Albany, Georgia, he had booked Johnny Jenkins and the Pinetoppers, featuring Otis Redding, for several parties. Jordan haggled with Walden over the band's $200 fee and was thrilled when he negotiated him down to $180, plus $20 for gas, only to realize he had been had. "I began to see why this guy was such a good agent," Jordan said.

Carter and his wife, Rosalynn, returned for another meeting with Walden, Wooley, and Fenter in 1973. Wooley recalled the nervous energy before the first couple's arrival: "people were running around vacuuming and dusting" the office, and Walden sent Carolyn Brown to "run down to the jewelry store and buy a nice tea or coffee set to serve them."

It must have made a good impression, because two weeks later the governor returned for another meeting, which ran for two hours rather than its scheduled fifteen minutes. Despite Capricorn's success and growing importance to Macon's economy and culture, Walden and company remained on the outside of the town's upper crust. He appreciated, even reveled in, the governor's attention and show of respect. Carter's acknowledgment of the music business's growing importance to Macon and the state of Georgia—something few politicians had been willing to embrace—was significant to Walden.

After talking to Walden, Graham relayed Dylan's acceptance back to Governor Carter's office, along with the singer's request for some "real down-home cuisine." Carter also invited the Allman Brothers Band, Walden, and other Capricorn executives to attend. Walden was joined by Frank Fenter and Alex Hodges, the Band, Graham, Carter's three sons, and some of the boys' closest friends.

Carter said that Dylan only asked him about his Christian faith. In five years, Dylan would announce himself as a born-again Christian and release the religiously themed album *Slow Train Coming*. At the governor's mansion, he was startled and moved by the realization that his songs had had an impact on Carter.

"The first thing he did was quote my songs back to me," Dylan said. "That was the first time that I realized my songs had reached into, basically, the establishment. I had no experience in that world. . . . He put my mind at ease by not talking down to me and showing me he had a sincere appreciation of the songs I had written. He's a kindred spirit to me, the kind of man you don't meet every day and are lucky if you ever do."

None of the Allman Brothers Band made it to the party. Dylan and his entourage traveled to the mansion in three long black limousines, and he declined offers of any drink other than orange juice or any food other than vegetables, despite his original request for Southern fare. *Rolling Stone* reported that the rest of the guests "ate grits, scrambled eggs and country ham, drank beer and wine and dipped fresh vegetables in a cheese sauce." Hodges said that it was "just a comfortable, casual early morning breakfast," similar to the kind of post-gig meals bands often enjoy at their hotel.

At the event, Carter told the Capricorn crew that he was planning to run for president, and Walden replied enthusiastically, pledging his support and assistance. He'd have to convince his artists to participate, but he could be very persuasive, and the Allman Brothers members tended to like Carter, anyhow.

Betts said that they could all feel the difference when he became governor and that they thought, "This guy's all right." "It was like the sun came out in Georgia," he said. "It was the Peach State instead of the 'afraid to drive through it to get to Florida' state."

The party had ended, and Dylan and the Band were on the way back to their hotels when Gregg rolled up to the governor's mansion in a limo. He had been rehearsing for his upcoming solo tour, and the night grew late. "We were in the studio and we shut it down at 11 and jumped in a limo to head to Atlanta," Allman said. "We got there just as the last guests were leaving."

Allman said that he told the driver to pull up to the security gate so it would be known he had tried to attend. "I wanted to let the record show we appeared," he said. "I got out and told the guard, who told me to wait a minute. As I was getting back in the limousine to go home, he called after me and said the governor wants to see me on the porch of the mansion."

Bunky Odom remembers the incident differently. He said that he was awoken by a call from Cloyd Hall, the governor's usual connection to the Capricorn crew. "If Dickey Betts got a speeding ticket from a state trooper, I'd call Cloyd to take care of it," Odom said. "He called me at one AM and said Gregg was at the guardhouse demanding to see the governor and wondering what he should do. I told him that was up to them."

The limousine was waved ahead. As it approached the governor's mansion, which was mostly dark, with just a porch light and one inside room lit up, Allman saw a solitary figure standing on the porch. Recalled Allman, "I saw this dude standing there in a pair of Levis, T-shirt, no shoes, wearing a white hat and thought, 'Who's this riff raff hanging around the governor's mansion?' Well, it was him!"

Carter described his outfit to *Rolling Stone* as "the way I always dress around the house." The governor blew Allman's mind by saying, "Come on in. I got some new Elmore James albums we can listen to." As they walked inside, Carter praised Allman's songwriting and started "rattling off the lyrics" to "Black Hearted Woman," "Midnight Rider," and "Don't Keep Me Wondering." The governor was clearly an educated, appreciative fan. If he was consciously wooing the rock star, he was doing a good job. Gregg said that they polished off a bottle of scotch, but Carter laughed that off, noting that he restricted himself to one or two drinks a night.

"We went in there and drank J&B scotch together and he said, 'By the way I'm running for President,'" Allman said. "I basically laughed, thinking, 'Okay. There ain't been a Southern president in how long, but you think you can be the one?'"

Allman thought it was absurd to think that his governor—this guy in the T-shirt sitting next to him sipping scotch and listening to Elmore James—would ever become president of the United States of America. But he truly liked Carter, admiring his gumption and his "just folks" appeal. He was ready to assist this Sisyphean effort. "What impressed me is not just that he cared so much about music—he knew all these lyrics—but also that he was a good guy," Allman said. "It was easy to sit and talk to him."

How many other governors would invite Dylan to a postshow party and how many such invitations would he accept? Was there another important politician, Allman wondered, "who would not care about the image of hanging out with people like us?" That kind of loyalty deserved to be returned, so when Carter said he "may need some money down the road" Gregg promised to bring the request to the rest of his bandmates.

"It was a friendship thing for me," Allman said. "I liked the guy, and if he told me he needed money to open used car lots, I probably would have helped him."

"We sat up all night and listened to records," Carter said.

A few nights after the Carter meeting, Gregg described his late-night soiree with the governor to a reporter simply: "He's really far out, man."

Earlier that night, when Carter told Walden, Hodges, and Fenter about his planned run, he added that "Hamilton has a plan." Shortly after Carter was elected governor in 1970, Hamilton Jordan had devised a comprehensive, eighty-page strategy memorandum for a long-shot, insurgent run for the presidency. It involved an intense focus on the Iowa caucuses, which were moved to be the first held in the nation in the Democratic Party's presidential nomination process in 1972 and had never before received the type of long, intense focus that soon became commonplace. The plan also included fundraising and awareness raising through rock concerts. Walden, of course, was the point of contact for some of the country's most popular bands, including the Allman Brothers Band and the Marshall Tucker Band, could help with the latter.

Fundraising was transformed in the 1976 presidential campaign, the first to be run under new campaign finance rules implemented after the Watergate scandal. These limited individual donations to $1,000 and authorized federal matching funds, which meant the government would give a dollar for every dollar raised, within certain limitations. It would be a huge

advantage to raise tens of thousands of dollars in one night at a concert—
which federal election funds would double. Walden took charge of these
efforts, choosing Atlanta native Tom Beard, then working as a banker, to
organize the concerts. Beard became an early employee of the Carter campaign, essentially at Walden's insistence.

"Phil called me up with this vision and told me this is what I had to
do," Beard recalled. "I hated being a banker and was lousy at it and I liked
Carter, so it sounded good to me. Phil called the campaign and made this
happen. It was 100 percent his vision and none of it would have happened
without him. He had a lot of grandiose ideas, and I was the one who was
supposed to get it all done."

Walden's drafting of Beard and involvement in the nascent campaign
was a logical step in a growing relationship that had started with Jimmy
and Rosalynn Carter's visits to Capricorn. "I was honestly skeptical of the
whole thing," said Wooley. "I was not on board at first, but Phil thought
Jimmy could be president and his enthusiasm was contagious."

Walden had his own interest in politics, though he understood that
his involvement in rock and R&B and dalliances with drugs ruled out his
running for office and he was happy to back Carter. The two charismatic
self-made Georgians got along well and had a distinct rapport. Walden
always insisted that he never asked for any favors in return for his support, though he did lobby the governor hard for a tough law against tape
piracy in Georgia, which was of great concern for the recording industry
at the time. (*Rolling Stone* estimated that record and tape piracy, mostly
sold cheaply at truck stops, cost the industry $10 million a year.) Carter
proposed one of the nation's toughest laws to prevent the sale of such boot-
legs. It was passed and signed into law after he left office.

Whatever business they discussed, Walden truly believed in Carter and
welcomed the opportunity for a new breed of Southerner to become via-
ble for national office. "I really don't think Phil had ulterior motives," said
Beard. "He just liked him."

In Walden's view, new thinking was particularly required on racial issues,
where he was embarrassed by notorious segregationist Lester Maddox, who
preceded Carter as governor after defeating him in the 1966 Democratic

primary. Maddox was nationally infamous for being a vicious racist. In 1964, he threatened Black activists with an axe handle when they tried to enter his Atlanta restaurant, a photo of which was seen across the country. He closed the restaurant rather than integrate. And while Carter did not select Maddox or run with him on a ticket, the former governor remarkably served as the new governor's lieutenant governor, a position he ran for after being limited to one gubernatorial term.

"I was so sick of racists like Lester Maddox representing our state and people thinking I was on board with that when I traveled anywhere and they heard my accent," said Walden, who had launched his career working with Black artists and felt forever grateful that they "shared their culture" with him. "I'd get in a cab in New York and the driver would hear me talk and say, 'You guys really know how to take care of those people down there.' That repulsed me. Civil rights, Black folks rights, were always a big thing for me. . . . I wanted someone who more represented my values to be visible to the world."

Many of Walden's peers shared his views on this issue, including some of the other white men in the rock and roll business who walked the line between the counterculture and the mainstream American business world.

"I'm a Southern boy, born and raised, and I had heard that [racist] crap all my life and saw this [campaign] as a way to get away from it," said Alex Cooley. The large, diverse festivals the promoter had put on were a "way to get away" from the stultifying racism locally, he explained. Helping Jimmy Carter gain exposure and maybe even the presidency was a pathway for similar progress nationally.

Carter shared these men's views on civil rights. In 1964, he and Rosalynn were alone among their fellow congregants in voting to admit Black people into the Carters' house of worship, the Plains Baptist Church. Maddox, on the other hand, had refused to allow Atlanta resident Martin Luther King Jr. to lie in state in the Georgia State Capitol following his 1968 assassination, prompting both outrage and widespread support, deepening the state's racial divides.

"When I got involved with Carter, I was preaching the gospel," Walden said. "I just thought [he] was going to be honest and straight and we would be able to be proud of our President and of our heritage again. I just believed in him."

Carter was an unlikely leader of the counterculture: a nerdy, cardigan-wearing, straight-A student who left his position as a United States Navy nuclear physicist to return to Plains, Georgia, population 650, to run the family peanut farm. Yet in his own odd way, he became the figurehead of a raggedy bunch of Southern musicians and promoters who wanted to be respected and taken seriously. They believed that the former governor provided a real opportunity to make progress on issues important to them. The year 1976 was barely a decade after passage of the Civil Rights Act of 1964 and the Voting Rights Act of 1965, which were arguably the most important statutes ever passed in the nation's efforts to guarantee rights to all its citizens so that it could become a true democracy.

Carter received another unexpected boost in the youth market from Hunter S. Thompson. The "gonzo journalist" had a huge following, writing for *Rolling Stone* and then, riding high, publishing his books *Fear and Loathing in Las Vegas* and *Fear and Loathing on the Campaign Trail*, which covered the 1972 presidential race. Thompson serendipitously heard the Georgia governor deliver what he called a "king hell bastard of a speech" at the University of Georgia law school's 1974 celebration of "Law Day."

Thompson was traveling with Massachusetts senator Ted Kennedy, who was scheduled to give the event's keynote speech in Athens. They had spent the previous night at the governor's mansion, where Kennedy found Carter, whom he was meeting for the first time, to be oddly unfriendly. What he didn't know was that the governor had been secretly running for president for eighteen months and assumed that the senator would be a primary opponent. He also "thought Ted wasn't as smart as his brothers and believed that his poor response to events at Chappaquiddick—where in 1969 Kennedy had driven his car off a bridge and fled the scene, leaving his young woman passenger to die—should disqualify him from the presidency," wrote Jonathan Alter in his Carter biography, *His Very Best: Jimmy Carter, A Life.*

At the last minute, Carter changed his mind about letting his potential rival fly to Athens on his plane, sending Kennedy rushing out in the morning to make it there in time. (Kennedy decided not to run, but severely damaged Carter's 1980 reelection chances by running against him in the party's nomination process to select its nominee for president.)

Arriving at the luncheon and realizing that his prepared remarks were too similar to the keynote speech Kennedy was set to deliver, Carter went to an adjoining room and quickly wrote out some notes. Then he gave a speech that unsettled the conservative legal establishment seated in front of him, while thrilling Thompson.

He uncorked a forty-five-minute speech that angered his crowd and thrilled much of the country's liberal voters once Thompson spread the word. Carter declared himself a governor "still deeply concerned about the inadequacies of the system of which it is obvious you're so patently proud" and attacked the lawyers for excessively punishing minor crimes. But what sealed Thompson's affections were the sources Carter cited for his sense of social justice. First, he mentioned theologian Reinhold Niebuhr, and then he added, "The other source of my understanding about what's right and wrong in this society is from a friend of mine, a poet named Bob Dylan."

Thompson, who had been sipping Wild Turkey in an iced tea glass throughout the luncheon, thought he must have misheard the governor, whose speech he was recording, but Carter continued:

After listening to his records about "The Ballad of Hattie Carroll" and "Like a Rolling Stone" and "The Times They Are A-Changin,'" I've learned to appreciate the dynamism of change in a modern society.

I grew up as a landowner's son. But I don't think I ever realized the proper interrelationship between the landowner and those who worked on a farm until I heard Dylan's record, "I Ain't Gonna Work on Maggie's Farm No More." So I come here speaking to you today about your subject with a base for my information founded on Reinhold Niebuhr and Bob Dylan.

Thompson didn't know much about Carter or his record as governor—that, for instance, he had recently signed a bill that provided new death penalty guidelines enabling state-sanctioned executions to resume after a four-year moratorium ordered by the U.S. Supreme Court. But he was wowed by the oratory and by Carter's willingness to deliver it mostly off the cuff in front of a hostile crowd. Thompson called the speech "the most eloquent thing I have ever heard from the mouth of a politician" and began urging *Rolling Stone* editor Jann Wenner to get behind the nascent Carter campaign. Thompson's advocacy also deeply impacted the young political reporters who revered him, and whose attention and favorable coverage the Carter campaign badly needed in order to be taken seriously.

Jimmy Carter officially announced that he was running for president in a December 1974 speech at the National Press Club in Washington, D.C.

19

LET NATURE SING

AFTER A WILDLY successful 1973, powered by the success of *Brothers and Sisters* and a triumphant run of end-of-year concerts, the Allman Brothers Band did not perform live for the first five months of 1974. Gregg Allman and Dickey Betts were both busy with solo projects. Betts was preparing to record his first solo album, while Allman was planning his initial tour in support of *Laid Back*.

Gregg's twenty-five-show, twenty-two-city tour in March and April 1974 would be neither a replication of the Allman Brothers Band nor a stripped-down solo outing. Allman had something much grander in mind: a twenty-eight-piece band, which included three background singers, a five-man horn section, and a fifteen-member string section. Always a fan of horn sections, he termed the orchestra "just a kick."*

Allman's 1974 band included Allman Brothers bandmates Chuck Leavell and Jaimoe, with Bill Stewart on drums, Scott Boyer and Tommy Talton on guitars, and saxophonist Randall Bramblett. "I borrowed Butch's larger

---

* Decades later, Allman told me that he was longing to take such a big band out on the road again. "It's not really economically feasible," he said, "but I might do it anyhow." Though Gregg never again took out a string section, the final version of his solo band included two saxophonists and a trumpet player. When Bobby "Blue" Bland passed away in 2013, Allman hired tenor saxophonist Art Edmaiston and trumpet player Marc Franklin from his hero's band and was thrilled to have them. He spoke reverently not only about Bland's singing but also about the large Joe Scott Orchestra that backed him during his 1960s prime.

kit for that tour because it was such a big orchestra that I felt I needed a bigger bass drum to support it," Jaimoe said.

The musicians had a great time on tour. "It was a good band and it even worked with the violins and singers," Jaimoe said. "To me it was like being back in the Apollo Theater with the R&B orchestras."

Most of the musicians had never played with strings or a band that large and had to adjust musically. "The string players were all New York cats, which made for a crazy combination," said Leavell. "They were mostly very talented classical players who had never worked with a rock band. We were playing some really innovative music, and everyone just enjoyed how fun and different the whole experience was."

The group also had to adapt to having so many people onstage and to relatively extensive props and scenery with translucent panels painted with trees dripping with Spanish moss. Walden hired Alice Cooper's production manager to design the set, a significant step up in production values from the Allman Brothers Band, who simply used spotlights on the singer or soloist. The members of Gregg's solo band were given suits to wear, which none of them particularly cared for. The idea behind all this, said Perkins, was to give immediate, clear visual signals that this was not the Allman Brothers Band.

The nationwide tour started on March 16 in Charlotte, North Carolina, with stops in some of the nation's most beautiful theaters, including Carnegie Hall. Most of the band, minus the strings and singers, also performed as Cowboy in the middle of the show instead of before it as an opener. "We did 45 minutes to an hour because Gregg wanted a little respite," said Talton. This was also clearly a way to give Cowboy more exposure, an effort that continued later that year when they released two tracks on *The Gregg Allman Tour,* the double album documenting the shows.

The entourage exceeded fifty, most of whom rode on one bus. Gregg flew on a chartered plane, and some of the crew rode in the equipment truck. "Guys would fight to get on the plane with us," said Perkins. "We had three other spots and we rotated who was on there. The bus was fun but crowded, and it wasn't even a real tour bus; it was like a 40s big band bus."

In the Broadway tradition, Gregg's shows opened with a beautiful instrumental overture, a medley of the songs to come. "That whole thing sprung from Chuck's creativity," said Talton. "He came up with that."

Leavell said he collaborated on the overture with string arranger Ed Freeman, who was with the tour conducting the orchestra, "to give a tease to the audience about what was to come." As the overture ended, Allman emerged from the wings and took a seat at his organ at center stage. These shows were the first time that Allman had ever performed as a solo act, and he admitted that he got "scared, up there by my damn self."

Reviewers compared the show in its large band and grandeur to Joe Cocker's Mad Dogs and Englishmen. "Each night when Gregg floated onstage, his long, blond hair streaming behind him, audiences hushed," *Circus* reported, adding: "The swelling of the strings, along with Gregg's plaintive, melodic crooning, made the event more than just rock and roll. It was a musical event of the first order."

Sandlin came out to record shows at Carnegie Hall on April 10 and 11 and at the Capitol Theatre in Passaic, New Jersey, on April 13 for what became *Gregg Allman Tour '74*. Sandlin left New York not only with an excellent recording but also with a very impressive new instrument for Capricorn Studios: Carnegie Hall's famed Steinway piano.

Setting up for the recording during an extended sound check, Sandlin and Leavell marveled at the piano's majestic sound. Sandlin wondered aloud if they could possibly buy it. It turned out that the piano was a favorite of many performers, and the Carnegie Hall manager had long declined all requests to sell it. The manager, however, had recently passed away, and Leavell and Sandlin were the first to ask the new man in charge about purchasing the piano. "Apparently the new manager was unaware of the situation, and agreed to sell it to us," Leavell said. "We were elated!"

That piano stayed in the Capricorn studio until the label's 1986 bankruptcy auction, when it was sold, along with most everything else. The last anyone heard of it, a church had purchased the instrument. This Sunday, a church in middle Georgia might feature music played on a Steinway grand beloved by everyone from Chuck Leavell to Vladimir Horowitz.

Each night on his solo tour, Gregg reassured attendees of one thing: "the Allman Brothers Band are still together" and a summer tour was forthcoming. At the tour's final show, in Cincinnati on April 25, 1974, with the fans stomping their feet for an encore after a two-hour show, Gregg returned and said, "I want to squelch a few rumors here and now." Betts, Trucks, and Williams walked out to join Gregg, Jaimoe, and Chuck, and the Allman Brothers Band played a ninety-minute encore.

"We all thought it was a good idea, which would indeed help put to rest any rumors of break-up," Leavell said. There was plenty of life left in the group.

AT APPROXIMATELY THE same time Gregg was touring, Betts entered Capricorn Studios with Sandlin to start work on his own solo debut, *Highway Call*. Like Gregg, Dickey saw no point in playing Allman Brothers–style music. "We're already doing what the Allman Brothers Band do as well as anyone can do it," Betts said. "Making a record on my own, it only ever made sense to do something really different."

Betts started the sessions with a core band of drummer David Walshaw, a former bandmate from the Jokers; bassist Stray Straton, another old friend; and Leavell, who was thrilled to be included.

"Dickey was the last one to really open up and welcome me into the Allman Brothers Band, so it meant a lot to me when he asked me to play on the record," said Leavell. "That's when we really became friends."

Sandlin had a similar experience. Though he had been around the Allman Brothers Band since its formation, Betts remained elusive. The guitarist only lived in Macon sporadically for the first three years of the band's existence, returning home to the Sarasota, Florida, area or to Love Valley, North Carolina, which Betts had fallen in love with when the band headlined a festival there in July 1970. Illustrating just how much of a lone wolf Betts could be, his cabin in Love Valley did not have a telephone. The band had an elaborate and rather old-fashioned means of reaching him to remind him about upcoming tour dates and communicate his flight information. (At the time, a ticket could be purchased by a third party and simply picked up at the gate.)

"Dickey's cabin was on the property of the mayor, whose house I would call when I needed to reach him," recalled Perkins. "I'd talk to the mayor's teenage son and relay the information about Dickey's flight from Charlotte. He would write it down and ride it up to Dickey on horseback. I was the only road manager to use Pony Express and I would always hold my breath that he would show up for flights, but he always did."

Betts had been contemplating a solo album for a while and, like Gregg, had a grand vision. His initial idea was to record instrumentals with Stéphane Grappelli, the French violin player who was jazz guitarist's Django Reinhardt's musical partner. Betts dreamed of recording an instrumental version of "Revival" with the violinist. Grappelli and Reinhardt were key influences on the harmonies Betts and Duane Allman played, and he wanted to replicate them with the source of his inspiration.

Traveling to Paris to record with Grappelli became too much of a logistical hurdle, and Betts pivoted toward another violin legend, who was much closer to home: fellow Floridian Vassar Clements, whom he'd met at a bluegrass festival. Clements added country to Betts's jazz guitar project, leading it toward the music genre where jazz and country intersect: western swing.

Clements joined Bill Monroe's Bluegrass Boys in 1949, when he was fourteen. He worked with a wide array of country and bluegrass artists through the 1960s. After taking time away from music to address his alcoholism, he played on the Nitty Gritty Dirt Band's 1972 *Will the Circle Be Unbroken* album, which exposed him and other traditionalist greats like Roy Acuff, "Mother" Maybelle Carter, Doc Watson, Earl Scruggs, Merle Travis, and Jimmy Martin to a wider audience. Clements was soon a member of Jerry Garcia's bluegrass project Old and in the Way, playing on its self-titled album and on the Grateful Dead's *Wake of the Flood,* both recorded in 1973.

"He was a musical giant," mandolinist David Grisman, a member of Old and in the Way and frequent Clements collaborator, said. "He had an incredible sound and imagination. He was a fountain of ideas and could execute them amazingly."

Clements played effortlessly with everyone, with a style that blended country, jazz, and western swing and that he called "hillbilly jazz."

Sandlin and Betts first brought Clements and pedal steel player John Huey to Macon to add to "Hand Picked," a Betts-composed slice of straight western swing. Huey was a top Nashville session player who had been to the studio before, playing on Alex Taylor's *Dinnertime* and country singer Kitty Wells's *Forever Young,* part of Capricorn's ill-fated attempt at a country division.

Both Clements and Huey had deep roots in and commanded the respect of the traditional country music and bluegrass worlds but were also modernists open to experimentation and to playing in almost any genre. They were also patron saints for a growing band of young bluegrass renegades like John Cowan, Sam Bush, John Hartford, and Tony Rice, who were putting their own stamp on the music, offering an updated, progressive take on the genre that became known as "new grass." Those young musicians felt a kinship with the Allman Brothers Band, who had done for blues what they wanted to do for bluegrass. They were thrilled by the commingling of their heroes. "We all shouted, 'Go Team!'" said Cowan.

While Clements already had a profile with rock audiences, thanks to his work with the Dirt Band and Garcia and the Dead, Huey was just starting to emerge in the spotlight. The pedal steel player was a Nashville session legend, largely for his work with Conway Twitty, and he was becoming a hero to the new generation of renegades.

"John produced his trademark 'crying steel' sound by playing two melodies on separate strings, one ascending and one descending, at the same time," said Cowan. "He and Vassar both had singular styles that combined outrageous technique with strong roots in traditional music but a modernist, almost jazz sensibility. They weren't afraid to play something 'out'—scales that don't necessarily match what the chord changes dictate."

With Clements and Huey on board, "Hand Picked" became a swinging hillbilly-jazz masterpiece, fourteen minutes of instrumental goodness that explored new ground and set the template for what the rest of the album would sound like. The song also featured the Nitty Gritty Dirt Band's Jeff Hanna on acoustic guitar. When Betts called Clements to invite him to record, the fiddler had just gotten off the road with the Dirt Band and suggested Hanna's involvement.

"Vassar was a genius musician and a super great hang who was always smiling and super positive, and he absolutely loved Dickey, whose musical sensibilities were right up his alley," said Hanna. "The twin lines they effortlessly played together were stunning. Dickey is a great collaborator who loves the process of working things out with a partner. It was a pleasure to watch the two of them come up with those harmony parts. My hands grew raw from chunking away on Dickey's Martin D28 over a couple of great days in the studio."

With animosity still lingering between Walden and Nitty Gritty Dirt Band manager Bill McEuen over Gregg's abandoning his contract with Liberty Records to join the Allman Brothers Band (Walden had to buy out the contract), Hanna said that he and Betts agreed not to tell their respective managers about their collaboration. "There was a real antagonism there and it scuttled some great opportunities for the Dirt Band and the Allman Brothers to play together," said Hanna. "Phil's reaction was always simple: no fucking way."

"Hand Picked" shared the second side of *Highway Call* with Clements's instrumental "The Kissimmee Kid." Betts wrote all the other material, including side 1's four songs. The album began with the upbeat "Long Time Gone," a country rocker that took the country rock leanings of "Ramblin' Man" one step further, leaning into Huey's weeping, soaring pedal steel.

Next up was "Rain," another upbeat tune on which Huey played harmony with Betts and added a wailing pedal steel counterpoint to a sweetly melodic guitar solo. The Rambos, a family gospel trio, harmonized with Betts's chorus vocal. The album's title track is a slow, moving ballad about the lure of the open road, highlighted by Leavell's piano solo, which flows like a summer rainstorm. It is not Leavell's flashiest playing, but it is some of his most dynamic and emotionally gripping. The Rambos provide an angelic chorus.

The first side ends with the sweeping "Let Nature Sing," which was inspired by Navajo medicine man Stewart Etsitty, whom Betts called "a helper, teacher and guidepost."

"I was seeking some guidance from Stewart and he said, 'Your life is too complicated, Richard. I don't know what to tell you except let nature sing,'" Betts said. "That's as Zen as it gets. He wouldn't say no more. And, man, he didn't need to. I wrote the song."

To capture the chirping birds that open and close the song, Sandlin took a four-track recorder to his house in the country, strung together multiple microphone cords, and ran into the woods each morning to record birdcalls. It was indicative of a loose, experimental recording process.

"The major sources of controversy that exist on a group record just weren't there," Sandlin said.

Betts was firmly in control; there would be no tiptoeing around who wrote or sang how many songs or debating whether a tune was too country to record. Also, the core band members were his friends, and the guests were all older, more experienced musicians whom Betts looked up to, thus encouraging his good behavior. Other musicians who performed on the album included the bluegrass trio the Poindexters, friends of Dickey's from Florida.

Reba Rambo, who was one third of the Rambos, along with her parents, Buck and Dottie, said Betts was a "perfect gentleman." Knowing a session with a rock musician was out of her parents' comfort zone, Dickey went out of his way to make them feel at home, banning smoking and drinking while they were in the studio. The prohibition even extended to Gregg when he visited the studio during the sessions. "When Dickey saw him coming in on the camera, he went to the door and explained they couldn't bring beer in, much to their surprise," said Rambo. "The whole experience of that album was a pleasure."

Betts took to calling Dottie "mom," and one of Reba's most enduring memories is watching the two of them—the rock guitar hero and the white country gospel star—playing guitar together during a pause, laughing and trading leads on a traditional string-music song.

Sandlin said that Betts gave the project his undivided attention, spending hours tinkering with his guitar tone to get the perfect sound. He was similarly devoted to his solos, which often required multiple takes, some of which were edited together, belying the overall jam-session vibe.

"We spent a lot of time trying to play passages without making a single error and some of the licks were complex," Sandlin said, "but he didn't get down on himself and turn violent in frustration as he would often do with the Brothers. The presence of John Huey and Vassar Clements helped keep him a lot calmer." Sandlin felt that these musicians "kept Dickey on his toes," much the way Duane had.

While the music was grounding and the studio experience relatively relaxed, Sandlin said that the swirling madness of mid-'70s Macon caught up with the *Highway Call* sessions as well. It was calmer, but it was far from totally clean. Early in the recording process, Dickey and his wife Sandy had such an epic fight that he started regularly sleeping on the couch in the studio office.

"He was virtually living in the studio," Sandlin said. "We'd get done from working all day and then go to my office and listen to music or play guitar together. We developed a nice rapport and were really getting to know each other."

Just as Sandlin and Betts's bond grew close, Betts and Sandy made up; she picked him up after a day's session, and he didn't return for six weeks. "It was a real shocker to spend twelve hours a day, seven days a week, with someone and one day he said 'see you tomorrow' and vanished for over a month," Sandlin said.

Highway Call was just a few degrees off from the outlaw country coming out of Nashville and Austin, from, among others, Willie Nelson and Waylon Jennings and his wife, Jessi Colter. At the very time when this new musical movement was starting to take hold, Dickey went a different route with his western swing–influenced approach. It was decidedly gentler and more musically complex and varied than the southern rock craze he helped spur with "Ramblin' Man," a song that was formational for outlaw country and part of its DNA.

If you doubt the influence of the Allman Brothers Band on musicians like Jennings, consider that his 1974 album was titled *The Ramblin' Man* and included a cover of "Midnight Rider." Betts had everything he needed to go to Nashville and slide right into the outlaw country firmament, but instead he remained on its fringe, with a more gentle, musically adventurous take on country on *Highway Call*. It was an approach that truly adhered to his own musical vision, which was decidedly nonconfrontational, both musically and lyrically. He was following the Navajo medicine man's advice to "let nature sing."

"I always felt like the acoustic music was what was in Dickey's heart—more so than the rock stuff," said Tommy Talton, who played on "Long Time Gone" and "Highway Call." (He, Leavell, and Sandlin were the only musicians to appear on both Gregg's and Dickey's solo debuts.)

As Talton recounted, "During these sessions, Vassar said, 'You know, Dickey, you play guitar like a fiddle player,' and he loved that and agreed. That stuff is what kept him playing music, not rock and roll and screaming Les Paul solos."

20

DOWN SOUTH JUKIN'

THE ALLMAN BROTHERS Band started inspiring musicians throughout the South from the day they formed, and their influence grew along with their popularity. Southern musicians took notice of their Macon-based success and their steadfast rootedness; they now had role models demonstrating that it was possible to make it on their own terms, without fleeing to New York or Los Angeles.

"It was a big deal for southern rock musicians to feel like we could stay in the region and succeed," said Warren Haynes, an Asheville, North Carolina, native. "We didn't have to move to the East or West Coast to play original music, which had been presumed to be the case."

After the Allman Brothers Band's ascension, the idea of bands playing original music became more palatable to Southern club owners, and groups could envision the possibility of having a thriving career without compromising musically. "Before the Allman Brothers, there wasn't anybody making it from these parts," the Marshall Tucker Band's Toy Caldwell said. He noted that the Allmans made it acceptable for the members of Tucker, or Mobile, Alabama's, Wet Willie to grow long hair, have beards, and play their own songs.

That approach went back to Duane, who was disgusted when Walden told him that some New York booking agents lost interest in the Allman Brothers Band before hearing them play a note, turned off by their simple, scruffy appearance. He told Walden that "if they wanted velvet pants and all that, they ought to go to a fashion show. This is a band that plays music. If you want to hear music, come hear us."

The success of *Brothers and Sisters* sent record companies into a frenzy to discover, sign, and promote their own southern rock bands. Capricorn, of course, was ahead of all of them, with a talent roster, studio, and infrastructure already in place. Capricorn's existing artists brought others to the label's attention, as Wet Willie did with Marshall Tucker and Betts did with country troubadour Billy Joe Shaver, his drinking buddy, and old friend Elvin Bishop. Bishop would go on to have one of Capricorn's biggest hits with 1976's "Fooled Around and Fell in Love."

As the label's roster grew, it became more and more common for Capricorn artists to play on one another's albums, and friends on other labels would often pop up as well. "There was nothing else to do except go fishing in Macon, so people would always end up playing on other folks' albums," said Paul Hornsby.

This is part of why Walden liked having his operation in the sleepy city, saying, "All they can do here is eat fried chicken and make music." Despite this, Walden was able to lure a host of national celebrities to Macon for his annual Capricorn Picnic and Summer Games, held at Lakeside Park, where guests engaged in jamming, hard partying, and intense games of volleyball. Revelers included Andy Warhol, Bette Midler, boxing promoter Don King, and Jimmy Carter, as well as out-of-town music business associates like Bill Graham, Tom Dowd, and Jim Koplik.

"The parties were infamous—athletic and party madness," Graham said. "Macon was an awesome party town for a while there."

When the band members weren't partying, they were usually recording. Jaimoe often hung around the studio. He was there when the Marshall Tucker Band recorded "Can't You See" and wanted to play congas, but the percussion instrument was nowhere to be seen, presumably having been borrowed by someone for a gig. The ever-inventive drummer flipped over an acoustic guitar and played on the back of it; he's credited on the original album with playing "guitcongas." He also recorded with Grinderswitch and the Charlie Daniels Band. The latter were never signed to the label but regularly recorded in the studio.

Betts played on tracks by Grinderswitch, Bishop, and Captain Beyond, which featured former Second Coming guitarist Larry Reinhardt and Johnny Winter And drummer Bobby Caldwell, a regular Allman Brothers Band guest. Betts also contributed a beautiful, melodic guitar solo to the Marshall Tucker Band's "Searchin' for a Rainbow."

For all the activity in and around Capricorn Studios and Records, Walden's enterprises did not hold a monopoly on Southern talent. The other band that would make the biggest impact, both commercially and culturally, was Lynyrd Skynyrd, from Jacksonville, Florida. The group's core members, singer Ronnie Van Zant and guitarists Gary Rossington and Allen Collins, abandoned baseball and turned to music in eighth grade after seeing the Rolling Stones on the *Ed Sullivan Show.*

Lynyrd Skynyrd rose right under Walden's nose and was managed by his younger brother Alan. This sibling relationship, however, made the band less, not more, likely to sign with Capricorn. If Phil had been able to overcome it, his label may have been much better positioned to weather the Allman Brothers Band's impending ups and downs. The Walden brothers had an intense rivalry that stretched back to at least 1965, when Phil returned to the States after sixteen months of being stationed in Germany with the U.S. Army. While he was gone, Alan and their father, C.B., ran Phil Walden Artists and Promotions, booking Redding and other acts. Alan expected a partnership when his brother returned, but Phil viewed him only as a placeholder. They worked together off and on after that but had frequent arguments that sometimes became physical.

"The third day I was in Macon, Alan and Phil had a fistfight, after which Alan just disappeared into his house for an extended period," said Bunky Odom. "It was a volatile relationship, and no one could wade into the middle of it."

Alan left Capricorn in April 1970 to start Hustlers Inc., a publishing and management company with his partner, singer Eddie Floyd ("Knock on Wood"). Wanting to enter the rock world and aware of the strength of the Jacksonville music scene, Alan Walden sent a local contact to observe a battle of the bands and pick the best ones to audition for him. Skynyrd was the obvious best in class. They signed a management and publishing deal with Hustlers, which took a 30 percent cut of their gross income, twice the industry standard, as well as all the publishing rights. It was a very unfriendly deal even for the time, and the one person who realized this was Rossington's mother, Berniece, who had to sign for him since he was a minor, like most of his bandmates.

"She actually read the contract carefully and wouldn't sign it," said Rossington. "She said we were giving all our rights away and Alan would own everything we do. She didn't think that any of us should sign, but we just wanted to get out of Jacksonville and get more and better gigs, and this felt like our only shot. We didn't even know what publishing was. I begged her to sign and cried and whined for a few days until she did. A few years later when we realized he owned 'Free Bird' and 'Sweet Home Alabama' and were hating on Alan, she did say, 'I told you so.'"

After signing, Lynyrd Skynyrd quickly went to Muscle Shoals to record their first demos, learning how to work in a studio and cutting the first versions of songs that included "Free Bird," "Gimme Three Steps," and "One More Time." Despite this great material, they couldn't get a record deal.

At various times, Van Zant and Rossington would say that they turned down a Capricorn offer because they worried about being able to establish themselves in the shadow of the Allman Brothers Band. However, the Walden brothers' rivalry precluded their being on the label, whether the members knew it or not.

The band played in a Macon club, and Phil Walden attended along with some other Capricorn executives and several members of the Allman Brothers Band. After the first set, Phil made it clear to his brother that he wasn't interested, saying, "Your lead singer's too goddamn cocky, he can't sing, the songs are weak, and they sound too much like the Allman Brothers."

Though they clearly had their own sound and musical vision, the members of Lynyrd Skynyrd had been greatly impacted by Gregg and Duane Allman. Seeing the Allman Joys at Jacksonville's Beachcomber in 1967 made Van Zant, Rossington, and Collins commit to making music their lives. Rossington said that they realized that to even approach the "unbelievable" standards they saw required a full-time commitment.

Duane and Gregg Allman were so much better than everyone else on the club scene, he said, that the Skynyrd members were not surprised when they resurfaced two years later with the powerful, nascent Allman

Brothers Band, playing free jams in Jacksonville's Willow Brook Park—especially since they had also loved Betts's and Reinhardt's dual lead guitars in Second Coming. "It was like we were waiting for them to show up," said Rossington.

Despite that direct inspiration, Lynyrd Skynyrd's music is more influenced by the riffy British blues rock of Free, the Faces, and the Rolling Stones than the jazz-rock attack of the Allman Brothers Band. Van Zant wrote and sang country-tinged songs that were like short stories, tales of working-class protagonists who could have wandered in from a Merle Haggard or Johnny Cash song. With that powerful combination of British blues-rock crunch and country-style vocals, Lynyrd Skynyrd evinced a distinctive sound from their earliest demos, driven by excellent songwriting and arrangements, unique vocals, and great playing. Still, they couldn't get any real record company's attention until producer Al Kooper happened to see them during a weeklong engagement at Atlanta's Funochio's bar in 1972.

Kooper had an impressive knack for being at the center of rock and roll history. In 1965 alone, he bridged the music's past and future, cowriting "This Diamond Ring," a number 1 hit for Gary Lewis and the Playboys, and laying down the distinctive Hammond B3 organ on Bob Dylan's "Like a Rolling Stone," despite never having played the instrument. For an encore, Kooper backed Dylan at the singer's groundbreaking electric performance at the 1965 Newport Folk Festival. He also founded Blood, Sweat & Tears, helping bring horns to rock, and was a stage manager at the landmark 1967 Monterey Pop Festival. Kooper also produced and played on *Super Sessions* with Michael Bloomfield and Stephen Stills and recorded with greats such as Jimi Hendrix and the Rolling Stones—that's his piano and organ on "You Can't Always Get What You Want."

Kooper had come to Atlanta's suburban Studio One to record with the Atlanta Rhythm Section, old friends he had met on the touring circuit when they were backing Roy Orbison. Kooper was impressed with everything about the setup—and with Atlanta. He liked the overall vibe and ease of life compared to his native New York, and the abundance of fantastic, unsigned musical talent blew him away.

"I'd go out and see these great bands from Atlanta and other regional places every night and they were all unsigned," Kooper said. "Capricorn was the only label that understood something was happening in the South. If they turned a band down, they had nowhere else to turn and just kept playing clubs."

He recognized an opportunity and decided to move to the city and see what he could make of the thriving but untapped music scene. Kooper saw Lynyrd Skynyrd several nights in a row from his usual perch in the Funochio's VIP balcony. They were polished and ready to record, already playing their great songs expertly. Yet they did not have a label deal.

"Can you imagine walking into a funky little bar where you could get shot, hearing the Rolling Stones and finding out they weren't signed?" Kooper asked. "I couldn't believe it."

The band knew who Kooper was and was momentarily starstruck when he introduced himself. But when he got up to jam, Van Zant called for "Mean Woman Blues" in C sharp, which made Kooper laugh. "I understood that he was testing me—and I appreciated it," Kooper said. "If a guy can't play, they definitely can't play in C sharp, a key which no one ever jams in."

In the three months it took him to convince the band and Alan Walden to sign with him, Kooper's vision expanded from doing a production deal to starting a new label, Sounds of the South, with Skynyrd at the center. He convinced MCA to back his new venture, telling them, "I'd like to be the guy bands come to after Capricorn turns them down—because they turned Skynyrd down."

Fenter and Phil Walden acknowledged their first-mover advantage and the fact that they were sitting on a gold mine. Right around the time Skynyrd was releasing their first album, Fenter entertained Australian journalist Ritchie Yorke in his office, pointed to a foot-high stack of submitted demo cassettes, and said, "That's a week's load of new Southern talent." They were not, he assured, concerned about competition. "Phil and I aren't worried about the major labels moving into Atlanta or Macon," Fenter insisted. "They're welcome to join us."

Kooper was at the head of this second wave of music industry veterans ready to tap the overflowing Southern talent. He signed his own deal with MCA, and then signed Skynyrd to his new Sounds of the South record imprint, a deal Alan Walden would eventually call "the biggest piece of shit" he had ever seen. The producer and label head would get 10 percentage points of sales, while the band got five to divide among members. Walden said that he told this to Van Zant, warning him it was an onerous deal, "worse than any R&B contract" he had ever seen. When the singer asked what the other options were—knowing the answer was "none"—his simple retort was, "Give me the Goddamn pen." The band signed their contracts on the hood of Walden's 1974 Ford pickup truck in the parking lot of the Macon Coliseum.

"We didn't have nowhere else to go," Walden said. "We had been fighting this thing for three years, trying to hold onto it."

The band also gave Kooper some latitude because he had fronted them $5,000 when their gear was stolen, leaving them temporarily unable to work. Kooper said that Van Zant told him then, "Al, you just bought yourself a band for $5,000." Once they were signed, the producer promptly got to work prepping Lynyrd Skynyrd for the studio—which didn't require much work at all.

"Skynyrd was ready to record, with all of their songs extremely well arranged," Kooper said. "One of the great things about them is that they had no improvisation whatsoever. All the guitar solos were composed, as was every background part. The jamming that the Allman Brothers did bothered me. It was just enough already! Skynyrd wrote great songs and had great arrangements that they could always replicate."

The precision with which they composed their guitar solos allowed Kooper to use a simple but very effective studio trick of doubling their guitar parts. In a contemporary digital recording setting, this can now be done by just laying together multiple tracks of a single part, but Kooper did it on tape the old-fashioned way: by having them play each solo twice and mixing them together. Any slight variation in note or rhythmic placement would be immediately apparent, but this was not a problem. Skynyrd was that tight.

"I could add a lot of heft to the sound with the doubling because they played the solos exactly the same every time," Kooper said. "It was a good idea, but it wasn't challenging with them at all."

Rossington agrees. "We doubled each other's parts all the time and worked them out meticulously in hours of rehearsal every day sitting in chairs looking each other in the eyes and playing together," he said. "It wasn't a big stretch to do that in the studio and to add the idea of doubling our own parts as well."

The band's maturity and readiness to record also made them prepared to stand up to their famous producer, most notably over "Simple Man," which Kooper did not want to include on the album, because he thought it did not fit. "We just ignored Al and when he wasn't around, we cut it alone with our engineer," said Rossington.

"We cut the whole tune without him," guitarist Ed King added. "When a band knows what it wants to do, it has to go with its heart and not listen to people on the outside."

Working together, Kooper and Skynyrd quickly crafted a polished, hard-hitting debut album. The producer played bass, sang harmony, and used a Mellotron to add an orchestral feel to "Tuesday's Gone." His work throughout the album helped the band create a sound that was uniquely balanced—simultaneously raw and polished. Skynyrd's songs were hard-hitting riff rockers, with swamp-blues influences and Van Zant's powerful presence and down-to-earth lyrics and vocals that carried the outlaw-country influence of Haggard, Cash, and Jennings.

When the band refused to change their name despite entreaties from Kooper and MCA, who were certain that no one would have any idea how to pronounce it, the label solved the problem by titling the debut *Pronounced Leh-nerd Skin-nerd*.

MCA launched Sounds of the South with a party at Richard's, Atlanta's top rock club, on July 29, 1973, the day after the Summer Jam at Watkins Glen. It was a Sunday, when local blue laws prohibited the sale of alcohol. Contending that it did not apply to a private party, the club secured a restraining order stopping the police and city attorney's office from interfering with the free-flowing booze. MCA flew label officials and press down from New York City for the event, which featured performances by Mose Jones and Lynyrd Skynyrd, two of Kooper's three signed bands. Displaying bravado, Skynyrd opened their performance with "Workin' for MCA," which Van Zant and King had written specifically for the occasion. The song stuck its thumb in the eye of their new label heads and playfully caricatured Kooper as a "Yankee slicker."

Kooper, a Jewish native of Queens, New York, played a huge role in setting the template for not only the band but also the entire emerging southern rock genre. He did this musically with Skynyrd's aggressive, harmonized guitars and swagger and culturally with the Sounds of the South name and its log cabin logo, which evoked a rustic, rural aesthetic.

Kooper also helped establish Skynyrd's rowdy image by designing a skull and crossbones logo, to which an MCA art director eventually added a rebel-flag bandanna. The label invested $100,000 in a Who Is Lynyrd Skynyrd? marketing campaign to launch the album. "No one would have ever heard of Lynyrd Skynyrd if it hadn't been for Al," said King.

Lynyrd Skynyrd's debut was released on August 13, 1973, the same week as *Brothers and Sisters,* and became a slow-burn success, going gold more than a year after its release. The band's take-no-prisoners live shows fueled its growing popularity, as did an extended run opening for the Who on its *Quadrophenia* tour. Their performances impressed not only the audience—who gave them standing ovations, rare for an unknown opening act—but the members of the Who themselves. Backstage at one show, Cameron Crowe reported, guitarist Pete Townshend stopped talking midconversation, listened to Skynyrd's set-closing "Free Bird," and observed, "They're really quite good, aren't they?"

THE BAND THAT toured behind the debut album was not the same exact one who recorded it. Just as they were about to enter the studio, bassist Leon Wilkeson, a devout Christian, panicked and quit the band. In need of an immediate replacement, Van Zant called Ed King, a founding member of Strawberry Alarm Clock, a 1960s psychedelic band with a single hit, "Incense and Peppermints," for which Skynyrd had opened on their first national tour.

King played bass on Skynyrd's first album, but Wilkeson returned immediately after the recording, and King, an accomplished guitarist, switched instruments. This allowed the band to duplicate the album's multiple guitar tracks when performing live. It wasn't planned, but Skynyrd's new three-guitar lineup became the next unique attribute of southern rock; if two lead guitars are good, three must be better.

Many of their imitators would abuse the three-guitar lineup by overplaying, but Skynyrd largely avoided overkill by continuing their practice of meticulously crafting their parts. The band's three guitarists used various methods to complement rather than crowd one another, playing harmony lines, arpeggiated chords, and complementary fills, and even sharing solos by trading bars.

"You just have to know how and when to stay out of each other's way," Rossington said. "We've always tried to work out our parts to prevent chaos, but we had to learn that. When Ed first started playing with us, we didn't know what to do and were all playing the same thing, but we worked really hard to figure it out until it became natural to us."

There was an immediate payoff to King's switching instruments: he wrote the riff to "Sweet Home Alabama" on his very first day as a Lynyrd Skynyrd guitarist. They were rehearsing at Hell House, the isolated, unair-conditioned one-room cabin in the woods outside Jacksonville where they put in long, regimented days of rehearsal and wrote most of their songs.

"We'd practice from about 8:30 in the morning 'til sundown," King said. "We did that every day and one of us would have to spend the night in that hot, nasty place because one time somebody stole some amps. We wrote new songs every day and threw half of them away. The ones we kept, we just played over and over until we knew them cold."

On that first day as a three-guitar band, Rossington came up with a simple but evocative, fingerpicked D-C-G progression—the root of countless folk and rock songs. Feeling like he was onto something, he kept playing the syncopated progression repeatedly. "Gary had been playing his riff for 15 minutes when I started throwing ideas in to bounce off of what he was doing," King said. "That was what you know as the 'Sweet Home Alabama' riff, and when Ronnie heard it, he locked in and wrote the words. That sort of sums up why I had to switch to guitar, really: I can write songs, but not on bass."

Rossington said that Van Zant completed the lyrics in an hour. They all knew they had struck gold with what King termed a "three-way collaboration." Rossington's picking inspired his riff, which inspired Van Zant's lyrics. The rest happened instantaneously. "I knew 'Sweet Home Alabama' was a classic the minute we wrote it," King said. "We all did. Ronnie turned to me and said, 'This is our Ramblin' Man.'"

They recorded the song in the summer of 1973, around the time their first album was released. It would be a year before "Sweet Home Alabama" would see the light of day on the band's follow-up, *Second Helping*. By then, they had bought out Alan Walden for a reported $250,000 and signed with the Who's manager, Peter Rudge, who also was part of the Rolling Stones' management.

"Rudge took note of the reaction they were drawing from the Who's crowd," said artist manager Charlie Brusco. "The guys in Skynyrd saw themselves as following in the footsteps of the Allman Brothers but Peter was looking for them to be an American-born-and-bred English band. He always saw them as more in the tradition of the Who or Thin Lizzy."

With their British-inspired guitar crunch—Rossington's North Star was Free guitarist Paul Kossoff—and Van Zant's country tinge and Southern swagger, Lynyrd Skynyrd was about to become both international superstars and avatars of a southern rock movement that traded on some very parochial and divisive cultural imagery.

21

SOUTHERN BLOOD

BY 1974, SOUTHERN rock was an established musical genre, fueled by the success of Lynyrd Skynyrd, the Marshall Tucker Band, and, of course, the Allman Brothers Band, who started it all but hated the label.

John Swenson, writing in *Crawdaddy*, summed up the situation and the inevitability of record labels and promoters glomming onto a naturally occurring scene and looking to label, pigeonhole, and market it: "The music industry is notorious for milking trends. Witness . . . 'the Liverpool sound,' 'the San Francisco sound,' 'the Detroit sound,' 'the Philadelphia sound,' not to mention 'folk rock,' 'acid rock' and 'glitter rock.' The corporate minds have outdone themselves in merchandising Southern music."

The runaway success of "Sweet Home Alabama"—with its clapback at Neil Young's poignant criticism of Southern racism in "Southern Man" and "Alabama"—drew more attention to the idea of a regional music genre. Rossington insists the "beef" with Young was all good-natured, and he's almost certainly being forthright about how the band viewed things. That's how Young himself took it, saying he was proud to have his name in a song by them. The singer in fact wanted Skynyrd to record some of his songs, passing demos of "Powderfinger," "Captain Kennedy," and "Special Delivery" on to them via Cameron Crowe, who said that "Neil loved the band and said they reminded him of Buffalo Springfield."

The song's Neil Young reference may have been tongue-in-cheek, but it was harder to justify the apparent defense of former Alabama governor

George Wallace. Wallace had been an archsegregationist as governor and ran for president several times, including in 1968, when he ran on the American Independent Party ticket, receiving ten million votes and winning five Southern states. In 1972, he won the Democratic presidential primary in Skynyrd's home state of Florida, capturing nearly 42 percent of the vote and taking all of the state's counties with the exception of Miami-Dade. (The father of Allman Brothers crew member Kim Payne was an officer in the Alabama State Police who served on Wallace's gubernatorial security team.)

The band members always insisted that the lyrics were not supporting Wallace, pointing to the "Boo boo boo" the background singers sing as an answer to Van Zant's "in Birmingham, they love the governor." "Ronnie was absolutely not political, and he was definitely not a Wallace supporter," says his friend Charlie Brusco.

When MCA started using the Confederate flag to promote Lynyrd Skynyrd's debut, the band didn't think much about it either way, according to tour manager Gene Odom (no relation to Bunky). Before long, however, Skynyrd embraced the flag, using it as a stage backdrop for decades. They also pushed the southern identity ever further, as it became a core part of their identity in a way that it never quite was for the Allman Brothers Band.

Still, they too, used the flag, a legacy its members have distanced themselves from over the years. Though they didn't like to be called southern rock, neither did they run away from the genre or its tropes as they were first gaining traction, despite having two Black members. Whether or not the ideas were theirs or those of someone in the music business, the band played along. Their 1974 tour was dubbed a Summer Campaign and its promotion used graphics of General Robert E. Lee on horseback and, for the first and last time in the band's history, the Confederate flag.

"We now realize that these are symbols we don't need to be promoting," said Leavell. "I don't remember it ever being brought up or thought about. It was more like we leave the poster art and T-shirts to others and we play the gigs."

Gregg Allman eventually expressed intense regret over using the flag, and took his views further, stating that no one should fly it. "I was taught how to play music by these very, very kind older black men," he said in 2015. "My best friend in the world [Chank Middleton] is a black man. If people are gonna look at that flag and think of it as representing slavery, then I say burn every one of them."

It's certainly true that cultural mores and awareness of the pain and divisiveness of Confederate imagery have changed over the years. As late as 1985, Tom Petty used the Confederate flag onstage for his *Southern Accents* tour and highlighted it by including an image of the giant backdrop behind the band on the centerfold of the live album *Pack Up the Plantation*. He ultimately apologized, expressing regret for these decisions. "I wish I had given it more thought," Petty said. "It was a downright stupid thing to do."

A decade earlier, Walden and the Allman Brothers Band had proudly and loudly supported Jimmy Carter for president, in large part to promote the "new" South and a more modern Southern man, even while using some of the most retrograde symbols of the old South. Some contemporaries noticed this dichotomy. Rick Brown of *The Great Speckled Bird*, the underground Atlanta newspaper, questioned the band's use of the flag in their promotions: "I'm wondering what the Black men in the band are feeling when they see the current promotional ad that featured a confederate flag complete with a confederate general on horseback riding to the glory of the old South," he observed. "Maybe they laugh all the way to the bank. Maybe they don't like it."

So, what did they think?

"We didn't give a shit about none of that," Jaimoe said. "Nobody was fucking with us, and we didn't really give it no never mind. The music was the dominant force for us and, as far as we were concerned, for the people coming to our shows, too."

Still, Williams often wore a jean jacket with a prominent Black Power patch. Lamar Williams Jr. describes his father and Jaimoe as "rebels of their own deep call."

"They were confident Black men walking in a world of whiteness," he said.

The first and last time the Allman Brothers Band and the original Lynyrd Skynyrd played together was on June 1, 1974. It was the second show of the Allman Brothers Band's Summer Campaign tour, and they headlined the Georgia Jam held at Atlanta–Fulton County Stadium, which also featured Grinderswitch and the Marshall Tucker Band. They were kicking off their last giant tour as one of the most popular bands in the country, packing stadiums and selling out multiple nights at arenas like the Nassau Coliseum and Boston Garden.

In July, they'd also make a rare trip to Europe for just two shows, in the Netherlands and England, where they headlined the first Knebworth Festival, topping a bill that also featured Van Morrison, the Doobie Brothers, the Mahavishnu Orchestra, and Gregg's old friend Tim Buckley. A twelve-show European run with the Marshall Tucker Band set for January and February had been canceled partly because spiking fuel prices in the face of an OPEC oil embargo made profits look impossible, as well as a general feeling that everything was too unstable to mount such an effort. The Allman Brothers Band never put in the time and effort to establish themselves in Europe, but they were certainly thriving back home.

More than sixty thousand fans filled the same Atlanta stadium where the Braves' Hank Aaron had broken Babe Ruth's major league baseball home run record on April 8, with Governor Carter in attendance. Aaron was subjected to vicious racism and received thousands of pieces of hate mail during the run-up to breaking Ruth's record. The threats were deemed real enough that his family received FBI protection—another reminder of the tense, hate-filled atmosphere within which bands were flying the Confederate flag.

The huge crowd on June 1 was there for a lengthy celebration of the exploding southern rock scene and roared their approval through the long, steamy day, despite rain showers on an uncovered stage that could have derailed the whole thing. After an excellent day of music by the openers, the headlining Allman Brothers Band were having problems just taking the stage for their second show after a five-month break.

Gregg arrived at the gig with someone no one else knew and whose name no one remembers. "Gregg would take these souls in and have a new best buddy who would come out on the road for a while and then disappear," Perkins said. "They were usually women but occasionally it was a guy, and that was the case that day in Atlanta."

The new friend, a bass player, was a heavyset man from Tennessee. He apparently arrived with the brilliant plan to audition for the bass role in the Allman Brothers Band in front of a packed stadium of drunk, sweaty, rain-soaked fans. He would do this by knocking Lamar Williams out of action, leaving him to ride to the rescue and play the show, making himself both the problem and the solution.

To accomplish this, he presented animal tranquilizer to Williams as heroin. Gregg walked into the room just as the Tennessee man cut some lines, and both he and Lamar had a taste. This wannabe bassist had effectively knocked out a third of the band because "he was after Lamar's gig," Allman explained. With Allman and Williams knocked out of commission, Willie Perkins and Twiggs Lyndon rushed to get medical help.

"They had all these trauma people for the show because they were anticipating a lot of drug overdoses, but they didn't know it was going to be the headliners," Perkins said. "Lamar was so far out that they'd hold up two fingers and he'd see 10."

"If we hadn't gotten him to a doctor, shit, Lamar could have died," Allman said. "I sure thought I was dying. Only reason I went on stage: I figured if I was going to die, I wanted to do it on my ax."

A weather delay benefited the Allman Brothers, who took the stage at 10 PM, needing every extra minute to figure out how they were going to perform. In desperate need of a bassist, the Allman Brothers Band turned not to the troublesome stranger but to reliable old friend Joe Dan Petty, who had left the crew and was now playing bass with Grinderswitch, the day's opening band.

"Joe Dan did a more than adequate job—he was terrific," said Leavell. "He had some chops."

Perkins, the nervous road manager, stood on the side of the stage hoping the band could simply get through the set and thus complete their obligation and collect their approximately $200,000 fee, one of their biggest paydays to that date. He looked out and saw a *Rolling Stone* reporter in the front row furiously taking notes and thought to himself, "My God, this is going to be awful."

A month later, he was surprised to read a positive review, which described a "45-minute first set with slow, precise, bluesy jamming from the band's first two albums." The band's set list had been altered to stick closer to the material Petty knew best, rather than the *Brothers and Sisters* tracks that they usually played. Reviewer Art Harris thought that the band was "fatigued from the wait"—if only he knew the truth!—and didn't seem to notice that after a twenty-minute break, Williams was back on bass. They played a forty-minute second set that leaned heavily on *Brothers and Sisters,* closing the show with an encore of "Ramblin' Man."

Though the band was white-knuckling it, essentially just happy to get through the show, it was received as a triumphant home-turf performance. "It was so tense backstage and onstage as the band came out," said A. J. Lyndon. "We were anticipating a disaster and that the crowd would be bummed out, but they were all high on music and happy."

Local coverage focused on the massive success of the event and the love shown for the Allman Brothers Band, with scant mention of the other acts who performed. "No other American band could have drawn so many people to Atlanta Stadium as turned out for the Allmans and there is considerable doubt that any of the legendary British bands—the Rolling Stones or The Who—could have done as well either," Scott Cain wrote in the *Atlanta Constitution.* The massive event, he said, "was a far cry from when the Allmans performed for free in Piedmont Park" five years earlier.

The paper primarily focused on the concert's size and success: the official crowd of 61,232 was the biggest ever for an Atlanta–Fulton County Stadium event, while the box office take was "the largest of any concert ever held in the South." The concessionaire reported that the day marked the most money ever generated in food and beverage sales, despite not selling beer since it was estimated that half the crowd was underage. No one doubted the no-booze wisdom in a stadium that sold 119,675 Coca-Colas, 16,000 hamburgers, 37,783 hot dogs, 10,362 servings of ice cream, and 12,574 popcorn boxes.

Regardless of the coverage, the band and their inner circle knew it was not a great performance and that they had dodged a bullet. "I think Lynyrd Skynyrd earned a lot of fans that day," said Bunky Odom. "They put on a great show, while the Allman Brothers Band was lucky to finish!"

Some news outlets also noticed the slippage. Even before that show, there were rumblings in the underground press that the Allman Brothers

Band was starting to show signs of stagnation. In a preview of the Georgia Jam, *The Great Speckled Bird*, which had been supportive of the band since they started performing free shows in Piedmont Park in May 1969, noted that "lately there have been a few murmurs about that Allman magic fading." In it, Rick Brown quoted R. Spangler of the *New Orleans Courier*, who described a recent show as lacking "spontaneity in a medium which depends so much on spontaneity and improvisation."

Those publications, which had been paying close attention to the group from its inception, were keyed into some important and unfortunate changes. As time marched forward, all of the challenges that the Allman Brothers Band had confronted in the past four years, including the deaths of original members, substance abuse, and strained relationships, increasingly took their toll.

22

TALES OF ORDINARY MADNESS

THE CHALLENGES MOUNTED, and the musical highs became less frequent as the years went on. There were fewer incandescent moments in 1974 than there had been in 1973, when the band was consistently hitting the note. Substance abuse and rivalries spurred rough nights, but so did an inescapable feeling among the musicians that they were chasing after the elusive magic of the original band, which many had called the greatest in the land.

"The music always had its moments, even in our worst years," Trucks said. "In spite of everything else, something magic always happened when we all were of one mind and decided to play. But there were too many nights when we didn't do that because one of us was going through a tough time or was too drunk—that was me or Gregg or Dickey, because Chuck was straight as a board, and Jaimoe and Lamar rarely had problems. The cocaine and drinking became a vicious, self-defeating circle."

Trucks himself readily admitted to "spending three years drunk," but pointed out that it rarely impacted his performances, since he did his heavy drinking after shows. Allman suffered mightily with alcohol and drug abuse, turning inward, hiding from his bandmates and the audience behind a four-hundred-pound piece of furniture, his Hammond B3. Also, no matter how much turmoil he had or how far down a hole he fell, music and the stage were consistently his ports of calm. There are countless stories of Gregg being unable to walk to the stage on his own, half-collapsed, arms around the shoulders of friends or handlers, only to sit down and perform beautifully.

"He transformed when he got onstage," said A. J. Lyndon. "It was just unbelievable. He was a consummate performer who was generally at his best onstage regardless of what was happening in his life."

Gregg never shied away from discussing the role the shows played in his life: he played "for peace of mind." He lived to play and played to live. "It's not that I need to get up in front of people," he explained. "If that were so, I wouldn't be hidden behind an organ. I'd have a guitar, or I'd be standing there with a microphone in my hand shaking my ass . . . but that's not my satchel at all. You've never seen anything funnier in your life than me trying to sing with a microphone. I tried it some with the Hour Glass and it was terrible."

But while Allman became ever more introverted when he was in bad shape, seeming to crawl inside himself, and Trucks was at the back of the stage and playing with a partner on the same instrument, Betts was front and center. He was the band's sole guitarist, a frequent singer, and the musical and visual focus of every performance. He could make the shows, and he could break them.

"If something went wrong—he couldn't get his guitar in tune, the sound was bad, something was off—Dickey would get so upset, so damn intense, that he could not play," Trucks said. "He'd get in this funk and he couldn't get himself out. He'd know we were counting on him and that the crowd was there and get down on himself—mad at *himself,* not at others—and it would be really difficult to do anything."

Trucks believed that this problem was intensified by the "omnipotent feeling" that comes with great success and crowds chanting your name. "In Dickey's case, that sometimes meant playing three licks then climbing behind an amp and sitting there all night or giving up after playing a few bad notes," Trucks said. "He'd get bummed out and quit, and he was too damn an important part of the show to be able to pull that off."

Betts's rage was almost always triggered by cocaine and alcohol, which could turn him from pleasant, engaged, and friendly into frighteningly violent on a moment's notice. "He's so bright but chemicals give him a problem," Phil Walden said. "They turn him into this redneck guy who he really isn't."

The guitarist would vanish into a fog for several nights in a row, leaving the band in a precarious position, with everyone trying to cover for the giant hole at center stage. Then he would snap out of his funk and play like the greatest guitarist in the world—which he arguably was in this era. When he was on top of his game, Dickey's playing was breathtaking, covering the wide gamut of his experiences and skills, from blues to country to "Django Reinhardt on acid," in the words of Warren Haynes. On those nights, Betts would take audiences for a ride, locked into the rhythm section, buoyed by Gregg's organ, and in constant conversation with Leavell's piano.

Betts himself beautifully described the experience of being lost in the music to writer Tom Nolan. "The energy level on that stage, the intensity of concentration, is so heavy that in the midst of something like that you can look at a guy and tell what he is thinking," he said. "If you see one dude who keeps thinking a bad thought you pull him aside and say, 'Come on man, forget that bullshit. Let's get on up and get over there and do something nobody else can do.' And we do it. When that music starts happening, mister, there's some real power there. And it don't have nothing to do with how you comb your hair or what you wear. It has to do with how much you can get with whoever you're with on that stage, with how much you love and understand them. . . . No smoke bombs. No glitter. Just guitars, pianos, voices. It's just a real human thing."

But the weight of the bad nights was challenging for a band battling other problems, including Trucks's own increasing alcohol consumption. In Mobile, Alabama, with a night off before an August 24, 1974, show at Ladd Memorial Stadium, Trucks was stewing in his hotel room, thinking that he "couldn't play one more show like that." He heard that Betts was in the hotel bar "drunk and raising hell" and decided the time had come to confront the guitarist and see what was bugging him. Maybe a confrontation could help snap Betts out of his deepening hole, but it would probably also cause him to lash out violently. Trucks said:

> I knew it could get rough and I ain't much of a fighter, so I drank a fifth of Jack Daniel's first. Then I went down to the bar and hauled off and slapped Dickey. He said, "That make you feel better?" and I

said, "Yeah, and I'm gonna do it again." Finally, after about five times, he had enough, jumped up and beat the shit out of me. He broke my nose, cracked three ribs, and knocked out a tooth. Scooter [Herring] jumped in and tried to end it, and Dickey knocked him down, and then he snapped out of it, and we said, "Let's sit down and talk."

When I asked for a drink, the bartender said, "Sorry we're closed," so I said, "The hell you are" and went behind the bar and poured us drinks and brought them back out. Dickey and I were sitting there having a drink and talking things out, and the police came in to take us to the drunk tank. Dickey said, "Fine. Please just put us in the same car." He wanted to talk, which we both knew we had to do.

But they put us in different cars, and I saw the other one rocking and jumping. He was kicking the doors out. They put us in a cell together. I was beat to shit and started crying, and we started talking and I told him what an asshole he was being, so he kicked my ass again. He was sitting there, and I was walking toward him, laying it on about how he was dragging the band down. He finally said, "Don't take another step." I did, and he kicked me in the ribs and came across my face before I could cover up. I never saw anyone do anything so fast in my life. I finally told myself to sit down. I was now sober enough to realize I better shut up before I got killed.

There was a guy laying there pretending to be asleep the whole time and when we were leaving, he said to Dickey, "You think you're pretty tough, don't you?" So Dickey kicked the shit out of him, too.

The next night Dickey got up there and played one of the best shows he'd played in years. I looked like Quasimodo, lips all swollen and everything, but he played his ass off. It just smoked. Walking off the stage, Rose Lane said to Chuck, "If that's what it takes to get him to play like that, you fight him next time." And that pulled Dickey out. I found out later that he found out some real bad stuff going on and he wouldn't talk about it. He holds it in and gets really depressed and he can't play, and it took something like that to snap him out of it.

Years later, Trucks admitted that he was probably blowing the frequency of bad nights out of proportion, that as rough as they could be, there weren't really that many of them. Most of the group's performances ranged from professionally competent to downright inspired, but when things went awry, they went totally off the rails. The performance would be not just flat but teetering on chaos. These nights were infrequent, Trucks conceded, but the problem was that he was comparing every show to June 26, 1971, the next-to-last night at the Fillmore East, which the band and everyone in attendance considered their finest performance ever. They were chasing a glowing, flickering, mythical memory of a golden moment.

Duplicating the magic of that performance was an elusive, even unachievable, goal. But its power resonated forever within all the four surviving original band members, an eternal flame that reminded them of how much they had lost, no matter what they achieved. From the minute Duane died, the band, and Trucks in particular, was chasing a ghost. From the moment of Oakley's death until his own passing on January 24, 2017, Trucks was Duane's greatest disciple.

"That night at the Fillmore we had that complete and total communication where you finish playing and the audience doesn't even applaud because they're stunned," Trucks said. "That level of religiousness—it was talking to God. Us and those people in front of us were the whole world. We were one of those lucky groups that had at least one moment like that, and we never quite got it again. That's what I was always chasing."

Jaimoe, too, grappled with the loss of special feeling, of levitation, that drove his percussion partner to such distraction, but he did it in a calmer, more philosophical manner. "The music is still spiritual, but in the beginning, it was even more spiritual," he said in 1975. "Several times I was so at peace with what I was playing that my spirit left my body, right on stage. That's a fact. Since Duane and B.O. have gone on, I have never experienced this while playing."

It was hard for the drummers to accept that the band they had believed in so much was no longer giving them that same thrill. And it was often baffling to experience so much success and, at the same time, to not feel inspired by the music in the way they had just a few short years ago.

"We more and more got away from that intense communication, talking to each other on stage," Trucks said. "I missed it because I loved that. After Duane died, we just slowly got away from that and it broke my heart."

The music suffered, with solos sometimes becoming self-indulgent and not being locked into the flow of the song or paying much attention to the other musicians. Group improvisation, the band's identity, which contributed tremendously to its uniqueness and success, no longer always ruled. "It got to where we all had to watch the length of our solos," said Leavell. "We were playing forty-minute versions of 'Les Brers,' and everyone was pointing a finger at one another as the music sometimes meandered around."

Even as they struggled to reclaim their past glories and enjoy their moment in the spotlight, the band's approach to performance was subtly but persistently shifting. Betts at times was vocal that Leavell was taking them too far in a jazz-fusion direction, changes Jaimoe and Gregg viewed as being a natural growth of a change in personnel. "Chuck did change the band," Gregg said. "We got more jazz going into it with him and Lamar."

Jaimoe welcomed the jazz flow and resented Betts's objections. "Dickey said Chuck took us too far into jazz but, shit, I thought it was cool!" Jaimoe said. "Chuck picked up stuff from everyone, including Mac [Dr. John], and introduced it into what we were doing, and it was fantastic. You don't change direction—you grow."

The band's conflict should be viewed holistically rather than parsed for the details of each member's complaints. The primary issue was that differences had emerged among the original members about the band's approach to live performance—which had always been its very reason for being. Tension flared around a fundamental, existential issue, whereas before there had been none. They had been known as one of rock's greatest performing bands, and it was a live album that elevated them to royalty status.

Betts's playing and singing were blossoming, but in ways that weren't always conducive to group improvisation and freedom. To sound their best, they often had to follow his lead, and a similar dynamic crept into Allman-led songs. This was profoundly different from the way the Duane-led band approached any song.

Jaimoe said that the group had become more traditional in the way they played around the singers instead of flowing together in an improvisational groove. "We had to play in a way that . . . didn't get in the way of what Dickey and Gregg wanted to do," he said.

The terrifying fight between Betts and Trucks revealed just how precarious the state of the band really was, and that a pause was in order. They played one more show after the fight, then would not play together as a band again for almost exactly a year. Rumors swirled that the group's increasing tensions meant that they might never reconvene, but the band members denied any impending breakup.

"You have all kinds of disagreements with your brothers and sisters and parents," Jaimoe said. "Does that mean you love them less?"

Everyone knew they needed a break from each other. Maybe some time off would help them recharge and create the musical magic one more time. In addition to the deaths and substance abuse that everyone acknowledged contributed to the outlandish behavior and musical inconsistency, exhaustion also had to be a major contributor to both the personal and musical decline.

IT WASN'T JUST the band that was out of control. With greater success feeding his delusions of grandeur, Walden was growing increasingly temperamental. Everyone working with him constantly walked on eggshells. Odom worked hard with Bill Graham and Crosby Stills, Nash, and Young manager Elliot Roberts to set up two shows at the hundred-thousand-seat Los Angeles Coliseum in the summer of 1974, alternating opening and closing slots between the two bands.

CSNY were reuniting for their first tour in four years and performing with them would have guaranteed the Allmans massive shows with large paydays, vast coverage, and serious cultural currency. It would also have been a huge help in better establishing the band on the West Coast, where they had never quite taken hold. When Odom called Walden to triumphantly inform him of the agreement, the manager demanded that the Allman Brothers Band close both shows.

"I told Phil that was not a fucking possibility, but he would not listen to me, so I had to pull out of the shows," said Odom. "That's the way he was sometimes; he was larger than the band."

As Trucks said, "Phil's attitude cost us all."

Years later, Bill Graham grew livid discussing these canceled shows and this aspect of Walden's approach, which he believed had caused irreparable harm to the Allman Brothers Band, a group he revered. "We tried to do giant shows with them where they would have made huge money," Graham said. He said that the guaranteed money could have been as high as $400,000 (approximately $2.4 million in 2023), with a chance to reach half a million dollars, but that wasn't good enough for Walden. The manager wanted a guaranteed five hundred thousand, period, no negotiations, which enraged Graham.

"What does he think I am? A little prick? It might rain. Anything could happen," Graham said. The guaranteed money, he said, was based on selling sixty thousand tickets, which he was confident about, but Walden was insisting on money based on selling eighty thousand, and the promoter, himself a famously tough negotiator, wouldn't budge. "The end result," he said, "is they didn't play, because he thought I'd give it to him sooner or later, which was just wrong."

Graham became even angrier when Walden passed his intransigence off on the band's own demands. "He'd say, 'Well, the boys want bigger,'" Graham said. "No, they don't. You who are representing them want bigger. They missed out on too many things because of this. They would have been better represented by a less smart person who thought of 'we' instead of 'me.' They could have been on TV shows, and management said their name has to be bigger. Why? Once you play, who gives a fuck how big your name is? The music is big."

The music of the Allman Brothers Band could have done the work for them, Graham insisted. But it had to be given a chance. He always felt that Walden and Capricorn took advantage of the Allman Brothers Band, and it always bothered him. "One problem with the Allman Brothers is they trusted people who knowingly messed with them and they paid a big price for it," he said. "They were seemingly good people who made people feel good. How could you betray them? You're a negative manipulator of decent people."

Graham acknowledged that the band members were adults who should have known better, but he felt that they believed that their job was to make music and they "trusted someone to take care of the rest. You're the manager and you deal in that world. This is what you do. They didn't know and couldn't know that tough street world of buy and sell, supply and demand.

They knew how to make people feel good and put their trust in someone else to take care of things."

Graham did not just mutter under his breath about Walden or merely complain about him to others. He took his feelings directly to the man himself. Graham began a lengthy telegram, sent to Walden on August 20, 1975, with these words:

> *I should like you to accept this telegram as a vehement protest regarding the prohibitive demands being made by the Paragon Agency on behalf of the Allman Brothers Band. Rather than go into detail, consider all the facts and then tell me that I am wrong in feeling so vehemently about what I consider to be a despicable display of disrespect and disregard for the professional producers.*

WITH THE ALLMAN Brothers Band taking a break from touring, and Betts's interest in the North American Indian Foundation flagging, Massarsky began to think that it didn't make sense to keep it active. Perkins estimates that they had distributed close to $200,000 to various Native entities on the strength of several benefit shows. The last was at the Boston Garden on July 26, 1974, which also featured the Eagles. Native American actor Chief Dan George (*Little Big Man* and *The Outlaw Josey Wales*) spoke between the two bands' sets.

"The money was being burned in overhead, which is common, but not something I wanted to do," Massarsky said. "I made a motion to shut the thing down and keep it alive on paper, in case someone did a benefit, but we weren't going to pay people to sit in an office and organize benefits."

Everyone agreed to disband the board in a meeting at Dickey's house on the farm. Once that happened, Walden tossed Massarsky aside as well.

"I eventually realized that the band had gotten to the point where they didn't want to do a lot of shows," Massarsky said. "So every time they would say to Phil, 'We're not ready to work,' Phil would say, 'Let's do an Indian benefit.'"

Once the band agreed to do a benefit, Walden would point out that it didn't make sense to do a single show, so they may as well do ten. This kept everyone happy, Dickey very engaged, and the band performing.

Now, with touring on hold, Walden promptly stopped paying Massarsky's law school tuition at Mercer, reneging on their previous deal, according to which Massarsky would stay in Macon rather than earn his law degree at Rutgers. A year later, Walden refused to even discuss why he had ended the tuition payments.

"Phil didn't need me anymore," Massarsky recalled. "There was no foundation, and I had no tuition. Every way he could screw me, he did."

Massarsky remained patient and insistent, and when Walden finally handed him a check to cover tuition, the disillusioned law student questioned how Walden could screw him over so badly. He asked what it might mean for their future relationship, and Walden shrugged.

"He said if he needs me again, he'd pay me more money than anyone else would and I would return," Massarsky recalled. "It was all money with Phil."

The lessons Massarsky took from his experience in dealing with Walden played a significant role in later years, when he became the lawyer and manager for first Betts and then the band. Working for his clients, he went after Walden and Capricorn for money due from unpaid royalties and other financial irregularities resulting from Walden's multiple conflicts of interest as an executive with other companies that did business with the band. Phil would come to regret the way he had treated Massarsky.

23

HIGHWAY CALL

NINETEEN SEVENTY-FOUR WAS the first calendar year since the Allman Brothers Band's formation that they did not record as a band. Both Betts and Allman were busy with their solo projects. Capricorn released Betts's *Highway Call* on August 7, 1974. The album rose to number 19. That fall, Gregg launched his second solo tour behind the double-live album *Gregg Allman Tour '74*, which peaked at number 50. This outing was scaled back, without the orchestra.

As the Allman Brothers–inspired southern rock genre became increasingly successful, Betts and Allman were steadfastly exploring their own distinctly less commercial musical visions: lush, orchestrated soul music for Allman and western swing for Betts. Neither was as well suited for Saturday-night beer drinking and hell-raising as Skynyrd or ZZ Top, the Texas trio whose 1973 debut album, *Tres Hombres,* included the boogie classic "La Grange."

Capricorn released a second Duane Allman anthology, comprised mostly of his session work, on the same day as *Highway Call,* a shortsighted decision bordering on cruel. Even three years after Allman's death, Betts couldn't quite escape his partner's shadow. *Rolling Stone* reviewed the two albums together, under the headline "Duane & Dick: Dueling Guitars." It was a thoughtful, mostly positive piece by writer and musician Tony Glover, who had written the extensive liner notes essay on 1972's *Duane Allman: An Anthology.* He deemed *Highway Call* an album "that grows on you" and noted that while "a lot of people seem to be jumping on the country bandwagon, Betts isn't one of them—he's just gone back to where he came from and produced a set that's not only honest and sincere but highly enjoyable."

Keen analysis couldn't overcome the overarching reality that for all his talent and success, it was difficult for Richard Betts—the name he started publicly using on *Brothers and Sisters* and under which *Highway Call* appeared—to be considered on his own merits. He was in Duane's shadow. And even Glover, a harmonica player who had not only written about the band for years but also played with them, didn't quite seem to realize this.

THE RICHARD BETTS American Music Show tour in support of *Highway Call* was an ambitious outing, featuring a thirteen-piece band, the heart of which was the album's core of Vassar Clements, John Hughey, bassist Stray Straton, and drummer David Walshaw. With Leavell touring with Gregg, Muscle Shoals great Spooner Oldham played keyboards. The band also included alto sax and mandolin players and a second drummer, who was added after the early shows felt shaky. "No one said anything to me, but one night we walked out and there was another drummer onstage," recalled Oldham.

Jaimoe was supposed to be the second drummer but pulled out at the last minute due to a flare-up of his chronic back problems. "It only seemed fair to tour with Richard since I had toured with Gregory, but I couldn't do it," he said.

Rounding out the group were two background singers and the Poindexters, a bluegrass band of brothers Leon, Frank, and Walter Poindexter, who had also appeared on *Highway Call,* and proved to be hard-drinking hell-raisers out on the road, according to Perkins. Betts compiled a very diverse band with the ambitious goal of presenting the history of American music in a two-hour serving.

"What I'm trying to do with the show is put together a concept. I wanted to show an evolution of the music," Betts told *Rolling Stone*'s Tim Cahill, who was out on the road in the fall of 1974 to do a cover story on both Betts's and Allman's solo tours. "We start with bluegrass, which is the music that came over to America from Europe . . . songs that go back to the

1800s. Then we do a Jimmie Rodgers tune, which is set in the 30s, and then a couple of Hank Williams numbers, which are up into the 50s. Then we ease into the electric set. We do some of the tunes that I wrote for the Allman Brothers and some from *Highway Call*. So the show is about evolution."

Throughout the tour, Betts got ever more into his own string-music background, even borrowing Clements's ancient violin at night to teach himself to play. The memories of his youthful experiments with various string instruments and his father's fiddle playing came back to him, Clements said. Betts "must have stayed up all night . . . because he figured out the scales." Clements had no doubt that he would have mastered the instrument with more focused practice. Their similar familial and musical backgrounds helped Betts and Clements form an immediate bond.

"His daddy and my daddy were both fiddlers," Clements said. "And that's why I think we're a lot alike." Betts figured that the only real difference between the two of them—why they took such different musical paths after similar upbringings—was the decade that separated them in age. "When I was sixteen, bluegrass wasn't cool," he said. "We were rock and rollers."

Playing together was fun for Betts and Clements because it brought out a different side in each of them and allowed Dickey to peer into an alternate version of himself; it's not a huge stretch to imagine him as a bluegrass picker rather than a rock guitar legend. "When we start exchanging riffs back and forth, we really get to talking to one another and it just feels so damn good," he said.

It's a shame that Betts and Clements never collaborated again, because they inspired each other. Though the shows were uneven, Betts deserves significant credit for creating such original music with *Highway Call* and attempting to bring it to life with a large ensemble. Unfortunately, while *Highway Call* sold respectably, the tour didn't do as well. Betts often played to half-filled halls—the same venues Gregg was selling out.

Tension began even before the first show. Betts was unhappy with an admittedly "piece of junk" tour bus and the fact that Gregg not only had Leavell but also the cream of the Allman Brothers Band road crew with him. To make it more equitable, Perkins shifted tours and Scooter Herring became Allman's tour manager. Herring was a motorcycle mechanic whom Gregg had met when he worked on one of his bikes. When they later ran into each other at a bar, they became buddies, and Gregg had the Allman Brothers Band hire him. He was Gregg's body man and drug connection. Now he was in charge of collecting and distributing money.

"There was no thieving, but this presented some obvious problems," said Perkins. "It was probably too big of a step for him to take and it would have been better to hire someone from the outside. He had trouble making that tour balance."

Herring was soon to become a surprisingly central figure in the band's history, but there were no major issues on Gregg's fall 1974 tour, which now had Lamar Williams on bass. Trucks was back in Macon, the only band member not on the road other than Jaimoe, who was resting his back. Bored and restless, Trucks joined up with an excellent Macon band, the Tall Dogs, rebranded with him as Butch's Brew, and played around the area, but downtime was rarely therapeutic for the drummer. Trucks spent most of his time sitting in his double-wide trailer on the farm drinking as his marriage to his first wife, Linda, fell apart, and he eventually counted himself lucky that his frequent drunk driving to and from town had not killed anyone.

Even with Perkins on board, Betts was not pleased with the overall crew, which was absent stalwarts like Red Dog and Twiggs, who were with Gregg. The motley crew included "Psychedelic Joe," Betts's gofer and handyman from the farm, who had previously worked as a strip club barker, luring customers in from the San Francisco sidewalk. Longtime Allman Brothers Band crew member Buffalo Evans served as the tour's advance man, but he ran off with a soon-to-be-well-known Hollywood actress in New York and wasn't seen for days.

While there was a rivalry between the Allman and Betts tours, *Rolling Stone*'s Cahill, who was shuttling between the two, reported that both bandleaders asked about the other and seemed genuinely eager to hear good news. Both went out of their way to compliment the other. "It was obvious each was concerned about the other's tour," he wrote. "They wanted to know who was pulling the biggest crowds (Allman was winning that one, hands down), what kind of new material the other was doing and how the other guy sounded."

All of this was big news because of even more swirling rumors that the Allman Brothers Band were going to break up and that the solo tours were a harbinger of the future. Everyone associated with the band worked hard to counter that impression. The separate Allman/Betts tours were just good business, Alex Hodges insisted. They could keep interest alive playing in smaller venues, while the Allman Brothers Band would wait for the summer, when they could play massive outdoor stadium shows. Cahill wrote an interesting, fair-minded story, but *Rolling Stone* screwed the organization again by putting a bare-chested Gregg alone on the cover, where Betts's name didn't even appear.

Even his solo efforts were being overshadowed by his more famous, more photogenic partner, and the two tours often danced around each other, despitre Paragon's best efforts to keep them separated.

The December 14, 1974 American Music Show at San Francisco's Winterland Ballroom was recorded for a planned live album that never saw the light of day. Bootleg versions that have circulated for years show that not everything Betts tried worked, but when it all clicked, the music was breathtaking. A few of the Allman Brothers Band songs didn't quite jell, but the *Highway Call* songs soared, and "Blue Sky" had a sloppy start before turning into a joyous romp with Betts, Huey, and Clements inspiring one another to great heights. The idea that drove the formation of that band was visionary, but its potential remained unfulfilled. It seems likely that with a bit more refinement and some more gigs under their belt, Betts's unique solo band would have been truly exciting.

24

DON'T ASK ME NO QUESTIONS AND I WON'T TELL YOU NO LIES

STEVE MASSARSKY, NOW back in New Jersey, went to see Betts at New York's Radio City on November 4, 1974, and a few days later at the Palace Concert Theater in Providence, Rhode Island. Speaking after the show, Betts perked up when Massarsky said he was now working at a New York law firm.

Massarsky recounts Betts saying, "You know, I've never had a lawyer. Nobody has ever looked at my relationships. Phil Walden as my manager negotiated with Phil Walden, president of my record company; with Phil Walden, president of the publishing company; and with Phil Walden, my investment counselor. I don't even know what most of my deals are, when they end, what I'm supposed to be doing. Will you look at them for me?"

Retained by Betts as his counsel, Massarsky wrote Walden requesting all relevant contracts for review. Walden responded that it was a bad idea for Massarsky to be looking into all this and there was certainly no need for it. The letter ended with a phrase that stuck with Massarsky forever: "Actions of this sort are hardly conducive to amiable relationships between mutually obligated parties."

He interpreted this line as, "if Dickey ever knows what the contracts said, he'd kill Phil Walden." When Massarsky responded that he still wanted to see Dickey's contracts, Walden sent him the documents with all the numbers blanked out, so they read, "this contract is for [BLANK] years at [BLANK] percent."

Betts was the first one to hire an outside advisor and take action, but he wasn't the only one in the band to face the same issues. Years later, every member expressed their unhappiness with, and regret over, their failure to fully review and understand their contracts and financial statements. Trucks claimed that they eventually came to realize that they were being charged for everything, including the nice Christmas presents Walden gave them every year, and that the long royalty statements, filled with many pages of deductions, were the product of creative bookkeeping that magically balanced out.

"They counted on no one really looking—and we didn't," Trucks said.

The band overlooked Walden's myriad conflicts of interest until Betts hired Massarsky. The move made everyone, band members and Capricorn staff alike, sit up and take notice.

"Phil not only managed us and owned our record company," Trucks said. "He also owned the booking agency, the publishing company that published all our songs, the liquor store where we bought all of our liquor, the merchandising company where we did our T-shirts. He even owned a travel agency where we booked all our flights from. Every dollar we made and much of what we spent funneled right through him."

Overriding all of that, most members believed, was a deeper, more fundamental, and inescapable problem: Walden viewed the band as nothing but Duane's sidemen, even after he was no longer alive.

"Phil always wanted it to be Duane Allman and his band," Gregg Allman said. "That's what they were used to and didn't know anything else. They weren't talking to Percy Sledge's keyboardist or Otis Redding's drummer."

Walden also manipulated the band members' insecurities and desire to be treated as talented and important in their own right. They all wanted his approval. "Phil called me once and said he thought I had as much talent as my brother and had thought so for a long time," Gregg said. "That meant a lot to me."

By March 1975, five months after Betts hired Massarsky, Walden still had not turned over his contracts. Massarsky became Betts's business manager a short time later, a further indication of Dickey's dissatisfaction with Walden. No member of the Allman Brothers Band had ever had their own management.

"We just didn't have no one to represent us," said Jaimoe. "We never had anyone in negotiations asking questions."

Once Massarsky became Betts's manager, they walked into Capricorn together and demanded the management, publishing, and record label contracts that Walden had refused to turn over. The guitarist and his attorney reviewed them together at Betts's house on the farm. They immediately saw that the management contract had expired the prior year and included a note saying, "We are continuing the management contract based on a gentlemen's agreement between us and the band."

Nobody recalled such an agreement ever being mentioned, much less agreed upon, and Massarsky also learned that Betts had signed three different concurrent publishing deals and that the Allman Brothers Band's revised 1972 record contract required them to record two albums a year for five years and stipulated that the label had the right to request additional sides. Simply put, Phil Walden, the manager, signed an onerous deal for the band with Phil Walden, the label owner, serving his own interests over those of his clients. It was nice work if you could get it, but now an outside lawyer was finally looking over these deals for the first time, and the power dynamic was shifting.

When Walden refused to reduce his 50 percent publisher's cut of the songwriting royalties in an October meeting, Massarsky said, Betts abruptly put the guitar he was playing back in its case and announced, "Since we can't get this resolved, there's something you need to know. I've got a really bad heroin problem and I'm heading out tomorrow to a rehab center in Tahiti. Since we have an Allman Brothers tour starting tomorrow [at the Omni in Atlanta], I would suggest you find out who is going to be playing guitar real quick and send them over to my house, so I can teach him some of the songs."

When Walden assented to all Betts had asked for, Betts changed his terms. "We didn't expect to get fucked that bad," he said. "We want 120 percent of what we asked for." Walden agreed, reducing his own cut in half and increasing Betts's songwriting royalties from 50 percent to 75 percent.

It still took four months for Betts to receive the new publishing and management contracts. Since the two deals had not been formally linked, Betts decided not to sign the management contract and tore it up. Massarsky would be his sole manager, and it was going to shake things up for everyone. The first thing he did was examine the Allman Brothers financial structure, Brothers Properties, and realize that "they all owed each other money" and that "Gregg and Butch had drawn so much out of the company that there was no way for Dickey and Jaimoe to get even."

He determined that the only way to make everyone whole would be to sell the farm, which they began the process of doing. Brothers Properties were also partners with Walden in various Macon real estate ventures, including a shopping center and an apartment complex. Jaimoe and Trucks said that they eventually realized they received smaller cuts of all such ventures than Betts and Allman—10 percent versus 15 percent—with Walden holding the other half of each investment. The larger issue was that the band owned 50 percent of the holding, but, Massarsky asserted, paid 100 percent of the sales price.*

As fast as Walden spent money, he was matched by the Allman Brothers Band, especially Allman and Trucks. "It was money in, money out for Phil as well as the Allmans," said Wooley. "The problems ramped up when it slowed, then stopped coming in."

As Massarsky reviewed the books, he learned that Brothers Properties had employees, including the entire road crew, who were drawing full salaries whether or not the band performed. He pulled Betts back from the band's business—clearly the right thing to do for his client, but also another significant crack in the group's foundation.

As the members of the Allman Brothers Band were starting to wonder where all the money was going, Phil Walden was living lavishly. He bought

---

* Jaimoe said that he didn't even know about these holdings until "the guy cutting my grass told me [he] had just come from our apartment building and I had to ask him what he meant."

He may not have realized what he owned, but on March 2, 1973, the *Macon Telegraph* reported a real estate transaction in a small item, noting that the band had purchased an apartment development on Napier Avenue for $447,500. It listed the band members (including Perkins) as owners, along with Walden and Capricorn treasurer Ted Senters.

his wife, Peggy, a white Rolls-Royce that previously belonged to actress Debbie Reynolds and had a Picasso hanging in his house. These were only the most publicly visible examples of his profligate spending.

"Phil's excesses got completely out of control," said Bunky Odom. "He had a house in Hilton Head, South Carolina, and he'd send his limousine on the two-hundred-mile drive there to meet his private plane."

Walden's chauffeured Mercedes 600 limousine had a TV and early video player, which was housed in the trunk, as well as a massive phone, which was an incredibly exotic luxury. A 1975 *Fortune* magazine feature by Louis Kraar noted this and toasted Walden as a capitalist success story who also "owns three elegant homes . . . and has a $750,000 collection of art and artifacts, ranging from Andrew Wyeth and Picasso to Walt Disney originals and a cigar store Indian." The story reported Walden's widespread control of his artists' revenue streams with something like breathless awe. Walden told the magazine that his gross income from all the various enterprises had doubled in the previous three years, to $15.7 million, while his personal net worth had "grown from approximately nothing to more than $5 million." Walden said that part of the label's success lay in "having Georgia expenses and earning New York dollars. . . . I'm not a Getty or an Onassis, but I'd like to be."

It doesn't seem to have occurred to Walden that his artists might be offended reading stories like this. The piece included pictures of a hirsute Wooley laughing as he talked on the phone, a bikini-top-clad secretary taking notes sitting on the arm of his chair, and of Cloyd Hall—Governor Carter's former fixer, who was then briefly working for Walden—sitting in the back of the limo. It noted that Hall was "leading a diversification drive that so far includes real estate, a nightclub and an amusement park," into which Walden said that he had invested over $3 million. The lead photograph was of the entire staff arrayed around the limo, holding up gold and platinum albums.

Walden told Kraar that he liked "to have a crisis atmosphere every day," which he said "made things bounce." Kraar attended a Capricorn executive meeting at Walden's house on Lake Sinclair, where the eight men present acted "more like fraternity brothers than businessmen." The gathering included copious amounts of J&B scotch, hours of conversation, steaks, more scotch, volleyball, more scotch, speedboat racing . . . and still more scotch.

THE FINANCIAL SHENANIGANS and shell games did not just relate to the Allman Brothers Band but to everyone working for and with Walden, some of whom were also starting to ask questions. After the Marshall Tucker Band's debut album became a hit, reaching 29 on the *Billboard* album chart, Paul Hornsby received a royalty check, supposedly to fulfill his producer's percentage as stipulated by contract. No explanation was provided regarding the amount of the check, and when he asked to see some accounting, Walden merely assured him that "it's fair."

"The album goes gold and I'm still making $175 a week," Hornsby wrote. "He gave me a few dollars extra but it wasn't enough to pay for a gold record. It was that kind of thing all the time."

Hornsby kept asking for a new deal, which Walden verbally committed to but repeatedly refused to put in writing. Hornsby quit Capricorn over the matter after showing up at Walden's office for a scheduled appointment, only to be told by Carolyn Brown that she was asked to pass on that there would be "no negotiations." Frank Fenter tried to talk him out of quitting, but Hornsby refused to reconsider without a new deal. "You know I can't do that," Fenter told him. "I can't convince Phil."

That was all Hornsby had to hear; he was done. During this time, southern rock was taking off, providing musicians and producers like Hornsby with significant financial opportunities. And he intended to pursue them.

Like Berry Gordy at Motown, Walden wanted his employees to be working for his label only. Quitting was the only way for Hornsby to work with others. "The name of the parent company was No Exit," Hornsby said. "So I just told Frank, 'I found the exit.'"

Liberated from working only for Capricorn, Hornsby produced the Charlie Daniels Band's *Fire on the Mountain* in 1974. Betts played dobro on the outlaw-country-rock manifesto "Long Haired Country Boy." The album also included "The South's Gonna Do It Again," which name-dropped a host of fellow musicians and became something of a southern rock anthem.

Fire on the Mountain was the Charlie Daniels Band's fourth album and the one where Daniels finally pulled his disparate threads together into a focused, bluesy country rock. The album established Daniels as a solo artist after his career as a Nashville session player, during which he compiled a lengthy résumé that included backing Bob Dylan on multiple albums. Hornsby helped Daniels establish himself and his band as cornerstones of southern rock. The producer said that in 1975 he had four records on the charts at once. He also continued to work for Capricorn, though no longer as an employee. He was liberated.

25
SUGAR SWEET

WHEN GREGG'S SOLO tour ended in December 1974, he went to Los Angeles with his good friend Chank Middleton for some rest and adventure. Just like every rock star before him, Gregg stayed at the Riot House on Sunset Boulevard. One afternoon, while cruising around town, Gregg and Chank stopped into the Troubadour in West Hollywood to visit Gregg's old friend, club owner Doug Weston.

Allman was excited that blues singer Etta James ("At Last," "I'd Rather Go Blind") was playing the next two nights, but Weston seemed anxious. He explained that he had just released his opening act so they could fulfill a recording commitment. Now he was in a bind. "I'll do it," Gregg blurted out.

"I was so scared, because I hadn't performed alone since elementary school," Gregg said. Weston peeled off a stack of fifty-dollar bills and threw them on the desk in front of Gregg, who added one stipulation: his name could not appear on the marquee. That last demand was summarily ignored, which turned out to have a major impact on Allman's life.

Gregg said that Cher's "secretary," Paulette Eghiazarian, drove by the Troubadour, saw his name on the marquee, and suggested they go.

"Who's Gregg Allman?" Cher replied.

Still, she ended up going to the Troubadour with her sister, Georganne LaPiere; Eghiazarian; actress Tatum O'Neal; and music executive and Cher confidant David Geffen. The club reserved a table just in front of the stage, and shortly before Allman was to begin, Middleton spotted them. "Man, Cher is down there looking good!" he told Gregg.

Allman had been quietly infatuated with Cher since 1967, when she and then partner Sonny Bono came to see Hour Glass at the Whisky a Go Go. "Isn't that the most beautiful woman you ever saw?" he asked Duane when he saw her walk by in a beaded leather dress.

Now, at the Troubadour, Gregg walked out and peered over the balcony at her. "Oh boy! Oh God!" he thought. Cher was a major star. She and Sonny had started having hit singles in 1965, and their ABC variety show *The Sonny and Cher Comedy Hour* was a smash from 1971 to 1974, before it was abruptly canceled when the couple split up.

Cherilyn "Cher" Sarkisian met Salvatore "Sonny" Bono, who worked as a producer for hitmaker Phil Spector, in November 1962. She was sixteen and he was twenty-seven. They became friends, then lovers, and eventually husband and wife. Bono had Cher work with the great studio musicians known as the Wrecking Crew on some of Spector's biggest recordings, including the Ronettes' "Be My Baby" and the Righteous Brothers' "You've Lost That Lovin' Feelin'"—the group Liberty producer Dallas Smith wanted Hour Glass to pattern themselves after.

Bono wrote, arranged, and produced a series of failed singles the couple put out under the name Caesar and Cleo before he penned "I Got You Babe," which they released as Sonny and Cher. It rose to number 1 in 1965, a year in which the duo had five songs in the top 20, and was followed by another hit in 1967 with "The Beat Goes On," featuring a simple but mesmerizing bass line by the Wrecking Crew's Carol Kaye.

With their success in decline by the end of the '60s, eclipsed by the growing counterculture, Bono relaunched the couple as a Vegas lounge act, with Cher playing the role of a glamorous, wiseacre singer constantly putting down her good-natured doofus of a husband, who was actually writing all their material. The act's popularity led to the TV show. Their separation and divorce, which would be finalized on June 26, 1975, was national news, splashed across the rising tide of new celebrity culture chroniclers like *People* magazine, which debuted in March 1974. "Half Breed," the lead single from Cher's second solo album of the same name, rose to number 1 in September 1973, blocking "Ramblin' Man" from the top spot.

Gregg, always enamored of both beautiful women and Hollywood, now stood looking down at Cher in awe. He overcame his nerves, took the stage, and played a short, moving set. "Everything came off perfect!" he said. "I was so scared, and I tried not to look at her, but I could just barely make her out in front of the stage."

The rock star, used to squealing fans trying to meet him, had been transformed into a nervous teen performing in front of his crush. "Suddenly, I was the groupie!" he said.

Back upstairs, Gregg nervously wrote a note to Cher and coerced Middleton into delivering it. Cher read it in the light of the cigarette machine and struggled to make out the words. It read in part, "Dear lovely lady, I'm not supposed to play here another night, but if you could come back, I would deem it an honor to play for you tomorrow night." As Cher noted, "Gregory was so flowery."

When he did not get a response, Gregg went downstairs and said hello to everyone at the table, including Geffen, whom he knew a bit from their mutual friend Jackson Browne. All inhibitions apparently gone, he leaned down toward Cher. "What's it gonna be?" he asked.

"I'll never forget: she was wearing a purple and black beaded shirt and God damn she looked so good! And she smelled so good," Gregg said. He was clearly smitten, but Cher merely said, "I'll get back to you." He retreated to the dressing room, but after the club cleared out, Middleton excitedly told him that Cher was still there. Gregg quickly packed up his guitar and "sauntered down, trying to play it cool," he said.

They chatted a bit before Gregg finally asked, "Why don't we have dinner?" To which she answered, "I don't know. Call my secretary," gave him a phone number, and walked away. The next morning, Gregg called Eghiazarian and they made a plan. He picked Cher up, and they went out for what he termed "the *Guinness Book of World Records'* worst date ever." Cher said they went to a party at Edgar Winter's room at the Riot House and a party at the Beachwood Canyon home of Judy Carne, a *Laugh-In* cast member who was a drug friend of Gregg's. Both these parties, Cher said, were populated by "horrible, drugged out people."

They went out for dinner, during which Gregg said they should go to Hawaii together, causing Cher to roll her eyes. Afterward, they returned to Carne's home, where Gregg retreated to the bedroom to do drugs, then took a long-distance phone call and talked for an extended period, leaving Cher alone. He walked out to see her leaving and followed her out the door to see where she was going. As she walked down the steps to a waiting car, she said, "I don't need this. This is a drag. Good night."

The next day, Gregg called Cher and said, "That was a world-class shitty date. It was so bad we have to do it one more time to make sure we're really that incompatible." Cher laughed and agreed, and the two went dancing. "We had a great time and I can't dance," Gregg said. "We laughed, we talked, and before the night was over we also fell in love. There's no book of rules about how things have to go, and that's what happened."

Things went better, Cher thought, because "Gregory wasn't trying to impress me this time. He was being himself."

Gregg soon moved into her Beverly Hills mansion, and Cher warned him of the difficulty of life under the Hollywood gaze. "She told me that the press would eat my ass alive," Allman said. "That meant nothing to me. Compared to what we had going? Fuck the press. Being in the paper never meant anything to me one way or another, but she was clear: 'Let the record show that I warned you.'"

He quickly found out that she was correct. He didn't understand Cher's level of fame. "I thought there were a lot of photographers around being an Allman Brother but I didn't know what it was until she and I went out together," he said. "Six or eight photographers would be waiting outside our gate twenty-four hours a day. I did not fall in love with her because she was famous. Famous did not turn me on. Famous is a pain in the ass."

After spending a lot of time together in Los Angeles, Allman returned to Macon for rehearsals for the long-overdue recording of the band's follow-up to *Brothers and Sisters*: *Win, Lose or Draw*. Cher wanted to join him, but he demurred. He knew he could no longer hide his heroin habit if she followed him "back down South." He was "still getting loaded but had been able to hide it from her," he explained. "I had it down to a science, using just enough for maintenance."

Allman was referring to an opiate dose big enough to prevent withdrawal symptoms and small enough to not appear high. He knew he would struggle to maintain the charade in Macon. Being in L.A. with Cher "kept my mind occupied," he explained.

He returned to Macon, and Cher joined him several days later. Her visit was front-page news in both the Macon and Atlanta newspapers. "It's the talk of the town," one anonymous Capricorn employee told the *Atlanta Constitution*. "Everyone is going nuts about her being here."

Gregg said that at the end of the third day, he told her, "Think of this as some sort of Disneyland. It was fun while it lasted. Now go home," and walked out the door. She was stunned and followed him out to his car, saying, "You're a son of bitch if you don't come talk to me." Gregg later said that he was telling her to leave "in lieu of telling her I was an addict," which he couldn't bring himself to do.

He drove away, but with Cher's words ringing in his ears, quickly returned and told her, "Okay, you asked for it. I've got some good news and some bad news. The good news is I'm crazy mad in love with you, but the bad news is I have a problem." He said that he cried for almost an hour before he could bring himself to explain the problem with these simple words: "I'm a junkie."

An admittedly naive Cher was unbothered. "That's okay," he recounted her saying. "We can beat that."

"You don't understand," Gregg replied. "I would steal your mama's TV."

Still, she was confident in her ability to help him overcome his drug problems, and Cher and Gregg recommitted to each other. Returning to Los Angeles, she was more focused on the band's deeply weird Macon existence. They all seemed to live on the Phil Walden plantation, she told Eghiazarian, and none of them realized how strange it really was.

Cher and Gregg publicly confirmed their relationship in a March 1975 *National Enquirer* interview. Gregg, who had been a public figure to some degree since he was sixteen and a leader of the country's most popular band for the past two years, had entered an entirely new level of celebrity, and he barely knew what hit him.

He appeared on Geraldo Rivera's *Good Night America* on August 14, wearing a white suit and tie and a JIMMY CARTER FOR PRESIDENT button.* Rivera had met Gregg and the Allman Brothers Band on the final night at the Fillmore East, June 27, 1971, and they remained friendly. He was surprised to see Gregg now struggling to find himself in an entirely different milieu.

"Cher is both a brilliant star and a handful, as was Gregg," said Rivera. "I had a lot of affection for Gregg and really thought of him as a pure heart. Other than his struggles with substance abuse, I never saw any negative aspects of his personality, but he was clearly uncomfortable and a little lost in the new world he found himself immersed in. He seemed like a fish out of water."

---

* His backing band for the two songs he performed included Jaimoe, Lamar, and Chuck, along with guitarist Davis Causey and drummer Bill Stewart.

26

WIN, LOSE, OR DRAW

S GREGG AND Cher attempted to settle into something approaching a normal life in Los Angeles, the Allman Brothers Band were trying to record in Macon. They needed a follow-up to *Brothers and Sisters*, and Capricorn desperately wanted them to deliver it.

The label should have been flush from the band's success in 1973 and 1974. According to *Fortune, Brothers and Sisters* cost $40,000 to produce and in its first two years had sold over two million copies, generating Capricorn a net income of $1.2 million. The band had made the long, hard climb out of the underground, and the company expected more of the same. Betts and Allman responded with solo albums that were artistic and commercial successes, but on a much smaller scale. Their mutual decisions to record, release, and tour behind these projects instead of another Allman Brothers Band album were a financial disaster for the company. *Fortune* reported that "the falloff in concerts alone has deprived Walden of about $500,000 in commissions."

The label's growing artist roster was not exactly setting the world on fire. Walden and company had made some good bets—Wet Willie had a top 10 hit with 1974's "Keep on Smilin'," and the Marshall Tucker Band was a legitimate hitmaker. But the newer bands they signed didn't pay off. The Florida hard rock band White Witch cost the label $123,000 for two albums that brought in just $8,000, *Fortune* wrote.

Phil Walden needed the Allman Brothers Band back in the studio and on the road as quickly as possible. Frank Fenter called it "the most frustrating and crazy thing. After years of struggle, we've got one of the hottest bands, but now it's tough to get them into the studio. They've got homes, cars and money coming, so it's hard to motivate them."

Of course, more than a lack of financial motivation slowed the band down. Gregg was in and out of town, often living in Beverly Hills with Cher. Jaimoe was still recovering from the back injury sustained during a serious car accident in August 1974, which caused him to back out of playing in Betts's solo band.

As the Allman Brothers struggled to get back in first gear, the southern rock movement they inspired was becoming ever more popular. The Outlaws, a Florida band who first made their mark as a preferred opening act for Lynyrd Skynyrd, signed with Arista Records, the first rock act on Clive Davis's new label. Phil's brother, Alan Walden, comanaged the Outlaws, in part because Ronnie Van Zant had given them a strong recommendation.

"Skynyrd was getting ready to leave Alan for Peter Rudge and Ronnie felt guilty," said Charlie Brusco, who was managing the Outlaws. A young Pittsburgh native who had come south and met the band in Tampa, Brusco was excited to add Walden as a comanager. He initially thought it could lead to a contract with Capricorn but quickly realized the opposite was true: Phil and Alan Walden didn't want anything to do with each other.

"Phil always told Alan that Lynyrd Skynyrd were a bunch of hillbillies who would never make it," said Brusco. "They had this big split but unfortunately one thing Alan learned from his brother was to ask the band for all the publishing and I was a very naive young manager running on adrenaline and love for the band. I made some mistakes early on, none bigger than letting Alan take all the publishing after he said, 'Don't worry; publishing is just pennies.' Everyone was giving up publishing and I knew more about live music and promotion than record contracts and publishing. I wasn't as smart as I thought I was."

Alan Walden readily admitted that the publishing was central to his interest in any band. He "very much expected to control the publishing," he wrote. "Publishing is everything. . . . You want to own the songs."

The Outlaws' publishing quickly became valuable when "Green Grass and High Tides" and "There Goes Another Love Song" became hits off their self-titled debut album. Emulating the Eagles as much as Skynyrd or the Allman Brothers, Clive Davis pushed the group to emphasize vocal harmonies. Had Phil and Alan Walden gotten along better, Capricorn may well have firmly controlled southern rock now, with a series of bands picking up when the others slowed down. It all clicked for the Outlaws in the summer of 1975 at a time when Skynyrd was getting burned out and the Allman Brothers Band was struggling to record—even just getting them to show up in the studio at the same time was difficult.

"Everyone blamed Gregg, and I didn't enjoy waiting for him, but you can't make someone sing when they're not ready to," Sandlin said. "And it wasn't just him; the whole band's schedule stifled creativity. Everyone got used to it and they had worked so hard for so long that I felt like they deserved some slack, as frustrating as it was."

When the Allman Brothers Band finally convened in Macon in February 1975 to begin recording, they had little new material and turned back to where it all began to try and recapture some of their past magic: Muddy Waters. Just as they did in 1969 with "Trouble No More," the band remade "Can't Lose What You Never Had" in their own image. "Can't Lose" came together quickly, and though it lacked the snap, drive, and originality of previous blues remakes like "Trouble No More," "One Way Out," and "Done Somebody Wrong," it got the new album off to a good start. Then the project stalled, with sessions continuing in fits and starts over the next five or six months, with different members showing up on any given night, and with Gregg often on the West Coast.

"We were barely in the studio at the same time," Allman said. While Gregg was wrapped up in his new life with Cher, the band recorded most of the tracks without him, requiring Sandlin to fly to L.A. to record Gregg's vocals at the Record Plant. It was a far cry from the Allman Brothers Band, 1969–73.

"There was definitely less interaction than there had been," said Leavell. "And I think you can hear it." Sandlin called *Win, Lose or Draw* "probably the hardest record I've ever done. It wasn't fun at all. It was just sad."

Jaimoe, Chuck, and Lamar always seemed ready to play, he said, but Dickey and Butch "struggled just to put anything into it," as did Gregg—when he was even around. Dickey refused to record on Thursday nights, when David Carradine's *Kung Fu* TV show aired. And while Gregg's absence was a problem, it was also something of a relief to Sandlin, who said that the "Dickey faction" and "Gregg faction" had split the band into two camps.

"You could just walk into the studio and feel all this tension," he said. "There might as well have been an electric sign warning you: THINGS COULD GET ROUGH IN HERE."

There's nothing unusual about single musicians working in a studio and layering their parts with the help of a producer. Many great rock records have been made that way, but it's not how the Allman Brothers Band had ever worked, and the approach was antithetical to their entire reason for being.

"This is not a band you cut one piece at a time, so we spent a lot of time waiting for someone to show up," said Sandlin. "Up to that point the band had recorded almost everything live—all the rhythm tracks and even most of the guitar solos. The difference was pretty profound."

Jaimoe, Lamar, and Chuck found themselves alone in the studio jamming so often that they began to call themselves We Three and joked about forming their own band, which they did the next year with Sea Level.

As the Allman Brothers Band continued to muddle along, seeking to complete the record, Gregg remained in Los Angeles trying to make things work with Cher, which was causing increasing frustrations and tensions within the band. On May 6, 1975, Madeline Hirsiger reported in the evening *Macon News* that the *Win, Lose or Draw* sessions had ground to a halt, saying that Gregg was in Los Angeles "gathering musicians to form a new band." She wrote that Allman was scheduled to record the final vocals but could not be persuaded to return to Macon. Hirsiger attributed the quotes to "employees of the band," sources she would have since her husband, Roger Cowles, was Capricorn's original head of publicity.

To be ready for a July release, Hirsiger reported, Gregg had to record three vocal tracks and the band had to totally recut one song. The band's crew had been given four weeks' notice, she said, indicating the end was near. Fenter, however, insisted that the Allman Brothers Band had just signed a new five-year contract with Capricorn. The new Los Angeles band, he said, was merely to back Gregg's solo outings. Jaimoe, the only member of the group to speak on the record, said, "If Gregg wants to pay a lot of money to get out of contracts, there won't be a band."

Capricorn officials denied any impending breakup in the next morning's *Macon Telegraph*. Publicist Mike Hyland said it wasn't true that Allman had refused to return to Macon, and Fenter insisted that the band had been recording the previous night.

ON JUNE 30, 1975, three days after Cher's divorce from Bono was finalized, Gregg said that she woke him up and asked what they were doing that day. "I had just gotten back from Macon and I didn't want to do anything," he recalled. "And she said, 'Well, I just thought, you know . . . we'd get married.'"

Gregg said that he laughed and rolled over to go back to sleep when she pushed ahead. "I'm serious," she said.

"She looked at me with those big brown eyes, and what could I say?" Gregg said.

The couple boarded a Learjet for Las Vegas with Paulette and Cher's sister, Georganne. They found a judge to perform the service in a honeymoon suite at Caesar's Palace. Describing the scene to Rivera in a TV interview just a year later, while the couple were still married, Allman started to say "coroner" instead of "judge," which the host called "the greatest Freudian slip ever."

"We pulled him out of court with his robe on and up to this purple-and-blue suite with a round bed and mirrors everywhere," Allman said. "We got in and out and got married and no one knew what was happening. Frank Sinatra was playing downstairs, and we headed home and immediately knew that we had made a huge mistake, that the party was over. We sat next to each other on the Learjet and didn't speak a word. It was like each of us was sitting next to the creature from the black lagoon. We somehow knew that all the fun was gone, and we were headed for a life of unadulterated, unstopping interruptions."

"I knew I was in trouble," Cher wrote. "I cried all the way home."

Their marriage fueled extensive coverage. "Cher Weds Macon-Based Rock Singer," blared a headline in the *Macon Telegraph*. The paper had always extensively covered the Allman Brothers Band as hometown heroes; if they prioritized Cher, imagine how the rest of the world viewed the couple's pecking order. They were just beginning the tabloid-frenzy stage of their relationship.

After nine days of marriage, Cher found Gregg's needles and filed for divorce. He was about to fly back to Macon to record and said he "was so out of it" that he didn't even realize what had happened until he turned on the TV in Georgia and learned that his wife wanted to end the marriage. "That threw me into a bad state, feeling like one dumb son of a bitch," Allman said. "I sat down and wrote the song 'One More Try' and went back out there to heal things up."

Capricorn representatives told the *Macon Telegraph* that the couple would work things out, but Cher's filing cited "irreconcilable differences." "Gregg and I made a mistake and I've always believed it's best to admit one's mistakes as quickly as possible," she said in a statement. "We just cannot live together as man and wife."

The quick divorce filing sparked rumors that they married solely to create publicity, but Gregg's efforts on his return to Los Angeles paid off, as Cher withdrew the divorce filing and the couple remained married.

Around the same time, the Allman Brothers Band finally finished *Win, Lose or Draw*. Of the album's seven tracks, only two originals remotely stood up to their best work: Allman's title track and the Betts instrumental "High Falls." Gregg wrote the moving ballad "Win, Lose or Draw" about his friend Chank Middleton, who had just gotten out of jail after serving two years for drug offenses. Gregg put him on the Allman Brothers Band payroll and moved him into his house upon his release.

"He called me into the bedroom and said, 'I got something I want you to hear,'" Middleton recalled. Allman played an early version of "Win, Lose or Draw" on his acoustic guitar, and Middleton thought it sounded like it was about him, but he wasn't quite sure. Then Gregg finished and said, "Bro, I started writing this about you when you first went to prison. Now that you're out, let's revise it."

Middleton opened up to his friend. "I started telling him about the experiences I had, as far as being addicted to heroin, being locked up in a county jail and going to prison, and the different things that had gone on in my life while I was in prison," Middleton said. "He took words that came out of my mouth and turned them into poetry."

Dickey's instrumental "High Falls" is an intricate composition with echoes of jazz fusion. "Dickey had been listening a lot to Coltrane, which inspired the song," said Jaimoe. "You can hear that influence in a lot of what he played in his solo. Dickey was a talented guy and [whatever] he got into, he was 200 percent into it, whether it was shooting a bow and arrow, Native American rights, or John Coltrane."

As good as the composition and final track are, the recording experience, Trucks said, was a nightmare. "We got obsessed with getting it perfect and worked it and worked it until it was sterile," he said. "One night we were jamming at Grant's and I did some coke someone gave me, but it turned out to be PCP. I made it back home to the farm, but I wrapped myself around the oak tree there, hugging it, with the woods screaming 'High Falls' at me for hours."

Allman contributed one other composition and vocal, "Nevertheless," an unusually slick track that pointed toward the direction he would take in his future solo career. Betts's "Just Another Love Song" and "Louisiana Lou and Three Card Monty John" sound like *Highway Call* outtakes. The album closed with Betts's vocal on Billy Joe Shaver's countrified blues romp "Sweet Mama," a fun, nonessential track highlighted by the guitarist's fluid slide playing.

Win, Lose or Draw is not a disaster, but neither is it nearly as good as any other album they had produced to that point. And it certainly is not a worthy follow-up to *Brothers and Sisters*. The band was in disarray and disinterested. Trucks and Jaimoe didn't even play on "Louisiana Lou" and "Sweet Mama," with Sandlin and Bill Stewart handling the drumming. "They weren't there when Dickey was ready and we needed to cut it when we had a chance," Sandlin said.

"The main problem with *Win, Lose or Draw* is simply that none of us were really into the music," Trucks said. "The thrill was gone and we quit surprising each other. It just wasn't fun anymore. When we heard the finished music, we were all embarrassed."

They were also annoyed that it had taken so long to complete. Speaking to Art Harris of *The Atlanta Constitution,* Jaimoe was again unusually blunt in pointing a finger at Gregg and Cher for the album's delay. "Things were in the wrong order," Jaimoe said. "A love affair can wait. It shouldn't have stopped what she's doing but that's the difference between someone who is already built and someone who is building and Gregg's still building. Cher's had gold albums out since I was a kid, so you know where the responsibility lies."

The cover of *Win, Lose or Draw* didn't exactly pull people in either. It was a manifestation of their turmoil, a picture lacking a visual center, taken in a bar at Atlanta Underground, a then thriving entertainment district. The Twiggs Lyndon–conceived image features the interior of an Old West saloon devoid of people. A poker table topped with half-empty whiskey bottles, cards, and chips sits front and center. Six empty chairs represent the then current Allman Brothers Band members. Two chairs lean against a small empty table in the background, representing Duane and Berry.

"I never really understood that cover," said Sandlin. "I've read a lot of interpretations but all I know is that it's eerie and kind of alarming."

Almost fifty years later, Leavell took a more philosophical approach to the album, seeing its shaky foundation as rooted in the band's troubled years. "Just think about everything that the band had gone through," he said. "They struggled for years, traveling in a van, sitting head to foot, foot to head for hundreds of days a year, crisscrossing the country to play one one-nighter after another. After all that, they finally had success, started playing arenas and inching towards stadiums and then . . . you lose the leader of the band, grieve, pick it back up again—and lose another founding member," said Leavell.

"You pick it up again—and have even bigger success. By the time of the *Win, Lose or Draw* sessions, everyone was exhausted. They were just tired. And when people get tired, other emotions like anger can go along with it. I just think the band had enough at that point."

27

DREAMS

ON AUGUST 31, 1975, nine days after the release of *Win, Lose or Draw,* the Allman Brothers Band played their first show in a year, at the newly opened New Orleans Superdome. They headlined the venue's first rock show, two days after Bob Hope inaugurated the building. Billed as the Pride of Dixie, the show also featured southern rock stalwarts Wet Willie, the Charlie Daniels Band, and the Marshall Tucker Band. The Allman Brothers were paid more than $100,000 for their performance.

Fans who feared the band's sixth album would never arrive greeted *Win, Lose or Draw* with relief. Old friend Tony Glover's *Rolling Stone* review acknowledged Betts and Allman had "seemed to be spinning off in separate orbits" in what was otherwise one of the record's few positive assessments. He wrote that it was "a record that grows on you. The more you hear it the more neat little subtleties you hear—the interplay is as tight as ever." Glover usually had great musical insight, but he was off base with this one.

Though *Win, Lose or Draw* rose to number 5 on the charts, it wasn't nearly the runaway success that *Brothers and Sisters* had been. Walden later joked that the album shipped platinum and returned gold, a sadly common record industry joke at a time of profligate spending and mass bootlegging. (Before there was actual scanning of sales, the record industry conferred gold records to any releases that *shipped* half a million copies and platinum to any that shipped a million. Record stores could return unsold vinyl for credit. Counterfeit copies of popular releases often flooded the market and were sometimes returned as well.)

The tour continued the momentum and strong sales that started with the Superdome show. The band almost instantly sold out the forty-five-thousand-seat Roosevelt Stadium in Jersey City for a September 13 show, but some fans and journalists were starting to notice a downturn. *Rolling Stone*'s review of the Roosevelt Stadium show ran under the headline "Jaded and Joyless in Jersey." As David McGee wrote, "Instead of any dynamic interplay between the instruments or exchange of provocative themes, the Brothers contented themselves with several pointless, undisciplined jams that gave each soloist a chance to play too long after he had run out of new licks." Of Betts, he wrote, "Though his suits are flashier than his playing these days, Betts remains the master purveyor of those loping, melodic oft-copied guitar lines which are the Allmans' trademark." Allman, he said, "shrank behind his organ, which was virtually inaudible."

One song was off of the playlist for the tour: "Blue Sky." Sandy had filed for divorce right before they hit the road. The split was acrimonious, and Betts flat-out refused to play the song he had written and named for her.

JIMMY CARTER WAS also touring hard in 1975, campaigning for two hundred and fifty days. He saved money by staying at the homes of friends and supporters and flying coach, but the outsider candidate was facing financial difficulties, with a $300,000 deficit in the fall. Carter would need assistance to remain in the race and fulfill his pledge to run in every Democratic primary and caucus of 1976. This sounds like a modest commitment given that candidates now declare years in advance of an election, but Carter's promise was truly significant at the time. There was a general belief that it would be a strong year for the party but there was no obvious front-runner and a lot of initial candidates; however, no one else matched Carter's commitment and most barely ran in half the states.

The 1976 Democratic primary was just the second time the voters in caucuses and primaries selected the party's nominee. In prior years, the party leader and elected officials selected the nominee in conventions held by states, with only limited primary elections and caucuses. In 1968, Vice President Hubert Humphrey had won the nomination without entering a single primary. Party leaders had vast authority to choose the candidate of their choice, but that began to change with reforms ushered in following the Democrats' divisive 1968 Chicago convention.

At the start of the 1976 race, Carter was viewed as an extreme long shot for the presidency, and many pundits suggested that he was really running for the vice presidency. But the former Georgia governor never expressed anything but confidence. "I don't see anybody on the horizon who can beat me," he said.

His supporters had the same conviction. "I thought he was going to win the day I met him," said Peter Conlon, who worked on Carter's campaign and later in the White House. (Conlon has been a prominent Atlanta music promoter ever since and the longtime chairman of Georgia for Live Nation.)

"You have to remember the very real backlash against Washington and Vietnam," he said. "Carter was an outsider, who saw a way that would appeal to young voters and the disenfranchised. And he had charisma; there was a notable change when he walked in a room. Jimmy Carter loves people and he would talk to and really engage with anyone."

Central to campaign strategist Hamilton Jordan's audacious plan to elect Carter was a focus on the Iowa caucuses, to be held on January 19, 1976. Two five-minute ads showed Carter at a Florida pulpit delivering a sermon centered on his honesty and trustworthiness. "I'll never tell a lie," Carter said. "I'll never make a false statement. I'll never betray the confidence you have in me and I won't avoid a controversial issue."

The themes of honesty and trustworthiness resonated with voters tired of the scandals of the Nixon administration, which had led to the president's resignation. The ads introducing him in a positive light to Iowa voters were funded by money Phil Walden helped the campaign raise with benefit concerts, starting in earnest with the Marshall Tucker Band at Atlanta's Fox Theatre on October 31, 1975.

The 1976 election was the first of the post-Watergate era. In the wake of the scandal, Congress passed new campaign finance laws designed to encourage smaller donations, greater disclosure of contributions, and public financing of campaigns through federal matching funds. These changes boosted nontraditional, reform-minded candidates like Carter over establishment politicians. The fundraising concerts started with some smaller local efforts that were nonetheless crucial because "they really kept him afloat when he was running out of money," said Tom Beard, Walden's handpicked coordinator of the campaign's benefit concerts. "Phil Walden and Alex Cooley kept the campaign going."

"The [first] concerts came at a time when we had trouble raising $1,000 a day," Carter campaign treasurer Robert Lipshutz said. Added Hamilton Jordan, "The shows were "the critical effort [that] established the campaign and kept it going financially when no one knew who he was."

Carter's embrace of scruffy rock and rollers was entirely radical for a politician at the time. Alex Cooley recalled eating in Mary Mac's Tea Room, an Atlanta institution, when then governor Lester Maddox walked in, spied the rock promoter, and turned tail to leave. He did not want to eat in the same establishment. Carter not only put up with the musicians but was a true fan who appreciated the music created by the Allman Brothers and the Marshall Tucker Band, and he appreciated, too, what they all were doing for him. He was even photographed wearing a *Win, Lose or Draw* T-shirt.

Some observers were surprised that a presidential candidate would so openly align himself with people so well known for their libertine lifestyles. Why indeed? "Well, what were the options?" asks Conlon. "The campaign needed money and these guys were willing to raise it. Carter did not see it as a threat to his candidacy. He was the first national figure to embrace rock and roll, while everyone else stayed away because of drugs and the overall image problem. He saw rock as a driving force, something that was not outside the bounds of what a presidential campaign could deal with."

Carter did more than accept the bands; he embraced them. "I'm proud of my relationship with the Allman Brothers Band," he said. "They are good people, they are my friends, and anybody who wants a President who doesn't like music like this, and who doesn't like people who make music like this, should just simply vote for another man."

The candidate also understood that the bands could help increase his visibility and popularity with younger voters who were angry and alienated over Watergate and Vietnam. The shows put his name and face in front of tens of thousands of concertgoers, many of whom didn't follow politics closely. "Carter wasn't an opportunist but he saw an opportunity and he was going to ride the tide," Conlon said. "He saw music as a way to reach out to a lot of disenfranchised people who wanted change."

Walden was the driving force behind this initial idea of integrating rock and roll into the campaign. He served on Carter's national finance and steering committees and worked to bring other music industry executives on board. It was a tough go. No one knew who Carter was. "It was not unlike trying to sell a new group," Walden said.

While Walden initially struggled to bring New York and Los Angeles music business executives into the campaign, he had a lot more success with his own bands. The few who initially hesitated were brought along. "Phil could be very persuasive," said Beard. "He did some cajoling."

Most musicians in the Capricorn family were relatively apolitical, but they liked and supported Carter, bonding with him over their shared southern heritage. A handful of performers leaned further right and objected to playing benefits; they were paid, which made it a regular gig for them. Even the musicians who did not particularly care about politics appreciated the respect Carter showed them.

"Jimmy Carter didn't mind being seen with us at all, despite being set up for ridicule by his opponents for hanging out with a bunch of hippie drug users," Allman said.

Carter was not naive about the musicians' drug use, and while he didn't approve of it, he also was not sanctimonious about it. "Carter hadn't just fallen off a pumpkin truck," said Beard. "He knew what was going on."

Beard recalled standing outside a Nashville benefit waiting for Carter to arrive as Charlie Daniels smoked a joint nearby. As Carter pulled up and approached them, another campaign staffer tried to redirect the candidate away from the toking musician, but it was too late; he was already walking toward Daniels to say hello.

"Charlie was holding a joint behind his back in his left hand and shaking Carter's hand with his right hand," Beard said. "Everyone knew that was part of the lifestyle, and Carter was never judgmental about people's lifestyles."

While there were risks involved in being associated with debauched musicians, the rock and roll connection helped Carter spruce up his nerdy, square, born-again Christian image. They helped him "overcome some of the stereotypes," Jordan said. The campaign needed a lot of help spreading the word and amplifying its message. They were working to elect a peanut farmer and former governor of Georgia with virtually no national profile to be president of the United States.

"Phil Walden and Capricorn Records were an important part of that effort," Jordan said. "Phil was responsible for introducing Jimmy Carter to the music and entertainment industry."

In the fall of 1975, with the January Iowa caucuses just months away, the Carter campaign faced an increasingly dire financial situation. They approached Walden about using his biggest gun: the Allman Brothers Band. Would they be willing to hold a benefit concert for Carter? Walden quickly put together a show on November 25, at the Providence Civic Center in Rhode Island.

In internal memos, the Carter campaign grappled with the complexities of complying with a recently passed law overhauling how candidates could raise money. Selling thousands of concert tickets provided the campaign with a great opportunity to secure large amounts of matching funds—but it would need to comply with the laws governing these contributions. To be eligible for matching funds, receipts for contributions of one hundred dollars or less needed a name and address. The law required the campaign to provide this information to the Federal Election Commission (FEC), which ensured the contributions qualified for matching funds. Thus, in the context of the concerts, the campaign was required to have the name and address of *each* ticket buyer to claim any matching funds. In addition, the new law prohibited any cash contribution of one hundred dollars or more, meaning it was a violation of campaign finance law to collect matching funds on any cash ticket sales over that amount.

If they overstepped in any way, campaign staffer Jim Gammill warned his colleagues, their opponents would be waiting to pounce. "What worries me most," Gammill wrote in a memo, "is the amount of bad press and trouble with the FEC we will get if we claim $75,000 from the Allman Brothers concert but have receipts for only half of it. It will be tough for us to justify accepting $40,000 that the Allman Brothers effectively raised for us without a single trace of where it came from. The enormous size of the thing is what makes us so vulnerable—any candidate will be drooling at the $40,000 and if they can delay us from spending it, they will try to do that."

Gammill's memo provides a concrete example of the logistical challenges the campaign faced in securing the matching funds from the concerts. It could not just accept the gross revenue minus expenses and benefit from the matching funds. The individual donations had to be separate, and the campaign needed the name and address of each person who "contributed" to the campaign. Cooley and Beard got creative, providing incentives for ticket buyers to fill out the forms by creating raffles to win tickets to future shows.

"People just needed to fill out the forms," said Beard. "It didn't matter why they did so. At one Toots and the Maytals concert we did in the Midwest, I was out there trying to get all these reggae people to sign the forms. It was a burden to the campaign, creating a lot of work and stress. I can now admit that I did a lot of the filling in as I asked people for their info."

Gammill also realized that the Allman Brothers Band was an incorporated entity, which meant that playing for free would constitute a corporate contribution and violate federal election law. As a workaround, the band agreed to be paid musicians' "union scale plus agreed upon expenses" for their performance. Grinderswitch received a grand total of $1,000 for opening. Backstage before the Providence show, Carter ran into Betts in a hallway and asked, "Goddamn, how are you, man?" They had been friendly since Carter stopped by Capricorn Studios during the recording of *Highway Call*.

Journalist Geraldo Rivera introduced Carter to the crowd as "an honest, open, progressive politician. He stands for the things that you and I believe in—civil rights and housing and the environment. Jimmy Carter's like a breath of fresh air coming out of Georgia, and he's sweeping the country, people . . ."

Beard had reminded Carter that afternoon that "the people are coming to see the Allman Brothers," urging him to keep his remarks brief, and he did so. Speaking to a smattering of boos, Carter raised his arms in the air and spoke quickly and wisely, saying: "I have just four things to tell you. My name is Jimmy Carter. I'm running for president. I need your help. I'm gonna win. And now I want to introduce some very good friends of mine from Macon, Georgia . . . the Allman Brothers."

The crowd erupted in cheers, and then the Allman Brothers Band performed a normal show for them in 1975. As Leavell remembers, "Once the music started, it was just another Allman Brothers show. We took pictures with Jimmy Carter beforehand, but onstage, nothing was different."

The campaign paid all expenses for the shows, ranging from the venue and stage rental to barricades, stage crew, backstage catering and bar, advertising, and security. Promoter Tony Ruffino billed them $14,931. The *St. Petersburg Times* reported that the Allman Brothers Band grossed $64,031 but netted the campaign just over $6,000. Because of the matching funds, the show generated a lot more money for the campaign. It is hard to say definitively how much cash the concerts raised. Lipshutz, the campaign treasurer, did not like the events, thinking they exposed the campaign to unnecessary risk and required too many hours of staff work. Beard and Conlon both say that, in response, he downplayed the yields, and he oversaw tabulating and releasing the campaign's financial data. Regardless of the exact amount raised, the concerts were a crucial source of cash when the campaign was in significant debt. "They created cash flow when there was virtually none," said Conlon.

The shows also had enormous public relations value. They provided awareness for a candidate who started out unknown outside his home region and exposed him to large numbers of young voters. "The Allman Brothers helped put me in the White House by raising money when I didn't have any," Carter said simply. "If it hadn't been for Gregg Allman, I never would have been president."*

WHILE THE PROVIDENCE benefit concert was a major success for the Carter campaign, the Allman Brothers Band themselves were limping through the end of their 1975 tour. Ticket sales and guarantees slipped throughout the run. Most ominously, they often were not clicking onstage, something they had largely managed to avoid through their first five years, no matter

---

* President Carter's loyalty to the Allman Brothers Band never wavered. He presented Gregg with an honorary degree to Mercer University in 2016 and attended Allman's funeral in Macon on June 3, 2017.

how crazy things grew around them. It all began with increasing offstage isolation from one another. Old friend and longtime advocate Bill Graham was terribly saddened to see them arrive in separate limousines at a show he promoted. "They played music as if in a commune, so the fact that they became so isolated said a lot," he said. "I blame many of their problems on the [Capricorn] guys, who could have been more righteous and made an attempt to help these troubled people when they needed it." But, he added, the distance that had set in between the band members was different. It was on them and it presaged a listless performance that alarmed Graham.

Jaimoe said that there were always differences between the band members, and some hung out offstage more than others, going back to day 1. It was never quite the full-on brotherhood that the band promoted and fans believed in, but they truly lived up to that ideal onstage and in the studio. "Everyone in the original band was so different from one another," he said. "But we had one goal that unified us." Once that unified vision and drive was gone, he said, it was easier for differences that had always been there to rise to the surface.

Exhaustion fueled by sorrow, fame, and drugs and alcohol contributed to the excesses. "We got away from talking to each other on stage," Trucks said. "It became about the limos and the star time. It was unnoticeable in real time. We weren't aware of what was going away. We were so caught up in the fantasy, but it wasn't all for the music anymore. It was playing the gig to sustain the lifestyle: the limos, suites, groupies, and cocaine."

"It's hard to accept success in a certain way," Gregg had told Geraldo Rivera in August. "The music business is so fast and it's all pressure. I went through a long state of depression this last year." He attributed pulling out of those struggles to his love for music—"if I couldn't play, I'd be dead"— and the love from his "good woman, Cher."

In 1975, the band traveled again on a chartered plane, which was smaller and less glamorous than the *Starship*, but still a considerable expense. They also had an ever-expanding crew, and thus payroll. Betts had two old Florida friends Buddy and Sid Yochim with him "to help him fight," said Odom, and Allman had both Scooter Herring and Chank Middleton as personal minders. "That was excessive, but we needed them both, just to keep going," said Perkins.

When crew members complained to him about Middleton's no-work job status, Allman suggested that he carry his guitar in and out of the venue every night, which he did. Middleton later acknowledged his real role was simply being Gregg's friend during the two years (1974–76) he was on the band payroll. "I'm going to be honest: I didn't do nothing for them," he said.

The expanding size of the crew became a growing expense. The joke that the roadies had roadies was based on truth; two hires were added in 1974 because the roadies needed a keyboardist and second guitarist for their own band, the Almost Brothers. The group featured Twiggs on guitar, Buddy Thornton on bass, and Red Dog and Mike Artz, sound engineer and Trucks's brother-in-law, on drums. They began by conducting sound checks for the Allman Brothers Band since the group never bothered to do so. David "Trash" Cole was tending to the horses on the Allman Brothers Band farm after Dale Betts had medical problems. Lyndon heard him play, realized he was a fine picker, and hired him ostensibly as a guitar tech, but really to join the Almost Brothers in place of Barry Richman, an excellent Atlanta guitarist.

At a show in Dallas, a young lady asked Lyndon if she could play Leavell's piano as he set the stage. Amazingly, he agreed, no doubt in part because Virginia Speed was a petite, attractive brunette. She sat down and played brilliantly and was immediately offered a crew job—so that she could become the Almost Brothers' keyboardist. With no actual crew position available, she was named the road laundry lady and left with them that night. With these reinforcements in place, the Almost Brothers advanced to playing shows around Macon and recorded a ten-song album, *A Band of Roadies,* at Capricorn Studios.

28

... AND JUSTICE FOR ALL

D ICKEY BETTS STARTED pursuing Cher's striking assistant, Paulette Eghiazarian, immediately after meeting her backstage at Roosevelt Stadium on September 13, 1975. He repeatedly invited her to the October 5 Omni show, an offer she consistently rebuffed. However, the day before the concert, she found herself in an Atlanta hotel with Cher after flying down to rescue her friend from a disastrous trip to Jamaica with Gregg. They were supposed to fly back to L.A., but Cher suggested they stay over for the concert.

With Gregg still absent, Dickey took them both out to Underground Atlanta and turned on the charm. Backstage at the Omni the next night, Paulette met not only Jimmy Carter, who introduced the band onstage, but also Dickey's mother, Sarah, and her twin sister, Eldora, as well as a variety of the guitarist's good friends.

"Cher made up with Gregory and they went off together and I ended up spending the night with Dickey," said Paulette. "I met and loved his family. His mother is one of my favorite people in the universe, one of the best human beings you could ever meet. With her there, I saw something in Dickey beyond the guy with bad pickup lines. He was on his best behavior, and nothing could be more of an aphrodisiac to him than a woman turning him down for a month."

Their romance blossomed throughout the rest of the year and into the next, and by May 1976, Paulette moved to Macon to live with Dickey over the objections of Cher, who vowed to never speak to her again if Paulette left Los Angeles. She did indeed quit speaking to her, just another conflict roiling in and around the Allman Brothers Band organization.

BY 1975, DICKEY had gotten Billy Joe Shaver signed to Capricorn, and the two regularly raised hell around Macon. One evening, Willie Perkins received a call from the city jail. They had Betts and Shaver in custody, where they continued carrying on. "Come down and get these guys out of there," the caller said. Their behavior was so out of line, even the jail didn't want them.

That incident stayed out of the news, but from 1975 to 1978, stories of the band's lawsuits against Capricorn and band members' legal, financial, and health problems filled the pages of Macon's two newspapers. Articles covered multiple alimony and child-support suits for Gregg, as well as his failure to pay travel agency bills; Betts's arrest for disorderly conduct and trashing jail cells; Trucks's multiple drunk driving accidents; and canceled tour dates allegedly due to Jaimoe's back problems. While the drummer really did have recurring lumbar issues that often made it hard for him to perform, the real reason the second leg of the 1975 tour was canceled was rising tensions during five fall California dates. At a show in Bakersfield, Betts asked, "What the hell is going on up here?" over the microphone, and in Los Angeles he and Allman screamed at each other backstage. Blaming it on Jaimoe's back was kinder and gentler.

Most ominous was a January 21, 1976, headline in the *Macon Telegraph*: "Allman Granted Immunity in Probe." Gregg gave testimony to a federal grand jury to determine if there was sufficient evidence to warrant indictment of an unnamed suspected offender. Though grand jury proceedings are supposed to remain secret, Gregg was too famous to hide in the two days he testified, especially in Macon.

The story wasn't yet a scandal or even major news. It appeared in small type at the bottom of the front page, blandly starting, "Rock superstar Gregg Allman was granted immunity from prosecution on federal drug charges last week and ordered to testify against some drug distributors in the Middle Georgia area." This straightforward report gave little hint of the trouble this case would soon cause Allman and his band. The article didn't make clear what Allman was testifying about in the case, described as an investigation into an "alleged multi-million-dollar international drug ring."

The story noted that prosecutors had granted Allman immunity in exchange for testimony after he had twice invoked his Fifth Amendment rights against self-incrimination. Allman, the article noted, provided evidence against local pharmacists and physicians and did not mention Allman Brothers Band crew member Scooter Herring, Gregg's right-hand man, who was also being pressured to testify in the case, against local crime boss J.C. Hawkins—in large part because of Herring providing drugs to Gregg.

After giving the grand jury testimony in January and before performing with the Allman Brothers at a one-off March 13 benefit for Geraldo Rivera's charity for developmentally disabled children, Gregg returned to Los Angeles to be with Cher, who was expecting their first child. He naively hoped the legal case would settle down with time and distance. That was not the case.

Allman said that his lawyer told him that the federal prosecutors threatened him with prosecution if he didn't testify, noting that they already had testimony from several people, including his ex-wife, Jan, implicating him in drug offenses. The prosecutors seemed determined to implicate someone associated with Capricorn or the Allman Brothers Band.

"It was terrible," Allman said. "I was up against the wall . . . backed in the corner."

The *Macon Telegraph* story about Gregg's testimony ran right below a top-of-the-page package of stories about Jimmy Carter's triumph in Iowa. Though Carter finished ten points behind "Uncommitted," his 27.6 percent support was double that of his closest challenger, Senator Birch Bayh of Indiana. Hamilton Jordan's plan was working. After Iowa, Carter was no longer an unknown underdog and was edging toward front-runner status. Throughout the winter and spring, his candidacy continued to gain steam, as did the federal drug case in Macon.

Rolling Stone reported that the federal grand jury investigation focused on "the local music scene of which Capricorn Records is at its center." Walden believed the investigation by the U.S. Attorney's Office, initiated by appointees of Republican president Gerald Ford, aimed to discredit the Allman Brothers, linchpins of the Carter campaign. "They wanted to get me so bad," Walden said. "They had people following me."

The idea that the drug prosecution was politically connected seemed less fanciful as it became ever more likely that Jimmy Carter would be President Ford's opponent in November. Mainstream press accounts hinted at the possibility; it wasn't just paranoia being expressed by Walden, who claimed to have discovered that law enforcement had as many as five people working undercover at Capricorn Studios and quickly issued a strict no-drugs policy to all his employees.

"It was a scary time in Macon," said Mark Pucci, who was a Capricorn publicist. "Everyone was paranoid that the feds were coming to their house next."

"The Republican Party in Macon thought that we were running drugs and they wanted to nab either Phil, Willie or me," said Bunky Odom.

With these concerns swelling and the grand jury taking testimony and evidence, Walden hired John Condon. The brilliant Buffalo, New York, defense attorney had defended Twiggs Lyndon in his 1970 murder trial and helped the band escape drug charges after an arrest in Jackson, Alabama, in March 1971. He now came to Macon with two associates to assist in preparation for the grand jury investigation, which Walden felt sure was targeting him, "a very logical thing for him to think," said attorney Thomas Santa Lucia, one of Condon's Buffalo associates.

Rumors about the drug probe were swirling when the band returned to Macon following their final tour date, May 4, 1976. They soon learned they were in a precarious financial position, spending money with the profligacy they had grown accustomed to even while they performed less and for smaller amounts. Their last stretch of touring had netted them a total profit of $100,000, though they had grossed $175,000 at the Superdome alone for the performance that launched their final run of shows. "They were blowing through money faster than we could make it," says Perkins. "It was precipitous."

ABOVE: The Grateful Dead's Jerry Garcia sat in for much of the Allman Brothers Band's New Years Eve, 1973, show at the Cow Palace in San Francisco, which was broadcast to a worldwide radio audience estimated at 40 million.

ABOVE "I always wondered what the other guys in the Brothers thought when Gregg started showing up in his white suit," said Cameron Crowe. Cow Palace, December 31, 1973.

ABOVE: Dickey Betts and Sandy "Blue Sky" Wabegijig were married in a traditional Native American ceremony on April 14, 1973, at the Allman Brothers Band farm in Juliette, Georgia.

AT LEFT: The bride and groom with Stanley Smith, a Creek medicine man and Baptist minister, who conducted their wedding ceremony.

TOP: The first leg of the Gregg Allman Tour 74, with the string section visible in the background. Guitarist Tommy Talton on the right, Scott Boyer on the left, with Bill Stewart on drums. Auditorium Theater, Chicago, March 22, 1974.
KIRK WEST

BOTTOM: Gregg Allman and Tommy Talton, second solo tour, November 9, 1974, Winterland, San Francisco. ALVAN MEYEROWITZ/© RETRO PHOTO ARCHIVE

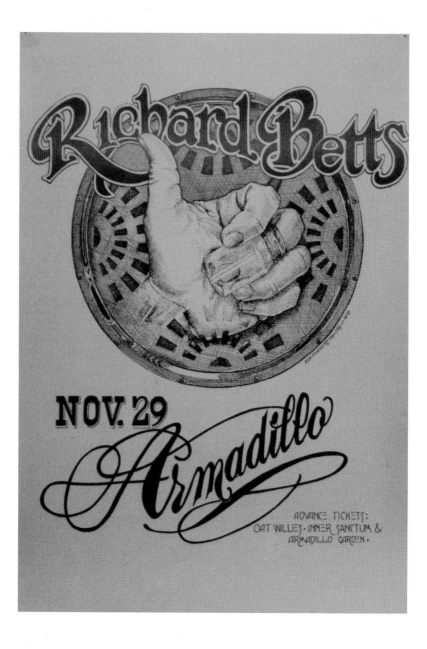

Poster for Richard Betts and the American Music Show at the Armadillo
World Headquarters, Austin, Texas, November 29, 1974.
COURTESY OF THE BIG HOUSE MUSEUM ARCHIVES

TOP: Dickey Betts and Vassar Clements with the American Music Show, December 14, 1974, Winterland, San Francisco.
ALVAN MEYEROWITZ/© RETRO PHOTO ARCHIVE

BOTTOM: The harmony lines that Dickey Betts and Vassar Clements "effortlessly played together were stunning," according to the Nitty Gritty Dirt Band's Jeff Hanna, who played with them on *Highway Call*.
SIDNEY SMITH/ALLMANBROTHERSBOOKBYSIDNEYSMITH.COM

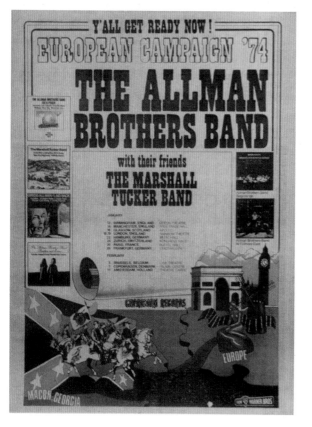

TOP: From 1973 through 1975, when the Allman Brothers Band were at the peak of their popularity, they rarely took group photos. Macon photographer Gilbert Lee spent two weeks camped out at their practice space trying to get one. By the time they all showed up, Dickey had a black eye, Gregg had a cast on his hand, it was over 100 degrees, and no one really wanted to pose. During his wait, Lee got a lot of informal smaller-group photos. This one is unusual because Allman and Betts were both present—one of them was usually the missing member. GILBERT LEE

BOTTOM: Jimmy Carter visited the Capricorn Studios while Richard Betts was recording his 1974 solo album *Highway Call*. Producer Johnny Sandlin is at the console. HERB KOSSOVER

ABOVE: Governor Jimmy Carter meeting with Phil Walden at the Capricorn Records offices, 1974.
SIDNEY SMITH/
ALLMANBROTHERSBOOKBYSIDNEYSMITH.COM

TOP LEFT: Phil Walden, Jimmy Carter, and unidentified attendee at the 1976 Capricorn Picnic and BBQ, Macon, Georgia.
JIMMY CARTER LIBRARY, CARTER FAMILY PAPERS

MIDDLE LEFT: From left: Watkins Glen promoter Jim Koplik (back to camera), promoter Larry Magid, Phil Walden, and Jimmy Carter at the 1976 Capricorn annual picnic.
JIMMY CARTER LIBRARY, CARTER FAMILY PAPERS

BOTTOM LEFT: Jimmy Carter and his sons, Chip (left) and Jeff, with Bob Dylan at the Georgia Governor's Mansion, January 2, 1974.
JIMMY CARTER LIBRARY, CARTER FAMILY PAPERS

"I'm proud of my relationship with the Allman Brothers Band," Jimmy Carter said. "They are good people, they are my friends, and anybody who wants a President who doesn't like music like this, and who doesn't like people who make music like this, should just simply vote for another man." JIMMY CARTER LIBRARY, 1976 CAMPAIGN FILES

TOP: The Allman Brothers Band had a close relationship with the Marshall Tucker Band. Dickey Betts and Toy Caldwell during a Betts sit-in with the MTB, Santa Monica Civic Auditorium, October 4, 1975. JOHN GELLMAN

BOTTOM LEFT: Late night drunken jam antics at Uncle Sam's Club, Macon, Georgia, late 1974. From left: Elvin Bishop, John Hammond Jr, the Marshall Tucker Band's Doug Grey, Wet Willie's Jimmy Hall, and Gregg Allman. SIDNEY SMITH/ALLMANBROTHERSBOOKBYSIDNEYSMITH.COM

BOTTOM RIGHT: Chuck and Gregg, jamming at Uncle Sam's Club, 1974. "Having two keyboardists was just so interesting," said Chuck Leavell. "It opened up a lot of possibilities. Gregg and I inspired each other." SIDNEY SMITH/ALLMANBROTHERSBOOKBYSIDNEYSMITH.COM

TOP LEFT: Gregg Allman and his mushroom-bedecked Hammond B3 organ and personalized Leslie speaker, Chicago Stadium, November 1, 1973. KIRK WEST

TOP RIGHT: The Allman Brothers Band, Winterland, September 26, 1973, the same night that Cameron Crowe did his famous interview. It was also the first time that Kirk West photographed the band. KIRK WEST

BOTTOM LEFT: Gregg appeared on Geraldo Rivera's *Good Night America* on August 14, 1975, played two songs with a band that included Jaimoe, Lamar Williams, and Chuck Leavell, along with guitarist Davis Causey and drummer Bill Stewart, and discussed the burdens of fame and his marriage to Cher.
COURTESY OF GERALDO RIVERA

BOTTOM RIGHT: Dickey Betts and Capricorn Records President Frank Fenter at the latter's La Brasserie restaurant, early 1976. HERB KOSSOVER

The drummer born Johnie Lee Johnson was nicknamed Jaimoe by Randolph "Juicy" Carter, with whom he played in the Percy Sledge Band, and went by various names over the years. Playing with Otis Redding, his bass drum read "Jai Johnny Johnson," and by the time of the Allman Brothers Band's 1969 debut, he had become "Jai Johanny Johanson." By any name, Johnson was the heart and soul of the Allman Brothers Band from their first note to their last.

TOP: Phil Walden and Gregg Allman review *Brothers and Sisters* cover art in the manager's Capricorn Records office. HERB KOSSOVER

ABOVE LEFT: Lamar Williams, Macon, 1973. "Berry's death was almost unbearable, but Lamar was the perfect replacement," said Gregg Allman. "It's amazing we found him." SIDNEY SMITH/ALLMANBROTHERSBOOKBYSIDNEYSMITH.COM

ABOVE RIGHT: Chuck and Rose Lane White Leavell were married July 26, 1973. She worked in the Capricorn office from 1970 through 1973. HERB KOSSOVER

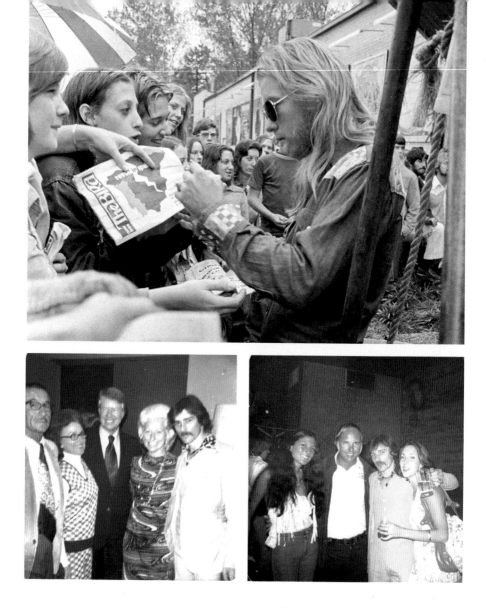

TOP: Gregg Allman signs autographs, including a copy of Atlanta's underground newspaper *The Great Speckled Bird*, upon arriving at an in-store appearance promoting *Win, Lose or Draw*, at Peaches Records, October 5, 1975. TOM HILL/GETTY IMAGES

BOTTOM LEFT: Backstage at the Omni, Atlanta, October 5, 1975. From right: Dickey Betts, his mother Sarah, presidential candidate Jimmy Carter, Sarah's twin sister, Eldora, and Eldora's husband. COURTESY OF PAULETTE HOWELL

BOTTOM RIGHT: Paulette Eghiazarian on her first date with Dickey Betts, backstage at the Atlanta Omni, October 5, 1975, with two unknown friends. COURTESY OF PAULETTE HOWELL

Kirk West recorded hundreds of hours of interviews with the members of the Allman Brothers Band and many friends, family, and associates in the mid-1980s for a book project. They gathered dust in his Macon, Georgia, office for almost forty years before he passed them on to author Alan Paul for use in this book in September 2021.

JACOB BLUMENSTEIN PAUL

TOP: Gregg, Cher, and family with the Freeze, Canisius High School, Buffalo, New York, October 20, 1976. Left to right: Mike Davis, Doug Cameron, Howie Bartolo, Gregg Allman, Cher, Ellard "Moose" Bowles, Gary Zamory, and Rick Cappotto.

BOTTOM: Gregg and Cher with three-year-old Chaz and the infant Elijah Blue, Canisius High School, Buffalo, New York, October 20, 1976.

On May 28, the band met to get more serious about their finances—"talking about getting rid of some of these roadies and the private plane and tightening up the money," Allman said. They also discussed the looming drug charges. Chank Middleton offered to take the rap, but Herring, already under investigation, said he would "take the heat." As if on cue, law enforcement officers entered the Capricorn offices to arrest Herring.

Willie Perkins resigned, hoping it would jolt the band, but they were now completely focused on legal matters. The grand jury indicted Herring on five counts of conspiracy to distribute narcotics that carried a potential maximum sentence of seventy-five years. Gregg said that when he realized he had full immunity only if he testified against his friend, he ran to his attorney's office and sat down with him and Herring, asking what they should do, and that Scooter said, "Tell the truth and I'll deal with it."

FIVE WEEKS AFTER the Iowa caucuses, Carter won the New Hampshire primary. Carter's victory led CBS's Walter Cronkite, the most trusted voice in American news at the time, to proclaim Carter the front-runner for the nomination. Thirty-three-year-old Joe Biden of Delaware became the first senator to endorse Carter.

Carter floundered to a fourth-place finish in Massachusetts before defeating former Alabama governor George Wallace by four points in Florida on March 9. Two weeks later, Carter topped Wallace by twenty points in North Carolina. These wins had great symbolic importance. Wallace represented the past that many Southerners, including Walden and the band, wanted to move away from. Carter represented an inclusive future.

First-term California governor Jerry Brown was a late entry into the race. The only other candidate to understand the power of rock and roll, he had the backing of much of the Los Angeles music industry. The Eagles, Jackson Browne, and his sometime girlfriend Linda Ronstadt were among those who helped Governor Brown raise money. He garnered momentum but did not enter the race until March. Despite winning Maryland, Nevada, and his home state, Brown was not able to slow Carter's march to the nomination. Gone were the days when a candidate could win over party bosses and be crowned at the convention. On the last day of the primary season, June 9, Carter won Ohio by a large margin and finished second to Brown in California. He had effectively won the nomination. Plains, Georgia, erupted in a party.

ALSO ON JUNE 9, 1976, the FBI took Gregg Allman into custody to ensure he did not skip town before the drug trial and also to protect him from those who stood to lose their freedom as a chain reaction. Allman had good reason to be wary. Scooter Herring's charges resulted from a federal investigation into drug trafficking and police corruption in Macon that pointed toward the Hawkins gang, the local branch of the "Dixie Mafia" (also called the Cornbread Mafia or Hillbilly Mob), an informal network of crooks and thugs with no formal ties to the better-known organized crime families. An agent in the intelligence division of the Fulton County District Attorney's Office described them as "a loose knit group of traveling criminals" operating in the Southeast. They were, he said, "notorious for contract killings" and, while he noted that there is no nice way to kill someone, the Dixie Mafia, he said, were "particularly sadistic."

J.C. Hawkins, the central Georgia crime boss, lived up to that description. He had a fierce reputation and a fondness for violence and had evaded prosecution for years. In May 1974, one of his lieutenants was shot to death before he could testify against Hawkins, who was heard on a federal wiretap saying, "That fink son of bitch won't be around much longer."

Gregg did not know Hawkins, but Herring did, and he refused to testify against the crime boss in the grand jury proceedings. Squeezing Allman to testify against his own security man and drug connection was likely part of an attempt to flip Herring to testify against Hawkins, but he wasn't having any of it. He preferred to do his time rather than find out what would happen if he became a government witness against J.C. Hawkins.

"They made it clear that they would kill him, inside prison or out," said Allman, who still refused to say the names over a decade later. "These were some bad boys."

Around the same time, the FBI arrested Hawkins and five others for violations of the Racketeering Influence and Corrupt Organization (RICO) Act, a new law established to prosecute organized crime. The indictment charged the gang with a host of offenses that included extortion, drug trafficking, insurance fraud, arson, counterfeiting, running a car-theft and truck-hijacking ring, and the murder of an associate turned witness.

The feds indicted Scooter Herring along with Joe Fuchs, the pharmacist who was selling illegal drugs on the side, including pharmaceutical cocaine. Fuchs quickly pled guilty to conspiracy to possess cocaine with the intent to sell and agreed to testify against Herring. Herring still refused to cooperate, maintaining loyalty both to Allman and to the fearsome Hawkins gang.

Jury selection began on June 21, and the trial, which would last just three days, commenced on June 23. With less than a month from indictment to trial, there was "virtually no time to prepare a defense," said Santa Lucia, Herring's lead attorney, who was paid by Capricorn. Condon remained Walden's counsel, in case he should get pulled in.

Herring's trial was a significant media event given Allman's stardom. The Macon federal courthouse was subject to strict security, with U.S. marshals frisking all attendees. No one from the band or label attended, though Willie Perkins, now an ex-employee, did. Allman testified on the afternoon of the first day of trial and part of the following day. Both Fuchs and Allman testified that Herring furnished cocaine and painkillers to Allman through January 1975. Fuchs also testified that in the summer of 1974, Herring balked at continuing to deliver drugs to Allman, saying that "Gregg was getting a drug problem."

Under cross-examination, Allman acknowledged that Herring had tried to get him to stop. When Santa Lucia asked Allman if Herring had ever saved his life when he was overdosing, he acknowledged that he had indeed overdosed in New York City in June 1973 but wasn't sure what had happened or who had saved him. "All I remember is waking up in an ambulance," he said.

Forty-six years later, on his ninety-second birthday, Santa Lucia recalled that he felt at a disadvantage as an outsider—a northerner in an insular Southern environment, with no real cultural understanding of the local population. His biggest, longest-lasting regret was hitting Allman too hard on cross-examination. He didn't understand "just how much the jury loved Allman," he said.

Allman was not feeling any love when he testified, however. His primary observation from his seat in the witness stand was that none of his band-mates or management were in the courtroom. He felt alone. "No one was out there except the press writing in their notebooks," he said.

Gregg's testimony was major news. The next day, June 25, would be the trial's last and most dramatic day, with Herring testifying in his own defense. A banner headline in the *Macon Telegraph* ramped up the al-ready circus-like atmosphere surrounding the trial: "Allman Under Heavy Guard. Death Threats Reported." A large photograph showed Allman being escorted into the courthouse by serious-looking men. The story reported that federal officials had confirmed that Allman had received threats on his life and that "stiff security measures" were in force.

Santa Lucia asked Judge Owens to poll every juror about whether they had seen the article, expressing concern that it was prejudicial; the implica-tion, he said, was that it was Herring who had threatened Allman. The judge refused, which inwardly thrilled the attorney, who now had an avenue for appeal. "It really seemed like a slam dunk request," he said. The case went to the jury, who deliberated for less than three hours, including a lunch break, before finding Herring guilty on all counts.

Almost a month later, on July 19, Judge Owens threw the book at Her-ring, sentencing him to the maximum fifteen years on each count, to run consecutively, not concurrently, which meant seventy-five years in prison. The judge did not shy away from admitting that he was punishing Herring for refusing to cooperate in building a case against Hawkins. "Without getting into specifics, your case involves other cases," he said. "You know that, your lawyer knows it, and the court knows it."

Judge Owens also lashed out against what was perceived to be a growing sentiment in the local community that Herring was a scapegoat, and he gave a speech defending the prosecutors' controversial decision to grant Allman immunity. "Let's be realistic," he said. "If somebody had not been given immunity you would not have been prosecuted. A whole lot of other people would not have been prosecuted. We would just have the public complaining about a larger number of people who had not been prose-cuted."

"It was a harsh sentence, but it wasn't surprising, and we all knew that Herring would never serve 75 years," said Santa Lucia. The judge would receive a report back from the Federal Bureau of Prisons in three months, when there would be another hearing to reconsider how long Herring would serve.

Several weeks after the trial, Santa Lucia filed an appeal centered on Judge Owens's failure to poll the jurors about the article, and he became eligible for bail. The band used a $125,000 royalty check from Warner Bros to put up the $100,000 necessary to secure Scooter's release.

Shortly after Herring's trial ended, that of J.C. Hawkins and his associates began. With Joe Fuchs one of the prosecution's chief witnesses, the gang was convicted of multiple charges, including conspiracy to commit murder. Hawkins was sentenced to eighty years in prison. His appeal was denied in 1981, but he was released in 1988, having served twelve years.

29

THE NIGHT THE LIGHTS
WENT OUT IN GEORGIA

GREGG ALLMAN LEFT Macon for Los Angeles after the trial, and it didn't appear likely that he would ever return. The entire rock world seemed to have excommunicated him for his testimony against his friend.

There were several opportunities for Herring's sentence to be reduced, no one knowledgeable expected him to serve anything near seventy-five years, and he was free on bail as soon as his appeal was filed. He would win the appeal, plead guilty to lesser charges, and be sentenced to thirty months in prison, but the public's impression was sealed the day the original sentence was delivered: to save himself, Gregg Allman had testified against his friend and drug dealer, who was sentenced to seventy-five years. That's what people believed, and the reaction was harsh.

"No one wanted anything to do with him," Walden said.

"When you get called to a grand jury, you better not lie, but no one wanted to hear it," said Bunky Odom. "The backlash against Gregg was so horrible."

Odom said that he spoke with Jerry Garcia and Grateful Dead manager Rock Scully and they only had one question: "Is Gregg a rat?" That reaction was the real reason why the rift between the Grateful Dead and the Allman Brothers Band never healed, and why Gregg made negative comments about the Dead in later years. The rift had little to do with music and everything to do with his feeling abandoned by friends and resentful at being shunned and publicly humiliated for being squeezed in a no-win situation that threatened his freedom. The list of rock stars who would do jail time to protect a crew member is short.

But being rejected by other bands or music business associates was the least important of the reasons why Allman was resentful of his fate. No one in the Allman Brothers would take Gregg's phone calls either, and they communicated their stance toward Gregg to the press. Gregg felt completely abandoned by his bandmates, the supposed brotherhood, during and in the immediate aftermath of the trial.

"The fact is, not one [member] of the Allman Brothers Band was at that trial," he told *Rolling Stone,* one of the group's prime methods of communicating to one another. "Therefore, I can only believe that they made up their minds on hearsay alone. They weren't there to see the pressure. They weren't there to see the cat holding my manuscript right in my nose just . . . fucking daring me to swerve off of it just enough to get me on a perjury charge."

All his bandmates would eventually acknowledge and express remorse over their failure to talk to Gregg or better understand his dilemma. "Though we were in Macon, we were getting our information by reading about the trial," Trucks said. "We thought Gregg had copped a plea and really didn't know he didn't have much of a choice. And we weren't talking enough to find out his story."

No band member other than Gregg seemed to understand Scooter's connection to the Dixie Mafia and so they did not grasp the pressure on Gregg, and none of them seemed particularly interested in learning more. The personal relationships were frayed and broken. Their time together had brought joyous musical highs and tremendous success, but the death, sorrow, and substance abuse finally became too much to bear.

"Everyone made too big a deal of the trial," Trucks said. "It was the final straw—a good enough reason to go our separate ways. It had all soured. No one was having any fun. If this had happened a few years earlier, Dickey and I would have been over there and known what was happening. We were all fed up with each other."

On August 19, 1976, the *Macon News* published a letter to the editor from Jaimoe, proclaiming that he could never play with Gregg again. He wrote, in part: "I love Gregg Allman, but for eight years I have watched him hurt the people who loved him for Gregg, not for the 'rock star' [which] people in money and groupie magazines proclaimed him to be. He wasted himself on the ones that did not give a darn more than they could get out of him. They are the vampires, leeches, etc. He overstepped his boundaries when he got a man who saved his life more than once a 75-year jail sentence—John Charles 'Scooter' Herring."

A couple of weeks later, Betts told *Rolling Stone*, "There is no way we can work with Gregg Allman again, ever." Leavell added, "As far as I'm concerned, the band has disbanded. When a band gets to the point where they can't or won't work, then it's time to just go and do something different."

Cher, then nine months pregnant, summed up her and Gregg's post-trial situation succinctly to *People*: "Our whole world was shot to ratshit."

And so the Allman Brothers Band broke up. The end came without an official announcement, a big fight, or a final tour or farewell concert. Instead, the band ended by publicly disparaging each other in print. Just two years after being the country's most popular band, rising from the ashes following Duane's and Berry's deaths, the Allman Brothers Band just kind of fizzled away. Capricorn publicity manager Mike Hyland said that "there was no chance of the band getting back together." They were no more.

Rolling Stone predicted it was the end of Gregg's musical career, implying that his violation of unspoken rock and roll code would lead to his eternal banishment. "It seems likely Allman will find it difficult to ever perform in public again," Patrick Snyder wrote.

One person who did not abandon Gregg or Capricorn was the one who had the most obvious reason to do so: Jimmy Carter. *People* chronicled Allman's struggles with heroin on its cover, yet Jimmy Carter, months away from a presidential election, refused to cut ties. "We didn't consider it to be our problem," said Peter Conlon of the Carter campaign. "People have problems in their lives and Jimmy Carter was not going to turn his back on a friend. He just wasn't going to do it."

Cher gave birth to her and Gregg's son, Elijah Blue, on July 10, 1976, three weeks after the trial and two days before the Democratic convention began at New York's Madison Square Garden. Carter called the couple with congratulations and did anything but back away from his rock and roll associations. Accepting his party's nomination on July 15, he said, "We have an America that, in Bob Dylan's phrase, is busy being born, not dying."

Even after the trial, and with the general election campaign against an incumbent president having begun, Carter did not put any distance between his campaign and the Allman Brothers Band. The connection was not missed by the press. The *Atlanta Constitution* directly said that the prosecution of Herring and Fuchs had "something to do with the behind-the-scenes aspects of presidential politics." And conservative *New York Times* columnist William Safire, a former speechwriter for Richard M. Nixon, opined that Carter's "Capricorn connection" needed scrutiny. "To what extent," he asked, was the candidate "indebted to Philip Walden?" The implications were that Carter's campaign had been funded by dirty money and that the connection should be explored by the Ford campaign.

The September 3 issue of *New Times* magazine went so far as to feature a cover illustration of a Bible-toting Carter standing with Walden and Allman holding a coke spoon to his nose. The cover line read, "Jimmy's friends in rock. Phil Walden, Macon's Music man, helped shape Carter's rise. Can he survive Gregg Allman's Fall?" Gregg called it a "terrible thing to do." The magazine had a wide reach in Washington circles, and the cover caused ripples of panic in Macon, but not, apparently, in the Carter campaign.

Carter continued to praise Walden and acknowledge his help even after there was little more to be gained from the relationship. It would have been politically expedient for Carter to distance himself from Walden to avoid negative publicity, but he appreciated the support Walden provided the campaign when he was a little-known candidate. The money kept the campaign alive at a time when it was in significant debt. Without it, the campaign may have had to fold its tent. The enormous public relations value and Carter's increased visibility and popularity with the nation's young voters lasted through the general election.

"How much money was raised is actually secondary to what Phil Walden [did] for the campaign," said Betty Rainwater, Carter's deputy press secretary. "It's my personal feeling that what Walden did was build a bridge of communication with a whole new group of people and that is far more important than any money that was raised."

Carter attended Walden's annual Capricorn picnic on August 19, about seventy-five days before the election and less than two months after the trial's conclusion. He walked through a surging crowd of six thousand with Walden, then turned to reporters and said, "[Walden] and his recording stars understand the consciousness of the American people, particularly young people. The rock music industry and its stars have helped make possible changes in attitudes that are beneficial to our country, bringing an end to wars, correcting some of the racial discrimination, alleviating pollution . . . and elevating the influence of young people in politics and government."

Carter was elected president on November 2, 1976, and there was speculation about whether Walden would receive any payback for his efforts. He scoffed at the idea. "People said I was a fool to not demand something in return from President Carter," Walden said. "Why would I want to be an ambassador? They could have had a flood of women and drug dealers at my confirmation hearing. I didn't want to embarrass him. I wanted him to be proud of me, as I was proud of him."

Every Allman Brothers Band member attended the inauguration on January 20, 1977. Sea Level—Jaimoe, Leavell, and Williams, along with guitarist Jimmy Nalls—played on the White House lawn, following one of Jaimoe's heroes, jazz great Buddy Rich. Betts and Allman were seated together at another event. It was the first time since the breakup that they saw each other, and things were still icy. They attended with their wives, former best friends Cher and Paulette, who still weren't speaking to each other. "None of us had anything to say to one another," said Paulette.

30

ONE MORE TRY

AFTER THE TRIAL, after the breakup, after being abandoned by most of his closest friends, allies, and bandmates, Gregg went to Buffalo to give rehab one more try. In the fall of 1976, he entered an outpatient rehab facility in the city that had ironically become the Allman Brothers Band's center for detox and stability after a terrifying and disturbing incident: Twiggs Lyndon's murder of a club owner in 1970 and his subsequent trial. Defense attorney John Condon then became the band's trusted fixer, and his hometown their rehab refuge. Gregg had failed to show up for the Duane-led 1971 hospital trip, but five years later he was all in for an extended stay to try and kick his addiction and save his marriage to Cher.

It didn't take long for word to spread among area music lovers that Allman was in town. Mike Militello, the senior class president at Buffalo's Canisius High, had the outlandish idea that the school's senior social committee should invite Gregg to visit their high school. Brian Procknal, one of the committee members, recalled that when the *Buffalo Courier Express* newspaper published a story about Gregg and Cher being in town, it included the name of the hospital where Gregg was receiving treatment. At a committee meeting, Militello said, "Gregg Allman is in town, and we have the address. Why don't we write him a letter and ask him to come here?"

The entire committee proceeded to write letters and send them to the hospital, but it was Procknal's that struck a nerve with Gregg. A few days later, his mother answered the family phone in the kitchen to hear a deep voice with a Southern drawl asking for her son. Procknal hurried to the phone, hoping it was the manager of the McDonald's where he had recently applied for a job calling to offer him the position; he couldn't imagine any other adult who would be phoning. When Allman identified himself, Procknal, sure it was a friend pranking him, cursed him out.

Once he realized that it really was Gregg Allman on the phone, the awed teenager apologized profusely and began to listen as the rock star opened up in a surprisingly intimate way. "I don't know what it is about your letter but there's something about it," Allman told Procknal. It had touched his heart, he said, because it was just so simple. "I don't know what I want to do, but I want to do something," he concluded.

Looking back, Procknal thinks that Allman was attracted to the fact that the letter didn't come off as fan mail. It wasn't the gushing of a fanboy— which made sense, since Procknal was only a casual fan. "I didn't go on and on about the Allman Brothers and how much I loved them, but just said that I'd heard that he was in town and if he felt like coming around, he could just talk or play a guitar or whatever," Procknal said. "There was no pressure or expectations."

They had a second phone conversation, during which Allman began speaking about a performance at Canisius High. "The second time he called, he said that he was going to get a band together and perform be-cause my letter had stuck with him like a sign," Procknal said. "It was the universe telling him to get back to what made him happy: playing music."

Allman told Procknal to keep this between them for now, and they scheduled a face-to-face meeting. The student picked a time and place near Canisius High, and Allman said he'd pick him up there so they could talk in person. It was the day of a big football game against rival Saint Joe's, and because Procknal was a member of the pep squad, his face was painted in the school's blue-and-gold colors. When he climbed into the back of the waiting stretch limousine, he said that "Gregg looked at me with alarm, like I was crazy, and just asked what the fuck was I wearing," Procknal recalled with a laugh.

"I told him it was a rally and then I guess he forgot about it and started talking, and he just bared his soul. He said that it was a really hard time in his life, that his brother and one other important person had died, and the band had broken up. He was lost and in turmoil."

As they drove around in the limousine, one of the world's biggest rock stars poured his heart out to a seventeen-year-old kid he had just met. Just as he had during his interactions with Cameron Crowe three years earlier, Allman seemed more comfortable showing emotional vulnerability to a teenager than to a peer. Gregg said that he was in a "tough place" and spoke a lot about God and spirituality. "He was very religious," Procknal said. "There was just something very sad about him. He seemed to be kind of broken."

Allman told Procknal that his family—the band—was split apart and he was trying to get back to a solid footing, "a good place," rooted in God, love, and family. Allman was searching for something, and Procknal's letter had connected with him, a bonding that continued in the car. He also may have sensed a vulnerability in Procknal, who was gay and struggling to realize his sexuality. Procknal believes that their shared pain and vulnerability created a bond and unlikely friendship between them.

"I think we were both suffering, in pain and afraid of what the future was all about—too afraid to even talk about it," said Procknal. "You do this thing where you just get it out of your head and don't think about it, which just makes it more painful until you learn to accept who you are. Of course, we didn't discuss any of this, but I think that Gregg sensed my anguish, which made me easier to talk to. Neither of us were being our authentic selves."

Conversations continued over the next week, with Procknal and Allman meeting once or twice more at night. Somewhere along the way, Allman said that he wanted to perform a full show at the school. He would put together a band, he said, but there was one condition: "It's got to be a secret," he said. "You can't tell anybody."

Struggling not to scream the news to his friends, Procknal called Militello and told him the show was a go, but it couldn't be announced publicly. Gregg was adamant that he didn't want any press there, which would be impossible if word leaked out.

"Of course, I wanted to tell people, but I was also good at not disobeying," said Procknal. "We went to a Jesuit high school and were used to people telling us what to do. Plus, Gregg Allman told me not to tell anybody, and I didn't want to dishonor this guy who was pouring his heart out to me and be the asshole who spread the word. I kept the promise that I made to him."

Now they just had to get their Jesuit institution to agree to host a secret concert by a rock star famous for his struggles with drug addiction. The committee met with the school principal, the Reverend Joseph Papaj, who told *The Buffalo News* that he never really hesitated or saw Allman's appearance as a problem. He was instead impressed that Procknal, Militello, and the other committee members had managed to pull off this seemingly impossible feat, that they had taken the initiative and made it happen. And Papaj also thought it was wonderful that Gregg Allman had "responded to a group of young people he didn't know."

GREGG WAS IN Buffalo for over a month, receiving outpatient care for drug and alcohol addiction while living in the home of one of the hospital's psychiatrists. He went out at night, sampling the city's nightlife. While nobody who was with him during that time said they saw him drink, he liked to check out local bands and became familiar with some of Buffalo's after-hours gambling emporiums, where he favored craps.

One night, he walked into a bar where a cover band was playing. Gregg jammed with them on "Whipping Post" and "One Way Out" and was impressed that violinist Doug Cameron could play Duane's trademark slide licks. He wanted to play with him more.

"He told me that he missed playing music and asked for my phone number," said Cameron, who was a student at the University of Buffalo.

Gregg called soon after and asked him to bring his violin over to jam. They had several extended sessions at the psychiatrist's house. Cher and their son, Elijah Blue, as well as her child with Bono, three-year-old Chaz, came for several extended visits. On one of them, Cameron went apple picking with the Allman family, driving out to Orchard Park in a stretch limousine.

"Cher and Gregg were climbing up ladders and around tree limbs and dropping apples down to the limo driver," Cameron recalled. "It was all pretty surreal for a kid who was a huge Allman Brothers fan."

Allman had also gotten to know the members of Freeze, a popular local band, when they backed him at a fundraiser for the Buffalo Philhar-
monic, which also featured the Bills' running back, O.J. Simpson. Shortly
after, Allman called the band's bassist, Ellard "Moose" Bowles, and said he
had another gig in mind: he wanted Freeze to back him at Canisius High
for an upcoming performance.

THE SCHOOL HAD to come up with a plan to get the entire student body into
their ornate auditorium on the afternoon of October 20, 1976, without telling them why. Rev. Papaj came up with the idea of announcing a manda-
tory assembly about "acoustical science." Before the performance, Allman,
unaware it was a boys' school, asked Procknal, "Where's the chicks?"

Procknal took the stage, announced there had been a change of plans,
and introduced Gregg, who walked out with an acoustic guitar, accompanied only by Cameron. They played "These Days," after which Gregg
thanked the screaming crowd and introduced himself as an "acoustical
scientist." He said that the show had come together very quickly and that
he was "nervous as can be."

Then he and Cameron played a gorgeous "Melissa" before an audience
of stunned and enthusiastically cheering teenage boys. Cher sat onstage
watching with the kids. Following the two acoustic songs, the second
curtain opened, revealing the members of Freeze, who launched into
the unmistakable opening riff of "One Way Out." The crowd exploded,
clapping, stomping, and cheering. This acoustical-science assembly was
now a full-tilt-boogie rock and roll show. "The kids went nuts," recalled
drummer Rick Cappotto.

Together, they performed "One Way Out," "Queen of Hearts," "Hot
'Lanta," and "Stormy Monday," after which an energized Allman said, "I
want to thank you again for letting us do this." He then introduced his
family, saying of his wife, "If it wasn't for this lady, I probably . . . wouldn't
be here." When he announced "Mrs. Cher Allman," the crowd went wild,
stomping their feet and rhythmically chanting, "Thank you! Thank you!"

Gregg said they'd play one more, and the band launched into "You Don't
Love Me." When they finished, the auditorium again rocked with applause;
the tapes of this show pulse with energy and enthusiasm, driven by the fact

that no one in the building—onstage or in the audience—could quite believe what had just happened.

All of those who performed with Allman at this surreal event would do so again. He even invited Cameron to relocate to Los Angeles, and the violinist did so in January, after completing his college term, moving into Cher's Beverly Hills mansion, where he found himself in the middle of the couple's often turbulent life.

"I was twenty-one and in over my head," he said. "Cher was a wonderful, hard-working woman who was very kind to me, but their relationship was rocky."

Freeze would also play with Allman again. Word had spread around the Buffalo rock scene that they were now Gregg's jamming buddies, and their popular Monday nights at Patrick Henry's bar became packed affairs, with Allman Brothers Band fans hoping for a sit-in. The band started posting a note on the door that read, "No, Gregg Allman is not performing tonight. Neither is Elton John or Paul McCartney."

But then one Monday Gregg and Cher walked in, and Allman took the stage and played a set with the band, returning the favor to a group that had backed him twice. While Gregg played, Cher sat at the bar and took it in. Cappotto thought they were enjoying the opportunity to just be a normal couple, as they had at Canisius. After that performance, Gregg and Cher had attended a faculty reception and charmed the Jesuits.

"I think they simply appreciated finding people who weren't trying to gain anything from them," Procknal said. "Gregg was at a point where he wasn't talking to anybody or doing anything creative. His life was full of sad shit, legal problems and addiction issues."

He seemed to appreciate that Procknal had reached out in such a simple, natural way without appearing to have a hidden agenda. And in Cameron and Freeze, Gregg had found what he needed in that moment: people to play music for music's sake with. The music, at least, would never let him down. He would always have that.

EPILOGUE

BY 1977, THE members of the Allman Brothers Band had all begun new projects. "We all just needed to get out of Macon and away from each other for a while," Trucks said. "We needed some space."

Betts formed a solo band and released *Dickey Betts & Great Southern,* but a legal settlement with Capricorn essentially forbade him from using any members of his former band or using the words "Allman Brothers Band" in any way to promote or describe the album. Gregg also put together a new group, based in Los Angeles, and put out his second solo album, *Playin' Up a Storm,* defying *Rolling Stone*'s absurd idea that his career might be finished. He followed that up with an album with Cher, *Two The Hard Way,* rather absurdly billed as Allman And Woman. Jaimoe, Williams, and Leavell formed Sea Level, a jazz fusion–tinged band that grew out of the many times they were the only three Allman Brothers Band members to show up for rehearsals. They released their self-titled debut and hit the road.

Trucks moved to Tallahassee with his wife, Melinda, and their expanding family, and reenrolled at Florida State University. He thought he might be done with performing in bands forever, and hoped to get a master's degree in music and work in the classical field.

In March 1978, Scooter Herring was on the road with Sea Level, serving as their tour manager, when a reporter from the *Macon Telegraph* called to tell him that he had won his appeal and that his conviction would be thrown out. The full truth was a little more complicated than that, but Herring ultimately pled guilty to lesser charges to avoid another trial and served thirty months.

Paulette Eghiazarian and Betts were married on May 15, 1977, and settled down on a beautiful piece of land outside Sarasota, Florida. When she gave birth to their son, Duane, in April 1978, Cher sent flowers and their friendship resumed, even as Cher and Gregg's relationship was coming to an end. That was in line with the reconciliations going on throughout Allman Brothers Band land.

The group reunited for the first time in August 1978, when Allman, Trucks, and Jaimoe joined Great Southern for a five-song set in New York City's Central Park. Eight days later, they played together again, this time with Leavell and Williams, at Capricorn's annual picnic. As the group decided to officially re-form and record a new album, the two newer members opted to stick with Sea Level, which slowly petered out. Jaimoe had only lasted one album, forced out by his recurring back issues, the start of several lineup changes as the group struggled to find a commercial foothold playing mostly instrumental music, a pursuit made more difficult by Capricorn's steady decline. That was hastened by the label losing a steady stream of lawsuits filed by musicians seeking redress for underpayment of songwriting and performing royalties. When the cash spigot slowed to a drip, all the flaws were exposed.

Everyone seemed to be suing everyone, but mostly Phil Walden and Capricorn—starting with Sandlin, then Betts, then Trucks. The latter's claim also sought money due from the sale of an apartment building, contending that Walden held a stake and took a profit despite contributing nothing to the purchase. Leavell sued the band, saying that the founding members reneged on an agreement to pay him royalties as a band member rather than to use him as a hired performer. The band sued Capricorn to try to prevent the release of another greatest hits package.

Williams relocated to Los Angeles and started suffering a series of debilitating health problems. He died tragically in 1983, a week after his thirty-fourth birthday, the victim of cancer almost surely caused by exposure to the defoliant Agent Orange during his service in Vietnam. By then, Leavell was touring with the Rolling Stones, eventually becoming their musical director, while also serving as a killer pianist-for-hire, performing or recording with Eric Clapton, David Gilmour, the Black Crowes, and many others over the ensuing decades. He would never again be a member of the Allman Brothers Band and rarely performed with any of them for over ten years. By the time Leavell appeared as a special guest for several shows at New York's Beacon Theatre in 2001, Betts was out of the band. A new generation of fans fell in love with the Allman Brothers Band without him as a member, an outcome that would have been impossible to even contemplate for anyone who saw them during their *Brothers and Sisters* heyday. They quit playing "Ramblin' Man," which remained their only true hit single.

The Allman Brothers Band would never again have a lineup like they did from 1973 to 1976, with a single guitarist and two keyboardists. Multiple incarnations before their 2014 retirement featured the original Duane-era formation of two lead guitarists and Gregg on B3 and vocals. They were a guitar band, and this *Brothers and Sisters* configuration faded into a distant memory, a time capsule locked in amber, an era that stood outside the rest of the band's timeline.

It's an odd fate for the years when the Allman Brothers Band elevated above their rock and roll peers to become an American institution, the most popular band in the country, a group that birthed a genre, had immense impact on country music, helped elect an American president, and stood at the center of the nation's culture—a band that really, truly mattered.

It didn't help that for decades the only officially available live recording of the era was *Wipe the Windows, Check the Oil, Dollar Gas*. It was a slap-dash double-album collection with a stupid title and vague, generic cover art.* Worse, it was released after the band had broken up, a clear cash grab by a reeling Capricorn, and reviews were dismissive, writing it off as an unnecessary live album that paled in comparison to *At Fillmore East*. *Wipe the Windows* almost immediately made it into record-store bargain bins, further diminishing its already low standing.

But the thing is, the album is very good! Some of the mixing is off, and there's a hodgepodge nature to having material from shows ranging from

---

* The phrase is a line in the Chuck Berry song "Too Much Monkey Business" and could be regarded as a clever title, but no one knew what it meant, and it was a mouthful.

1972 to 1975, but the first five tracks are from the September 26, 1973, Winterland performance—the night of Crowe's famous interview with Allman—and they are all fantastic, including the best-ever live version of "Ramblin' Man."* "Come and Go Blues" from Watkins Glen also sparkles. It's an album that deserves a new listen, and the initial reaction to it is a case study in how contemporary impressions impact the experience of a listener—and even of musical creators themselves.

Almost fifty years after its release, Jaimoe was giving drum lessons to a young man who brought over a copy of *Wipe the Windows,* enthused about his new discovery. "Why would we listen to that?" Jaimoe asked. Then he sat back and listened to the music pouring out of his studio speakers. Far removed from the emotions of the moment, the discontent, the feelings that things used to be different, he was stunned by the vitality and originality he heard. The band's cohesion shocked him. Some of the era's bad memories had overwhelmed his recall of the music's strength.

"God damn we were good!" Jaimoe exclaimed in an excited phone call to me. "That Chuck/Lamar band could turn on a dime, everyone was forming grooves and pockets with one another and playing off each other, and Richard was playing his ass off. It's far out. We really had something going on there."

---

* This whole excellent show was released as a bonus disc on the 2013 deluxe edition of *Brothers and Sisters.* It's not clear why they didn't just make it a live album the first time; "At Winterland" would have worked well.

ACKNOWLEDGMENTS

This book has been both the most difficult and the most fun of the four I have written, which is a great combination! So many people helped me in the process and I thank all of them, especially everyone who took the time to do interviews, answer queries, or point me in the right direction to find the answers I sought. I apologize to anyone whose name I missed and I am eternally grateful to a few key people from the band who were always available, notably Jaimoe and Chuck Leavell. Their willingness to consistently answer phone calls, texts, and emails and sometimes to even make additional inquiries on my behalf was a tremendous resource.

My hours spent talking to Jaimoe in the decade since I first started writing *One Way Out* are among the highlights of my life. A simple phone call with a yes/no question can become an hours-long conversation about the history of jazz drumming or whatever else is on his mind. The man is an American treasure and I am blessed to have spent so much time in his presence.

This book would be a shadow of itself without the invaluable information and enlightening quotes from the hundreds of hours of interviews Kirk West did with the Allman Brothers Band members and associates, mostly in 1986 and 1987. I am forever grateful that he volunteered them to me, trusted me to treat them properly, and allowed the world to have the incredible insights contained therein. Listening to Kirk interview Gregg, Dickey, Butch, Jaimoe, Chuck, and all the rest was incredibly enlightening. I learned so much and hope that I have conveyed that knowledge to you. I also gained tremendous insights from interviews with Dickey Betts, Phil Walden and Bill Graham by Kirsten West, Bill Ector, and John Ogden, respectively.

Kirk was also part of my counsel of wise men, who were with me every step of the way, along with The Big House Museum's John Lynskey and ABB manager Bert Holman. They not only were incredibly helpful, but the non-stop text banter was a lot of fun! Kirsten West is an invaluable ally and friend and a wonderful Macon hostess. Willie Perkins was also consistently available to answer questions—and he kept all his financial books, the kind of thing that can make an author weep with joy. Bunky Odom was another font of knowledge, insight, and amusement. He is a wonderful conversationalist.

This book would not exist without Brad Tolinski, who set me right when I earnestly suggested I was done writing about the Allman Brothers Band. He thought *Brothers and Sisters* remained largely unexplored and our conversation and his enthusiasm got me started on this path.

Richard Brent has been a friend, ally, and huge help for many years and I appreciate him and the fantastic Big House Museum in Macon, a great source of both material and inspiration. Bob Beatty is a brother in research and writing about the Allman Brothers Band. I was happy to give an early read to his excellent book, *Play All Night!*, and he in return provided me research materials, helpful conversations, and an excellent final read. Richard Rosenzweig came out of nowhere and was a valued, thoughtful reader and research assistant.

Alex Hodges, Rose Lane Leavell, Buck Williams, Jonny Podell, Dick Wooley, Jon Landau, Buddy Thornton, Trash Cole, Paul Hornsby and the Lyndon brothers—Skoots, AJ, and John—all helped me understand Capricorn and the ABB better. Bob Weir, Phil Lesh, Sam Cutler, Blair Jackson, Dennis McNally, Dan Healy, Rick Turner, David Browne, and Hawk Semins provided insight into the Grateful Dead universe and the band's relationship to the Allman Brothers. The two bands' interactions felt like a topic long overdue for an unpacking. Gary Rossington, Paul T. Riddle, Ed King, Al Kooper, Charlie Brusco, and Henry Paul helped me understand the story of southern rock.

I truly appreciate the support and assistance of Gregg's manager Michael Lehman, Dickey's manager David Spero, and the band family members who trusted me to tell the story and assisted me in doing so, including: Marian Williams, Sandy Wabegijig, Catherine Fellows, Donna Betts, Linda Miller, Paulette Howell, Melinda Trucks, Duane Betts, Devon Allman, Lamar Williams Jr., Vaylor Trucks, Melody Trucks, Cajai Johnson, Elise Trucks, Berry Duane Oakley, James Williams, Leroy Johnson, and Julia Negron. Thank you also to Stacey Maranz.

Laid Back has long been one of my favorite albums and it was a pleasure to interview many of the people who helped Gregg Allman craft that classic, including Bill Stewart, Tommy Talton, Charlie Hayward, the late Scott Boyer, and Johnny Sandlin. Jeff Hanna was a wonderful, insightful source and I really enjoyed our lengthy conversations.

Tom Beard, Peter Conlon, Jonathan Alter, and the Carter Center archives were invaluable in understanding Jimmy Carter and his relationship to Phil Walden and the Allman Brothers Band. Brian Procknal, Rick Capotto, and Doug Cameron were huge resources in helping me tell the story of one amazing night at a Buffalo high school. The Allman Brothers Band archives at the Macon Library were also a wonderful resource.

Thank you to all the photographers whose images grace these pages, especially Sidney Smith and Neal Preston, who are also part of the story. Randy Houser and Myron Sharvan supplied photos that were like manna from heaven, of Watkins Glen and Gregg's Buffalo high school appearance, respectively. Marian and the Williams family opened their photo archives to me. My son Jacob Blumenstein Paul was a fantastic photo editor. I truly appreciate and value Cameron Crowe's support and encouragement, and the many wonderful articles he wrote in 1973 for various publications were essential sources.

Thank you to my agent, David Dunton, and my editor, Marc Resnick, both of whom understood and embraced the concept of this book right away. St. Martin's has been a great home through three books, which is a real luxury for any author. Thanks to the team there, including Lily Cronig, designer Robert Grom, who has now created three covers I love, publicist Kathryn Hough, and marketing gurus Martin Quinn and Paul Hochman. It takes a lot of work in solitude to write a book and it sure is nice to have so much excellent help in getting it out to readers.

I have been in constant communication with the ABB fan base and the wonderful extended family around the band ever since *One Way Out: The Inside History of the Allman Brothers Band* came out in 2014, and it has been a consistent pleasure. I've learned so much from so many and enjoyed our countless interactions.

Thank you to my entire family for a lifetime of support. My parents, Suzi and Dixie Doc always gave me the freedom to explore and find myself, even when it required prodigious biting of the tongue. My in-laws; brother and sister; nephews, nieces, and cousins have all been a bedrock foundation, along with my immediate family: wife, Rebecca Blumenstein, and our kids: Jacob, Eli, and Anna Paul. Rebecca has been a source of mutual inspiration and support for many decades. Thanks always to the Maplewood Squad and the shtetl—the village that helped raise our children and continues to be our rock. Thank you to *The Wall Street Journal's* Gary Rosen, Adam Kirsch, and Warren Bass for the opportunities to profile dozens of musical giants.

The spirits of Gregg Allman, Butch Trucks, and Bruce Hampton have stayed with me since the very horrible first months of 2017 when we lost all three of them. Gregg's artistry touched me early, an inspiration that never left, and I am thankful that he trusted me to tell his story over decades of interviews. I always appreciated the faith that Butch placed in me to tell the band's story and how much he shared with me. I lost count of how many times I wanted to share a tale or ask him a question while writing this book. Bruce was a friend and inspiration who pushed me to write my first book, *Big in China*. Rest in peace to Gary Rossington, Chank Middleton, Skoots Lyndon, and Louise Hudson, who passed while this book was being written, and to Duane, Berry, Lamar, Woody, Dan, Farmer, Joe Dan, Red Dog, Twiggs, Phil, Frank, and every other fallen ABB soldier.

It has been an honor and a pleasure to share the musical legacy of the Allman Brothers Band with my wonderful band, Friends of the Brothers. It is ever thrilling to play this music with Junior Mack, Andy Aledort, Craig Privett, Lee Finkelstein, Dave Diamond, Mike Katzman, Peter Levin, Eric Finland, and Lamar Williams Jr., as well as Eric Krasno, Ron Holloway, Brandon Niederauer, Tash Neal, and everyone else who has shared a stage with us. Thanks to C. J. Strock and Mint Talent for helping us get out in the world. Support live music!

NOTES

PREFACE

xii   *Duane described* . . . : Laurel Dann, "The Last Interview with Duane Allman," *Creem*, December 1973.

CHAPTER 1: BEGINNINGS

1   *"I told Duane* . . .": Tom Nolan, *The Allman Brothers Band: A Biography in Pictures and Words* (Sire Books, 1976).

1   *"To call military school* . . .": Gregg Allman interview with Kirk West, 8/10/87.

1   *Duane didn't make it* . . . : Galadrielle Allman, *Please Be with Me: A Song for My Father, Duane Allman* (Random House, 2014).

2   *"It was the summer* . . .": Gregg Allman interview with Kirk West, 8/5/87.

3   *A fed-up Duane* . . . : Galadrielle Allman, *Please Be with Me.*

4   *"It was the only time* . . .": Gregg Allman interview with Kirk West, 8/5/87.

4   *"couldn't understand* . . .": Joel Selvin, "The Allman Brothers Band: What Southern Boys Can Do with Rock," *San Francisco Chronicle*, February 14, 1971.

4   *"He liked that* . . .": Gregg Allman interview with Kirk West, 8/5/87.

5   *"a steep expenditure* . . .": Richard Albero, "A GP Tribute to Duane Allman. Just Rock On, and Have You a Good Time," *Guitar Player,* May/June 1973.

5   *over the phone*. . . : Phil Walden interview with Bill Ector, 5/26/05.

5   *Walden immediately headed* . . . : Ibid.

6   *"Phil was regarded* . . .": Louis Kraar, "How Phil Walden Turns Rock into Gold," *Fortune*, September 1975.

6   *Working with primarily white artists* . . . : Bob Beatty, *Play All Night!: Duane Allman and the Journey to Fillmore East* (University Press of Florida, 2022).

6   *saw this* . . . : Phil Walden interview with Bill Ector, 5/26/05.

7   *"My brother didn't* . . .": Gregg Allman interview with Kirk West, 8/5/87.

CHAPTER 2: THE BOYS IN THE BAND

10   *Duane sought additional . . . :* Phil Walden interview with Bill Ector, 5/26/05.

12   *"Dickey's a real . . .":* Gregg Allman interview with Kirk West, 8/5/87.

13   *remaining rooted . . . "feeling of the blues":* Dickey Betts interview with Kirsten West, 7/22/94.

13   *For the first time . . . :* Butch Trucks, foreword, *One Way Out: The Inside History of the Allman Brothers Band,* by Alan Paul (St. Martin's Press, 2014).

14   *"They were majestic . . .":* Phil Walden interview with Bill Ector, 5/26/05.

14   *"He said that . . .":* Ibid.

15   *Gregg said that . . . :* Nolan, *Allman Brothers Band.*

16   *"It was the first time . . .":* Gregg Allman interview with Kirk West, 8/5/87.

16   *Duane called Walden . . . :* Phil Walden interview with Bill Ector, 5/26/05.

17   *"Duane inspired everyone . . .":* Bruce Hampton interview with Kirk West, 8/7/87.

CHAPTER 3: END OF THE LINE

19   *"Duane had incredible drive . . .":* Ritchie Yorke, "Macon, Georgia," *ZigZag,* March 1974.

19   *"You know what . . .":* Dickey Betts interview with Kirk West, 1987.

20   *"Nobody had a clue . . .":* Rose Lane Leavell interview with Kirk West, undated.

21   *Producer and father figure . . . "kill you, too":* Gregg Allman with Alan Light, *My Cross to Bear* (William Morrow, 2012).

22   *"Gregg definitely needed . . .":* Joe Dan Petty interview with Kirk West, 5/14/86.

22   *The whole enterprise . . . :* Galadrielle Allman, *Please Be with Me.*

22   *"Duane and Otis . . .":* Phil Walden interview with Bill Ector, 5/26/05.

23   *"He kept me busy . . .":* Gregg Allman interview with Kirk West, 1984.

23   *"We knew that . . .":* Dickey Betts interview with Kirk West, 1987.

23   *Betts described the . . . cheering them on:* Patrick Snyder-Scumpy, "The Allman Brothers: Boogie or Bust," *Crawdaddy,* October 1973.

24   *"I think replacing . . .":* Cameron Crowe, "The Allman Brothers Story," *Rolling Stone,* December 6, 1973.

24   *"He showed more strength . . .":* Gregg Allman interview with Kirk West, 3/5/87.

24   *Sadly, in the same interview . . . :* Ibid.

24   *"The time after . . .":* Cameron Crowe, "The Allman Brothers Band Together," *Hit Parader,* June 1974.

25   *"Within that one . . .":* Dickey Betts interview with Kirk West, 1987.

CHAPTER 4: WILL THE CIRCLE BE UNBROKEN?

27   *"knew them . . .":* Bill Ector, "Sessions with Tom Dowd: The Making of *Eat a Peach,*" *Hittin' the Note* 37 (2003).

28   *Gregg had introduced . . . :* Jon Landau, "Bandleader Duane Allman Dies in Bike Crash," *Rolling Stone,* November 25, 1971.

28   *rarely interacting with . . . :* Ector, "Sessions with Tom Dowd."

29   *Gregg said that . . . :* Gregg Allman interview with Kirk West, 3/5/87.

29   *Trucks described the . . . :* Crowe, "Allman Brothers Story."

29   *"It was obvious . . .":* Butch Trucks interview with Kirk West, 9/3/87.

30   *"We all knew . . .":* Gregg Allman interview with Kirk West, 3/5/87.

30   *"That year of . . .":* Ibid.

30   *"It was sad . . .":* Ibid.

31   *"He was a brother . . .":* Butch Trucks interview with Kirk West, 9/3/87.

31   *"We didn't know . . .":* Gregg Allman interview with Kirk West, 3/5/87.

31   *"There's a little part . . .":* Ibid.

31   *"It ate at him . . .":* Candace Oakley interview with Kirk West, undated.

31   *"He was paranoid . . .":* Butch Trucks interview with Kirk West, 9/3/87.

32   *Betts spoke to . . . :* Roy Carr, "Allman Brothers: Duane Is Dead, but His Spirit Lives on Every Time the Band Goes on Stage," *New Musical Express,* April 22, 1972.

32   *"I didn't really accept . . .":* LifeLines Radio interview, date unknown.

CHAPTER 5: YOUNGER BROTHER

33   *Trucks had architectural . . . :* Butch Trucks interview with Kirk West, 9/3/87.

34   *Gregg said that . . . :* Madeline Hirsiger, "The Allman Band: No Stars," *Macon Telegraph,* September 30, 1973.

34   *Gregg, exhausted from . . . :* Gregg Allman interview with Kirk West, 3/5/87.

35   *"It took me . . .":* Ibid.

35   *Allman asked his friend . . . :* Gregg Allman, *Laid Back,* deluxe edition reissue, liner notes by John P. Lynskey.

35   *Gregg said that . . . :* Gregg Allman interview with Kirk West, 3/5/87.

36   *"Quite frankly . . .":* Lynskey, *Laid Back* liner notes.

39   *"Jerry Wexler had delivered":* Landau, "Bandleader."

38   *"His eulogy was . . .":* Butch Trucks interview with Kirk West, 9/03/87.

39   *Rose Lane Leavell said . . . :* Rose Lane Leavell interview with Kirk West, undated.

39   *"Anyone will leave . . .":* Kraar, "How Phil Walden."

40   *"Dickey was a little . . .":* Gregg Allman interview with Kirk West, 3/5/87.

41   *"Everything was completely different . . .":* Butch Trucks interview with Kirk West, 9/3/87.

42   *"Blue Sky" wasn't . . . :* Dickey Betts interview with Kirk West, 1987.

43   *Betts said the . . . :* Cameron Crowe, "Ramblin' Man," *Rolling Stone,* October 25, 1973.

43   *"I was going to show . . .":* "Dickey Betts interview with Kirk West, 1987.

43   *"Hell, that song . . .":* Chris Charlesworth, "An Interview with Gregg Allman," *Melody Maker,* January 26, 1974.

44   *"One day," Betts recalled . . . :* Marc Meyers, "Anatomy of a Song: 'Ramblin' Man," *Wall Street Journal,* February 13, 2014.

44   *As Trucks said . . . :* Butch Trucks interview with Kirk West, 9/3/87.

45   *Allman said that . . . :* Gregg Allman interview with Kirk West, 3/5/87.

CHAPTER 6: TROUBLE IN MIND

47   *The producer said . . .* : Johnny Sandlin interview with Kirk West, 9/22/87.

49   *"Duane was very . . ."*: John P. Lynskey, "Lamar Williams Tribute—Out of the Shadows," *Hittin' the Note*, Issue 17, 1998.

49   *Gregg was in . . .* : Gregg Allman interview with Kirk West, 8/5/87.

49   *"Berry's death..."*: Jaimoe interview with Kirk West, 9/9/87.

49   *"It was so hard . . ."*: Crowe, "Allman Brothers Story."

50   *Walden said that . . .* : Phil Walden interview with Bill Ector, 5/26/05.

52   *Said Leavell . . .* : Lynskey, "Lamar Williams."

52   *"Berry's death was . . ."*: Crowe, "Allman Brothers Band Together."

CHAPTER 7: TROUBLE NO MORE

54   *Williams's enlistment was . . .* : Gerald F. Goodwin, "Black and White in Vietnam," *New York Times*, July 18, 2017.

55   *Williams was initially . . .* : Jim Schwartz, "Sea Level: Rock, Funk, and Blues from the South," *Guitar Player*, January 1980.

55   *as many as . . .* : James P. Sterba, "Saigon Army Desertions Up Nearly 50% in Spring," *New York Times*, July 27, 1970.

56   *mainly came . . .* : "Lee Robins' Studies of Heroin Use Among US Vietnam Veterans," Wayne Hall and Megan Weier, NIH National Library of Medicine, January 2017.

57   *"I like to . . ."*: Schwartz, "Sea Level."

57   *"If somebody played . . ."*: Chuck Leavell with J. Marshall Craig, *Between a Rock and a Hard Place* (Mercer University Press, 2004).

CHAPTER 8: BROTHERS AND SISTERS

60   *"Deciding to record . . ."*: Johnny Sandlin interview with Kirk West, 9/22/87.

60   *"It was almost . . ."*: Ibid.

61   *Betts said that . . .* : Crowe, "Ramblin' Man."

63   *Levon Helm felt . . .* : Levon Helm with Steven Davis, *This Wheel's on Fire* (Chicago Review Press, 1993).

66   *"It got real . . ."*: Butch Trucks interview with Kirk West, 9/3/87.

69   *"We were so . . ."*: Ibid.

69   *"We needed a . . ."*: Ibid.

69   *Capricorn's head of publicity . . .* : Cameron Crowe, "Brothers and Sisters Album Ambles On In," *Circular*, August 6, 1973.

CHAPTER 9: ALL MY FRIENDS

73   *Young's guitar playing . . .* : Dann, "Last Interview."

75   *From the street . . .* : Ben Edmonds, "Snapshots of the South," *Creem*, November 1972.

77   *"Everything on* Laid Back *. . ."*: Lynskey, *Laid Back* liner notes.

79   *Browne preferred Allman's . . .* : Jackson Browne statement following Gregg Allman's death.

79   *Allman "unlocked a power"* . . . : Interview with Jackson Browne, KGSR radio Austin, October 10, 2002.

82   *Atlantic's Jerry Wexler* . . . : Jerry Wexler, *Rhythm and the Blues: A Life in American Music* (Knopf, 1993).

82   *"For the first time . . .":* "A Sinner's Second Chance," Steve Oney, *Esquire,* November 1984.

CHAPTER 10: BROTHERS IN ARMS

85   *Promoter Alex Cooley* . . . : Patrick Edmondson, "A Bus Stops in Piedmont Park," Strip Project, http://www.thestripproject.com/TheStripProject/Hippies _Stories/Entries/200Patrickd Edmondson, 7/5/19_Dead_in_Piedmont_Park .html.

87   *"Duane was very . . .":* Andy Aledort, "Big Brother," *Guitar World,* April 2007.

87   *Hearing a recording . . . "opening those doors":* Peter Richardson, *No Simple Highway: A Cultural History of the Grateful Dead* (St. Martin's Press, 2015).

90   *Garcia suggested* . . . : Blair Jackson, *Garcia: An American Life* (Penguin, 1999).

92   *"There's a lot . . .":* Lisa Robinson, "Grateful Dead Band Interview," *Creem,* December 1970.

94   *The Fillmore staff* . . . : Bill Graham with Robert Greenfield, *Bill Graham Presents: My Life Inside Rock and Out* (Da Capo Press, 2004).

94   *"You put that . . .":* Bill Graham interview with John Ogden, 10/25/91.

94   *"The Allman Brothers . . .":* Graham and Greenfield, *Bill Graham Presents.*

94   *On the way* . . . : Phil Lesh, *Searching for the Sound: My Life with the Grateful Dead* (Back Bay Books, 2007).

95   *"When the Dead . . .":* Graham and Greenfield, *Bill Graham Presents.*

95   *"They both had . . . were transported":* Bill Graham interview with Kirk West, 1/31/86.

95   *"For sure . . .":* Joseph L. "Red Dog" Campbell, *The Legendary Red Dog: A Book of Tails* (2001).

95   *Lesh was pleasantly* . . . : Lesh, *Searching.*

96   *During the quiet. . . :* Ibid.

96   *"I had a tom-tom . . .":* Graham and Greenfield, *Bill Graham Presents.*

97   *As the band* . . . : Lesh, *Searching.*

97   *But the crowd* . . . : Graham and Greenfield, *Bill Graham Presents.*

97   *Garcia, Lesh, and Weir came out* . . . : "The Dead and Allmans," Dead Essays, January 2019.

97   *After the dazed* . . . : Lesh, *Searching.*

98   *"Peter Green . . .":* Jim Brodey, "A Moment Captured in Time: The *Crawdaddy* Interview with Duane Allman," *Crawdaddy* 4, no. 5 (1970).

98   *Owsley described* . . . : Owsley Stanley, liner notes for *The Allman Brothers at the Fillmore East 11, 13 and 14 Feb 1970.*

98   *"The Dead arrived . . .":* "Atlanta Sports Arena, May 10, 1970," Dead.net.

98 *"I had to borrow . . ."*: John Dauphin and Kirk West, "The Road Lesh Travels," *Hittin' the Note* 29 (2000).

99 *The Great Speckled Bird . . . *: Miller Francis Jr., "Allman Brothers, Hampton Grease Band Twice," *Great Speckled Bird*, May 18, 1970.

99 *"I love the Dead!"*: Duane Allman interview with Dave Herman, WABC-FM, New York, December 9, 1970.

99 *Lesh said that . . . *: Dauphin and West, "Road."

100 *When* Melody Maker *. . . *: Chris Charlesworth, *Melody Maker* interview, January 1974; available on his blog: https://justbackdated.blogspot.com/2014/08 /the-allman-brothers-band-my-1974.html.

101 *The first scheduled . . . *: "Happening on the Green: Ontario Speedway Sets Rock Concert," *Pomona Progress-Bulletin,* May 8, 1973.

101 *Two weeks later . . . *: "Time Limits Cancel OMS Rock Concert," *Pomona Progress-Bulletin,* May 22, 1973.

101 *"The Dead were . . ."*: John Lynskey, "Watkins Glen Remembered: A Conversation with Bunky Odom," *Hittin' the Note* 79 (2013).

CHAPTER 11: BIG BOSS MAN

103 *office of Peter Yarrow . . . *: All Steve Massarsky quotes throughout the book are from Kirk West interview of 3/7/96, unless otherwise noted.

105 *over 300 handwritten . . . *: Madeline Hirsiger, "Wedding Rites Were Authentic," *Macon News*, April 20, 1973.

105 *"Finding a duck . . ."*: Ibid.

106 *In June 1974 . . . *: Cathy Yarbrough, "Allmans Concert in City to Aid Indians," *Atlanta Constitution*, June 7, 1973.

108 *"Fillmore East just . . ."*: Rose Lane Leavell interview with Kirk West, undated.

108 *"Anything we needed . . ."*: Butch Trucks interview with Kirk West, 9/3/87.

109 *"There was no . . ."*: Ibid.

110 *Paul Hornsby described . . . *: Paul Hornsby, *Fix It in the Mix* (Mercer University Press, 2021).

110 *He had met . . . *: Jonathan Gould, *Otis Redding: An Unfinished Life* (Crown, 2017).

110 *"Phil was a . . ."*: Ahmet Ertegun, interview, YouTube, https://www.youtube .com/watch?v=zfC26KHTCQ4.

111 *His wife . . . *: Robyn Passante, "Southern Rock and Style," *South,* June 3, 2015.

111 *"Frank was Executive Vice President . . ."*: Rose Lane Leavell interview with Kirk West, undated.

111 *Fenter took to . . . *: Yorke, "Macon."

112 *"Frank had a lot . . ."*: Rose Lane Leavell interview with Kirk West, undated.

113 *Melody Maker feature . . . *: Chris Charlesworth, "Southern Rock: Under the Sign of Capricorn," *Melody Maker*, February 2, 1974.

113 *That represented significant . . . *: Scott B. Bomar, *Southbound: An Illustrated History of Southern Rock* (Backbeat Books, 2014).

113 *Said Rose Lane Leavell . . .* : Rose Lane Leavell interview with Kirk West, undated.

114 *"Absolutely nothing else . . .":* Ibid.

CHAPTER 12: AMERICAN BEAUTIES

115 *"Every rock & roller . . .":* Gordon Fletcher, "East Coast Rocks at DC Concerts," *Rolling Stone,* July 19, 1973.

115 *"If 2,000 kids . . .":* Tom Zito, "Grateful Dead and the Allman Brothers Band," *Washington Post,* June 8, 1973.

115 *The next day's . . .* : "Concert Camp Out," *Washington Post,* June 9, 1973.

116 *Police blocked that . . .* : Lawrence Feinberg and Tom Zito, "53,000 Rock Fans Jam RFK," *Washington Post,* June 10, 1973.

116 *"Marijuana was plainly . . .":* Tom Zito and Megan Rosenfeld, "Days and Nights in the Stadium," *Washington Post,* June 11, 1973.

117 *Dead tape archivist . . .* : https://ia800206.us.archive.org/8/items /MonteBarrygd73-06-09.AUD.fob.barry.flac/Latvala730609notes.jpg.

117 *After a stage turnover . . .* : https://deadessays.blogspot.com/2019/01/the-dead -and-allmans.html.

117 *Cutler again introduced . . .* : Ibid.

117 *The* Post's *review . . .* : Feinberg and Zito, "53,000 Rock Fans."

117 *The* Post *described . . .* : Ibid.

118 *impressed* Rolling Stone's *. . .* : Fletcher, "East Coast."

118 *A few months later . . .* : Cameron Crowe, "The Grateful Dead Flee Big Business," *Circus,* October 1973.

122 *what* Rolling Stone *termed . . .* : Charles Perry, "Alembic: Sound Wizards to the Grateful Dead," *Rolling Stone,* September 27, 1973.

CHAPTER 13: NEW SPEEDWAY BOOGIE

126 *"It was not . . .":* Lynskey, "Watkins Glen."

128 *"We didn't want . . .":* Barney Hoskyns, *Across the Great Divide: The Band and America* (Hyperion, 1993).

128 *Red Dog described . . .* : Campbell, *Legendary Red Dog.*

129 *"The sound from . . .":* Perry, "Alembic."

129 *"My assignment was . . .":* Janet Furman, "A History of Furman Sound and Its Grateful Dead Roots," http://www.furmanhistory.com/.

130 *Conflict erupted over . . .* : Anathalee G. Sandlin, *A Never-Ending Groove: Johnny Sandlin's Musical Odyssey* (Mercer University Press, 2012).

132 *Writing in* Crawdaddy *. . .* : Snyder-Scumpy, "Allman Brothers."

133 *A week before . . .* : Les Ledbetter, "Rock Promoters Expect 150,000 at Watkins Glen Fete July 28," *New York Times,* July 19, 1973.

135 *He was "petrified" . . .* : Charlesworth, "Interview with Gregg Allman."

135 *"By Friday night . . . heroes were there":* Joel Siegel, "Watkins Glen Jam Tops Woodstock: 600,000 Fans," *Rolling Stone,* August 30, 1973.

136   *Betts described the crowd . . .*: Dickey Betts interview with Kirk West, 1987.

136   *"It looked like . . ."*: Hoskyns, *Across the Great Divide.*

CHAPTER 14: EYES OF THE WORLD

141   *"I'd rather deal . . ."*: Siegel, "Watkins Glen."

141   *"All through . . . saw a fight"*: Ibid.

141   *Facilities and resources were . . .*: Snyder-Scumpy, "Allman Brothers."

142   *Sandlin looked out . . .*: Johnny Sandlin interview with Kirk West, 9/3/87.

143   *"Watkins Glen was . . ."*: Snyder-Scumpy, "Allman Brothers."

144   *Cutler released the following . . .*: Siegel, "Watkins Glen."

144   *"We usually do . . ."*: *Late Night with David Letterman* interview with Bob Weir and Jerry Garcia, September 17, 1987.

144   *John Swenson, reviewing . . .*: John Swenson, "Allman Brothers Band, the Band, the Grateful Dead: Summer Jam at Watkins Glen," *Village Voice*, August 9, 1973.

144   *The break helped . . .*: Jonathan Taplin, *The Magic Years: Scenes from a Rock and Roll Life* (Heyday, 2021).

144   *Meanwhile, some of . . . stopped the rain"*: Helm, *This Wheel's.*

145   *The performance made . . .*: Charlesworth, "Gregg Allman."

145   *"There was an . . . eight years"*: Hoskyns, *Across the Great Divide.*

146   *The crowd, which . . .*: Swenson, "Allman Brothers."

146   *"At times the scene . . ."*: Grace Lichtenstein, "Festival at Watkins Glen Ends in Mud and Elation," *New York Times*, July 30, 1973.

146   *as Swenson wrote . . .*: Swenson, "Allman Brothers."

146   *"It was an awesome . . . trouble from starting"*: Butch Trucks interview with Kirk West, 9/3/87.

148   The New York Times *described . . .*: Lichtenstein, "Festival."

148   Rolling *Stone said . . .*: Siegel, "Watkins Glen."

149   Rolling Stone *reported . . .* Ibid.

149   *Shortly after takeoff . . .*: Sandlin, *Never-Ending Groove.*

149   *Garcia took a helicopter . . .*: Jackson, *Garcia.*

150   *headline reading . . .*: Lichtenstein, "Festival."

150   *But the headline . . .*: Sharyn Kane, "Allmans Get Record Pay at Mammoth Rock Festival," *Macon Telegraph*, August 1, 1973.

150   *The British magazine* Melody Maker *. . .*: Michael Watts, "The Allman Brothers Are What the Grateful Dead Were in '67," *Melody Maker*, August 25, 1973.

CHAPTER 15: ALL IN THE FAMILY

151   *"The family is . . ."*: Crowe, "Allman Brothers Band Together."

152   *Said bassist Lamar Williams . . .*: Madeline Hirsiger, "Country Sound Added by Betts," *Macon News*, October 2, 1973.

152   *The title* Brothers and Sisters *. . .*: Crowe, "Allman Brothers."

153   *Betts was pleased . . .*: Crowe, "Ramblin' Man."

154   *The mixing of the song . . .*: Johnny Sandlin interview with Kirk West, undated.

154   *As the song began . . .* : Snyder-Scumpy, "Allman Brothers."
154   *"We went into . . ."*: Dickey Betts interview with Kirk West, 1987.
155   *Gregg gave a . . .* : Charlesworth, "Interview with Gregg Allman."
155   *"When 'Ramblin' Man' . . ."*: Dickey Betts interview with Kirk West, 1987.
155   *Betts's accomplishment . . .* : Phil Walden interview with Bill Ector, 5/26/05.
156   *Bob Dylan . . . "one hell of a compliment"*: John Lynskey, "Dickey Betts: Lookin Forward, Moving On," *Hittin' the Note* 31 (2001).

CHAPTER 16: DOWN THIS ROAD BEFORE

157   *That performance sealed . . .* : All Phil Walden quotes in this chapter from his Walden interview with Bill Ector, 5/26/05.
159   *"the greatest exposure . . . living in Spartanburg"*: Cameron Crowe, "Marshall Tucker: The South Also Rises," *Rolling Stone*, March 14, 1974.
160   *"We were . . ."*: Crowe, "Marshall Tucker."
161   *"I have never . . ."*: Tom Beard, Alex Cooley, and Peter Conlon interviewed by David Barbe, Callie Holmes, and Christian Lopez, April 10, 2013. Oral History Documentary Collection at the Richard B. Russell Library for Political Research and Studies, University of Georgia Libraries.
162   *Podell said . . .* : Kirk West, "Jon Podell: Booking the best Band in the Land," *Hittin' the Note*, Issue 25.
162   *He told* Melody Maker *. . .* : Charlesworth, "Southern Rock."
163   *Decades later . . .* : Hudson, "Q&A: Butch Trucks of the Allman Brothers Band Talks Phil Walden, Reunion, Bruce Hampton," *Atlanta Business Journal*, December 15, 2016.
163   *"Phil was . . ."*: Gary James, "Steve Massarsky Interview," Famous Interviews .com, http://www.famousinterview.ca/interviews/steve_massarsky.htm.
164   *"The importance of . . ."*: Dickey Betts interview with Kirk West, 1987.

CHAPTER 17: HITTIN' THE NOTE

165   *As Cameron Crowe . . .* : Crowe, "Allman Brothers Story."
166   *Tom Dowd described . . .* : Ector, "Sessions."
166   *"The differences between . . ."*: Butch Trucks interview with Kirk West, 9/3/87.
166   *"My role was . . ."*: Chuck Leavell interview with Kirk West, 5/7/86.
167   *"My job got . . ."*: Steve Rosen, "Gregg Allman, Rock Organist," *Contemporary Keyboard*, August 1976.
167   *Listening to Stevie . . .* : Ibid.
168   *"Dickey Betts contributed . . ."*: Joe Dan Petty interview with Kirk West, 5/14/86.
169   *After witnessing . . .* : Charlesworth, "Interview with Gregg Allman."
169   *Fenter reflected . . .* : Yorke, "Macon."
170   *"We had some . . ."*: Wade Tatangelo, "Dickey Betts on the Real Allman Brothers Band Stories Behind the Film 'Almost Famous,'" *Sarasota Herald Tribune*, August 16, 2020.

170   *Trucks summed up . . .* : Butch Trucks, "Whipping Post," Letter to the Editor, *New York Times,* May 8, 2005.

171   *The young writer . . .* : John Dauphin, "Reflections from Cameron Crowe," *Hittin' the Note* 32 (2001).

172   *"I took to . . ."* : Tatangelo, "Dickey Betts."

172   *"I always felt . . ."*: Angie Martoccio, "Cameron Crowe Digs into the 'Almost Famous' Archive for the 20th Anniversary," *Rolling Stone,* September 11, 2020.

173   *In the process . . .* : Dauphin, "Reflections."

173   *"Gregg was unlike . . ."*: Neal Preston, *Exhilarated and Exhausted* (Reel Art Press, 2017).

173   *"There's an air . . ."*: Hirsiger, "Allman Band: No Stars."

175   *"We did a . . ."*: Martoccio, "Cameron Crowe."

175   *Allman told . . .* : Bozza, "Boy's Life."

175   *"Why did Gregg think . . ."*: Stephen K. Peeples, "'Almost Famous': Neal Preston Recalls the Interview Tape Hostage Crisis," Stephenkpeeples.com, September 13, 2021.

176   *"We were both . . ."*: Ibid.

176   *But, the writer knew . . .* : Bozza, "Boy's Life."

177   *"We had our story . . ."*: Martoccio, "Cameron Crowe."

177   *"The real question . . . inside your head"*: Crowe, "Allman Brothers Story."

181   *Allman was also . . .* : Tim Cahill, "A Tale of Two Tours," *Rolling Stone,* January 16, 1975.

181   *Deep into the morning . . .* : Corry Arnold, "December 31, 1973, Cow Palace, Daly City, CA: Allman Brothers Band with Jerry Garcia, Boz Scaggs and Bill Kreutzmann," Lost Live Dead blog, https://lostlivedead.blogspot.com/2012/12/december-31–1973-cow-palace-daly-city.html.

CHAPTER 18: HE WAS A FRIEND OF MINE

183   *"He asked me . . ."*: Phil Walden interview with Bill Ector, 5/26/05.

184   *Carter's young . . .* : Hamilton Jordan, *A Boy from Georgia: Coming of Age in the Segregated South* (University of Georgia Press, 2015).

184   *two weeks later . . .* : Wesley G. Rippert, "Macon-Plains Connection Ties Campaign to Youth," *St. Petersburg Times,* October 5, 1976.

185   *"The first thing . . ."*: *Jimmy Carter: Rock and Roll President,* directed by May Wharton, written by Bill Flanagan, 2000.

185   Rolling Stone *reported . . .* : Paul West, "Bob Dylan in Atlanta: 'Great to Be in Joe-Jah!'" *Rolling Stone,* February 28, 1974.

185   *Betts said . . .* : David Browne, "How Jimmy Carter (Literally) Rocked the Presidency," *Rolling Stone,* September 8, 2020.

186   *Allman said that . . .* : Gregg Allman interview with Kirk West, 8/5/87.

186   *Allman saw . . .* : Ibid.

186   *Carter described . . .* : West, "Bob Dylan."

186   *Gregg said . . .* : Wharton and Flanagan, *Rock and Roll President.*

186 *"We went in . . . talked to him"*: Gregg Allman interview with Kirk West, 8/5/87.

187 *"It was a . . ."*: Ibid.

187 *"We sat up . . ."*: Robert T. Garrett, "Blue Skies over Georgia," *Harvard Crimson*, December 8, 1975.

187 *A few nights . . .* : Gregory Jaynes, "We Made Some Music Last Night That'd Blow Your Hat in the Creek," *Atlanta Constitution*, January 30, 1974.

188 *Walden always insisted . . .* : Joe Klein and Dave Marsh, "Rock Meets Politics in 1976," *Rolling Stone,* September 9, 1976.

188 Rolling Stone *estimated . . .* : Art Harris, "Candidate Jimmy Carter: Rock's Good Ol' Boy," *Rolling Stone,* December 4, 1975.

189 *In 1964, he . . .* : John Meroney, "How to Elect a President: Jimmy Carter, Two South Georgia Political Novices, and the Unpredictable Road to the White House," *Atlanta*, March 9, 2020.

189 *"I was so sick . . ."*: Phil Walden interview with Bill Ector, 5/26/05.

189 *"I'm a Southern boy . . ."*: Tom Beard, Alex Cooley, and Peter Conlon interviewed by David Barbe, Callie Holmes, and Christian Lopez, April 10, 2013. Oral History Documentary Collection at the Richard B. Russell Library for Political Research and Studies, University of Georgia Libraries.

189 *In 1964, he and Rosalynn . . .* : Browne, "How Jimmy Carter."

189 *"When I got . . ."*: Phil Walden interview with Bill Ector, 5/26/05.

190 *Thompson was traveling . . .* His Very Best: Jonathan Alter, *His Very Best: Jimmy Carter—A Life* (Simon and Schuster, 2020).

191 *Thompson, who had . . .* : Hunter S. Thompson, *The Great Shark Hunt* (Simon and Schuster, 1979).

191 *"After listening . . ."*: Text of speech read at Jimmy Carter Presidential Library.

191 *Thompson didn't know . . .* : Alter, *His Very Best.*

192 *Thompson called . . .* : Thompson, *Great Shark Hunt.*

CHAPTER 19: LET NATURE SING

195 *These shows were . . .* : Cahill, "Tale."

195 *Reviewers compared . . .* : Chris Charlesworth, "Gregg Allman: Carnegie Hall, New York City," *Melody Maker*, April 20, 1974.

195 *"Each night when . . ."*: Steve Faines, "Gregg Allman Live—The Tour That Saved the Allman Brothers," *Circus*, October 1974.

196 *"We're already doing . . ."*: Crowe, "Allman Brothers Band Together."

197 *"He was a . . ."*: Matt Schudel, "Fiddler Vassar Clements Dies," *Washington Post*, August 17, 2005.

199 *Navajo medicine man . . .* : Dickey Betts interview with Kirsten West, 7/22/94.

201 *Early in the . . .* : Johnny Sandlin interview with Kirk West, 9/3/87.

CHAPTER 20: DOWN SOUTH JUKIN'

203 *"Before the Allman Brothers . . ."*: Cameron Crowe, "Capricorn: Five Years Later—The Sound of the South Sounds Fine," *Circular*, August 12, 1974.

203   *who was disgusted . . .* : Dave Kyle, "Remembering Duane Allman," *Vintage Guitar,* January 1997; additional interviews published online at https://www .duaneallman.info/rememberingduaneallman.htm.

204   *"There was nothing . . ."*: Hornsby, *Fix It.*

204   *This is part of why . . .* : Jaynes, "We Made."

204   *"The parties were . . ."*: Bill Graham interview with Kirk West, 1/31/86.

206   *After the first . . .* : Michael Ray Fitzgerald, *Jacksonville and the Roots of Southern Rock* (University Press of Florida, 2020).

208   *"Can you imagine . . ."*: Lee Ballinger, *Lynyrd Skynyrd: An Oral History* (Spike, 1999).

208   *Fenter entertained . . .* : Yorke, "Macon."

209   *Walden said . . .* : Mark Kemp, *Dixie Lullaby: A Story of Music, Race and New Beginnings in the New South* (University of Georgia Press, 2004).

209   *The band signed . . .* : Alan Walden and S. E. Feinberg, *Southern Man: Music and Mayhem in the American South* (Jawbone Press, 2021).

209   *"We didn't have . . ."*: Kemp, *Dixie Lullaby.*

209   *The band also . . .* : Al Kooper, *Backstage Passes and Backstabbing Bastards* (Backbeat Books, 1998).

210   *MCA launched . . .* : Gene Odom with Frank Dorman, *Lynyrd Skynyrd: Remembering the Free Birds of Southern Rock* (Broadway Books, 2002).

211   *Kooper also helped:* Kooper, *Backstage Passes.*

211   *Backstage at one . . .* : Lynyrd Skynyrd, *One More from the Road,* liner notes by Cameron Crowe.

CHAPTER 21: SOUTHERN BLOOD

215   *John Swenson summed . . .* : John Swenson, "Southern Rock: Gone with the Trend," *Crawdaddy,* July 1975.

215   *That's how Young . . .* : Crowe, *One More from the Road* liner notes.

216   *Alan Walden has said . . .* : Walden and Feinberg, *Southern Man.*

216   *When MCA started . . .* : Odom and Dorman, *Remembering.*

216   *Gregg Allman eventually . . .* : Radio.com interview with Gregg Allman, 2015.

217   *He ultimately apologized . . .* : Andy Greene, "Tom Petty on Past Confederate Flag Use: 'It Was Downright Stupid,'" *Rolling Stone,* July 14, 2015.

217   *Some contemporaries noticed . . .* : Rick Brown, "Southern Rock at Its Best," *Great Speckled Bird,* June 3, 1974.

219   *This wannabe bassist . . .* : Cahill, "Tale."

219   *"If we hadn't . . ."*: Ibid.

219   *a positive review . . .* : Art Harris, "Singing in the Rain," *Rolling Stone,* July 4, 1974.

220   *Local coverage . . .* : Scott Cain, "Allmans Sound a Lucrative Note," *Atlanta Constitution,* June 2, 1974.

221   *In a preview of . . .* : Brown, "Southern Rock."

CHAPTER 22: TALES OF ORDINARY MADNESS

223 *"The music always had . . ."*: Butch Trucks interview with Kirk West, 9/3/87.

224 *Gregg never shied . . .* : Nolan, *Allman Brothers.*

224 *"If something went wrong . . ."*: Butch Trucks interview with Kirk West, 9/3/87.

224 *"In Dickey's case . . ."*: Ibid.

224 *"He's so bright . . ."*: Phil Walden interview with Bill Ector, 5/26/05.

225 *Betts himself beautifully described . . .* : Nolan, *Allman Brothers.*

225 *Trucks was stewing . . . "snap him out of it"*: Butch Trucks interview with Kirk West, 9/3/87.

227 *"That night at . . ."*: Ibid.

227 *"The music is . . ."*: Nolan, *Allman Brothers.*

227 *"We more and . . ."*: Butch Trucks interview with Kirk West, 9/3/87.

228 *"It got to . . ."*: Chuck Leavell interview with Kirk West, 5/7/86.

228 *"Chuck did change . . ."*: Gregg Allman interview with Kirk West, 8/7/87.

228 *Jaimoe said . . .* : Nolan, *Allman Brothers.*

229 *As Trucks said . . .* : Butch Trucks interview with Kirk West, 9/3/87.

229 *Years later, Bill Graham . . . "music is big"*: Bill Graham interview with Kirk West, 1/31/86.

230 *He always felt . . . "take care of things"*: Bill Graham interview with Kirk West, 1/31/86.

231 *Graham began . . .* : Telegram from Bill Graham to Phil Walden, August 20, 1975, viewed at the Big House Museum Archives.

CHAPTER 23: HIGHWAY CALL

233 Rolling Stone *reviewed . . .* : Tony Glover, "Duane & Dick: Dueling Guitars," *Rolling Stone,* October 10, 1974.

234 *"What I'm trying . . ."*: Cahill, "Tale."

235 *"His daddy and . . . rock and rollers"*: Ibid.

235 *"When we start . . ."*: Ibid.

236 *While there was . . .* : Ibid.

CHAPTER 24: DON'T ASK ME NO QUESTIONS AND I WON'T TELL YOU NO LIES

240 *"They counted on . . ."*: Butch Trucks interview with Kirk West, 9/3/87.

240 *"Phil not only . . ."*: Hudson, "Q&A."

240 *"Phil always wanted . . . meant a lot to me"*: Gregg Allman interview with Kirk West, 8/5/87.

243 *Walden's chauffeured . . . still more scotch*: Kraar, "How Phil Walden."

244 *After the Marshall Tucker Band's . . . "I found the exit"*: Hornsby, *Fix It.*

CHAPTER 25: SUGAR SWEET

247 *"I'll do it"*: All Gregg Allman quotes in this chapter are from his interview with Kirk West, 8/5/87, unless otherwise noted.

248 *Allman had been . . .* : Jim Jerome, "Now That Cher Has Helped Show Him the Way, Gregg Allman Takes to the Road Again," *People Weekly,* September 8, 1975.

249   *He overcame . . . :* West, 8/5/87.

249   *As Cher noted:* Jeff Coplon, *The First Time: Cher as Told to Jeff Coplon* (Pocket Books, 1998).

249   *Both these parties . . . :* Ibid.

250   *Things went better . . . :* Ibid.

251   *Her visit was:* Art Harris, "Cher in Macon? With Gregg?" *Atlanta Constitution,* February 13, 1975.

CHAPTER 26: WIN, LOSE, OR DRAW

253   *According to* Fortune . . . : Kraar, "How Phil Walden."

253   *"the falloff . . .":* Ibid.

253   Fortune *wrote:* Ibid.

254   *Frank Fenter called . . . :* Ibid.

254   *Alan Walden readily . . . :* Walden and Feinberg, *Southern Man.*

255   *"Everyone blamed Gregg . . .":* Johnny Sandlin interview with Kirk West, 9/3/87.

255   *"We were barely . . .":* Gregg Allman interview with Kirk West, 8/5/87.

256   *On May 6, 1975 . . . :* Madeline Hirsiger, "Allman Band Album Grinds to Halt," *Macon News,* May 6, 1975.

256   *To be ready . . . :* Ibid.

257   *Capricorn officials denied . . . :* "Officials Deny Allman Breakup," *Macon Telegraph,* May 7, 1975.

257   *"I had just . . .":* All Gregg Allman quotes about Cher, including Cher's recounted dialogue, from Kirk West interview, 8/5/87, unless otherwise noted.

257   *Describing the scene . . . :* Geraldo Rivera, *Good Night America* Episode 22, August 14, 1975.

257   *"I knew I was . . .":* Coplon, *First Time.*

258   *"Gregg and I . . .":* Christopher Bonner, "Cher Suing for Divorce," *Macon Telegraph,* July 10, 1975.

258   *The quick divorce filing . . . :* Ibid.

258   *"He called me . . . into poetry":* "All My Friends Part III: Jack Pearson, Chank Middleton and Bert Holman," Relix.com, August 10, 2017.

259   *"We got obsessed . . .":* Butch Trucks interview with Kirk West, 9/3/87.

259   *Speaking to Art Harris . . . :* Art Harris, "Waiting for Gregg: Slow Beat," *Atlanta Constitution,* August 6, 1975.

CHAPTER 27: DREAMS

261   *Old friend Tony Glover's . . . :* Tony Glover, "Win, Lose or Draw," *Rolling Stone,* November 6, 1975.

262   Rolling Stone's *review . . . :* David McGee, "Jaded and Joyless in Jersey: The Allman Bros Draw a Blank," *Rolling Stone,* October 24, 1975.

263   *But the former . . . :* "A Long-Shot Candidate Who Will Run in Every Race," *US News and World Report,* September 22, 1975.

264   *"The [first] concerts . . .":* Rippert, "Macon-Plains Connection."

264   *"the critical effort . . .":* Jordan, *Boy from Georgia.*

264   *Alex Cooley recalled . . . :* Tom Beard, Alex Cooley, and Peter Conlon interviewed by David Barbe, Callie Holmes, and Christian Lopez, April 10, 2013. Oral History Documentary Collection at the Richard B. Russell Library for Political Research and Studies, University of Georgia Libraries.

264   *"I'm proud of . . .":* Garrett, "Blue Skies."

265   *"It was not . . .":* Klein and Marsh, "Rock."

265   *"Jimmy Carter didn't . . .":* Gregg Allman interview with Kirk West, 8/7/87.

266   *They helped him . . . :* Jordan, *Boy from Georgia.*

266   *In internal memos . . . :* Fall 1975 memo from Jim Gammill to Carter campaign; documents reviewed at the Carter Presidential Library.

266   *If they overstepped . . . :* Fall 1975 memo from Jim Gammill to Carter campaign.

267   *Grinderswitch received . . . :* Providence benefit contracts; documents reviewed at the Carter Presidential Library.

267   *Backstage before the . . . :* Garrett, "Blue Skies."

267   *Speaking to a smattering . . . :* Ibid.

268   *The campaign paid . . .* Providence benefit contracts.

268   *"The Allman Brothers . . .":* Jimmy Carter: Rock and Roll President.

269   *Old friend and longtime . . . :* Bill Graham interview with Kirk West, 1/31/86.

269   *"We got away":* Butch Trucks interview with Kirk West, 9/3/87.

269   *"It's hard to . . .":* Geraldo Rivera, *Good Night America,* Episode 22, August 14, 1975.

270   *When crew members . . . :* "Leave My Blues at Home," *Savannah,* September/October 2017.

CHAPTER 28: . . . AND JUSTICE FOR ALL

272   *Most ominous was . . . :* Randall Savage, "Allman Granted Immunity in Probe," *Macon Telegraph,* January 21, 1976.

272   *The story wasn't yet . . . :* Ibid.

273   *"It was terrible . . .":* Patrick Snyder, "The Sorrowful Confessions of Gregg Allman," *Rolling Stone,* November 4, 1976.

273   Rolling Stone *reported . . . :* "Allman Reportedly Testified in Drug Probe," *Rolling Stone,* March 11, 1976.

275   *"talking about . . .":* Gregg Allman interview with Kirk West, 8/10/87.

275   *Gregg said that . . . :* Ibid.

276   *An agent in . . . :* Russell Baker, "Georgia Hunt for Bodies Is Linked to 'Dixie Mafia,'" *New York Times,* April 19, 1974.

276   *In May 1974 . . . :* Scott Burnstein, "Drug Trial, Dixie Mafia Ties Led to Break-Up of the Allman Brothers," *Gangster Report,* June 11, 2015.

276   *"They made it clear . . .":* Gregg Allman interview with Kirk West, 8/10/87.

276   *FBI arrested Hawkins . . . :* Scott Burnstein, "Dixie Mafia in Macon, GA, Killed Jimmy Reeves in Years Leading Up to Trying to Kill Rocker Gregg Allman," *Gangster Report,* May 29, 2017.

277 *Both Fuchs and . . . :* Jim Lee, "Defendant Furnished Cocaine, Allman Said," *Atlanta Constitution*, June 25, 1976.

277 *Under cross-examination . . . :* Peter Vandevanter, "Allman Under Heavy Guard," *Macon Telegraph*, June 25, 1976.

277 *When Santa Lucia asked . . .* Lee, "Defendant Furnished Cocaine, Allman Said."

277 *His primary observation . . . :* Gregg Allman interview with Kirk West, 8/10/87.

278 *A banner headline . . . :* Vandevanter, "Allman Under Heavy Guard."

278 *Almost a month later . . . "not been prosecuted":* Peter Vandevanter, "Herring Sentenced to 75 Years in Drug Case," *Macon Telegraph*, July 20, 1976.

CHAPTER 29: THE NIGHT THE LIGHTS WENT OUT IN GEORGIA

281 *"No one wanted . . .":* Phil Walden interview with Bill Ector, 5/26/05.

282 *"The fact is . . .":* Snyder, "Sorrowful Confessions."

282 *"Though we were . . .":* Butch Trucks interview with Kirk West, 9/3/87.

282 *"Everyone made too . . .":* Ibid.

282 *On August 19, 1976 . . . :* Jaimoe, Letter to the Editor, *Macon News*, August 19, 1976.

283 *A couple of weeks . . . :* Barr Nobles, "More Talk of Allman Brothers Band Breakup," *Rolling Stone*, September 9, 1976.

283 *Cher, then nine months . . . :* Snyder, "Sorrowful Confessions."

283 *Capricorn publicity manager . . . :* "The Allmans: Southern Discomfort," *Rolling Stone*, August 26, 1976.

283 *"It seems likely . . .":* Snyder, "Sorrowful Confessions."

284 *The* Atlanta Constitution *. . . :* David Morrison, "The Capricorn Connection," *Atlanta Constitution*, November 4, 1976.

284 *And conservative . . . :* William Safire, "The List That Never Was," *New York Times*, October 4, 1976.

284 *The September 3 . . . :* Robert Sam Anson, "Jimmy's Friends in Rock," *New Times*, September 3, 1976.

284 *Gregg called it . . . :* Snyder, "Sorrowful Confessions."

284 *"How much money . . .":* Morrison, "Capricorn Connection."

285 *Carter attended . . . :* Rippert, "Macon-Plains Connection."

285 *"People said I was . . .":* Phil Walden interview with Bill Ector, 5/26/05.

CHAPTER 30: ONE MORE TRY

290 *The committee met . . . :* Sean Kirst, "How Gregg Allman and Cher Stunned Canisius High 'Assembly' in 1976," *Buffalo News*, June 4, 2017.

EPILOGUE

293 *"We all just needed . . .":* Butch Trucks interview with Kirk West, 9/3/87.

293 *He thought he might . . . :* Madeline Hirsiger, "It Was Fun While It Lasted," *Macon Telegraph*, October 3, 1976.

BIBLIOGRAPHY

INTERVIEWS

By the Author

Many of the following subjects were interviewed multiple times over many years. Others were interviewed just for this book.

Gregg Allman, Dickey Betts, Jaimoe, Butch Trucks, Chuck Leavell, Warren Haynes, Derek Trucks, Oteil Burbridge, Marc Quiñones, Dan Toler, Jimmy Herring, Jack Pearson, David Goldflies, Kirk West, Phil Walden, Bert Holman, Willie Perkins, Vaylor Trucks, Sandy Wabegijig, Paulette Howell, Duane Betts, Berry Duane Oakley, Marian Williams, Lamar Williams Jr., Delaney Bramlett, Bonnie Bramlett, Leroy Johnson, James Williams, Ginger Williams, Alex Hodges, Buck Williams, Jonny Podell, Red Dog, Kim Payne, Mark Pucci, A. J. Lyndon, John Lyndon, Skoots Lyndon, Buddy Thornton, David "Trash" Cole, Tom Dowd, Johnny Sandlin, Paul Hornsby, Bunky Odom, Joe Dan Petty, Brian Farmer, Chank Middleton, Linda Oakley Miller, Gary Rossington, Ed King, Rickey Medlocke, Al Kooper, Charlie Hayward, Bill Stewart, Scott Boyer, Tommy Talton, Buzzy Feiten, John McEuen, Ben Fong-Torres, Cameron Crowe, Neal Preston, John Swenson, Dick Wooley, John Lynskey, Richard Brent, Bill Levenson, Jon Landau, Don Law, Vince Gill, Bob Weir, Phil Lesh, Robert Hunter, Bill Kreutzmann, Steve Parish, Sam Cutler, Dan Healy, Hawk Semins, Jim Koplik, Shelly Finkel, David Browne, Blair Jackson, Dennis McNally, Robert Greenfield, Jay Blakesberg, Rick Turner, Mama Louise Hudson,

Bruce Hampton, Robbie Robertson, James Taylor, David Crosby, Mac Rebennack, John Hammond Jr., Charlie Laquidara, Robin Fenter, Gilbert Lee, Sidney Smith, Henry Paul, Charlie Brusco, Jonathan Alter, Julia Negron, Geraldo Rivera, John Cowan, Toy Caldwell, Paul T. Riddle, Reba Rambo, Jeff Hanna, Peter Levin, Scott Sharrard, Andy Aledort, Peter Conlon, Tom Beard, Thomas Santa Lucia, Sean Condon, Spooner Oldham, Brian Procknal, Elvin Bishop, Jimmy Hall, Matt Burt, Edward Steven Weissman, Joe Rosenberg, Bruce Kaufer, Bill Irvine, Becky Chalk, Brad Perkins, Karen Dibble Whitman, Jeff Schein, Mary Moulthrop Heidemann, Tom Tobin, Jay Corcoran, Jackie Avery Jr., Richard Price, Reese Wynans, Rick Capotto, Doug Cameron.

By Kirk West

Interviews with Steve Massarsky, 3/7/96; Butch Trucks, 9/3/87; Gregg Allman, 7/27/84, 3/5/87, 8/5/87; Dickey Betts, 1987; Joe Dan Petty, 5/14/86; Bruce Hampton, 7/7/87; Bill Graham, 1/31/86; Jaimoe, 9/9/87, 9/10/87, 9/13/87; Geraldine Allman, 8/31/87; Chuck Leavell, 5/7/86; Jonny Podell, 10/24/91; Rose Lane Leavell, Johnny Sandlin, Jimmy Hall, and Candace Oakley (all undated).

By Others

Phil Walden, interview by Bill Ector, 5/26/05; Dickey Betts, interview by Kirsten West, 7/22/94; Bill Graham, interview by John Ogden, 10/25/91.

BOOKS

Allman, Galadrielle. *Please Be with Me: A Song for My Father, Duane Allman* (Random House, 2014).

Allman, Gregg, with Alan Light. *My Cross to Bear* (William Morrow, 2012).

Alter, Jonathan. *His Very Best: Jimmy Carter—A Life* (Simon and Schuster, 2020).

Ballinger, Lee. *Lynyrd Skynyrd: An Oral History* (Spike, 1999).

Beatty, Bob. *Play All Night!: Duane Allman and the Journey to Fillmore East* (University Press of Florida, 2022).

Bomar, Scott B. *Southbound: An Illustrated History of Southern Rock* (Backbeat Books, 2014).

Campbell, Joseph L. "Red Dog." *The Legendary Red Dog: A Book of Tails* (2001).

Cohodas, Nadine. *Spinning Blues into Gold: The Chess Brothers and the Legendary Chess Records* (Iconoclassic Books, 2012).

Coplon, Jeff. *The First Time: Cher as Told to Jeff Coplon* (Pocket Books, 1998).

Fitzgerald, Michael Ray. *Jacksonville and the Roots of Southern Rock* (University Press of Florida, 2020).

Freeman, Scott. *Midnight Riders: The Story of the Allman Brothers* (Little, Brown, 1995).

Gordon, Robert. *Respect Yourself: Stax Records and the Soul Explosion* (Bloomsbury, 2013).

Gould, Jonathan. *Otis Redding: An Unfinished Life* (Crown, 2017).

Graham, Bill with Robert Greenfield. *Bill Graham Presents: My Life Inside Rock and Out* (Da Capo Press, 2004).

Hagan, Joe. *Sticky Fingers: The Life and Times of Jann Wenner and Rolling Stone Magazine* (Vintage Books, 2017).

Helm, Levon, with Steven Davis. *This Wheel's on Fire* (Chicago Review Press, 1993).

Hornsby, Paul. *Fix It in the Mix* (Mercer University Press, 2021).

Hoskyns, Barney. *Across the Great Divide: The Band and America* (Hyperion, 1993).

Jackson, Blair. *Garcia: An American Life* (Penguin, 1999).

Jordan, Hamilton. *A Boy from Georgia: Coming of Age in the Segregated South* (University of Georgia Press, 2015).

Kemp, Mark. *Dixie Lullaby: A Story of Music, Race, and New Beginnings in the New South* (University of Georgia Press, 2004).

Kooper, Al. *Backstage Passes and Backstabbing Bastards* (Backbeat Books, 1998).

Leavell, Chuck, with J. Marshall Craig. *Between Rock and a Home Place* (Mercer University Press, 2004).

Lesh, Phil. *Searching for the Sound: My Life with the Grateful Dead* (Back Bay Books, 2007).

McNally, Dennis. *A Long Strange Trip: The Inside History of the Grateful Dead* (Broadway Books, 2002).

Myers, Marc. *Anatomy of a Song: The Oral History of 45 Iconic Hits That Changed Rock, R&B and Pop* (Grove/Atlantic, 2016).

Nolan, Tom. *The Allman Brothers Band: A Biography in Pictures and Words* (Sire Books, 1976).

Odom, Gene, with Frank Dorman. *Lynyrd Skynyrd: Remembering the Free Birds of Southern Rock* (Broadway Books, 2002).

Paul, Alan. *One Way Out: The Inside History of the Allman Brothers Band* (St. Martin's Press, 2014).

Perkins, Willie. *No Saints, No Saviors: My Years with the Allman Brothers Band* (Mercer University Press, 2005).

Preston, Neal. *Exhilarated and Exhausted* (Reel Art Press, 2017).

Richardson, Peter. *No Simple Highway: A Cultural History of the Grateful Dead* (St. Martin's Press, 2015).

Sandlin, Anathalee G. *A Never-Ending Groove: Johnny Sandlin's Musical Odyssey* (Mercer University Press, 2012).

Streissguth, Michael. *Outlaw: Waylon, Willie, Kris, and the Renegades of Nashville* (It Books, 2013).

Taplin, Jonathan. *The Magic Years: Scenes from a Rock and Roll Life* (Heyday, 2021).

Thompson, Hunter S. *The Great Shark Hunt* (Simon and Schuster, 1979).

Walden, Alan, and S. E. Feinberg. *Southern Man: Music and Mayhem in the American South* (Jawbone Press, 2021).

Wexler, Jerry. *Rhythm and the Blues: A Life in American Music* (Knopf, 1993).

MAGAZINE ARTICLES

Aikin, Jim. "Grateful Dead: Wired for Sound." *Guitar Player,* July 1973.

Albero, Richard. "A GP Tribute to Duane Allman: Just Rock On, and Have You a Good Time." *Guitar Player,* May/June 1973.

Aledort, Andy. "Big Brother." *Guitar World,* April 2007.

"Allman Reportedly Testified in Drug Probe." *Rolling Stone,* March 11, 1976.

"The Allmans: Southern Discomfort." *Rolling Stone,* August 26, 1976.

Anson, Robert Sam. "Jimmy's Friends in Rock." *New Times,* September 3, 1976.

Ball, Oneida. "Gregg Allman Takes the Big Plunge." *Circus,* August 1974.

Bozza, Anthony. "A Boy's Life (in Sex, Drugs and Rock & Roll)." *Rolling Stone,* October 12, 2000.

Brill, Steven. "Jimmy Carter's Pathetic Lies." *Harper's,* March 1976.

Brodey, Jim. "A Moment Captured in Time: The *Crawdaddy* Interview with Duane Allman." *Crawdaddy* 4, no. 5 (1970).

Browne, David. "How Jimmy Carter (Literally) Rocked the Presidency." *Rolling Stone,* September 8, 2020.

Cahill, Tim. "A Tale of Two Tours." *Rolling Stone,* January 16, 1975.

Carr, Roy. "Allman Brothers: Duane Is Dead, but His Spirit Lives On Everytime the Band Goes on Stage." *New Musical Express,* April 22, 1972.

Charlesworth, Chris. "Gregg Allman: Carnegie Hall, New York City." *Melody Maker,* April 20, 1974.

———. "An Interview with Gregg Allman." *Melody Maker,* January 26, 1974.

———. "Southern Rock: Under the Sign of Capricorn." *Melody Maker,* February 2, 1974.

Crowe, Cameron. "The Allman Brothers Band Together." *Hit Parader,* June 1974.

———. "The Allman Brothers Story." *Rolling Stone,* December 6, 1973.

———. "*Brothers and Sisters* Album Ambles On In." *Circular,* August 6, 1973.

———. "Capricorn: Five Years Later—The Sound of the South Sounds Fine." *Circular,* August 12, 1974.

———. "The Grateful Dead Flee Big Business." *Circus,* October 1973.

———. "Marshall Tucker: The South Also Rises." *Rolling Stone,* March 14, 1974.

———. "Ramblin' Man." *Rolling Stone,* October 25, 1973.

Dann, Laurel. "The Last Interview with Duane Allman." *Creem,* December 1973.

Dauphin, John. "Reflections from Cameron Crowe." *Hittin' the Note* 32 (2001).

Dauphin, John, and Kirk West. "The Road Lesh Travels." *Hittin' the Note* 29 (2000).

Duncan, Robert. "Rhett Butler After the Fall: Dickey Bett[e]s Brushes Himself Off." *Creem,* March 1977.

Ector, Bill. "Sessions with Tom Dowd: The Making of *Eat a Peach*." *Hittin' the Note* 37 (2003).

Edmonds, Ben. "Snapshots of the South." *Creem,* November 1972.

Edwards, Gavin. "Nothing Weighs as Much as the Heartache: 30 Years of Ups and Downs with the Allman Brothers Band." *Rolling Stone,* November 25, 1999.

Faines, Steve. "Gregg Allman Live—The Tour That Saved the Allman Brothers." *Circus,* October 1974.

Farren, Mick. "Dickey Betts: Movin' On Out of the Macon Mess." *New Musical Express*, June 11, 1977.

Fletcher, Gordon. "East Coast Rocks at DC Concerts." *Rolling Stone*, July 19, 1973.

Glover, Tony. "Duane & Dick: Dueling Guitars." *Rolling Stone,* October 10, 1974.

———. "Win, Lose or Draw." *Rolling Stone*, November 6, 1975.

Goldman, Peter, and Eleanor Clift. "Carter on the Rise." *Newsweek,* March 8, 1976.

Greene, Andy. "Tom Petty on Past Confederate Flag Use: 'It Was Downright Stupid.'" *Rolling Stone*, July 14, 2015.

Gross, Michael. "The Death of the Allman Brothers Band." *Swank,* 1977.

Harris, Art. "Candidate Jimmy Carter: Rock's Good Ol' Boy." *Rolling Stone*, December 4, 1975.

———. "Singing in the Rain." *Rolling Stone*, July 4, 1974.

Hendrickson, Matt. "Gregg Allman's Restless Soul." *Garden and Gun*, April/May 2011.

Hoskyns, Barney. "Southern Men: The Long Tall Saga of the Allman Brothers Band." *Mojo*, December 2002.

Hudson, Phil W. "Q&A: Butch Trucks of the Allman Brothers Band Talks Phil Walden, Reunion, Bruce Hampton." *Atlanta Business Journal*, December 15, 2016.

Jerome, Jim. "Now That Cher Has Helped Show Him the Way, Gregg Allman Takes to the Road Again." *People Weekly*, September 8, 1975.

"Jimmy Carter: Not Just Peanuts." *Time*, March 8, 1976.

Klein, Joe, and Dave Marsh. "Rock Meets Politics in 1976." *Rolling Stone,* September 9, 1976.

Kraar, Louis. "How Phil Walden Turns Rock into Gold." *Fortune*, September 1975.

Landau, Jon. "Bandleader Duane Allman Dies in Bike Crash." *Rolling Stone*, November 25, 1971.

"Leave My Blues at Home." *Savannah*, September/October 2017.

"A Long-Shot Candidate Who Will Run in Every Race." *US News and World Report*, September 22, 1975.

Lynskey, John. "Lamar Williams Tribute—Out of the Shadows." *Hittin' the Note*, Issue 17, 1998.

———. "Watkins Glen Remembered: A Conversation with Bunky Odom." *Hittin' the Note* 79 (2013).

———. "Dickey Betts: Lookin Forward, Moving On." *Hittin' the Note* 31 (2001).

Martoccio, Angie. "Cameron Crowe Digs into the 'Almost Famous' Archive for the 20th Anniversary." *Rolling Stone*, September 11, 2020.

McGee, David. "Jaded and Joyless in Jersey: The Allman Bros Draw a Blank." *Rolling Stone*, October 24, 1975.

Meroney, John. "How to Elect a President: Jimmy Carter, Two South Georgia Political Novices, and the Unpredictable Road to the White House." *Atlanta*, March 9, 2020.

Nobles, Barr. "More Talk of Allman Brothers Band Breakup." *Rolling Stone*, September 9, 1976.

Oney, Steve. "A Sinner's Second Chance." *Esquire*, November 1984.

Palmer, Robert. "Allman Brothers Band: A Great Southern Revival." *Rolling Stone*, May 3, 1979.

Passante, Robyn. "Southern Rock and Style." *South*, June 3, 2015.

Perry, Charles. "Alembic: Sound Wizards to the Grateful Dead." *Rolling Stone*, September 27, 1973.

Robinson, Lisa. "Grateful Dead Band Interview." *Creem*, December 1970.

Rosen, Steve. "Gregg Allman, Rock Organist." *Contemporary Keyboard*, August 1976.

Schwartz, Jim. "Sea Level: Rock, Funk, and Blues from the South." *Guitar Player*, January 1980.

Scoppa, Bud. "Allman Brothers Band: *Win, Lose or Draw*." *Phonograph Record*, October 1975.

Siegel, Joel. "Watkins Glen Jam Tops Woodstock: 600,000 Fans." *Rolling Stone*, August 30, 1973.

Snyder, Patrick. "The Sorrowful Confessions of Gregg Allman." *Rolling Stone*, November 4, 1976.

Snyder-Scumpy, Patrick. "The Allman Brothers: Boogie or Bust." *Crawdaddy*, October 1973.

Swenson, John. "Allman Brothers Band, the Band, the Grateful Dead: Summer Jam at Watkins Glen." *Village Voice*, August 9, 1973.

———. "Southern Rock: Gone with the Trend." *Crawdaddy!*, July 1975.

Thompson, Hunter S. "Fear and Loathing on the Campaign Trail '76: Third-Rate Romance, Low-Rent Rendezvous." *Rolling Stone*, June 3, 1976.

Uhelszki, Jaan. "Beat the Devil: The Allman Brothers." *Creem*, December, 1975.

Watts, Michael. "The Allman Brothers Are What the Grateful Dead Were in '67." *Melody Maker*, August 25, 1973.

West, Kirk. "Jon Podell: Booking the Best Band in the Land." *Hittin' the Note* 25 (1999).

West, Paul. "Bob Dylan in Atlanta: 'Great to Be in Joe-Jah!'" *Rolling Stone*, February 28, 1974.

Yorke, Ritchie. "Macon, Georgia." *ZigZag*, March 1974.

Zwerling, Andy. "Workingman's Dead." *Rolling Stone*, July 23, 1970.

NEWSPAPER ARTICLES

Baker, Russell. "Georgia Hunt for Bodies Is Linked to 'Dixie Mafia.'" *New York Times*, April 19, 1974.

Ball, Millie. "Maddox Call for Reawakening." *New Orleans Times-Picayune*, October 17, 1976.

"Band Members Buy Development." *Macon Telegraph*, March 2, 1973.

Bonner, Christopher. "Cher Suing for Divorce." *Macon Telegraph*, July 10, 1975.

Brown, Rick. "Southern Rock at Its Best." *Great Speckled Bird*, June 3, 1974.

Burger, Frederick. "Allman's Death Machine Sold at Public Auction." *Macon Telegraph*, April 30, 1972.

Cain, Scott. "Allmans Sound a Lucrative Note." *Atlanta Constitution*, June 2, 1974.

Camp, Arklette. "Cher Weds Macon-Based Rock Singer." *Macon Telegraph*, July 1, 1975.

"Concert Camp Out." *Washington Post*, June 9, 1973.

Feinberg, Lawrence, and Tom Zito. "53,000 Rock Fans Jam RFK." *Washington Post*, June 10, 1973.

Fisher, Robert. "Herring Trembling with Joy over Ruling." *Macon Telegraph*, March 2, 1978.

Francis, Miller, Jr. "Allman Brothers, Hampton Grease Band Twice." *Great Speckled Bird*, May 18, 1970.

Garrett, Robert T. "Blue Skies over Georgia." *Harvard Crimson*, December 8, 1975.

Goodwin, Gerald F. "Black and White in Vietnam." *New York Times*, July 18, 2017.

"Happening on the Green: Ontario Speedway Sets Rock Concert." *Pomona Progress-Bulletin*, May 8, 1973.

Harrington, Richard. "The Selling of Rock on the Megabucks Music Circuit." *Washington Post*, September 24, 1989.

Harris, Art. "Cher in Macon? With Gregg?" *Atlanta Constitution*, February 13, 1975.

———. "Waiting for Gregg: Slow Beat." *Atlanta Constitution*, August 6, 1975.

Hirsiger, Madeline. "Allman Band Album Grinds to Halt." *Macon News*, May 6, 1975.

———. "The Allman Band: No Stars." *Macon Telegraph*, September 30, 1973.

———. "Country Sound Added by Betts." *Macon News*, October 2, 1973.

———. "It Was Fun While It Lasted." *Macon Telegraph and News*, October 3, 1976.

———. "Wedding Rites Were Authentic." *Macon News*, April 20, 1973.

Jaimoe. Letter to the Editor. *Macon News*, August 19, 1976.

Jaynes, Gregory. "We Made Some Music Last Night That'd Blow Your Hat in the Creek." *Atlanta Constitution*, January 30, 1974.

Kane, Sharyn. "Allmans Get Record Pay at Mammoth Rock Festival." *Macon Telegraph*, August 1, 1973.

King, Bill. "Betts Bets on Allman Band Unity." *Atlanta Constitution*, September 28, 1978.

Kirst, Sean. "Gregg Allman, His Canisius High Show and Lives That It Changed." *Buffalo News*, June 21, 2017.

———. "How Gregg Allman and Cher Stunned Canisius High 'Assembly' in 1976." *Buffalo News*, June 4, 2017.

Ledbetter, Lez. "Rock Promoters Expect 150,000 at Watkins Glen Fete July 28." *New York Times*, July 19, 1973.

Lee, Jim. "Defendant Furnished Cocaine, Allman Said." *Atlanta Constitution*, June 25, 1976.

Lichtenstein, Grace. "Festival at Watkins Glen Ends in Mud and Elation." *New York Times*, July 30, 1973.

Lyman, Rick. "Hamilton Jordan, Carter's Right Hand, Dies at 63." *New York Times*, May 21, 2008.

Morrison, David. "The Capricorn Connection." *Atlanta Constitution*, November 4, 1976.

"Officials Deny Allman Breakup." *Macon Telegraph*, May 7, 1975.

Popson, Tom. "Capricorn Records and Phil Walden Back in the Game." *Chicago Tribune,* July 19, 1991.

Rippert, Wesely G. "Macon-Plains Connection Ties Campaign to Youth." *St. Petersburg Times,* October 5, 1976.

Safire, Willliam. "The List That Never Was." *New York Times,* October 4, 1976.

Savage, Randall. "Allman Granted Immunity in Probe." *Macon Telegraph,* January 21, 1976.

Schudel, Matt. "Fiddler Vassar Clements Dies." *Washington Post,* August 17, 2005.

Selvin, Joel. "The Allman Brothers Band: What Southern Boys Can Do with Rock." *San Francisco Chronicle,* February 14, 1971.

Sterba, James P. "Saigon Army Desertions Up Nearly 50% in Spring." *New York Times,* July 27, 1970.

Strout, Richard L. "How Jimmy Carter Did It." *Christian Science Monitor,* June 17, 1976.

Sverdlik, Alan. "Jailbound Herring Forgives Old Friend." *Macon Telegraph,* August 20, 1979.

Tatangelo, Wade. "Dickey Betts on the real Allman Brothers Band Stories Behind the Film 'Almost Famous.'" *Sarasota Herald Tribune,* August 16, 2020.

"Time Limits Cancel OMS Rock Concert." *Pomona Progress-Bulletin,* May 22, 1973.

Trucks, Butch. "Whipping Post." Letter to the Editor, *New York Times,* May 8, 2005.

Vandevanter, Peter. "Allman: 'I Got Very High.'" *Macon Telegraph,* June 24, 1976.

———. "Allman Under Heavy Guard." *Macon Telegraph,* June 25, 1976.

———. "Herring Sentenced to 75 Years in Drug Case." *Macon Telegraph,* July 20, 1976.

Vejnoska, Jill. "Jimmy Carter & Gregg Allman's Story Goes Way Back. And It Involves Cher." *Atlanta Journal-Constitution,* May 17, 2016.

Yarbrough, Cathy. "Allmans Concert in City to Aid Indians." *Atlanta Constitution,* June 7, 1973.

Zito, Tom. "Grateful Dead and the Allman Brothers Band." *Washington Post,* June 8, 1973.

Zito, Tom, and Megan Rosenfeld. "Days and Nights in the Stadium." *Washington Post,* June 11, 1973.

LINER NOTES

Allman Brothers Band. *The Allman Brothers at the Fillmore East 11, 13 and 14 Feb 1970,* liner notes by Owsley Stanley.

———. *Dreams,* box set, liner notes by John Swenson.

Allman, Duane. *Skydog,* box set, liner notes by Scott Schinder.

Allman, Gregg. *Laid Back,* deluxe edition reissue, liner notes by John P. Lynskey.

Lynyrd Skynyrd. *One More from the Road,* liner notes by Cameron Crowe.

ARCHIVAL DOCUMENTS

Fall 1975 memo from Jim Gammill to Carter campaign. Documents reviewed at the Carter Presidential Library.

Providence benefit contracts. Documents reviewed at the Carter Presidential Library.

Telegram from Bill Graham to Phil Walden, August 20, 1975. Viewed at the Big House Museum Archives.

FILM

Jimmy Carter: Rock and Roll President. Directed by May Wharton, written by Bill Flanagan, 2020.

TV SHOW

Rivera, Geraldo. *Good Night America,* episode 22, August 14, 1975.

WEB ARTICLES

"All My Friends Part III: Jack Pearson, Chank Middleton and Bert Holman." Relix .com, August 10, 2017.

Arnold, Corry. "December 31, 1973, Cow Palace, Daly City, CA: Allman Brothers Band with Jerry Garcia, Boz Scaggs and Bill Kreutzmann." Lost Live Dead, https: //lostlivedead.blogspot.com/2012/12/december-31–1973-cow-palace-daly-city .html.

"Atlanta Sports Arena, May 10, 1970." https://www.dead.net/show/may-10–1970.

Burnstein, Scott. "Dixie Mafia in Macon, GA. Killed Jimmy Reeves in Years Leading Up to Trying to Kill Rocker Gregg Allman." *Gangster Report,* May 29, 2017.

———. "Drug Trial, Dixie Mafia Ties Led to Break-Up of the Allman Brothers." *Gangster Report,* June 11, 2015.

"The Dead and Allmans." Dead Essays, January 2019, https://deadessays.blogspot.com /2019/01/the-dead-and-allmans.html.

"The Dead in Piedmont Park." http://www.thestripproject.com/TheStripProject /Hippies_Stories/Entries/2007/5/19_Dead_in_Piedmont_Park.html.

"Dick Latvala's Notes from 6/9/73." https://ia800206.us.archive.org/8/items/Monte Barrygd73-06-09.AUD.fob.barry.flac/Latvala730609notes.jpg.

Fulce, Jay. "African Americans in the Vietnam War: Project 100,000." Jay-harold.com, October 13, 2015.

Furman, Janet. "A History of Furman Sound and Its Grateful Dead Roots." http://www .furmanhistory.com/.

Hall, Wayne, and Megan Weier. "Lee Robins' Studies of Heroin Use Among US Vietnam Veterans." NIH National Library of Medicine, January 2017.

Heisler, Bret. Interview with Dickey Betts, Phil Zone, http://www.philzone.com /interviews/dickey/index.html.

Kyle, Dave. "Remembering Duane Allman." *Vintage Guitar,* January 1997, additional interviews published online at https://www.duaneallman.info/rememberingduaneallman .htm.

Peeples, Stephen K. "'Almost Famous': Neal Preston Recalls the Interview Tape Hostage Crisis." Stephenkpeeples.com, September 13, 2021.

VIDEOS

Tom Beard, Alex Cooley, and Peter Conlon, interviewed by David Barbe, Callie Holmes, and Christian Lopez, April 10, 2013. Oral History Documentary Collection at the Richard B. Russell Library for Political Research and Studies, University of Georgia Libraries.

"Duane Allman & Jerry Garcia Jam WBCN 1970." YouTube, https://youtu.be /FuU0aTdHI4A.

Ahmet Ertegun. Interview. YouTube, https://www.youtube.com/watch?v=zfC26KHTCQ4.

Bob Weir and Jerry Garcia. *Late Night with David Letterman*, September 17, 1987. YouTube, https://www.youtube.com/watch?v=fTut68r_Q-E.

COURT CASES

United States of America v. James Alford Elliott, Jr., Robert Ervin Delph, Jr., William Marion Foster, Recea Howell Hawkins, John Clayburn Hawkins, Jr., a/k/a J. C. and John Frank Taylor, United States Court of Appeals (5th Cir., April 21, 1978).

United States of America, Plaintiff-appellee v. John C. Herring, A/k/a Scooter, Defendant-appellant, United States Court of Appeals (5th Cir., March 1, 1978).

INDEX

Aaron, Hank, 218

Agent Orange, 294–95

"Ain't Wastin' Time No More," 27, 28, 155

Alaimo, Steve, 28

Aledort, Andy, 131–32, 138, 143

Alembic, 122–23

"All My Friends," 78–79

Allman, Duane, 4, 6, 40, 50, 54, 98
  Allman, Gregg, and, 14–15, 22
  Betts, Dickey, and, 10–12, 29, 233–34
  in Castle Heights Military Academy, 1–2
  death of, xi–xii, 19–20, 47, 100–101, 170
  funeral of, 23, 38
  Garcia and, 96, 99
  Grateful Dead and, 99–101
  as guitarist, 3, 11
  Jaimoe and, 9–10, 17
  as leader, 19–20, 47–48, 86
  Walden and, 22–23, 109–10, 168

Allman, Elijah Blue, 283–84, 290

Allman, Geraldine, 1

Allman, Gregg, 1, 3–4, 40, 178, 269, 277
  alcoholism of, 223–24
  Allman, D., and, 14–15, 22
  Betts, Dickey, and, 12, 47–48, 69, 255–56
  in Buffalo, 290–91
  Carter, J., and, 186–87
  Cher and, 248–51, 257–59, 290–91

on Confederate flag use, 216–17
  covers by, 78–79
  Crowe on, 173–78
  drug probe against, 272–78, 282–83
  on *Laid Back,* 78–80
  Leavell, C., and, 63–64
  Los Angeles and, 72–74
  marriage to Cher, 257–58
  musicianship of, 63–64, 166–67
  on Oakley, B., 30–31
  in rehab, 287–90
  as singer, 14–15, 65, 71–72

Allman, Janice Blair, 174

the Allman Joys, 1–2, 13, 41, 206

the Almost Brothers, 270

Almost Famous, 173

Altamont, 90, 126

AM radio, 155

American Beauty, 89, 91–92

"American Pie," 81–82

Ampex, 122–23

"And We Bid You Goodnight," 181

"Angel from Montgomery," 79

Aoxomoxoa, 90

Artz, Mike, 138, 270

At Fillmore East, xii, 17, 19, 20, 28, 56, 104, 108, 295

Atkins, Chet, 158

Atlanta International Pop Festival, 85, 161

Atlantic Record, 6

"Attics of My Life," 93

Bach, J. S., 145

Balin, Marty, 90

the Band, 144–48

Bangs, Lester, 20

Beard, Tom, 188, 265, 267, 278

Beat Generation, 87

"The Beat Goes On," 248

Beatty, Warren, 104

Beck, Jeff, 82

"Been Gone Too Long," 3

Berry, Chuck, 100

"Berry's Tune," 61

"Bertha," 144

Betts, Dale, 34*n*, 38, 40, 60, 152, 262

Betts, Dickey, 19–20, 25, 28, 43, 44, 105, 226

    Allman, D., and, 10–12, 29, 233–34

    Allman, Gregg, and, 12, 47–48, 69, 255–56

    on Allman Brothers Band, 151

    on *Brothers and Sisters*, 65

    on business, 164

    Clements and, 235

    on Crowe, 172–73

    divorce of, 262

    Dudek and, 62–63

    Dylan and, 156

    Eghiazarian and, 271–72, 294

    as frontman, 224, 228

    on Garcia, 87

    Garcia and, 93–95, 121, 122–23, 181

    on Grateful Dead, 102

    as guitarist, 62, 122–23

    Jaimoe on, 13, 23–24, 63, 259

    as leader, 23–24, 47–48

    Love Valley cabin of, 196–97

    marriage of, 152

    Massarsky as lawyer for, 239–42

    on Native American culture, 104–7

    outfits of, 165–66

    personality of, 12

    Petty on, 168

    on "Ramblin' Man," 44–45

    solo debut of, 196–201

    as songwriter, 68

    Trucks on, 224

    Wabegijig, S., relationship with, 152

Betts, Jessica, 104

Beverage Baron, 132

Bickwit, Bonnie, 142

Bishop, Elvin, 204

"Black Hearted Woman," 155, 186

Blair, Janice, 45, 49

Bland, Bobby, 67, 71

von Blixen-Finecke, Ulla, 111

Blood, Sweat & Tears, 94, *94,* 207

Blue Sky. *See* Wabegijig, Sandy

"Blue Sky," 27, 42–43, 104, 262

bluegrass, 92–93, 197–98

Bluegrass Boys, 197

Bono, Chaz, 290

Bono, Sonny, 248

Born to Run, 112

Bowles, Ellard "Moose," 291

"Box of Rain," 92, 93

Boyer, Scott, 13, 22, 37, 75, 76, 193

Bramblett, Randall, 193

Bramlett, Delaney, 86

Brantley, Larry, 138

Brecker Brothers, 51

"Les Brers in A Minor," 27, 28, 61, 180–81

"Broken Arrow," 73

Brothers and Sisters, xii, 61, 64, 77, 120, 123,

    150, 165, 204, 211, 295

    Betts, Dickey, on, 65

    country music on, 153–54

    production costs, 253

    recording of, 59–60, 69–70, 151

    success of, 152, 153, 193

Brothers Properties, 242

Brown, Carolyn, 49, 114, 244

Brown, David, 13

Brown, Jerry, 275

Brown, Rick, 217, 221

Browne, Jackson, 36, 71, 72–73, 78–79, 249
Brusco, Charlie, 213, 254
Buckley, Tim, 71, 74
Buffalo Springfield, 73
Burbridge, Oteil, 57, 89
Burroughs, William S., 87
Burt, Matt, 131

Caesar and Cleo, 248
Cahill, Tim, 234, 236
Caldwell, Bobby, 205
Caldwell, Tom, 203
Caldwell, Tommy, 157
Caldwell, Toy, 157, 158, 159
Callahan, Mike, 120
Cameron, Doug, 290, 292
"Can't Lose What You Never Had," 255
"Can't You See," 159, 204
Canyon, Laurel, 71–72
Cappotto, Rick, 291
Capricorn, 38, 50–51, 109, 112, 113, 120,
    157–58, 162–64, 204
Capricorn Picnic and Summer Games, 204
Capricorn Studios, 75–76, 204–5
Captain Beyond, 204
"Captain Kennedy," 215
Carne, Judy, 249
Carr, Roy, 32
Carter, Clarence, 112, 271
Carter, Jimmy, xi, 283
    Allman, Gregg, and, 186–87
    on Allman Brothers Band, 264–68
    campaign of, 262–63, 266
    on civil rights, 189–90
    Conlon on, 264–65, 268
    Dylan and, 184–85
    election of, 285
    fundraising campaign of, 187–88
    primary victory of, 275
    Thompson on, 190–92
    Walden, Phil, and, 183–84, 188–89,
        284–85
    Carter, Rosalynn, 184, 188

Carter, Rudolph, 30n, 56
"Casey Jone," 91
Cassady, Neal, 87
Cassidy, Ed, 86
"Cast Off All My Fears," 72
Castle Heights Military Academy, Allman,
    D., in, 1–2
Chalk, Becky, 132
Charles, Ray, 66
Charlesworth, Chris, 100, 113
Charlie Daniels Band, 37, 163, 180, 204, 244
Cher, 155, 247, 255, 269, 283–84, 287
    Allman, Gregg, and, 248–51, 257–59,
        290–91
    marriage to Allman, Gregg, 257–58
Chess Records, 164
"Chest Fever," 145
Chicago (band), 86
civil rights, Carter, J., on, 189–90
Civil Rights Act of 1964, 114, 190
Clapton, Eric, 4, 106
Clavinet, 167
Clements, Vassar, 93–94, 197, 198–99, 200,
    235
Cobham, Billy, 51
Cole, David, 270
Coleman, Linda, 10
Collins, Allen, 205
Colter, Jessi, 201
Coltrane, John, 259
"Come and Go Blues," 64, 66, 74, 146, 147
Condon, John, 17, 274
Confederate flag, 216–17
Conlon, Peter, 161–62, 263, 264–65, 268
Cooley, Alex, 85, 161, 189, 264
Cooper, Alice, 194
Corcoran, Jay, 145
country music, on *Brothers and Sisters*,
    153–54
Cow Palace, 149–50, 179
Cowan, John, 198
Cowb, 171
Cowles, Roger, 256

Criteria Studios, 36
Crosby, David, 91
Crowe, Cameron, 160, 165, 170–71, 180, 289, 295–96
  on Allman, Gregg, 173–78
  Allman Brothers Band and, 172–73
"Cumberland Blues," 91
Cur, John, 128
Cutler, Sam, 86–87, 88, 90, 125, 127, 139
  on Allman Brothers Band, 149–50
  on Grateful Dead, 101–2, 121, 149–50

"Dark Star," 96, 99
Davis, Clive, 255
Day on the Green, 101
Delaney & Bonnie and Friends, 86
Densmore, Julia, 50
Derek and the Dominos, 19
Derringer, Rick, 12
Dick's Picks, Volume Four, 98
Dillon Stadium, 100
Dinnertime, 37, 197
"Dire Wolf," 91
Dixie Mafia, 276
"Done Somebody Wrong," 255
Donovan, 29, 95–96
"Don't Keep Me Wondering," 186
"Don't Mess Up a Good Thing," 78
the Doors, 2
"Double Cross," 66
Doucette, Thom, 11, 23, 47–48, 89
Dowd, Tom, 21, 27, 36, 60, 166
Dr. John, 37–38
"Dreams," 15
drummers, 13
Dudek, Les, 38, 44, 62–64, 123, 165
Dylan, Bob, 91, 127, 145, 183, 207, 245
  Betts, Dickey, and, 156
  Carter, J., and, 184–85
  on "Ramblin' Man," 156

"Early Morning Blues," 64, 65, 68
Eat a Peach, 27, 29, 39, 41, 60, 69, 155

Eckstine, Billy, 67
Edmonds, Ben, 75
Eghiazarian, Paulette, 247, 249, 251, 271–72, 294
"Endless Highway," 144
English, Joe, 34*n,* 152
Ertegun, Ahmet, 21, 110
Etsitty, Stewart, 199
Evans, Gerald, 106
"Expecting to Fly," 73

FAME Studio, 4, 6
Farlow, Tal, 158
The Farm, 33
Feiten, Buzy, 81
Fenter, Frank, 110–11, 114, 154, 158, 169, 208, 244, 254
  Jaimoe on, 113
  Leavell, C., on, 113
  Walden, Phil, and, 112–13
Fetcher, Gordon, 115
Fillmore East, 94–98
Finger Lakes, 125
Finkel, Shelly, 125–26, 127, 130, 141
Fire on the Mountain, 244–45
5'll Getcha Ten, 78
Fleetwood, Mick, 96
Fleetwood Mac, 95
Fletcher, Gordon, 115, 118
Floyd, Eddie, 205
FM radio, 155
Fong-Torres, Ben, 171–72, 176
For Everyman, 78–79
Free, 213
"Free Bird," 206
Freeman, Ed, 81–82
Freeze, 291, 292
"Friend of the Devil," 93
Fuchs, Joe, 277, 279
Furman, Janet, 129

Gaillard, Slim, 145
Gammill, Jim, 266

Garcia, Jerry, 179, 197, 281–82
    Allman, D., and, 96
    amps of, 122*n*
    Betts, Dickey, and, 87, 93–95, 121, 122–23, 181
    court case of, 149
    Cutler on, 127
    on Kerouac, 87–88
    leadership of, 86
    on Watkins Glen, 144
Gary Lewis and the Playboys, 207
The Gattlinburg Tapes, 43
Geffen, David, 248
"The Genetic Method," 145
George, Dan, 231
"Gimme Three Steps," 206
Ginsberg, Allen, 87
Glover, Tony, 261
"God Rest His Soul," 28
"Going Down the Road Feeling Bad," 100
Good Night America, 251–52
Gordy, Berry, 244
Graham, Bill, 20, 94, 96, 101, 127, 128, 130, 137, 179, 204, 229–30
Grand Funk Railroad, 95
Grand Ole Opry, 72
"La Grange," 233
Grappelli, Stéphane, 197
the Grateful Dead, xi, 4, 48, 90–91, 148
    Allman, D., and, 99–101
    Allman Brothers Band and, 85–87, 95–99, 115–16, 126–28, 135, 149–50, 179–80
    Betts, Dickey, on, 102
    Cutler on, 101–2, 121
    sound crew of, 121, 128–29
    on touring hiatus, 150
    Trucks, B., on, 88–89
Gray, Doug, 158
Great Southern, 294
The Great Speckled Bird, 99, 221
Green, Grant, 158
"Green Grass and High Tides," 254–55

Greenfield, Robert, 137
The Gregg Allman Tour, 194–95
Gregg Allman Tour '74, 233
Grinderswitch, 204, 219
Grossman, Albert, 104

Haggard, Merle, 90–91
"Half Breed," 155, 248–49
Hall, Cloyd, 186, 243
Hall, Rick, 4, 7
Hampton, Bruce, 17, 98
Hampton's Grease Band, 86, 98
"Hand Picked," 198–99
Hanna, Jeff, 3, 71–72, 168–69, 198–99
Harris, Art, 259–60
Hart, Mickey, 88, 91, 96
Hartwick, Kenny, 44
Hawkins, J. C., 273, 276, 277
Haynes, Warren, 80, 203, 225
Hayward, Charlie, 37, 78
Healy, Dan, 121, 128, 129–30, 143
    stage design of, 136
    on Watkins Glen, 133
Heidemann, Mary Moulthrop, 141, 148
Hell's Angels, 90
Helm, Levon, 63, 145
Hendrix, Jimi, 85, 207
heroin, 20–21, 56, 250
Herring, Scooter, 175, 178, 226, 235–36, 269, 273, 275, 293–94
    Allman, Gregg, and, 277
    indictment of, 277
"Hey Bo Diddley," 100
"Hey Jude," 5–6
"High Falls," 259
Highway Call, 77, 94, 196, 199, 201, 233, 234, 259
"Highway Call," 201
Hines, Earl, 67
Hirsiger, Madeline, 173, 256
History of the Grateful Dead, Volume One (Bear's Choice), 98
Hodges, Alex, 162, 163, 185, 237

Hornsby, Paul, 7, 75, 85, 204
  MTB working with, 158
  on Walden, Phil, 110
Horowitz, Vladimir, 195
"Hot 'Lanta," 61, 291
Hour Glass, 2–3, 10, 72–73
Howe, Deering, 35
Hudson, Garth, 145
Huey, John, 197, 198, 200
Hunter, Meredith Curly, 90
Hunter, Robert, 90
Hustlers Inc., 205
Hyland, Mike, 69, 171, 283

"I Got You Babe," 248
Idlewild South, 17, 60, 78
improvisation, 88
"In Memory of Elizabeth Reed," 43, 61, 97,
    180
"Incense and Peppermints," 211
International Society for Krishna
    Consciousness, 117
Irvine, Bill, 131
"It Hurts Me Too," 100
"It's Not My Cross to Bear," 15

Jaimoe, 25, 57, 100, 227, 272, 285, 295
  Allman, D., and, 9–10, 17
  on Allman, Gregg, 64
  on Allman Brothers Band differences, 269
  on Betts, Dickey, 13, 23–24, 63, 259
  on drumming, 53
  on Fenter, 113
  on jazz, 228
  Leavell, C., and, 167
  marriage of, 106
  on Oakley, Berry, 49
  on racism, 217
  on Trucks, B., 14
  Walden, Phil, and, 108–9
  on Watkins Glen, 136
  Williams, L., and, 51–52, 53–54
  on *Win, Lose, or Draw,* 259–60

James, Elmore, 100
James, Etta, 247
jazz, 9, 228
Jefferson Airplane, 90
"Jelly Jelly," 67, 68
Jenkins, Johnny, 9
Jennings, Waylon, 121, 201
"Jessica," 61, 62–64, 69, 117, 146, 165
John Coltrane Quartet, 89
"Johnny B. Goode," 100, 147
Johnson, John Lee. *See* Jaimoe
Johnson, Leroy, 56
Jones, Elvin, 14
Jordan, Hamilton, 184, 187, 266
Jordan, Luis, 66
"Just Another Love Song," 259
"Just Like a Woman," 183

Kath, Terry, 86
Kaufer, Bruce, 98
Kaye, Carol, 248
"Keep on Smilin'," 253
Kennedy, Caroline, 116
Kennedy, John F., 116
Kennedy, Ted, 190–91
Kerouac, Jack, Garcia on, 87–88
King, B. B., 62, 85, 93, 211
King, Ed, 210, 212
King, Martin Luther, Jr., 189
Kirwan, Danny, 96
"The Kissimmee Kid," 199
Knebworth Festival, 218
Kooper, Al, 207–11
Koplik, Jim, 125–26, 127, 130, 141
  on Watkins Glen, 133–34, 137, 148–49
Kossoff, Paul, 213
Kraar, Louis, 243
Kreutzmann, Bill, 86, 88, 90, 91, 137, 149

Ladds Memorial Stadium, 225–26
Laid Back, 35, 36, 38, 39–40, 69, 71, 74
  Allman, Gregg, on, 78–81
  lead guitar on, 82

Leavell, C., on, 77
original compositions on, 81
recording of, 76–77
release of, 169
tour support for, 193
Landau, Jon, 111–12, 164
Lapiere, Georganne, 247
Laquidara, Charles, 99
Layla and Other Assorted Love Songs, 19
Leavell, Chuck, 20, 37, 38, 43, 45, 47, 52,
    80–81, 193–94, 195, 216, 268, 294–95
  Allman, Gregg, and, 63–64
  in Allman Brothers Band, 40–41
  on Allman Brothers Band interactions,
    255–56
  on Fenter, 113
  Jaimoe and, 167
  on *Laid Back,* 77
  musicianship of, 166–67
  Oakley, B., and, 47
  on songwriting, 64
  Trucks, B., on, 41–42
  on Watkins Glen, 134–35
  on *Win, Lose, or Draw,* 260
Leavell, Rose Lane, 20, 39, 108, 112
Led Zeppelin, 85
Les Paul, 122–23
Lesh, Phil, 57, 86, 88, 93, 95–96, 98, 99
"Let Nature Sing," 199
Levin, Peter, 64, 65
Lewis, Grover, 169–70, 176
Liberty Records, 2, 3, 109
"Light My Fire," 2
"Like a Rolling Stone," 207
"Little Martha," 27, 68
Little Milton, 71
Live at Watkins Glen, 147
Live Dead, 90
"Lonely Avenue," 82
"Long Haired Country Boy," 244
"Long Time Gone," 199, 201
"Looking for Another Pure Love," 82
Los Angeles, Allman, Gregg, and, 72–74

"Louisiana Lou and Three Card Monty John,"
    259
Love Valley, 196–97
Lyndon, A. J., 120–21, 138, 205, 224, 274
Lyndon, Twiggs, 16–17, 120, 138, 139–40,
    151, 236, 270
Lynyrd Skynyrd, xi, 163, 208–11, 217–18, 254

Macon Telegraph, 120
Maddox, Lester, 188–89, 264
"Mama Tried," 90–91
Manuel, Richard, 144
Marshall Tucker Band (MTB), 171, 180, 204,
    215, 253
  Hornsby working with, 158
  success of, 160
  Walden, Phil, and, 157–59
Mass Gathering Act, 141
Massarsky, Steve, 103–5, 106
  Allman Brothers Band and, 107
  in law school, 160
  as lawyer for Betts, Dickey, 239–42
  Walden, Phil, and, 107–8, 163–64
  Walden and, 231–32
McCartney, Paul, 34n
McCorkle, George, 157
McEuen, Bill, 2, 72, 199
McGee, David, 262
McGovern, George, 104
McKernan, Ron "Pigpen." *See* Pigpen
McLean, Don, 81–82
McTell, Blind Willi, 68, 93
"Mean Woman Blues," 208
"Melissa," 4, 27, 28, 43, 74, 155, 291
Melody Maker, 150
Middleton, Chank, 217, 247, 258, 269, 270
"Midnight Rider," 35, 74, 79–80, 155, 169,
    186, 201
Mile High Stadium, 164
Miles, Buddy, 100
Militello, Mike, 287
Mitchell, Joni, 72
Mitchell, Mitch, 36

Monroe, Bill, 197

Montgomery, Wes, 158

Montrose, Ronnie, 117

"Morning Dew," 4

Mount Holly, 149

"Mountain Jam," 29, 95, 99, 100, 147, 181–82

Mullaney, Jack, 132

"Multi-Colored Lady," 74, 78

Muscle Shoals, 4, 6, 54

My Cross to Bear (Allman, Gregg), 174

Nadjiwon, Carol, 104–5

Nalls, Jimmy, 285

Nash, Graham, 91

Nashville Skyline, 91

Nelson, David, 92

Nelson, Willie, 201

New Orleans Superdome, 261

New Riders of the Purple Sage, 90

The New York Times, 132, 150, 170

Newman, David, 81, 82

Nico, 72–73

"Night Time Is the Right Time," 82

Nitty Gritty Dirt Band, 2, 3, 71–72, 168, 199

Nixon, Richard, 153

Nolan, Tom, 225

North American Indian Foundation, 103, 231

"Not Fade Away," 100, 147

Oakley, Berry, xii, 10, 20, 33, 36, 61, 63, 97

    Allman, Gregg, on, 30–31

    as bassist, 57

    death of, 48–50, 100–101

    depression of, 30–31

    Jaimoe on, 49

    Leavell, C., and, 47

Oakley, Berry Duane, 50

Oakley, Brittany, 50, 151

Oakley, Candace, 31, 106

Oakley, Linda, 33, 50

Odom, Bunky, 19, 51–52, 68, 101, 126, 150, 186, 205, 229, 281

    on Walden, Phil, 161

    at Watkins Glen, 134, 139–40

Odom, Gene, 216

Old and in the Way, 197

On the Road (Kerouac), 87

"Once I Was," 74

"One More Time," 206

One Way Out (Paul), 13

"One Way Out," 29, 43, 155, 255, 291

O'Neal, Tatum, 247

Orbison, Roy, 207

the Outlaws, 254–55

"Outskirts of Town," 65

Papaj, Joseph, 290

Paragon Booking Agency, 162

Parish, Steve, 100

Payne, Kim, 119, 120

Perkins, Willie, 30, 33, 39–40, 108, 120, 132, 140, 178, 218, 235–36, 269, 274, 277

Peter, Paul and Mary, 103–4

Petty, Joe Dan, 50–51, 168, 219

Petty, Tom, 217

Phillips, Tuffy, 119, 120

Pickett, Wilson, 4–5, 6

Piedmont Park, 85

Pigpen, 93, 96–97

Pinera, Mike, 36

Playin' Up a Storm, 293

"Please Be with Me," 78

"Please Call Home," 78, 79, 82

Podell, Jonny, 162

police, at Watkins Glen, 148

"Pony Boy," 68–69, 153

Popwell, Robert, 36

"Powderfinger," 215

Power of Love, 3

Preston, Neal, 173, 175, 176

Procknal, Brian, 287–89, 291, 292

Pronounced Leh-nerd Skin-nerd, 210

Pryor, Richard, 95

publishing income, 63

Pucci, Mark, 274

"Queen of Hearts," 35, 78, 81, 82, 291

racism, 188–89, 216, 217

Racketeering Influence and Corrupt
    Organization (RICO) Act, 276–77

"Rag Mama Rag," 145

"Rain," 199

Rainwater, Betty, 284

Raitt, Bonnie, 79

Raizene, Mark, 128

"Ramblin' Man," 42–43, 47, 61, 69, 117, 123,
    146, 150, 165, 199, 213, 295

    Betts on, 44–45

    Dylan on, 156

    mixing of, 153–54

    recording of, 44

    Sandlin on, 154

    success of, 154–55

The Ramblin' Man, 201

Rambo, Reba, 200

the Rambos, 200

Record Plant, 130

Red Dog, 95, 128, 139–40, 176, 236, 270

Redding, Otis, 5, 17, 22, 108–9, 183

Reeve, Judi, 151

rehab, 21

Reinhardt, Django, 61, 197, 225

Reinhardt, Larry "Rhino," 10, 205

"Revival," 155

RFK Stadium, 115, 118–19, 125, 164

Rich, Buddy, 285

Richman, Barry, 270

RICO Act. *See* Racketeering Influence and
    Corrupt Organization Act

Riddle, Paul T., 158, 159

Riot House, 247, 249

"Ripple," 93

Rivera, Geraldo, 251–52, 267, 273

Roberts, Elliot, 229

Robertson, Robbie, 63, 128, 145–46

"Rock and Roll, Hoochie Koo," 12

Rodgers, Jimmie, 235

Rolling Stone, 149, 172

    Allman Brothers Band grudge against,
        169–70

    Trucks, B., on, 170

the Rolling Stones, 207

Rosenberg, Joe, 97

Rossington, Gary, 205, 206, 207, 209–10, 212

royalties, 63

Rudge, Peter, 213

Ruffino, Tony, 268

Russell, Leon, 127

Ruth, Babe, 218

Ryman Auditorium, 72

Safire, William, 284

Sahm, Doug, 116

Sandlin, Johnny, 2, 7, 27, 37, 49, 65–66, 120,
    195, 196, 197, 200

    on Allman Brothers Band schedules,
        255–56

    on *Idlewild South,* 60

    as producer, 60, 76

    on "Ramblin' Man," 154

    Talton on, 76

    at Watkins Glen, 142–43

Santa Lucia, Thomas, 274, 277–79

Scaggs, Boz, 165, 181

Schein, Jeff, 135

Scully, Rock, 127

Sea Level, 285, 293, 294

Seabreeze High, 1

"Searchin' for a Rainbow," 205

Second Coming, 10–11, 16

Second Helping, 213

Sgt. Pepper's Lonely Hearts Club Band, 73–74

Shaver, Billy Joe, 204, 259, 272

SHIT. *See* Stone Harbor Island Trash

Siegel, Joel, 141

Simon and Garfunkel, 171

"Simple Man," 210

Simpson, O. J., 291

Sir Douglas Quintet, 116

Sledge, Percy, 108–9

Slow Train Coming, 185

Smith, Dallas, 3

Smith, Sydney, 178–79

Smith, Willard, 142

"Smokestack Lightning," 97

Snyder-Scumpy, Patrick, 132, 141, 143, 283

So Many Roads, 148

The Sonny and Cher Comedy Hour, 248

"Southbound," 60, 117, 146

Southern Accents, 217

Southern Blood, 74

"The South's Gonna Do It Again," 244

Spartanburg, 157, 159–60

"Special Delivery," 215

Spector, Phil, 248

Spirit, 86

Springsteen, Bruce, 112

St. Petersburg Times, 268

"Stand Back," 27

Stanley, Owsley "Bear," 94–95, 98, 122, 128

"Stateboro Blues," 24

Stax, 6

Stewart, Bill, 35, 75

Stills, Stephen, 71, 91

Stone Harbor Island Trash (SHIT), 145

"Stormy Monday," 291

Strawberry Alarm Clock, 211

"Sugar Magnolia," 92, 93, 99–100, 144

Sumlin, Hubert, 97

Summer Jam at Watkins Glen. *See* Watkins Glen

"Superwoman," 82

"Sweet Home Alabama," 206, 212–13, 215

"Sweet Mama," 259

Swenson, John, 144, 146

Talton, Tommy, 37, 68–69, 78, 80, 193, 195, 201–2

   on Capricorn Studios, 75–76

   on Sandlin, 76

Taplin, Jonathan, 144

Tatum, Art, 145

Taylor, Alex, 37, 197

Taylor, James, 37

"Teach Your Children," 91

Texas Flood (Paul & Aledort), 131

"There Goes Another Love Song," 255

"There Is a Mountain," 29, 95–96

"These Days," 76, 78–79, 174

the 31st of February, 4

"This Diamond Ring," 207

Thompson, Hunter S., 190–92

Thornton, Buddy, 45, 68, 75, 120, 122, 270

Three Dog Night, 159

Ticketmaster, 125

Ticketron, 125–26

Tobin, Tom, 142

Toots and the Maytalls, 267

Townshend, Pete, 211

Travis, Merle, 158

Tres Hombres, 233

Trouble No More, 147

"Trouble No More," 29, 255

"Truckin'," 93

Trucks, Butch, 4, 13, 19, 20, 29, 31, 34, 96, 109, 136, 166, 227

   alcoholism of, 223–24, 225–26

   on Allman Brothers Band lifestyle, 269

   on Betts, Dickey, 224

   on contracts, 163

   on drug trial, 282

   on Grateful Dead, 88–89

   Jaimoe on, 14

   on Leavell, C., 41–42

   on *Rolling Stone,* 170

   on Walden, Phil, 108, 240

   on Watkins Glen, 146, 147

   on Williams, L., 52

   on *Win, Lose, or Draw,* 259

Trucks, Melinda, 293

Trucks, Vaylor, 151

"Tuesday's Gone," 210

Turner, Rick, 123, 128

Tuttle, Lyle, 174

Twitty, Conway, 198
Tyner, McCoy, 89

"Unchain My Heart," 82
"Uncle John's Band," 91
"Uncommitted," 273

Van Zant, Ronnie, 205, 209, 210, 211,
    212–13, 216, 254
the Velvet Underground, 72–73
Vietnam War
    heroin use in, 56
    Williams, L., in, 54–56, 294–95
Voting Rights Act of 1965, 114, 190

Wabegijig, Rolland, 104–5
Wabegijig, Sandy, 104, 106, 111. *See* Blue Sky
    Betts, Dickey, relationship with, 152
    divorce filing, 262
Wake of the Flood, 197
Walden, Alan, 205, 213, 254
Walden, Peggy, 243
Walden, Phil, 5–7, 14–15, 22, 41, 50, 77, 140,
    155, 208, 261
    Allman, D., and, 22–23, 109–10, 168
    business practices of, 239–41, 244–45
    on Capricorn business approach, 162–64
    Carter, J., and, 183–84, 188–89, 284–85
    Conlon on, 161–62
    Fenter and, 112–13
    Hornsby on, 110
    Jaimoe and, 108–9
    Landau and, 111–12
    Massarsky and, 107–8, 163–64, 231–32
    money problems of, 242–43, 253–54
    MTB and, 157–59
    Odom on, 161
    Redding and, 108–9
    temper of, 161–62
    Trucks, B., on, 108, 240
    Wet Willie and, 157
    Yarrow and, 103
Walker, T-Bone, 93

Wallace, George, 215–16
Walshaw, David, 196
The Waltons, 153
"Wasted Words," 42, 45, 47, 61, 146, 180
Waters, Muddy, 36, 163, 255
Watkins Glen, 120, 121, 126, 128, 131, 165,
    210
    aftermath of, 148
    crowd at, 132–33, 136
    environment at, 143–44
    expenses of, 149
    finale of, 146–47
    Garcia on, 144
    ground transportation at, 137
    Healy on, 133
    Jaimoe on, 136
    Koplik on, 133–34, 137, 148–49
    Kreutzmann on, 137
    Leavell, C., on, 134–35
    The New York Times on, 150
    Odom at, 134, 139–40
    police at, 148
    recording of show, 146–48
    Sandlin at, 142–43
    toilets at, 141
    Trucks, B., on, 146, 147
    turnout at, 133–34
    Weir on, 142–43
Weir, Bob, 87, 89, 92, *94*, 131
    on Watkins Glen, 142–43
Weiser, Mitchel, 142
Weissman, Edward Steven, 116
Weldon, Casey Bill, 66
Wells, Kitty, 197
West, Kirk, 155
Weston, Doug, 247
Wet Willie, 118, 157, 171, 253
Wexler, Jerry, 5–6, 21, 38, 39, 82
"Whipping Post," 28, 35, 63, 65, 117,
    146
White, Tony Joe, 112
White Witch, 253–54
the Who, 211, 213

Wickersham, Ron, 122–23, 128

Wilkeson, Leon, 211–12

Will the Circle Be Unbroken, 197

"Will the Circle Be Unbroken," 78, 80,
    181–82

Williams, Hank, 43, 235

Williams, Lamar, 53–54, 123, 217, 219, 236,
    285
    on Allman Brothers Band, 151
    as bassist, 57
    death of, 294–95
    Jaimoe and, 51–52
    marriage of, 106
    musical influence of, 166
    Trucks, B., on, 52
    in Vietnam War, 54–56, 294–95

Williams, Marian, 152

Win, Lose, or Draw, 250
    cover art of, 260
    Jaimoe on, 259–60
    Leavell, C., on, 260
    recording of, 258–59
    sales of, 261–62
    Trucks on, 259

"Win, Lose, or Draw," 258

Winter, Edgar, 249

Winter, Johnny, 205

Winters, Shelly, 42, 45

Wipe the Windows, Check the Oil, Dollar Gas,
    147, 295–96

With Friends and Neighbors, 37

Womack, Bobby, 163

Wonder, Stevie, 82, 167

Woodstock, 132, 134

Wooley, Dick, 110, 113, 119, 154, 180

Wooley, Joan, 160

"Workin' for MCA," 210–11

Workingman's Dead, 89, 91

Wrecking Crew, 248

Yarrow, Peter, Walden, Phil, and, 103

Yorke, Ritchie, 208

"You Can't Always Get What You Want," 207

"You Don't Love Me," 291–92

Young, Neil, 215

Yowell, Albert, 115

ZZ Top, 233